ONE WEEK LOAN

Rural Englands

Labouring Lives in the Nineteenth Century

Barry Reay

First published 2004 by
PALGRAVE MACMILLAN
Houndmills, Basingstoke, Hampshire RG21 6XS and
175 Fifth Avenue, New York, N.Y. 10010
Companies and representatives throughout the world

PALGRAVE MACMILLAN is the global academic imprint of the Palgrave
Macmillan division of St. Martin's Press, LLC and of Palgrave Macmillan Ltd.
Macmillan® is a registered trademark
in the United States, United Kingdom and other countries.
Palgrave is a registered trademark in the European Union
and other countries.

ISBN 0–333–66918–5 hardback
ISBN 0–333–66919–3 paperback

This book is printed on paper suitable for recycling and made from fully
managed and sustained forest sources.

A catalogue record for this book is available from the
British Library.

Library of Congress Catalogue-in-Publication Data

Reay, Barry.
    Rural Englands: labouring lives in the nineteenth century/Barry Reay.
        p. cm.
    Includes bibliographical references and index.
    ISBN 0-333-66918-5 —ISBN 0-333-66919-3 (pbk.)
        1. Working class—England—History—19th century. 2. Agricultural
    laborers—England—History—19th century. 3. Rural men—
    Employment—England—History—19th century. 4. Rural women—
    Employment—England—History—19th century. 5. Rural children—
    Employment— England—History—19th century. 6. Rural industries—
    England—History—19th century. 7. England—Rural conditions—19th
    century. 8. England—Economic conditions—19th century. I. Title.

    HD8399.E52R43 2004
    305.5'63'094209034—dc22
                                                        2004043357

10   9   8   7   6   5   4   3   2   1
13   12   11   10   08   07   06   05   04

Printed in China

Contents

List of Illustrations

List of Maps

List of Figures

Acknowledgements

The origins of this book lie with two other works of rural history, *The Last Rising of the Agricultural Labourers* (1990) and *Microhistories* (1996). They dealt with rural labouring society and culture on a small stage – a group of parishes not far from Canterbury, in Kent, to be precise. *Rural Englands* is my attempt to make sense of the nineteenth century on a much wider scale, including those workers who abandoned the Old World for the New. Given that this history does not ignore labouring emigrants just because they left their country (indeed, we will see that their leaving is highly significant), my own mental and physical distance seems rather appropriate. I was born in England (Isle of Wight, no less), raised in Australia, and now live in New Zealand.

I have accumulated many debts during the making of this book, but there are a few that I want to acknowledge in particular. The first is to Athina Tsoulis and our children, Alexa and Kristina Tsoulis-Reay. Like all partners and children of academics, they have had to face the perpetual preoccupations and absences, and, in their case, have coped by means of a wonderfully ambiguous blend of encouragement and disdain. Our daughters have grown up, and have fled back across the water to Australia; Athina still has to manage. My parents, Ken and Gladys Reay, have always been supportive, if sometimes perplexed. ('Why can't you write about beautiful things?' my poor mother once asked.) My Scarborough-born father will be gratified by the occasional inclusion of Yorkshire; my Scottish mother will be mortified that this is another book on England.

My thanks go to a variety of colleagues. Sally Alexander, Meg Arnot, Alun Howkins and Keith Snell have offered entertainment, friendship and intellectual stimulus during my research forays from the other side of the globe. David Levine and Keith Wrightson have also been constantly encouraging. I am grateful to several recent and current graduate students who have engaged in research related to the topics covered in this book, and who have tried to keep me on my toes: Laurel Flinn, Li-Ming Hu, Jill Wrapson and Stephanie Wyatt. I owe a great deal to various people in the Department of History at Auckland and in the faculty and university more widely, who have, in their various ways, made life more interesting. I am particularly grateful to Barbara Batt, James Belich, Malcolm Campbell, Caroline Daley, Raewyn Dalziel, Kim Phillips, Nalini Srinivasan, Doug Sutton and Joe Zizek. Giles Margetts of the University Library has been unfailingly helpful with the microfilm and official papers collections. Christine Jackson and others in the Interloans section of the Library have dealt with my constant requests for urgent material from libraries around the world. Igor Drecki of the School of Geography and Environmental Science very kindly produced the digital mapping.

I also have a substantial institutional debt. The Marsden Fund of the Royal Society of New Zealand awarded the three-year funding that made the research for this book possible, and enabled the hiring of a talented research assistant, Li-Ming Hu. If it had not been for the Marsden Fund, there would be no *Rural Englands*.

Finally, I would like to express my thanks to the following sources of illustrative material and/or permission to reproduce it: Art Gallery of South Australia: Plates 9, 20, 25; Auckland Art Gallery Toi o Tamaki: Plate 5; University of Auckland Library: Plate 13; The Bridgeman Art Library: Plate 24; Brown University Library: Plate 6; George Eastman House International Museum of Photography and Film: Plates 1, 2, 4, 14–16; © Manchester Art Gallery: Plate 10; Board of Trustees of the National Museums and Galleries on Merseyside (Walker Art Gallery, Liverpool): Plate 8; Courtesy of the Director, National Army Museum, London: Plate 7; Plymouth City Museums and Art Gallery: Plate 24; Public Record Office Image Library: Plate 17; Rural History Centre, University of Reading: Plates 12, 21; Mrs Jane K. Smith, London: Plate 11; © Tate, London: Plates 11, 19, 23; Master and Fellows of Trinity College, Cambridge: Plate 3; La Trobe Collection, State Library of Victoria: Plates 18, 22. (Every effort has been made to trace the copyright holders, but if any have been inadvertently overlooked, the necessary arrangement will be made at the first opportunity.)

Some of this research was carried out at the height of the Foot and Mouth scare in the UK, when large sections of the countryside were virtually closed off to outsiders and televisions relayed nightly images of slaughtered and burning piles of animal carcases. It was an interesting time for a rural historian: the rural, normally the object of nostalgia and romanticization, became portrayed in terms of contagion, decay and death. I trust that comparable touches of interest, drama and contagion are conveyed in the pages ahead.

B. R.

Preface

There are many general histories of nineteenth-century rural England, but surprisingly few that focus on the life of workers, and even fewer historians (Alun Howkins is an important exception) who take seriously the work of women and children.[1] The only systematic modern history of the English rural worker is primarily economic in its approach, relentlessly charting the adult male wage, and treating labour, it has been observed by one reviewer, almost as an 'unspeaking commodity'.[2] It demonstrates little awareness of the overlapping spheres of peasant farming, rural crafts and the household economy, and the vital contributions of women and children. It is a history of *farm labourers* rather than rural workers.

This relative neglect of the rural workforce is somewhat ironic, given that the most representative English male worker in the mid-nineteenth century was the agricultural labourer, and the typical female worker was either the domestic servant or also someone earning a living from the land.[3] Let us be clear that this is a book dealing with a large segment of English society. There were over two million agricultural workers in the mid-point of the nineteenth century, nearly 600 000 of whom were women, and 250 000 of whom were small farmers. The total comprised some 25 per cent of the entire workforce.[4] Moreover, these figures do not include non-agricultural rural occupations, domestic servants or the families of the rural industrial and agricultural workers, so we are dealing with many more people. Alan Everitt calculated that in the 1860s about a third of the population of England and Wales were 'still directly or indirectly dependent on agriculture for a livelihood'.[5] In other words, on the eve of their occupational decline, our subjects, rural workers and their families, numbered some six or seven million people.

We are covering a time of immense change, with a periodization still disputed: stagnation, crisis and repression in the period to the 1840s, stability in the 1850s and 1860s, depression from the 1870s to the 1890s.[6] It was a century which saw massive shifts in literacy, changes in mortality and fertility, a transformation in the complexion of the rural workforce, including the decline of female farm labour, increased mechanization, large-scale

emigration, rural depopulation, significant alteration in poor-law administration, the rise and fall of rural unionism, and the economic impact of
imported wheat, meat and dairy products. At all times, these changes were
complicated by regional, gender and class variation. Did the landlords
suffer most in the agricultural depression of 1873–95? Did labourers' wages
rise in real terms during the same period, given the fall in food prices? Were
the farm workers of the north cushioned from the traumatic experiences of
labourers in the south and east? However, the approach taken in *Rural
Englands* is thematic rather than chronological. While it by no means
neglects change, its primary aim is to sketch out the contours of a vanished
world, and it therefore crosses chronological boundaries in order to achieve
its goals.

Nor is this a comprehensive history of rural labour. Purists may detect
some silences, though I am not about to make the reviewer's job easier by
listing them here. The intention is to produce a series of arguments about
English rural workers, insights on a range of crucial topics, and engagements with assumptions and orthodoxies that have long irritated this
writer. The result, I think, is a fresh perspective on England's rural past,
reintroducing those often excluded from more traditional historical
approaches, and stressing the diversity of working communities and the
richness and dynamism of rural life. Although it focuses on the nineteenth
century, the book spills into the period up to 1914, where appropriate (the
long nineteenth century). I have already intimated that social history does
not recognize strict chronologies.

As for the irritable engagements, the reader will encounter them soon
enough. But he or she – you! – will hopefully notice that I do not think that
rural England is typified by the southern village (or the village, for that
matter), am unhappy with the equation of rural work with agricultural
labour, am unimpressed by economic histories that are limited to the male
wage, do not hold much brief for arguments for the poverty of rural leisure
and the absence of rural protest, and am continually fascinated by the ability of nineteenth-century artists, writers and folk-song collectors to remain
so oblivious to the lives of those around them, even when they attempted
to represent them. The reader should also get the message that rural
England was a nation of incredible local variation. So much so, that there is
justification for seriously thinking in terms of plurality rather than the
singular. This is a book about rural *Englands*.

One is tempted – and many historians succumb – to write of the 'real'
worker, hidden from history, either ignored or obscured by a romantic
haze. But there is no such entity. The 'real' worker is nothing more than a
rhetorical device. The intention in the chapters that follow is not to contrast

image and reality, naively counterposing the false nostalgia of past observers with the realist empiricism of the present historian. The rural worker is as 'mobile and malleable' as the 'rural' he or she inhabited.[7] I am aware that the outcome of my research and writing will be yet another construction – my re-presentation.

Introduction: Locating Rural Workers

During the folk-song revival of the late nineteenth and early twentieth centuries, middle-class enthusiasts went into the villages of the south, west and Midlands to tap the authentic, but disappearing, culture of the English.[1] 'The folksingers of today', wrote one of the leading figures of the revival, 'are the last of a long line that stretches back into the mists of far off days.' Folk music proceeded 'from out the heart and soul of a nation, it embodies those feelings and ideas which are shared in common by the race which has fashioned it.'[2] If this era was particularly productive for British classical music – Gustav Holst, Percy Grainger and Ralph Vaughan Williams were part of the movement – it is less helpful in terms of charting the culture of rural workers. The collectors had a rather limited sense of what they considered legitimate folk culture. They were willing to edit and bowdlerize collected material in order to protect the sensibilities of readers and hearers: 'Mr Marson has re-written the words, retaining as many lines of Mrs Hooper's song as were desirable.'[3] Editorial notes are scattered with explanations of expurgation: 'objectionable'; 'impossible to print'; 'very gross'; the 'coarseness of the original words obliged me to re-write the song'.[4]

Performers must often have censored themselves in anticipation of perceived sensibilities. An old carter told a female collector that he knew 'a many songs' that he would not even sing to a 'gentleman' because they 'be outway rude'.[5] There is certainly a huge contrast between the muted sexual content of the songs assembled in the 1890s and the 1900s and the far more explicit 1960s portfolio of Ewan MacColl and Peggy Seeger, collected from travellers born during the earlier period:

> For I am a hedger and ditcher
> I'm up to the airse amang snaw,
> And the de'il took a-hold o' my pintle
> And he swore that he'd never let go.[6]

The character of the singers presumably influenced the difference in tone, but it must also have been affected by the approach of the respective collectors.

The earlier folk-song enthusiasts approached the elderly disproportionately, for they saw them as the repositories of folk culture. 'I have learned that it is, as a rule, only waste of time to call upon singers under the age of sixty. Their songs are nearly all modern; if, by chance, they happen to sing an old one, it is so infected with the modern spirit that it is hardly worth the gathering.'[7] Anything smacking of commercial influence (the printed ballad and contact with the music hall) was anathema: 'A few weeks ago I was hunting for songs on Exmoor, and had spent two or three hours one afternoon listening to and noting down several exquisite melodies that were sung to me by an old man, eightysix years of age. In the evening of the same day, my peace was rudely disturbed by the raucous notes of coarse music-hall songs, shouted out, at the tops of their voices, by the young men of the village, who were spending the evening in the bar of my hotel.'[8] There was absolute denial of the complexity of cultural interaction, the hybridity of orality and literacy, tradition and modernity, the very issues that cultural historians are so preoccupied with today.

It was, then, a very partial view of the culture of rural workers, and there are some hilarious examples of cultural encounters. George Butterworth began his field trip from Cheyne Gardens in good spirits: 'Sat. April 13th, 1912. *Bicester* – Seems a good place to start a hunt from!' But his quest for the Oxfordshire morris ran into trouble as soon as he took off his bicycle clips: 'Morris at L[aunton] stopped about 50 years back & all the dancers are dead.' Much of his ethnography consisted of drunken conversations and dismissals of the quality of his informants: 'Visited the workhouse – nearly all the inmates are admitted under the head of "senile decay", so there's not much to be got there.' He was shown the tree where a famous morris-pipe player had been tied whenever he was too drunk to stand. A couple of survivors of the Bucknell morris attempted to revive it for their guest. The result 'of course, was chaos'.[9]

This historian would also have loved to be the metaphorical fly on the wall when 'The Hog's Eye Man' was sung to Percy Grainger:

> With a cunt for a jolly boat and a prick for an oar,
> O come along rollocks and row me ashore.[10]

Among the collectors, however, Grainger was the least likely to be shocked by sexual innuendo. He prided himself on his unorthodox sexuality, and his archives are a strange mix of documentary material for the historian of sexuality as well as those interested in the collection of folk music. The man responsible for the song *Country Gardens* ('An English Country Garden') took photographs of his own lacerated body: 'self-whipped in Kansas City, Feb. 9, 1933'.[11] Grainger was the first collector in England to actually record, rather than transcribe, the voices of his musical informants, and he resisted the temptation to rewrite the songs so that they conformed to some sort of collectors' ideal.[12] Yet we cannot really declare that with Grainger we finally have the voice of the people. His methods of recording must have dampened spontaneity; one man referred to his experience with Grainger's phonograph as 'like singing with a muzzle on'.[13] Grainger and his companions, the writer H. G. Wells, the painter John Singer Sargent, the politicians Alfred Lyttleton and Arthur Balfour, sallied forth from Lady Elcho's country home – in Balfour's new car – trawling country lanes and workhouses in search of new material, surely an alienating introduction to informants. 'It was fun to see an amusing farm labourer sing into the phonograph, while Balfour, Lyttleton, Sargent, Lady Elcho, Lady Wemys, etc. listened to it.'[14] Nor should we assume too much empathy. Grainger wrote in 1906 that the Lincolnshire country folk had 'nice interesting animal-like goat-bearded faces'; they were 'nice people, big hearted and amusing, but (naturally) dirty-handed and filthy, and sometimes I did not feel strong enough to find pleasure in an otherwise happy, so-called "nature life" like that'.[15] After a trip to Gloucestershire in 1909, collecting songs and observing morris dancing, he remarked: 'How can folk think that any niggers smell stronger than English country folk? I know now [*sic*] human stench so sickening searching sickly as the latter's. Even when I get into an empty railway carriage on a countrified stretch I niff at once the unfleeable whiff. Not that I mind. It isnt [*sic*] sweat smell I mean, but the real fleshsmell of them.'[16]

* * *

Rural workers are simply absent in many famous works of literature.[17] In Jane Austen's *Mansfield Park* (1814) and a string of other nineteenth-century, country-house novels, there are horses but no horsemen, pheasants' eggs but no peasants. Austen's agricultural labourers are hidden, except when their harvest work prevents the transport of a harp, or when their cottages trouble the aesthetics of the village. The closest the genteel characters in *Mansfield Park* come to labouring life is to contemplate the part of the cottager's wife in a drawing-room play – and that role is deemed demeaning, 'an insult'.[18]

Elizabeth Gaskell's short stories and novels are mostly about farmers' daughters.[19] Those first published in the 1840s and 1850s include a cloying, moralizing story about the disgraced daughter of a small farmer who went to Manchester and supported her illegitimate child through prostitution, and a melodrama about the love and endurance of a widowed mother after her daughter's terrible accident ruins her marriage prospects.[20]

They can hardly be said to be about labouring lives. The only poverty in Gaskell's *Cranford* (1853) is genteel poverty, for the main subjects of this novel are gentlewomen. The faithful servant, Martha, hovers in the background, brought on only to convey some information or as an object of amusement regarding her courtship practices.[21]

Alternatively, rural workers are caricatures.[22] George Eliot (Mary Anne Evans) is generally accepted as a realist in her fiction writing, and her novel *Adam Bede* (1859) is certainly remarkable in that it takes seriously the lives of a village carpenter and all those around him – including, significantly, central characters who are labouring women. It is difficult to disagree with Valentine Cunningham's endorsement of the novel as speaking up for (that overworked phrase) 'ordinary people', previously 'more or less disenfranchised as citizens of the English novel'. But surely he exaggerates Eliot's realism, her 'insider' status for the cultures that she charts.[23] Whatever her social origins, Eliot is most at ease with descriptions of farmers, clergy/curates, and gentry, more self-conscious when she descends below that level, and too often tempted by stereotyping. Agricultural workers 'slouch'; their gaze is 'bovine'.[24] 'Adam was not a man to be gratuitously superstitious; but he had the blood of a peasant in him as well as of the artisan, and a peasant can no more help believing in a traditional superstition than a horse can help trembling when he sees a camel.' There is not much feel here of the insider.[25] Any empathy conveyed elsewhere through use of dialect (though I remain to be persuaded about the realism of the verbal interactions of Eliot's characters) and the centrality of humble protagonists is undermined by a distancing collusion between narrator and most potential readers.

The doomed Hetty Sorrel may represent the voice of the inarticulate, the female inarticulate, but she is also the archetypal dairymaid of nineteenth-century pastoral. Her domain was 'a scene to sicken for with a sort of calenture [delusional fever] in hot and dusty streets – such coolness, such purity, such fresh fragrance of new-pressed cheese, of firm butter, of wooden vessels perpetually bathed in pure water'. Sorrel blushes, and pats her butter with a 'coquettish air'. She is all dimples and smiles, ringlets, and pouting lips. Hers was a beauty 'like that of kittens, or of very small downy ducks making gentle rippling noises with their soft bills, or babies just beginning to toddle and to engage in conscious mischief – a beauty with which you can never be angry, but that you feel ready to crush for inability to comprehend the state of mind into which it throws you'.[26] The reader could be forgiven for thinking that they were being introduced to a small pet rather than a hard-working farm servant.

Eliot's *Silas Marner* (1861) is about a village weaver, but all the characters, including Marner, are even more one-dimensional than those of *Adam Bede*. The village of Raveloe is isolated from modernity. Although superficially it displays the structures of 'an important-looking village', with church, churchyard and substantial farms, and is certainly not isolated from 'civilization', its inhabitants are trapped in time. Their minds are 'pressed close by primitive wants', their imaginations 'almost barren of the images that feed desire and hope'. Theirs is the archetypical 'rude mind' of the peasantry.[27] The labouring characters in Eliot's first novel, *Scenes of Clerical Life* (1858), are the least connected of all. Poll Fodge, Mr Fitchett, Mrs Brick, Dame Ricketts, and the other inhabitants of the poorhouse and Bridge Way, would not have been out of place in Hardy or Charles Dickens.[28] Henry James was cruelly discerning when he referred to Eliot's 'trick of seeming to humour benignantly her queer people and look down on them from the heights of analytic omniscience'.[29]

Despite his reputation for rural verisimilitude, and his own essay against the stereotyping of Hodge as 'a degraded being of uncouth manner and aspect, stolid understanding, and snail-like movement', Thomas Hardy repeatedly used the agricultural labourer for comic relief.[30] As Keith Snell has demonstrated, the scenes in *Far from the Madding Crowd* (1874), where Bathsheba pays her labourers and when the workers drink in the Buck's Head after the death of Fanny Robin, the descriptions of the inhabitants of Mixen Lane in *The Mayor of Casterbridge* (1886), and the portrayal of Tess's parents in *Tess of the d'Urbervilles* (1891), trivialize rural workers as simple, ignorant, clodhopping fools.[31] Henry James was perceptive again, writing that 'Mr Hardy puts his figures through a variety of comical movements; he fills their mouths with quaint turns of speech; he baptizes them with odd names', so that ultimately 'the only things we believe in are the sheep and the dogs'.[32] Some of Hardy's sympathetic characters are very improbable. In his ludicrous short story, 'The Romantic Adventures of a Milkmaid', Hardy has a farm servant changing into a gown in a hollow tree so that she can join a baron at a country-house ball.[33]

Richard Jefferies crossed genres, writing both fiction and observations on what he termed wild life 'on the borderland of nature'. His brief included 'the tillers of the soil'.[34] Though he wrote like an angel, and was critical of the failure of the visual arts to capture 'the force of truth and reality' in their portrayal of the rural, it would be a mistake to look to him for correction.[35] His *Hodge and his Masters* (1880) is primarily about the masters (farmers, squires, curates) rather than Hodge (the farm labourer).[36] Jefferies' interests lay firmly with the flora and fauna rather than with his 'tillers of the soil', hence the page after page on larks, hares, ants, downs, forests, hedges, flowers, jackdaws, the beauty of wheat, starlings, thrushes, martins, orchards, foxes, snakes, woodpiles, lizards, rabbits, corncrakes, hedge fruit, copses, nightingales, hedgehogs, moorhens, reeds, ferrets, forests, squirrels, deer, hawks, rooks, chaffinches, wrens, peewits, crows, cuckoos, spiders, wasps, frogs, toads, kingfishers, herons, mussels, roach, jacks, sticklebacks, wood-cocks and eagles.[37]

* * *

So-called documentary accounts have been little more successful in their encounters with labouring culture. Even the sympathetic Alexander Somerville encountered hostility from some of the rural workers he ques-tioned for his reports to the *Morning Chronicle* in the 1840s. In response to enquiries about how he lived on his meagre wages, a Dorset labourer retorted: 'Suppose, rather than I tell thee, that thou tries. Take thee to break-ing flints and making roads at eight shillings a-week for a year, do thee think thou could tell what thee lived on?' Clearly, the man viewed Somerville as a superior and an outsider: 'I see you ha' got a good coat on your back, and a face that don't look like an empty belly; there be no hunger looking out atween your ribs I'll swear. You either be a farmer or somebody else that lives on somebody else.'[38]

The famous surveys of rural life are, almost without exception, views from the top down, heavily weighted in favour of the opinions of employ-ers and clergy rather than the workers themselves.[39] James Caird's survey of 1850–51 used only one labourer as an informant.[40] H. Rider Haggard's famous *Rural England* (1902) was notoriously farmer-centred in its opinions and approaches. One (heavily edited) 'grateful reader' pointed out to Haggard, 'With only one or two exceptions landlords, farmers, land agents, auctioneers and others of the owning and employing fraternity have been your informants.'[41] A reviewer in the *Economic Journal* (1903) observed that 'of the three classes connected with the land' Haggard 'has had more inter-course with landlords and with farmers than with labourers'.[42]

George Sturt's book about his gardener, Frederick Grover, originally published in 1902, has been hailed as a picture of life 'as it was really lived among the agricultural poor'.[43] Yet Sturt's position in *The Bettesworth Book* is that of a distanced observer, Grover's employer. Although he claimed that 'there grew up between us a curious, and to me a most refreshing fellow-ship, in which social distinctions were forgotten', Sturt's very denials inscribe that distinction. *Change in the Village*, Sturt's famous account of village life near Farnham, Surrey, is essentially a eulogy of the passing of an old order, 'the home-made civilization of the rural English', an idealized peasant community in which the virtues of self-sufficiency and industriousness shaped the character of the 'poorest labourer'.[44] This was the organic community attractive to twentieth-century critics of modernity and mass society. However, rural workers were so close to nature, so much part of the environment, so organic, that they were dehumanized:

> One may . . . imagine dimly what the cumulative effect of it must have been on the peasant's outlook; how attached he must have grown – I mean how closely linked – to his own countryside. He did not merely 'reside' in it; he was part of it, and it was part of him. He fitted into it as one of its native denizens, like the hedgehogs and the thrushes . . . But I lose the best point in talking of the individual peasant; these things should rather be said of the tribe – the little group of folk – of which he was a member. As they, in their successive generations, were the denizens of their little patch of England – its human fauna – so it was with traditional feelings derived from their continuance in the land that the individual peasant man or woman looked at the fields and the woods.[45]

The distancing is also evident in Sturt's journals. In 1890, when reflecting on the impact of the printed ballad on rural culture, he described the 'rural working class' as 'intellectually quite undeveloped – barbarous, – almost *primitive*'.[46] He was frustrated by his inability to breach rural working culture. In 1898, he observed that he knew that Farnham Fair was important to village life – 'part of the unknown life of these village people' – but felt incapable of more than what he actually termed observation 'from the outside'. 'I looked at it as in the Zoo one looks at animals, knowing nothing of the inner life going on.'[47] By 1907, Sturt was criticizing the novelist Thomas Hardy for not managing to get close to the rural labourers, despite his claims to have done so, yet was also admitting his own defeats: 'I find it more and more difficult to get upon terms of camaraderie with my working-class neighbours. Between my mind and theirs a great gulf widens: between mine the objectivating and theirs the subjective.' Hence, the context for his better-known observation, 'No-one knows the labourer.'[48]

Edwin Grey's evocative account of village life in Harpenden (Hertfordshire) in the nineteenth century was written in the 1930s, when Grey was in his seventies. Although it has much interesting information on material life (clothing, housing, water, heating, food, the cottage pig, even smoking) and rural culture (games, courtship, weddings, burials, fairs, rough music, religion, superstitions, dialect), it is essentially cottage life seen through the eyes of a child, recounted – like most oral history – by an elderly person. As F. M. L. Thompson has observed, apart from discussions of gleaning and straw-plaiting, both tasks carried out by children, there is relatively little information about the lives and occupations of rural workers.[49] Grey himself said that although many of his friends were from a labouring background, his 'own home was not that of an agricultural worker', and he must have become somewhat removed from his subjects by his status as a superintendent at the nearby Rothamsted Experimental Station. (He mentions that he was a census enumerator in the 1890s, another indication of his status in the local community.) Indeed the words 'quaint', picturesque', 'amusing', appear in Grey's text from time to time, indicating a certain bemused detachment from his subjects.[50]

Walter Rose's account of life and work in Haddenham, Cambridgeshire, first published in 1942, is yet another book that looks back nostalgically to the vanishing rural world of village England. *Good Neighbours* is dedicated to 'All who love the English village', and is set vaguely in the late nineteenth and/or early twentieth century (the timescale is rather indistinct), the period of his boyhood and youth. The book is certainly compelling, with remarkably atmospheric passages – used elsewhere by this author – about the clothing and demeanour of rural workers, and the smells of their work environments. '[T]o pass from the stable into the cowhouse was to enter another world altogether. Instead of the strong ammoniated smell of the stable, one became conscious of a pervading essence of meadows; the laxative quality of green grass in semi-fluid manure, and sweet smelling milk.' The carpenter's workshop was 'a palace of craft . . . Its music was the sound of tools and the voices of men working well together: its whole air was charged with the smell of wood.'[51] However, *Good Neighbours* is unadulterated nostalgia, heightened by the childlike drawings that illustrate the work: 'the authentic stuff, good crusty bread, home baked', according to an enthusiastic and predictable endorsement from *Country Life*![52]

The most sensitive and empathetic observers faced what Christopher Holdenby termed the 'challenge of silence'. 'I was like a man travelling in a foreign country . . . I soon found that I was not alone: I saw people living in the country – even on their hereditary estates – who had no knowledge or conception of the cottage life around them.'[53] This book will be concerned with the lives that so evaded these contemporaries.

1 Rural Worlds

Ken Worpole recalled that when he was growing up in twentieth-century urban England, he was fed a steady diet of English rurality: 'The world, we were led to believe, was really a large farmyard.'[1] For much of the modern past, the 'imagined community' of England has been rural.[2] Whatever the role of agriculture in the economy – indeed one is tempted to posit an inverse relationship – the myth of the rural has exerted a powerful hold on modern English culture. The rural has been a constantly moving signifier. It has served as a refuge from the pressures of modernity. It has been a site for fashioning ideals of domesticity and femininity. It has become the contested and refashioned essence of Englishness. It has offered consolation in the face of loss of Empire. It has provided melancholic

1 P. H. Emerson, *Cantley: Wherries Waiting for the Turn of the Tide* (1886)

This photograph of a village in the Norfolk Broads provides evidence of the varied environments of rural workers. From P. H. Emerson and T. F. Goodall, *Life and Landscape on the Norfolk Broads* (London, 1886)

compensation for those who have left the countryside for life in the towns or overseas.[3] But if the imagined community of England has been persistently rural, it has also unceasingly focused on the south, producing 'a deformed nationalism', centred on the culture, landscape and representation of the significantly named 'Home Counties'. Whole communities have been excluded by this selective sense of national identity.[4] As we shall see in this chapter, England's rural worlds, the environments of its rural workers, were far more complex than this.

* * *

When A. D. Hall toured through Britain from 1910 to 1912, 'with the view of learning something of the diversity of British farming', he moved from the large sheep and dairy holdings of the chalk country of Wiltshire, 'the home of the capitalist farmer', to the small farming Vale of Somerset.[5] He saw contrasts within as well as between counties: the Sussex corn belt, with its large farms and well-paid day-labourers – 'no farming we had seen so far had given us the same impression of a busy manufactory of produce' – versus the self-supporting, smallholding community of chicken-crammers at Heathfield.[6] Hall visited the large potato farms of Lincolnshire, which had squeezed out the smaller farmers during the price crisis of the 1880s. He wrote about the old open-field farms of the Isle of Axholme, with their strips of crops in individual holdings scattered throughout the parish. This was the traditional home of the opium poppy, 'its cultivation . . . maintained by the habit of taking opium and laudanum which existed as long as the agues hung about the marshes'.[7] Durham and the southern parts of Northumberland were 'counties of violent contrast, so rapidly does one exchange purely pastoral or agricultural country for densely populated colliery areas or that still more dreary land where the coal has been won and farming is being resumed in a half-hearted way'.[8] Hall's tour included milk production in Cheshire and upland Derbyshire, sheep-breeding in the Lake District, and fruit and vegetable cultivation in the Vale of Evesham.[9] The general picture is of variation and adaptability.

Such diversity had obvious implications for the patterns of rural labour. The large arable farms of the Yorkshire wolds, with their sheep- and bullock-fattening, employed farm servants. It was 'a district of yearly hirings', with a male labouring culture that had a reputation for heavy drinking.[10] Hop-growing in the Kent/Sussex border area was 'more like manufacturing than farming', providing work for women and supporting the 'most numerous and best-paid body of labourers in the countryside'.[11] In contrast, the farmer and his family did all the work on the small dairy farms of West Cornwall. If there were no grown sons, a man was hired and his wife did the milking.[12] Finally, there were the worker peasants on the outskirts of the New Forest: 'all kinds of little holdings, with weird bungalows . . . each with a strip of land on which the occupier hopes to make a living out of fruit or poultry or even bees'.[13]

* * *

'Scripture says, "The earth is the Lord's and the fullness thereof"', wrote an agricultural labourers' union correspondent in 1877, 'but the locality for many miles round appears to be the exception, as my keenest observation leads me to the supposition that the land belongs to the Duke [of Rutland].'[14] Although they are not directly the concern of this book, the rural élites figured large in the material and mental lives of rural workers. John Buckmaster, a former agricultural labourer, encountered the power of local landed magnates when he traversed the villages and market towns of the west and south-east, campaigning against the protectionist Corn Laws. The 'Olives' were one such Hampshire family. 'The place, body and soul, had belonged to the Olives since the Flood . . . The Olives had represented the place undisputed since the Saxon Heptarchy. The Olives were the chief landowners. The Olives were everybody, and everybody had to be for the Olives. A meeting against the Corn Laws was one of the most impudent and insulting things ever attempted in the land of the Olives.'[15] The son of a farm labourer, who grew up in a village in the early 1900s, said something similar. The principal landowner, Lord Postern, 'entered the consciousness of every child as soon as he knew anything more than how to eat and drink, and walk about. Lord Postern was the ultimate earthly influence. He owned the houses we lived in. In an indirect way, through the farmers, he settled how everybody was to work, and what they were to get for it . . . He was the boundary to everybody's thinking.'[16]

As James Obelkevich once observed, the families of the squires 'were the parochial version of a royal family'.[17] Sir Edwyn Dawes, a shipping magnate and pioneer of the frozen-meat industry with global economic interests, owned a quarter of the land in the late nineteenth-century Kent villages and hamlets of Dunkirk and Hernhill. When H. Rider Haggard visited Dawes in 1901 during his tour of rural England, Sir Edwyn told him that his 2000-acre farm was 'the pleasantest of recreations, giving me health and pleasure far beyond yachting and horses'.[18] Dawes employed over a hundred agricultural labourers, and was landlord of at least eight farms, two potteries, and almost eighty cottages and houses.[19] By national criteria, the Dawes family would have been relatively small fry, but from the perspective of the son of a local farm worker, they 'were very rich and they seemed to own practically all of Kent'.[20]

There were just over 4000 families in England and Wales in the 1870s with over 1000 acres. Together they owned just over half of England.[21] In 1895, over 70 per cent of the total acreage of English agricultural holdings was held by 20 per cent of landholders.[22] Naturally, there was tremendous variation in the extent of landed wealth and influence in the various localities. In Wiltshire, over 40 per cent of farmland was occupied by a mere 5 per cent of farmers.[23] In 1895, there were 87 properties of over 1000 acres in Wiltshire, 58 in Norfolk, 48 in Lincolnshire, and 31 in Northumberland, but only 1 each in Cornwall, Derbyshire, Herefordshire, Lancashire, Shropshire, Worcestershire and the North Riding.[24] The Duke of Northumberland had the greatest acreage: 186 000 acres.[25] The Second Earl of Lonsdale (1787–1872) owned over 67 000 acres in Cumberland and Westmorland.[26] The Earl of Yarborough was proprietor of 55 000 acres in Lincolnshire in the 1870s, almost a third of the Lincolnshire wolds. The Yarboroughs inscribed their power on the landscape with a mausoleum, memorial arch and 12-million-tree woodland on their estate at Brocklesby.[27] Yet there were landed families in Kent whose estates numbered in the hundreds rather than the thousands of acres.[28]

Every settlement had its hierarchy. In what has aptly been termed the 'iconography of social division', architecture proclaimed the configurations of class in the mansions of the gentry and the topography of the larger farms and farmhouses.[29] Some landowners controlled their surroundings to the extent of creating their own villages. The nineteenth century saw the invention of the picturesque village, cottages built around a village green to house the workers of the occupant of an adjoining castle or manor house. Blaise Hamlet, near Bristol, had steep-roofed, tiled and thatched cottages with elaborately decorated chimney stacks, and doorways facing in different directions to discourage gossiping. Somerleyton, near Lowestoft (Suffolk), was said to have paid 'rare attention to the comfort and morality of Peasant Families'. Old Warden, in Bedfordshire, had honey-coloured thatched cottages, with red doors to match 'the red cloaks and tall hats' of the inhabitants![30]

However, for many communities it is necessary to look below the level of the landed élite to the farmers, the 'little kings' of village life and a kind of pseudo-gentry in many nineteenth-century rural parishes.[31] Alan Everitt has traced what he has termed 'dynasties' of farming families in Kent and Norfolk, mostly operating within the boundaries of their counties and linked by their respective networks of intermarriage and kinship (they reminded him of the 'gentry clans of the seventeenth century').[32] In England in 1895, nearly 75 per cent of agricultural land consisted of substantial hold-ings of more than 100 acres – county percentages varying from nearly 90 in Northumberland and Wiltshire to 37 in Lancashire and around 50 in Derbyshire, Cornwall, Cheshire and the West Riding of Yorkshire.[33] These farmers were the power brokers of local society with whom the labouring population had most contact as major employers. Moreover, large farm-houses could visually dominate a hamlet, standing out among the small cluster of cottages that housed the farmers' workers. Farms were important markers in the labouring population's conceptions of their community. The oral histories of a small fenland village are punctuated with references to the principal farmer and employer in the region.[34] Farmers could also be men (and women) of some means. One of the Yarborough's tenants at Brocklesby, a farmer of 1400 acres, was reputed to have an estate of £80 000. As Charles Rawding has put it, wealthy farmers like this were the hegemonic group in rural society.[35]

* * *

Geographers, historians and contemporaries have spent considerable time on the typologies of English rural settlement. Villages, settlements around a central point or strung out along a road or common, were dominant in the south and east, while the north and the west were farmstead-based, consisting of isolated farms or collections of a few houses in tiny hamlets.[36] One of the problems with such models is their tendency to equate rurality with village, hamlet and farm, ignoring not only combinations of these forms but also – as we shall see – larger settlements of people in urban concentrations of varying sizes.

The open-close model of rural settlement has fallen from favour in recent historiography, but it has been an influential way of seeing nine-teenth-century parishes in terms of land-ownership. In close parishes, ownership was concentrated and limited, and a single landlord or a few propertied families were in a position to exercise great power over the vari-ous aspects of the lives of fellow parishioners. Land-ownership in open parishes, on the other hand, was more dispersed, characterized by small rather than large farms, and less likelihood of control by a minority. The attraction of this typology – what sociologists call an 'ideal type' – was that it provided a foundation for a whole range of further economic, social and cultural classifications. Close parishes were politically conservative, Church-dominated, nucleated village settlements, unlikely to be involved in rural manufacturing. Open parishes were scattered communities of small farmers and rural industry, resistant to control and susceptible to political radicalism and religious nonconformity. The weakness of this typology is that few communities actually corresponded to the ideal types.[37]

Alternatively, divisions of the nation into regions – south and south-east, East Anglia and the fenlands, the Midlands, the north, and the south-west – can obscure as much as they reveal. The south and south-east was divided into areas of mixed corn and sheep/corn and cattle, grazing and dairying, and arable. East Anglia overlapped with the south-east, and was similarly divided into highly different patterns of land use, but with the added complication of the fens (in itself a geographically divided region). And the Midlands, where north meets south, is an almost arbitrarily defined region, divided into corn/grazing and high wage/low wage sectors, and containing grain production, dairying and market-gardening, as well as significant rural industry. It is not necessary to work through each region to demonstrate, as Sarah Wilmot observed of the south-east, the 'great contrast in farming regimes and agricultural history' within these so-called regions.[38] The south Lindsey area of Lincolnshire alone can be divided into eight 'well-defined' regional environments.[39] The workers of rural England inhabited diverse worlds.

* * *

Although historians habitually separate the agricultural from the industrial, and the urban from the rural, the situation in nineteenth-century England was by no means so straightforward.[40] Where do we place the inhabitants of the Staffordshire Potteries, where the bulk of women and children worked in the potteries, and the men in the ironworks, potteries and coal mines? The perpetually blackened and smoke- and fume-filled landscape around Stoke-on-Trent had all the appearance of a huge conurbation by the 1860s, but was really a series of villages and hamlets as well as the six rapidly expanding towns. The workers in the famous Wedgwood potworks, for example, lived in the village of Etruria with a population of less than a thousand.[41] The bottle ovens, mills, collieries, brickfields, lime kilns, and ironworks were scattered untidily, encroaching upon the contrasting fields around to produce what has been aptly described as a stark incompatibility in land use.[42]

Many such populations contained industrial as well as agricultural occupations. In the west, for example, the 1850s Cotswold settlement of Wotton-under-Edge (Gloucestershire) was made up of the 'town' of Wotton (1200 people), the adjoining villages of Simwell and Bradley, and the 700 inhabitants of the hamlets and villages of Wortley, Huntingfield and Combe. Wotton's population was employed in agriculture and in dyeing and silk and clothing manufacture. It was a hybrid rural–urban settlement. Despite the presence of four mills in the parish in 1854, Wotton was described as predominantly agricultural.[43] In the next valley, north-east of Wotton, the hamlets and villages of the Vale of Nailsworth contained varying occupational blends of workers engaged in agricultural labour, weaving and the wool industry. Although the clothing industry was strong in all the settlements in this area at mid-century, some villages were highly industrialized, while others contained larger proportions of agricultural labourers.[44] The Wiltshire parish of Corsley was also a community of cloth workers and farm workers until the decline of the clothing industry in the mid-nineteenth century. Inhabitants in Corsley's nine or so hamlets were employed in local clothing and silk factories, and in a large mechanized dye-works – older inhabitants in the 1900s remembered the workers leaving the factories 'stinking of the dye'.[45]

There are other examples of mixes of agriculture and industry in the Midlands. The economic region of the Black Country around Birmingham contained communities of nailers, lock makers, and needle and fish-hook manufacturers, carrying out their trades in villages and hamlets still noticeably agricultural, yet in an area renowned for its industrial and metropolitan development.[46] The inhabitants of the cluster of hamlets and villages around Heanor in Derbyshire and Eastwood in Nottinghamshire had 'avocations ... of a very mixed character', including agricultural work, mining, framework-knitting, and lace-manufacturing.[47] Darley's population (also in Derbyshire) supported itself through work in the market-gardens, flax mill, lead mines and stone quarries, and at hand-loom weaving, flax dressing and carting stone.[48] 'The principal avocations' of the inhabitants of the market town, villages and hamlets of nearby Alfreton were in the collieries, ironworks, framework-knitting and agriculture.[49] The Belper area, just north of Derby, was described in the 1890s as a mix of agriculture and mining: 'The small agricultural villages are everywhere kept separate by the obtruding of large mining communities, and there are no villages of any considerable extent in the union that are not, to some extent, inhabited by miners, or those engaged in industrial pursuits.' Industries included collieries, wire works, sewing-thread works, railway works, hosiery, silk, cotton and wool factories, quarries, tile and fire-clay works, and ironworks. 'There is probably no union in England with a greater variety of important industries side by side with purely agricultural communities.'[50]

J. D. Marshall and J. K. Walton have charted the range of small industries in the Cumbrian countryside – mining, quarrying, hoop-making, bobbin-making, basket-making, metalworking, nail-making, toolmaking, silk, woollen and flax manufacture, paper-making – all in a region where the 'major industry' was agriculture.[51] Similarly, Christine Hallas has demonstrated the importance of rural industries in the north Yorkshire Pennine areas of Swaledale and Wensleydale, where lead-mining, quarrying and the woollen industry (knitting, spinning and weaving) were 'integrally linked' with farming for much of the nineteenth century, and dual occupations were common.[52] Such mixes and interactions were dynamic. The occupational structure of the nineteenth-century communities of the Craven region of the West Riding of Yorkshire changed because of the growth of towns and a widening separation between agriculture and industry. Yet agricultural employment lingered in the textile-dominated townships, and mining and textile working could be found in predominantly agricultural villages.[53] Michael Winstanley's fascinating study of small farming in nineteenth- and early twentieth-century Lancashire has argued for a symbiosis between farming and urbanization and industrialization in the textile and mining regions of Derbyshire, Lancashire and Yorkshire. The small farmers of the north were adaptive products of the new industrial economy, combining family and wage labour, and agricultural and non-agricultural employment.[54]

While such fusions were most common in the north and the Midlands, they were not confined to those regions. The Cambridgeshire fenland town of Littleport had a mixed occupational profile in 1891. 70 per cent of males were farm workers or farmers; and nearly 50 per cent of the employed women were shirt-factory machinists or laundresses, or shirt seamstresses. Here was a clear case of husbands and sons working as agricultural labourers, and wives and daughters earning a living either as factory workers or as outworkers – one can see it street by street in the district enumerations.[55] One of the great strengths of Pamela Sharpe's study of working women in adjoining Essex is her recognition of the intersection between the urban and the rural; 'employment opportunities in both affected the same women'.[56] The traditional distinction between the urban and the rural, town and country, takes insufficient cognizance of a host of hybrid communities.

* * *

Instead of using village and town as essential divides, it makes better sense to consider spheres of influence and interaction based on networks of towns and surrounding villages. The work of Charles Phythian-Adams has stimulated a rethinking of local interaction: from the smaller local society, widening outwards to what he has termed the cultural province, and, ultimately, the nation.[57] For an individual rural community, the pull towards its associated urban settlement may have been stronger than its links with an adjoining village, which itself may have been part of a competing 'nucleated' urban society.[58] Jacqueline Cooper's study of nineteenth-century Saffron Walden demonstrates the intimate connections between this country town and its rural hinterland of Essex villages, observable in a range of economic, cultural and administrative interactions.[59]

It was similarly said of the town of Banbury that it was a 'metropolis' for some 140 settlements in a ten-mile radius.[60] Before its decline in the late nineteenth century, the straw-plaiting and hat- and bonnet-making industry linked the cottage producers of the villages and hamlets of Hertfordshire to the markets and industrial producers of the town of St Albans, and the rural straw-workers of Bedfordshire to the dealers and manufacturers in the towns of Dunstable and Luton. As an observer noted in 1850, 'The district to which the straw plait may be said to be confined is within a circle of about 12 or 14 miles around Dunstable, and within that area the whole labouring population may be said to be employed upon the straw plait.'[61] Identical matrixes tied village lace-workers and small dealers in Buckinghamshire and Oxfordshire to the large entrepreneurs of High Wycombe, and the market towns of Bedford, Newport Pagnell (Buckinghamshire) and Honiton (Devon) to lace villages as far as 15 miles away from these respective centres.[62]

In Oxfordshire in the 1860s, sewing gloves provided home employment for the wives and daughters of agricultural labourers in villages within a seven-mile radius of Woodstock. Slopping (finishing machine-sewn clothes) filled an analogous function in an identical ring around Abingdon.[63] Similar arrangements prevailed in the glove-making villages of south Somerset, where women and girls sewed either in large groups in the homes of overlookers or alone in their own cottages, trekking once a week to the towns to deliver their product to the manufacturers.[64] The Midland hosiery industry was scattered across the villages and hamlets of Nottinghamshire, Leicestershire and Derbyshire. It was estimated in the 1850s that only about one-fifth of the knitting frames were situated in the towns of Nottingham, Leicester and Derby; the majority were housed in the small rural settlements. A series of middlemen linked the branches of the trade together.[65]

The interactions were numerous. People moved into the towns in the winter and out to harvest work in the summer. Welsh and northern miners, Black Country smiths, London factory girls and white-lead workers left town to work in the market-gardens or at haymaking, fruit-picking, or hopping. The London lodging houses emptied and then, as winter approached, the wanderers returned 'with the instinct which sends some birds of passage southwards at the same season', as one contemporary put it, filling the lodging houses once again. Men worked as agricultural labourers from June to September, and as maltsters from October to May.[66] Rural builders' labourers and stoneworkers retreated to the big cities when winter closed their opportunities in the villages. A survey of the influx of rural workers into London noted that the 'employments most overrun by countrymen seem to be the building trades'.[67] Countrymen, originally brought in as scab labour during a dispute, worked the Millwall Dock, unloading corn and timber.[68] In the early twentieth century, former agricultural labourers comprised substantial sections of the labour force in several major London breweries, the South Metropolitan Gas Company, sections of the Great Northern Railway, and all the large municipal corporations.[69] The London Metropolitan Police actively recruited rural workers for their perceived health and political docility; nearly half the recruits in the late 1880s came from villages and country towns.[70]

Generations of London workers were employed as hop-pickers in Kent each year. Between 80 000 and 150 000 hands were required for the Kent hop harvest by the mid-nineteenth century. An estimated 75 000 workers were employed there in 1908. There was also work in picking currants, gooseberries, raspberries and strawberries.[71] Men, women and children from the Black Country were brought into Herefordshire in the 1890s, in specially scheduled trains, to assist in the hop harvest. Nail-makers from Cradley Heath (near Birmingham) explained that they treated the working excursion as a 'cheap family outing'.[72] Shropshire pitwomen worked periodically in the market-gardens near London – their men calling out to them to keep their legs closed until they got back![73] Nineteenth-century agricultural labourers from Norfolk and Suffolk moved annually to the ports of Yarmouth and Lowestoft to work the herring fleets, and, much further afield, to Burton-on-Trent, Staffordshire, to employment in the maltings.[74]

Such interactions were multifaceted. Railway construction and iron-working in the north-west of England drew men away from farm work; but railway labouring also brought large numbers of urban workers temporarily into the countryside. The population of the dale village community of 'Wanet' doubled in the second half of the nineteenth century with the arrival of the railway navvies, creating shanty towns and providing opportunities for enterprising locals. Over 70 per cent of the more than a thousand excavators and labourers were 'offcomers' (outsiders).[75] One of the most dramatic and violent interactions between the urban and the rural took the form of the town-based poaching gangs of nineteenth-century Lancashire – miners, canal men, glass-blowers, weavers, and other urban/industrial workers – who embarked on forays into the countryside.[76]

Fourteen thousand agricultural labourers lived in towns, according to the census of 1871, and must have travelled daily to their work in the fields.[77] The town of Maidstone in Kent in the 1860s contained over 700 agricultural labourers who worked in the surrounding farms.[78] Stephen Hussey's oral history of rural workers in the Chiltern villages of Buckinghamshire in the early decades of the twentieth century, reminds us that the 'morning and evening processions of men on bicycle and on foot journeying ... between their village homes and High Wycombe's furniture factories represented a labour force that was now urban in its place of employment but continued to be rural in its place of residence'.[79] Alfred Williams's classic study of Swindon's huge railway factory describes the way in which many of its 12 000 workers trooped backwards and forwards from the village and hamlets that surrounded the turn-of-the-century Wiltshire town. The coach-washers, bricklayers, apprentice turners, and forgemen were often village men and boys. The rural communities would wake at 4 a.m. to allow time for the walk to work; 'I have many a time, as a boy, run from the village to the factory, four miles distant, in thirty-five minutes, as the result of oversleeping.'[80]

Therefore, we should not envisage hard-and-fast divisions between town and country. As Marshall and Walton have written of nineteenth-century Cumbria, 'a man did not change overnight because he moved from a farm servant's attic to a coalmine'. Towns 'did not represent microcosms with a sense of abiding separation from the rural reality beyond their streets'.[81] In 1881, 1.3 million of London's 3.8 million people were born outside the city, predominantly from rural counties in the south-east and west.[82] Almost 40 per cent of migrants living in Bethnal Green in London in 1881 came from the counties of Essex, Suffolk and Norfolk.[83] A survey of such immigrants noted migration bridgeheads established by enterprising individuals, who then, in turn, encouraged kin and former neighbours to leave their villages for the city. '[A] country nucleus once established in any particular district in London, grows in geometric ratio by the importation of friends and relations. We find one village sending the flower of its youth to Finsbury, another to Hornsey, a third to a big establishment in Cheapside. So, if an employer is Welsh, we may find a Welsh colony near his works; if from Devon, a colony of Devonshire men.'[84] The pauper letters of the early nineteenth century, left by poverty-stricken workers seeking relief from their parishes of settlement, also show the movement of rural labourers into towns and cities in search of work. Many of the Essex poor, writing home from London, were petty traders.[85] Women from rural areas were employed as urban domestic servants; indeed their rurality was a requirement.[86] Norfolk women supplied servants to the richer suburbs of London.[87]

We are also dealing with a moving target. Economy and society were constantly in flux, as one decade's village became another's town. The towns and villages of the Potteries increased their population by over 800 per cent over the nineteenth century to become an area of extensive and 'continuous development to the point of near physical linkage'.[88] The pottery villages of the eighteenth century had become the 'six towns', linked together by a pall of smoke.[89] There are numerous other examples. We see the villages and hamlets of the Warwickshire parishes of Nuneaton and Chilvers Cotton drawn into the economies of coal-mining and ribbon manufacture in nearby Coventry, converting Nuneaton 'from a village into a town'.[90] We catch the transformation of Willenhall, Staffordshire, from a settlement of fewer than 150 people in 1801 to a coalmining and metal-manufacturing town of 16 000 in 1871.[91] We glimpse Bacup, a sprawling community of spinners and power-loom weavers riding the Lancashire cotton wave, 'an immensely overgrown village' of 8000 to 10 000 in 1851, and 17 000 in 1871.[92] We observe Wallasey, Cheshire, little more than a 'rural village' in 1841, incorporated into ever-expanding Liverpool, on the other side of the Mersey. Wallasey's population was nearly 15 000 by 1871.[93]

The intent, then, is not to deny England's movement from a rural to an urban nation. The population of England and Wales doubled from 1801 to 1851, and then doubled again by 1911, increasing, in total, from just fewer than 9 million to 36 million.[94] From 1841 to 1911, the natural increase in the population of the rural areas was nearly 90 per cent, but almost all of this increase was lost in migration. Consequently, the 'rural residues' had a net population increase of a mere 13 per cent over the period 1841 to 1911, while London and the northern industrial towns expanded at the rate of 200 per cent and more.[95] In 1801, 66 per cent of the population was rural (defined in terms of residence in settlements of under 2500 people). In 1851, the rural quotient was 46 per cent. By 1911, the corresponding figure was a mere 21 per cent.[96] This is the history of a rapidly shrinking sector.

*　*　*

The correspondents of the *Morning Chronicle*, who surveyed labour in England and Wales in 1849–51, described manufacturing villages in the countryside around Manchester, where two or three streets were 'clustered around the mill, as in former times cottages were clustered around the castle'. 'A "rural factory"! To how many will the phrase seem a contradiction in terms! In the minds of how many are even the best features of the cotton mill associated with the worst features of a squalid town. And yet, thickly sprinkled amid the oak-coppiced vales of Lancashire ... are to be seen hundreds on hundreds of busily working cotton mills.' For mile after mile, the Saddleworth area of Yorkshire manufactured flannel and cloth in a mixture of factory and home workshop. 'The eye wanders over clumps of oak and through straggling woods of sombre fir – from cottage to cottage, and hamlet to hamlet, and mill to mill – the former often perched high upon the hills, where the green of the pasture begins to give place to the brown sterility of moss and moor, and the latter invariably nestled in the bottom of the glen, each beside its lakelet of clear water, damned up from the rapid stream of the Thame.'[97] The *Morning Chronicle* correspondent also wrote of the surprising rurality of 'the great northern coal region' of Durham and Northumberland: 'In traversing that undulating region, the spectator will cast his eyes over vast ranges of country, of peculiarly soft and wavy outline, dotted with those buildings and scaffold apparatus which denote that beneath each of them a mine shaft sinks into the earth, but totally unmarked by that luxuriant crop of towns which the power loom has called into being. The collier population is scattered, because the pits are scattered.'[98]

They were indeed diverse landscapes. The rural worlds that we will be traversing in this book include the often-excluded north, 'England's Other'.[99] The environments of the nation's rural workers were far more wide-ranging than the archetypal southern village of agricultural labourers' thatched cottages around the village green.

2 Working Men

When Alexander Somerville wrote his sympathetic reports on rural labour in a series of articles for the *Morning Chronicle* in the 1840s, he cleverly contrasted the beauty of England's landscape with the poverty and quiet desperation of its inhabitants.[1] In a memorable few pages, Somerville wrote about a young Oxfordshire farm servant on an estate near Abingdon owned by a member of the House of Lords. Framed by the Thames, the Chilterns and Cotswolds, the 'picture in which this young Englishman is a

2 P. H. Emerson, *Coming Home from the Marshes* (1886)

Emerson wrote about ways of getting a living on the Norfolk Broads: shooting waterbirds, eeling, mowing marsh hay, the reed harvest, breaking up ice to sell at Yarmouth, and growing garden produce. From P. H. Emerson and T. F. Goodall, *Life and Landscape on the Norfolk Broads* (London, 1886)

subordinate' consisted of beechy woods and blue skies, meadows and farm-yards, village churches, birds and blossoms. The 'rural beauty of England' contained 'young farming-men whose bedclothes are changed once a-year; who do two-thirds of all the work on the farm; and who have for breakfast "bread and lard" – for dinner "bread and lard" – for supper "bread and lard"'.[2] In this chapter and those that follow, we will move beyond the landscape to look a little more closely at the people who worked the woods and tilled the land, and did much more besides.

* * *

The conventional division of rural society into landlord, tenant farmer and landless labourer no longer adequately describes the nineteenth-century situation. Revisionists have stressed the roles of farm servants, peasant smallholders and women in the rural workforce. The new theme is of 'a complex variety of experiences for those who worked the land'.[3] We can see this quite graphically in the recent work of A. J. Gritt on the agricultural labouring force in Lancashire in 1851, where, according to the demands of the local economy, employment consisted of various blends of family labour, day-workers and farm service. In the Ribble Valley, over 60 per cent of the farm labour force consisted of family members, over 20 per cent of farm servants, and only 15 per cent of day-labourers. This was an industrial area where pastoral farming was combined with hand-loom weaving. In the arable south-west of Lancashire, however, over a third of the workforce consisted of agricultural labourers, only 16 per cent were farm servants, and nearly a half was family labour.[4]

The small farmers were the real peasantry of the nineteenth and early twentieth centuries. Recently described as worker peasants, they survived with the labour power of their own families, but supplemented it through the employment of occasional outside help and also by their own work in other occupations.[5] Historians have used various ways of trying to locate and measure their strength in the nineteenth century. Using the employment of family labour as a proxy, 36 per cent of farms in England in the 1830s were family farms, varying from 50 to 60 per cent in Rutland, Westmorland, Derbyshire, Lancashire and the West Riding, to 20 per cent or less in Suffolk, Oxfordshire, Buckinghamshire and Essex.[6] If we plot the percentage of the farm workforce, county-by-county, according to the strength of family labour, there is a clear division in 1871 between the north and west as areas of worker-peasant strength and the day-labour favoured in the south and east. (See Map 2.1.) Using 50 acres as the defining limit of the small family producer, nearly 70 per cent of farms in England in 1895

Map 2.1 Family labour as a percentage of the agricultural workforce, 1871
(male and female combined)

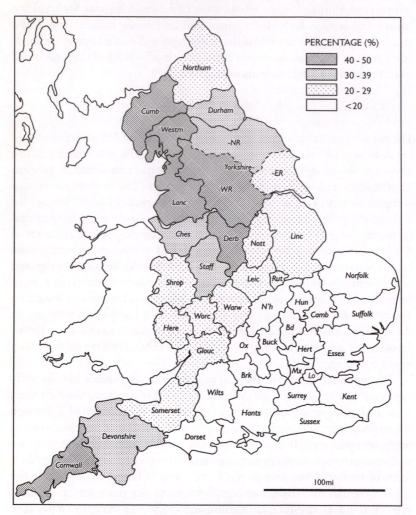

Source: My calculations from census of 1871: *Parliamentary Papers*, 1873, lxxi, part 1.
Family labour is defined as that where the census occupation is given as farmer's
son, daughter, and other relative, or wife of farmer. The agricultural workforce
consists of the total of family labour, agricultural labourers, and farm servants.
Farmers are not included in the calculation.

were less than 50 acres, and these smallholdings comprised 14 per cent of agricultural land. There was great regional variation. In the small farming strongholds of Lancashire and Derbyshire, 34 per cent and 27 per cent (respectively) of agricultural land consisted of holdings of less than 50 acres, compared to a national figure of 14 per cent and county rates as low as Northumberland's and Wiltshire's 7 per cent.[7] Within Lancashire itself, the extent of small farms varied from the 22 per cent of fell farms in the High Furness that were less than 50 acres to the 77 per cent for the industrial Blackburn district of central Lancashire.[8] In the Ravenstonedale area of Westmorland, 50 per cent of *all* households were headed by farmers, many of whom were classified in 1891 either as self-employed small farmers or as also earning a living as wage labourers.[9]

Definitions varied from locality to locality.[10] In the south Midlands, 60 acres was the demarcation between 'family and capitalist farms'.[11] In north Lancashire, 50 acres 'marked the limit of farms that were as a rule farmed using family labour'.[12] In Lincolnshire, most of the farmers who employed outside labour in 1851 had properties of more than 40 acres.[13] The Royal Commission on Labour in 1893–94 said that in the St Neots district in Huntingdonshire 10 acres or more of market-garden vegetables provided a living, whereas in Hampshire those who farmed fewer than 40 acres 'generally worked for wages or otherwise earning money apart from their land' (carting or dealing, for example).[14] In the Kent parishes of Boughton, Dunkirk and Hernhill, 25 acres seems a far more likely cut-off point in the nineteenth century. Holdings below 25 acres relied heavily upon family labour, were less likely to hire labour than the larger farms, and were often dependent on some other form of activity to contribute towards the household economy.[15] In other words, the rural workforce included those who held small plots of land, and the families of these people, given that their basic economic unit was household production. Although he gravitated towards the aristocracy and the substantial farmers, H. Rider Haggard was intrigued by the smallholders of the Bewdley district in Worcestershire. Of several hundred landholders in the area in the 1900s, nearly 70 per cent farmed properties smaller than 20 acres. These holdings, not very far from Birmingham, survived by combining fruit-growing with basket-making, fowl-raising, egg-producing, breeding bulldogs, and varieties of dealing. The contribution of wives and children was expected.[16]

Moreover, it is difficult to separate such worker farmers from the agricultural labourer. A Staffordshire farm labourer recalled how in the 1880s and 1890s he had rented a 12-acre farm which his wife managed while he worked for other farmers and broke stone in the parish quarry.[17] It was said of the small Lincolnshire marsh parish of Mumby in 1886 that 'most of the

farmers are of the labouring class'.[18] The St Neots market-gardeners who
farmed holdings of from two to ten acres worked for larger farmers 'in busy
seasons'.[19] Hampshire smallholders in the woodland areas near
Basingstoke, who had originally carved tiny two- or three-acre plots out of
the common land, earned a living through a mixture of piece-work in the
nearby woods in winter, working their own land, haymaking and harvesting for other farmers, and travelling to the London market-gardens and the
fruit and hop gardens in Kent.[20] The son of a small farmer in the Blean area
of Kent recalled helping his mother look after the family acres in the
summer when his father worked for wages in other farmers' orchards and
hop-grounds. His father was both wage-earner and wage-payer. He hired
women to harvest his own fruit crop. He kept pigs; two would be killed
each year for the household, the rest were sold to the butcher. His mother
took in a lodger, an old woman who paid 18d each week.[21] The situation was
further complicated in those areas where the allotment system took hold at
the end of the nineteenth century.[22] In Midland villages, men would work
irregularly at a craft or trade, or at farm work and spend the rest of their
time cultivating their plots. If the bulk of their time was taken up with paid
work, the labour would either devolve upon their families or they would
hire others to work their land; 'it is becoming common for men in regular
employment to cultivate their allotments largely by hired labour'.[23] Thus,
agricultural workers hired other agricultural workers, including small
farmers. The employed were also employers!

* * *

It is crucial to include the crafts and trades in a history of rural work.
Indeed, it is likely that employment in this sector increased relative to work
in agriculture in the nineteenth century. E. A. Wrigley has estimated that
two-fifths of new employment in the male workforce in the countryside in
the first half of the nineteenth century was provided by retailing and hand-
icrafts rather than by growth in employment in agriculture. In 1851, 18 per
cent of the rural male population aged 20–64 was employed in ten major
trades and crafts: baker, blacksmith, bricklayer, butcher, carpenter, mason,
publican, shoemaker, shopkeeper and tailor.[24] Over 100 000 blacksmiths
worked about 25 000 forges in urban and rural England in the 1870s.[25] We
should not think of the rural worker as synonymous with agricultural
labour. Take the coppice and underwood workers, for example.
Concentrated in the south, the west Midlands, and the Lake counties, these
workers were responsible for the harvesting, processing and crafting of the
wood used for fuel, tanning, farming (hop-poles, fruit-stakes, gates and

fences), tools and tool handles, bobbins, hoops, baskets and packaging. They were the woodmen, wood dealers, charcoal burners, bobbin-makers and basket-makers, some 30 000 to 40 000 in all, listed in the nineteenth-century censuses. Much of the work in this agricultural industry was seasonal winter work and therefore underestimated by the census. E. J. T. Collins has pointed out that in Kent alone the acreage of coppice implies a workforce of more than 1000 woodmen, yet only a quarter to a half of that number are recorded in the census. Many of those who worked with wood were recorded as 'agricultural labourer', 'labourer' or 'farmer'.[26]

We know that in the heathland areas of Dorset there were whole labouring communities where labour supply outstripped demand; the men found farm work only in summer and had to scrape a living in the woods in the winter. They travelled long distances in search of such work.[27] The broom-dashers (broom-makers) of Berkshire lived in huts on one- to two-acre plots in the fir and moorland parish of Finchampstead, earning a 'hard living' to cover the 10s to 15s per week rent on their small properties.[28] In the Basingstoke area of north Hampshire, agricultural workers regularly worked at piece-work in the woods in the winter. The common pattern was for farmers to lay off the bulk of their workforce during the lull in the agricultural year, knowing that they would find employment in the woods and be available when needed again.[29] In Tadley, in this same woodland area, employment consisted of various combinations of piece-work (agricultural, and wood and timber cutting), wood-related crafts (broom-making, hoop-making and charcoal burning), and forms of self-employment (small farming and wood dealing, for example). There was a clear split between winter wood work and summer farm work, with 'a large part of the labouring population of Tadley and adjoining villages . . . spending 40–60 per cent of the year working in other districts'.[30]

Weaving is another example of non-agricultural rural work. Geoffrey Timmins's important study of the Lancashire hand-loom weavers has shown that the decline in hand-weaving in the Lancashire cotton industry was more protracted than has normally been assumed. While the focus of hand-weaving shifted to the urban areas in the early nineteenth century, and its replacement by the power loom (also in the towns) was assured by the 1860s, until then hand-loom weaving offered 'high earning potential' for large numbers of rural women, children and men. Its survival was particularly pronounced in the hamlets and villages around Blackburn. In a group of 11 Lancashire villages in 1851, the proportion of dwellings occupied by hand-weavers ranged from 20 per cent to as many as 80 per cent.[31] Weaving also had associations with farm-work. The hand-loom weaving villages of nineteenth-century Lancashire combined weaving with farming, harvesting and agricultural labour. Fathers would farm or work as agricultural labourers, while wives and children were occupied at the hand-loom. Alternatively, as it was observed in 1840, young men combined weaving with 'field-work in harvest-time . . . the produce of their potato settings . . . fishing; and occasional employment in various capacities'.[32]

The miner, a twentieth-century icon of industrial development (and decline), is rarely discussed in connection with rural work. Yet nineteenth- and early twentieth-century mines were located rurally. Many mining settlements were villages or even smaller nucleated rural settlements.[33] Mining and agriculture frequently appeared together. In the Truro area of Cornwall in the 1890s, miners occupied 'an exceptionally large number of small holdings', making it difficult for agricultural labourers to get a toehold on the land.[34] In the Swaledale area of north Yorkshire in the nineteenth century, it was usual to combine mining with farming, and up to a half of lead-mining households kept dairy cows.[35] In the ironstone-mining villages and hamlets of south Yorkshire, inhabitants in 1851 included agricultural workers as well as miners.[36] Both the lead-miners of Derbyshire and the colliers of Staffordshire commonly combined mining with agricultural labour.[37] Small farmers in Cumberland villages worked on their 20- or 30-acre farms and carted for the collieries and iron-mines: 'This class of men can scarcely be called farmers, although they are occupiers of land', one observer noted in the 1860s.[38] Melvin Bragg's grandmother, Elizabeth Armstrong, born in 1898 in a pit community near Wigton, Cumberland, described herself as 'part country and part town'. 'We knew about farming as well as mining.' Her father began as a farm worker and then became a miner; her mother worked in the fields. Her brothers went into farm service and then became miners when they married. Elizabeth was a farm servant before she married a miner/farm worker.[39]

The Reports to the General Board of Health on sanitary conditions in England's towns and villages in the 1840s and 1850s are an under-utilized source for early Victorian economic history. Repeatedly, inspectors described mixed economies or small centres of rural industry. (See Table 2.1.)

While its decline over the period from 1830 to 1914 is indisputable, rural industry should not be written out of English economic history. When, in 1915, in an effort to stimulate their revival, J. L. Green surveyed the recent past of once-viable rural industries, he was able to list off an incredible range before he ran out of impetus at Northamptonshire. They included the manufacture of ribbons, velvets and clothing, spinning and weaving, hurdle-making, and bell foundries in Berkshire; lace-making, straw-plaiting and needle-making in Buckinghamshire; silk-weaving and

Table 2.1 Rural industry in the 1840s and 1850s

County	Village/Parish	Population	Occupations
Cumberland	Keswick	2500	Woollen workers, pencil manufacturers, tool-makers, and tourist servicers
Derbyshire	Litton	900	Framework-knitters, cotton-mill workers, farmers and farm workers
Durham	Crook and Billy Row	3000	Colliers and coke-drawers
Essex	Halstead and Grinstead Green	5700	Silk-factory hands, velvet and satin home-workers, straw-plaiters, paper-mill workers and agricultural labourers
Lancashire	Denton	3000	Hat-makers, cotton spinners and silk weavers
Leicestershire	Wigston Magna	2500	Factory and home-workshop stocking-makers
Northumberland	Warkworth	6000 (in 12 villages and hamlets)	Pitmen, agricultural workers and fisherfolk
Somerset	Street	1600	Stone-quarry employees, agricultural workers, sheepskin-rug manufacturers and boot- and shoemakers
Staffordshire	Tamworth	8600	Agriculturalists and tape- and paper-mill workers
Wiltshire	Ashton Keynes	1300	Brick- and tile-makers, potters, glovers and farm workers
Yorkshire	Castleford	1400	Glass-manufacturers and potters

Sources: R. Rawlinson, *Report to the General Board of Health ... of the Township of Keswick* (London, 1852), pp. 15–16; W. Lee, *Report to the General Board of Health ... of the Township of Litton* (London, 1851), pp. 4–5; T. W. Rammell, *Report to the General Board of Health ... of the Township of Crook and Billy Row* (London, 1854), pp. 6–7; T. W. Rammell, *Report to the General Board of Health ... of the Parish of Halstead* (London, 1852), pp. 7–11; W. Ranger, *Report to the General Board of Health ... of the Township of Denton* (London, 1857), pp. 3–4; A. L. Dickens, *Report to the General Board of Health ... of the Parish of Wigston Magna* (London, 1850), p. 8; R. Rawlinson, *Report to the General Board of Health ... of the Townships of Alnwick and Canongate* (London, 1850), pp. 70–2; T. W. Rammell, *Report to the General Board of Health ... of the Parish of Street* (London, 1853), pp. 6–7; W. Lee, *Report to the General Board of Health ... of the Borough of Tamworth* (London, 1853), pp. 8–10; T. W. Rammell, *Report to the General Board of Health ... of the Parish of Ashton Keynes* (London, 1852), pp. 6–7; B. H. Babbage, *Report to the General Board of Health ... of the Township of Castleford* (London, 1850), pp. 8–9.

fustian-cutting in Cheshire; weaving and pencil-making in Cumberland; gloving, and cloth-, carpet-, lace-, button-, thread- and woollen-making in Devon; basket-making, cloth manufacture, straw-plaiting, silk-weaving and shoemaking in Essex; weaving, cloth making, pin-making, herb-distilling and hosiery, hat and felt manufacture in Gloucestershire; cloth 'of various kinds', wood crafts and watch-spring- and chain-making in Hampshire; cotton- and silk-weaving, hat-making, file-making and watchmaking in Lancashire; framework-knitting, stocking-making, gloving and wickerwork in Leicestershire; weaving and cloth-making in Norwich; silk-weaving, stay-making, lace-making, gloving, basket-making and parchment manufacture in Northamptonshire. Green was recording their demise, but the point remains that these industries were productive for much of the period covered in this book.[40] Indeed, an enquiry in the early 1920s again revealed that while rural industry was in decline, it was by no means dead.[41]

One of the abiding themes of the period, then, was the 'relative buoyancy of so many traditional crafts and trades in the face of a late industrialising society', and the fact that rural industry and manufacturing remained resilient until the turn of the century.[42] The use of a reserve army of cheap labour, which we will see so evident in the experience of agricultural workers, was equally applicable to rural industrial outwork. Cotton became factory- and town-based, but some industries (wool and lace) retained a strong rural component, while others (gloving, hosiery, tailoring and hatting) increased as 'rural/urban hybrids' based on the cheap employment of women.[43] A 1920s survey found that such outwork was widespread in the rural areas, particularly in the Midlands 'where there are few villages which are not within reach of a factory'.[44] Shoemaking also adapted to mechanization, with outwork in village settlements around urban manufacturing concentrations: Leicestershire and Northamptonshire shoemaking was strongly village-based in 1911.[45] Although their trade declined in the latter part of the nineteenth century, nail-makers plied this form of outwork in villages in Staffordshire, Warwickshire and Worcestershire.[46] Brickmaking, often in tandem with farming or agricultural labour, and commonly on the outskirts of towns, was another rural industry until late in our period of interest. Small brickworks were widespread in Kent and in the rural belt around Manchester, for example, and it was said in the 1870s that 'almost every parish' in Staffordshire had a brickfield.[47] In short, not only did rural work include mixed occupations, but also our definition of rural worker needs to include communities of weavers and colliers as well as agricultural labourers and subsistence farmers. The village was the industrial village as well as the agricultural village that has dominated so many accounts of the rural.[48]

* * *

Some descriptions of the rural social structure place the crafts and trades in 'the middle ground between the farmers and labourers'.[49] However, the trades and crafts ran the scale in terms of status and social condition. They included the substantial employer, the small master with one or two helpers, the self-employed with no help other than family, and the man (or woman) who worked at a trade or craft for someone else. In Corsley in the 1900s, two builders employed the bulk of the artisans in this Wiltshire community of about 800 people. One wheelwright and builder provided work for 40 men, half of whom came from outside the village. These workers earned from 20s to as much as 27s per week, though these rates assumed a total of 59 hours.[50] But the point is that the category includes employers as well as workers. Working-class autobiographers could be scathing about the difference that the word 'master' made to a man's sense of worth; a former potter wrote of one man as a 'little tyrant', a 'human bantam', puffed up with self-importance because he was a petty employer.[51]

In Boughton in 1851, a Kent village of about 1500 inhabitants, over a quarter of the working male population was employed in a trade or craft: as shoemakers, carpenters, wheelwrights, butchers, grocers, blacksmiths, thatchers, charcoal and lime burners, sawyers, brick- and tile-makers, plumbers and glaziers, millers, bakers, victuallers, bricklayers, tailors, dealers of various sorts, drapers, builders, potters, weavers, and as a harness-maker, hairdresser and perfumer, watchmaker and chemist.[52] In Kington, a Herefordshire country town of 2000 people, there were at least 60 master craftsmen engaged in over 30 different trades in the 1840s.[53] Tradesmen and artisans headed 16 per cent of households in Corsley in 1905–06.[54] Although one would not want to extrapolate from one village to the whole nation, and local economic specificities were always important, other studies suggest that Boughton's broad male occupational composition was representative. For example, 25 per cent of the male working population in the small Essex agricultural village of Elmdon in 1861 were craftsmen or tradesmen.[55] Nigel Goose's detailed analysis of mid-nineteenth-century Hertfordshire shows other village populations where the percentages of men occupied in the crafts and trades were from 20 to 25 per cent. Small communities near towns had lower proportions thus employed, presumably because of their size and because such services were provided in the urban centre nearby.[56] A survey of a large group of Warwickshire villages, published in the *Economic Journal* in the 1890s, found that the proportions varied from up to 25 per cent in the larger villages to 10 per cent in smaller communities (the average for the 56 villages was 16 per cent).[57]

B. H. Fagg was a blacksmith living and working in Harbledown in Kent during the early decades of the twentieth century. His father was a wheelwright, carpenter and undertaker, whose shop was just across the street from the forge where Fagg junior started work in 1908 at the age of 14. Fagg described his father's work radius as about three or four miles, and he would walk to a job with an old handcart for his material and tools. Like craftsmen everywhere, Fagg senior catered for the various needs of the local economy. He made carts and waggons – four-wheeled waggons, dung carts, timber tugs, tradesmen's vans (which he also painted) and small traps to take the children to the fields for fruit, hop and potato picking, as well as ploughs – Kent ploughs, and little wooden ones used by cottagers for furrowing and planting potatoes. He made gates and fences, ladders for the orchards, and troughs for bakers. Nor was he above a bit of plumbing and general household repair (his son recalls roof-tiling, wallpapering, and carpet-laying). Finally, he was the local undertaker, measuring the corpse, constructing the coffin and organizing the bearers and the digging of the grave.

The younger Fagg's work as a blacksmith was somewhat more specialized. The bulk of his work involved caring for horses. He made and fitted shoes, curing, as an unofficial 'animal doctor', ailments such as swollen feet or rotting hooves; he could describe the anatomy of a horse's hoof and the intricacies of 'frost-nailing' in the winter or shoeing for 'drop foot'. But he also made tools (hoes, chisels, forks), fitted handles to spades and shovels, set scythes ('Practically every different man had a different way of swinging a scythe, so you had to set the scythe to suit him, not to suit yourself'), and tended to the various metal fittings of ploughs, hop-washers, carts and waggons. Fagg plied his trade in an arc not unlike that of his father: from Harbledown down to St Dunstans, and then up to Dunkirk at the top of Boughton Hill, and across to Chartham Hatch. He did not cover the village of Blean because there was a blacksmith there – 'you didn't step on his ground'.[58]

Some of these households farmed as well. In Hernhill, the parish's carpenter, wheelwright, blacksmith and shoemaker all farmed smallholdings.[59] This was also the pattern in Melbourn, Cambridgeshire, where many of the smallholders had other occupations: publican, plumber and glazier, grocer and draper, tailor and publican, shoemaker, shoemaker and beerhouse keeper, pig dealer, blacksmith and publican, carpenter, bricklayer, builder, harness-maker, baker, carrier, and butcher.[60] Because much of the work in a public house or beer shop could be undertaken by the women of a household, victualling was frequently combined with farming or a craft.

* * *

However, the bulk of the employable male population in rural England worked as labourers and agricultural labourers. There were close to one and a half million male agricultural labourers, labourers and farm servants in England and Wales according to the censuses of 1851–71.[61] Most areas of England had some sort of seasonal agriculture and therefore required a reserve army of labour – female and male, adult and child – for the various harvests. There were intricate hierarchies among farm workers, as lovingly charted by rural working-class oral informants as any élite explanation of the difference between barons and baronets. Kent workers and census-takers distinguished between the levels of servant in husbandry: waggoner, second man, third man, waggoner's mate, second boy, third boy, and so on.[62] When an agricultural commissioner listed the wages of the employees on a large Dorset farm in 1868, he started from the top down: 1st carter, 2nd carter, 3rd carter, 4th carter, 1st shepherd, 2nd shepherd, cowman, ordinary labourers, ploughboys, carter boys, shepherd boy, cow boy, extra men, extra women.[63] In east Yorkshire, as Stephen Caunce has explained, the terminologies varied, but the essential distinctions were either between the foreman, the waggoner, second waggoner, third waggoner (or second and third lads), down to the box lad; or between foreman, waggoner, third lad (or thirdy), fourther, fiver . . . ('They were never called *third* or *fourth waggoner* and there was no *seconder*'). Then there were the separate orders of the beast-men and shepherds and their lads, responsible for the care, respectively, of cattle and sheep rather than horses. These hierarchies 'governed life on every farm'. 'The lads identified with their role on the farm to the extent that those working together commonly called one another by their titles, such as wag, fourthy, sixer, etc., and not by their names.'[64]

Such differentiations were important – and it would be possible to provide all sorts of regional refinements – but it is also necessary to impose some structural order on the category. W. A. Armstrong has divided farm workers into farm servants, regular outdoor labourers and casual labourers.[65] Although we need to note the complexities acknowledged above, his basic divisions are a useful starting point.

Ann Kussmaul once wrote of the 'rout' and 'extinction' of farm service in the nineteenth century, but notices of its decline are proving somewhat premature.[66] Farm service was the practice, normative in England in the early modern period, of hiring young men and woman as live-in agricultural workers. Service was characterized by the contractual nature of the employment (for a period of several months or a year), its mobility (servants tended to regularly change their farms), its 'continuously available labour' (residence in the farmhouse or outlying buildings), and the youth of the workforce. It was also a transitional form of employment; it provided training in agriculture, but servants in husbandry did not expect to live their whole lives in service.[67] One simple difference between farm servants and their employers and fellow-workers was age. In England and Wales in 1871, almost 60 per cent of male farm servants were under the age of 20. Nearly 90 per cent were under the age of 35, compared with fewer than 50 per cent of agricultural labourers and only 15 per cent of farmers.[68]

The pattern of the supposed nineteenth-century demise of male farm service was regional. England's south-east experienced the greatest decline – although service was resilient in parts of Sussex and Kent.[69] In the north and west, farm service was relatively strong, adapting and even expanding as an institution of employment.[70] In north Lancashire, 'farm service met the labour requirements of stock rearing small farmers in an area of scattered settlement with few cottages'.[71] In the East Riding, it was common practice to employ boys and single men on yearly contract as live-in farm servants, responsible for the daily upkeep and working of the horses. Here, working with horses was characterized by youth. Farm workers started as unmarried servants ('horse*lads*'), and then married and became agricultural labourers. In contrast, 'horse*men*' in the south and east of England had custody of the horses; they were the more experienced, older workers, the 'aristocrats' of farm workers.[72]

As Kussmaul has put it, by 1851 'England had been divided between the low-service agricultural south and the high-service industrial north and west.'[73] In 1871, the last census distinguishing farm service, 85 per cent of England's male farm servants – nearly 110 000 in all – lived either in Cornwall or Devon or in counties north of a line drawn between the Wash and the Severn. Over a quarter of the nation's farm servants came from the Ridings of Yorkshire and Lancashire alone. Farm servants comprised nearly 60 per cent of hired male farm workers in Westmorland, 52 per cent in Cumberland, 43 per cent in the North Riding of Yorkshire, 41 per cent in the West Riding – all well above England's average of 13 per cent – but less than 10 per cent of workers in all the counties of the south-east.[74] (See Map 2.2.) The north-west/south-east division is clear.

We need to be careful not to minimize the role of farm service, even in areas where farm servants were numerically insignificant in the census. It is emerging that the county census figures miss live-in farm servants more clearly identifiable in individual parish enumerations. Goose has found that

Map 2.2 Farm servants as a percentage of male farm workers, 1871

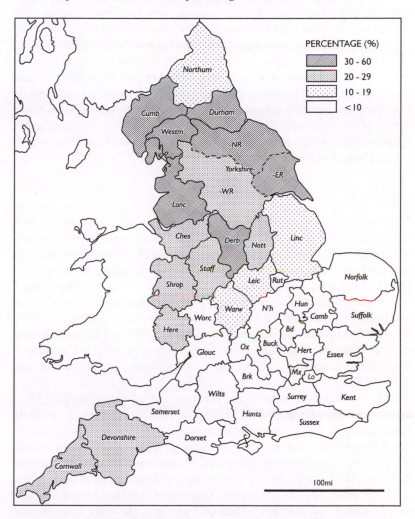

Source: My calculations from census of 1871: *Parliamentary Papers*, 1873, lxxi, part 1. Male farm workers are defined here as the total number of agricultural labourers and farm servants. The intention is to compare the relative strengths of these two types of male farm labour. Family labour is not included in this calculation.

almost 25 per cent of agricultural workers were farm servants in the St Albans area of Hertfordshire, whereas the county figure was less than 10 per cent according to the census of 1851.[75] In the Kentish Blean, the proportions of males employed as farm servants were insignificant, yet farm servant was the most important occupation after agricultural labourer and labourer for unmarried males aged 15 to 24. When we focus on this younger sex and age category, farm service assumes an importance masked by broader occupational structures. Indeed there were ten Blean farm servants for every thirteen labourers in that age group.[76] Farm service was also far from extinct in the formative work culture of Sussex labouring men. About a third of young, unmarried men were employed as farm servants in the Weald in 1851, and this generation would continue to work on farms as agricultural labourers for much of that century.[77]

* * *

The majority of farm workers were classified as 'agricultural labourers' in the nineteenth- and early twentieth-century censuses. The north-west/south-east division that we noted of the distribution of farm service is applicable to non-service labour, though with a reversal of weightings. (See Map 2.3.) Over 60 per cent of the nation's nearly 750 000 agricultural labourers recorded in the census of 1871 lived in the counties east of Devon and Cornwall and south of that notional line between the Wash and the Severn. In the south-east, 97 per cent of males employed as farm workers were described as agricultural labourers. Over a quarter of the nation's agricultural labourers came from Sussex, Kent, Essex, Suffolk and Norfolk.[78]

Len Austin was an agricultural labourer for his entire working life, a highly experienced one, who could describe the complexities of work with horses and the care of sheep, the skills associated with harvesting and the threshing machine and with hop and fruit growing, as well as the intricacies and hidden struggles of piece-work. 'When you went to work, a proper farm worker was supposed to be able to do anything there was on that farm ... Look after bullocks today, pigs tomorrow, get two horses to go to harrow tomorrow, next day perhaps go and help the brick layer, mix up cement, next help the chap on the roof doing the guttering. Don't matter what you do, stacker, thatcher, anything. Hop drier, you had to learn to do anything. If you was on that farm long enough.'[79]

The relative preponderance of agricultural labourers at a grass-roots level obviously varied from community to community. In predominantly agricultural villages – as in Elmdon (Essex) and the Blean parishes – some

Map 2.3 Agricultural labourers as a percentage of the agricultural workforce, 1871 (male and female combined)

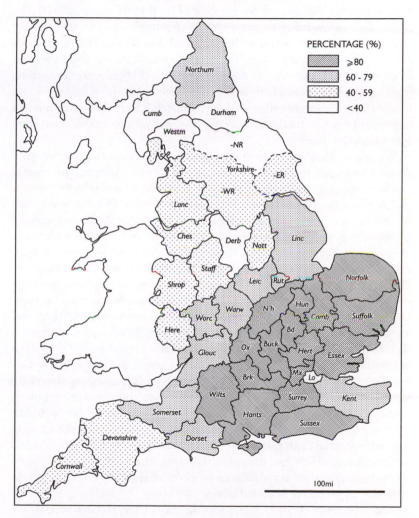

Source: My calculations from census of 1871: *Parliamentary Papers*, 1873, lxxi, part 1. The agricultural workforce consists of the total of family labour, agricultural labourers, and farm servants. Farmers are not included in the calculation.

50 to 60 per cent of the male workforce were so employed.[80] In J. B. Priestley's Godshill, on the Isle of Wight (now an archetypal 'olde worlde' tourist village), 54 per cent of employed males were classed as agricultural labourers in 1891.[81] In strongly agrarian Norfolk and Suffolk, the percentages were even higher: over 60 per cent of total male occupations.[82] The proportions were lower in more mixed economies. In the lead-mining village of Hennock in Devon in the 1850s and 1860s, from around 30 to 40 per cent of working males were employed in agriculture and from about 20 to 40 per cent in mining.[83] In mining/agricultural Highley in Shropshire, from 20 to 40 per cent of employed men were agricultural labourers and nearly 40 per cent were colliers.[84] Approximately a third of households in a large area of agricultural/lime burning Midland villages in the 1890s were agricultural labourers.[85]

When considering agricultural workers, we need to distinguish between the few 'constant men' and the vast bulk of casual labour. The regular outdoor labourer, the 'constant man', employed on a regular basis, perhaps on a yearly contract, could live quite comfortably. This élite, the 'aristocrats of rural labour', was comprised of men with particular skills or expertise – waggoners, ploughmen, cowmen, shepherds – or those with a wide range of abilities – hedging, ditching, thatching, working with horses, or hop-drying.[86] A summary of the data published by the Royal Commission on Labour in the 1890s stressed the regularity of labour for horsemen and stockmen employed on either a yearly or half-yearly contract in most English counties.[87] The account book for a Kent farm shows that there was a wide range of regular work for a few skilled men.[88] Those who, along with their families, worked more or less permanently earned from £35 to £57 a year in day-work, plus £4 to £14 extra for the harvest and hopping, a weekly average of from 15s to 25s.[89] It is likely that most communities of agricultural workers consisted of a mix of constant men and those less regularly employed. Work on the wage books of a Derbyshire farm shows a minority group of two men who worked more than 300 days each in 1840, eight men who worked from 100 to 270 days, and a cohort of nine who worked for from just 17 to less than 100 days in the year.[90] Lancashire farm accounts similarly demonstrate a dual reliance on a core of regularly employed workers and a 'large reserve of casual labour'.[91]

The experience of the majority was therefore likely to have been different from that of the labouring élite. Most farm workers in the 1890s were hired by the week or by the day.[92] When the Blean census of 1851 was taken in March and April, and farmers were asked how many men they employed, the total number that they gave was 54 per cent of the number of men and boys described as agricultural labourers or farm servants. The implication is that about half the male labouring population was out of work in the spring, and presumably even more in the winter.[93] In the south Midlands in 1831, half of the agricultural labourers 'were unemployed for most of the year'.[94] If there was such a thing as a typical agricultural worker, the occasional or casual labourer has a strong claim.

Rural workers were a socially static group. Quantitative work on national marriage registers for the period 1839–1914 indicates that those males categorized as 'Class V', unskilled (our workers), followed their fathers' example at the time they married. More than 70 per cent of unskilled grooms came from that specific class background. They tended to marry into that group as well: over 60 per cent of unskilled grooms married a woman whose father was from the same class background.[95] At the local level, work on both Kent and Suffolk rural parishes has revealed a similar pattern. The majority of women from labouring households married agricultural labourers and labourers. The majority of young labouring men who stood before the altar were the sons of labourers and farm workers.[96] Of those Kentish male labouring household heads in the census of 1851 whose backgrounds are known from family reconstitution, over 80 per cent had fathers who had earned their living in the same way.[97] The figures for Jean Robin's study of the Essex village of Elmdon are almost identical: almost all the fathers of agricultural labourers were agricultural labourers themselves.[98] Nor was there much individual mobility. Local studies make it possible to trace household heads throughout their life-course to determine movement in occupational status. Some labourers became bailiffs, took up a craft or a trade, or, if they were the kin of farmers, inherited a small block of land. Roughly a quarter changed occupation or status in some way at some stage. However, the vast majority – almost 75 per cent of the Kent sample – remained wage labourers.[99] When B. Seebohm Rowntree and May Kendall published their study of rural labour, they emphasized this stasis in comparison to rural workers on the Continent. Not only were agricultural workers in England and Wales predominantly paid labourers – 'having no direct financial interest in the success or otherwise of the work in which they are engaged' – but their state of alienation from the land that they tilled was a permanent rather than a temporary 'state of things'.[100]

* * *

There is no denying the importance of the male wage for working-class households. In the nineteenth century, male earnings comprised some 70 to 80 per cent of family incomes.[101] Indeed, knowledge of the male wage is one of the indicators of the gendered culture of rural workers in the nine-teenth and twentieth centuries, for male oral-history informants invariably knew what their fathers had earned, even though they were looking back to their own childhoods. (Girls were less clear, though more knowledgeable on other matters.) Men were aware of skilled and unskilled differentials and average earnings over long periods, and they often provided detailed infor-mation on piece-work or task-related earnings.

Academics have spent much time debating trends of standards of living during the industrial revolution, though somewhat less time on the relative fate of rural workers. There were both shorter-term fluctuations and longer-term trends. The impact of unionism in the 1870s almost certainly increased farm wages in the short term, but by 1880 they had returned to their previous level.[102] From a wider perspective, agricultural labourers' wages increased over the nineteenth century, although the increase was less dramatic than the wage improvements of the British worker as a whole. If average full-employment wages are converted to full-employment real earnings (adjusted in terms of the cost of living index), agricultural work-ers' real wages increased by less than 20 per cent by mid-century, compared to British workers' 33 per cent. By the end of the century, the increase for agricultural labourers was just over 40 per cent, compared to the general average of 70 per cent. (See Figure 2.1.) Charles Feinstein has interpreted his adjusted figures for British worker averages as evidence for 'the very moder-ate rate of improvement in full-employment real earnings', 'a long plateau in material standards' until the 1860s. Improvement for the agricultural labourer was even more modest.[103] The experience of other rural workers is often ignored. There seems little doubt, for example, that the situation of the hand-loom weavers declined: they were amongst the 'losers' in the industrial revolution.[104]

Those interested in such things were constantly perplexed at the impos-sibility of generating meaningful wage averages – and far more circumspect than some more recent commentators. 'It is extremely difficult . . . to get at the ranges of nominal weekly wages and estimated average weekly earnings the year round . . . the variations in the value of payments in kind and other perquisites are so puzzling that an immense amount of research and calcu-lation is necessary in order to give the total earnings during the year, and the weekly averages.'[105] There are indeed numerous problems with the nominal wage as a gauge of household income. First, normal wage-rates underestimate earnings, as A. L. Bowley signalled when he distinguished between 'wages' of 13s 4d and 'earnings' of 15s 9d for the general average in 1892–93 in his chart of agricultural labourers' wages. Often the male wage-rate does not include extra harvest earnings, piece-work, or perquisites.[106]

Figure 2.1 Agricultural labourers' real earnings, 1795–1880

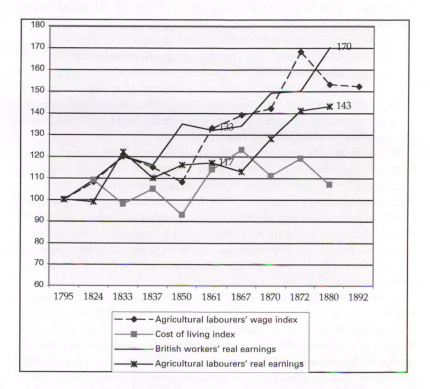

Sources: Based on a reworking of A. L. Bowley, 'The Statistics of Wages in the United Kingdom During the Last Hundred Years. (Part 1) Agricultural Wages', *Journal of the Statistical Society of London*, 61 (1898), pp. 706–7; and C. H. Feinstein, 'Pessimism Perpetuated: Real Wages and the Standard of Living in Britain During and After the Industrial Revolution', *Journal of Economic History*, 58 (1998), pp. 652–3.

Yet the nominal wage also *overestimates* earnings, particularly for casual labour – note that the figures in Figure 2.1 are average *full-employment* earnings. Averages are what their name suggests: averages that can mask huge variations in personal and group experience. The average weekly earnings on a large Dorset farm in 1868 varied from the 1st carter's 16s to the ordinary labourer's 10s.[107] In the Wiltshire parish of Corsley in 1905–07, the average earnings (not wages) of carters was 16s 9d but individual incomes varied from 20s 6d to a mere 10s. The average earnings of ordinary agricultural labourers was 15s 4d but some earned 17s, while others received 12s 6d per week.[108] An early sociological study of an English village noted the discrepancy between the county wage-rates of the official statistics and agricultural earnings on the ground: 'After a very careful examination of Mr. Fox's figures, I cannot help thinking that in working out his averages, he has not allowed enough for the enormously greater number of the lower grade of labourers over the higher grades.'[109] Moreover, national averages disguise substantial regional variations. A survey of a large number of Warwickshire villages in the 1890s noted wage differentials of up to 5s per week in comparable villages a mere 25 miles apart: 'The local variations in the rate of wages are often very remarkable.'[110]

When the weekly earnings of agricultural labourers are plotted, county by county, for three moments over the nineteenth and early twentieth centuries (1867-70, 1898 and 1907), the result is an upward trend, but with a large range in county experience. The difference between the highest and lowest wage counties was always between roughly 40 and 60 points in a 100-point index. (See Figure 2.2.) Gregory Clark has recently demonstrated that agricultural wage improvements in the nineteenth century were far stronger for the north and Midlands than they were for the south-east and the south-west.[111]

Wage security could not be taken for granted in the labouring world, and it may be a distortion to assume constant weekly employment throughout the year when rural workers could be without paid work because rain, frost or snow made work impossible, or when they were in receipt of lower wages. In the 1830s, the churchwarden of Titchfield, Hampshire, distinguished between about a quarter of workers 'often out of work' and earning only £10 to £15 a year, and the remainder whose income (excluding family earnings) was £30 to £35.[112] In East Grinstead, Sussex, agricultural labourers were divided into the two-thirds in regular hire, with wages of £34, and a third, out of work, who earned a mere £16 per annum.[113]

Opinions differed on the issue of lost time. When one rural investigator asked two Bedfordshire farmers what the annual income of their farm workers was, they said £36 to £40, whereas a meeting of labourers claimed that the figure was closer to £30.[114] One of the returns to the Poor Law Commissioners of 1834 allowed for eight to 12 weeks' loss of work through 'sickness, bad weather, and scarcity of employment'; others calculated five weeks each lost through bad weather and lack of work, and one week 'in looking out for work' (a total of 11 weeks).[115] In the 1870s, labourers told the Kent union activist, Alfred Simmons, that days lost amounted to as much as three months' worth of weekly wages per year (in effect, reducing a weekly wage of 15s 6d to just over 11s).[116] The various late nineteenth-century commissions of labour, on the other hand, normally stressed the

Figure 2.2 Index of agricultural labourers' weekly earnings, 1867–1907

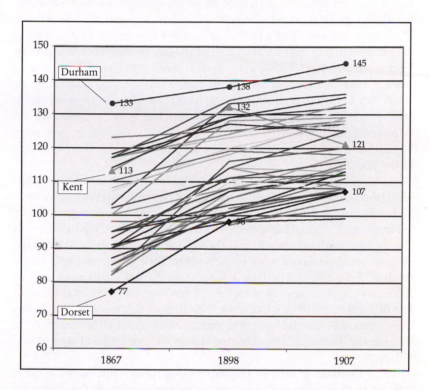

Source: Based on data in E. H. Hunt, *Regional Wage Variations in Britain 1850–1914* (Oxford, 1973), pp. 62–3. The weekly earnings have been indexed (15s in 1867 = 100).

relative lack of loss of work due to the wet and winter (or illness): two to three weeks per person was the most that they would acknowledge.[117] A survey of agricultural villages in the Midlands in the 1890s allowed only three and a half weeks a year from bad weather for a man in regular employment – and that included 'work on allotments, and holidays'.[118] More recently, Gregory Clark has claimed that male agricultural labourers enjoyed practically *full* employment in the nineteenth century, 'typically employed for 300 days or so per year'.[119]

It is hard to see how Clark's claims would stand against much of the evidence of rural labouring experience in the nineteenth century. Half of the agricultural labourers in the south Midlands in 1831 were out of work for the bulk of the year.[120] Certainly, 'loss of time in wet weather' was central to

discussions of late nineteenth-century agricultural labour; the mere fact
that it featured in both the *Daily News* survey of rural life in 1891 and the
Royal Commission on Labour in 1893–94 demonstrates the importance
of the issue.[121] Even Clark's own data for the Essex parish of Ardleigh in
1821 demonstrates 'significant unemployment in the months between
December and July' with up to 10 per cent of the workforce out of
work.[122] Poor law records also attest to the pronounced seasonality of
relief.[123] In Ampthill (Bedfordshire) in the 1820s and 1830s, labourers were
fully employed during the harvest months but heavily dependent on
poor relief for the rest of the year. The parish, like many others in
England at that time, 'was plagued by surplus labour for three-quarters
of the year'.[124]

As suggested earlier, the crucial distinction is between casual and long-
term labour. Too many of the calculations of farmers and commissioners –
and perhaps Clark's own – were based on information regarding the
'constant men'. Casual labour enjoyed no such security. Day-labourers in
Cumberland in the 1890s said that they lost at least one day a week in the
summer and two days a week in the winter. Their estimates imply yearly
totals of from 208 to 234 days, a long way off Clark's 300 and closer to
Simmons's figures mentioned earlier.[125] There was also the added factor of
loss of pay through illness. Using the friendly societies' records, James Riley
has calculated individual sickness durations of about *eight weeks* for the
Foresters of Abthorpe, a Northamptonshire shoemaking and agricultural
village.[126]

Local variation is vital to the national picture. While parish returns
differed in their estimates of labouring unemployment in the 1830s, the
Poor Law Report of 1834 indicates that rural fates were extremely localized.
The percentages of rural labourers out of work in the winter ranged from
the lows of 'none' for individual parishes in Staffordshire and Somerset to
highs of 40 and 60 per cent in some Sussex and Oxfordshire parishes.[127]
Labourers in Willington (Bedfordshire) were seldom out of employment,
'except the disabled and the infirm': all the labourers in Battle (Sussex) were
reported to be out of work for 'about four months' during the winter.[128]
With somewhat misplaced confidence in the quality of this data, one
economic historian has calculated an estimated 17 per cent of agricultural
labourers out of work in winter in the early 1830s.[129] Many of these families,
while not getting a wage, would have been in receipt of some form of poor
relief, of course.

Oral accounts provide supplementary evidence for the winter desperation in some labouring homes. A fenland woman recalled that her farm-
worker husband only had work in the spring and summer. 'No work in the

winter. February, that were the longest month of the year. No work, nor nothing.' Not surprisingly, he took to poaching.[130] Frank Pack's father was out of work for a 'couple of months' each winter. He never forgot those times 'we were all out of work': 'And we were starving, there's no doubt about it.'[131] P. H. Mann, who was the first person to apply Charles Booth and Seebohm Rowntree's social-survey methodologies to an English rural community, found in his study of the Bedfordshire village of Ridgmont that just over a third of the population were living in what he termed 'primary poverty': that is, their household income was insufficient to maintain basic physical health. Of the reasons given for this poverty, the predicament of over 50 per cent of the affected families, was attributed to either irregular work or low wages.[132]

The more astute social commentators were aware of what they termed the mortgaging of the summer wage to get by in winter. Edward Stanhope recalled that one labourer had challenged his employer's simple division of his total yearly earnings by 52 to arrive at his weekly income. He made the point that this did not take into account the fact that he worked eight or nine hours longer each day in the summer, lost time when it was wet, and had to cover the cost of purchase and wear on tools as well as the expense of subcontracted casual help. Stanhope said that the common pattern was for families to be a year or more behind so that the earnings in summer were used to catch up for the losses of the previous winter rather than being set aside for subsistence during the next.[133] It was not just farm work that was affected. Maidstone brickmakers, quarrymen and agricultural labourers, who often interchanged their occupations and who worked in the hamlets and villages outside this major Kent town, were out of work for two or three weeks every winter. The curate of a mission complained in the 1860s that not only were they 'in wretchedness themselves', but they absorbed 'much of the assistance which ought to go to the town labourers'.[134] Raphael Samuel once referred to the 'two economies' of the brickmakers and builders of the Oxfordshire village of Headington Quarry: the summer economy of relative abundance and opportunity, and the winter economy of slump and desperation.[135]

Although the problems of winter seem undeniable, we should not be too complacent about summer experiences. Several of the informants in the Poor Law Commission of the 1830s noted other slack times in the agricultural year. From 60 to 70 labourers were out of work during the winter in Westoning, Bedfordshire (population: 630), but 30 to 40 were 'often unemployed' 'during the rest of the Summer half-year', before the harvest.[136] In Hambleden in Buckinghamshire, out-of-work labourers were on poor relief in winter and for 'two months in the spring'.[137] In Enstone,

Oxfordshire, a fifth of labourers were out of employment in the summer, and were 'very badly maintained'.[138] The levels of unemployment in Boldre in Hampshire in the spring were almost as high as those in the winter.[139]

But perhaps the best way of demonstrating the gap between the surface message of average wages and the lived experience of actual weekly earnings is through the individual example. A graph of the annual earnings of an agricultural labourer in 1891–92, based on data in a table provided by the Royal Commission on Labour, shows clear fluctuations in annual earnings, from the harvest high of 33s in the last week of September to the winter low of 6s 6d in one grim March pay. From mid-October to May, the man, from Hollingbourne in Kent, was earning less than his average of 15s 6d a week. (See Figure 2.3.) Only 16 of the 52 weeks – less than a third of the year – saw earnings over his weekly average. And this was for someone who had day-work every week of the year.

* * *

Rural work was extremely fluid. Workers in nineteenth-century Kent moved from paper-mill to fruit and hop picking, from fishing to farm service, and from fieldwork to brickmaking and woodcutting.[140] In northern 'Wanet', the local economy was characterized by what Nigel Rapport has termed 'occupational bricolage'; 'the small farmer or artisan combined a number of economic activities, as suited to his particular skills . . . and the labour he could muster according to the developmental cycle of his family. Knitting, quarrying, mining, stock-rearing, cheese- and butter-making were all turned to as partial means of securing economic survival.'[141] When machinery undermined the livelihood of the nailers of Catshill, near Birmingham, who had manufactured nails in sheds attached to their cottages, they were able to acquire tiny smallholdings. The result, as one observer expressed it in 1902, was that 'instead of forging iron, they are growing strawberries for the Birmingham market.'[142]

Although agricultural workers are important to the history of English rural labour, this chapter has made it clear that they are only part of the story. In Headington Quarry, the male workforce of 1891 was evenly divided into quarryworkers and stoneworkers, brickmakers and their labourers, general labourers, agricultural labourers and miscellaneous trades and crafts. Farm workers only made up about 13 per cent of male occupations.[143] In the Forest of Dean rural community of Berry Hill, woodworkers and stoneworkers were each as numerous as agricultural labourers (8 per cent), and the largest group of male workers (27 per cent) was the miners.[144] These miners were rural workers. Indeed, they were the men with pale faces, blue

Figure 2.3 Weekly earnings of a Kent agricultural labourer, 1891–1892 (in shillings)

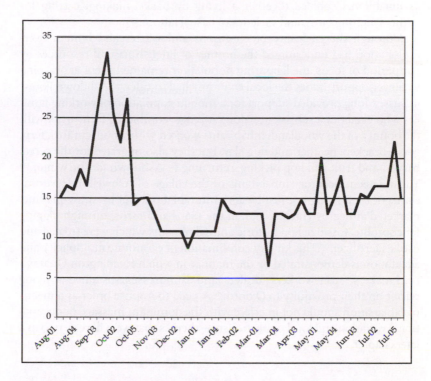

Source: *Royal Commission on Labour: The Agricultural Labourer: Reports ... Upon ... Selected Districts, Parliamentary Papers*, 1893–4, xxxv, p. 681. The man earned an average of 15s 6d a week.

coal scars, and the silicosis rattle, immortalized by the writer Dennis Potter.[145]

It has been suggested that we need to keep in mind a range of rural trades and industries. The framework-knitters of the Nottinghamshire village of Calverton, for example, adapted their household economies throughout the nineteenth century, responding to the demand for specialized work, and surviving into the twentieth century. Pam Sharpe was able to tap into a 'living memory' of the trade as late as the 1980s.[146] Nor should we neglect rural fishing villages like nineteenth-century Marshside, near Southport (Lancashire), which depended heavily on the harvesting of shrimps, with its men, women and children involved in the various stages of catching, shelling, cooking, potting and selling. During the slack season, its inhabitants cobbled together a living by basket-making, carting for farmers, netting birds, and varieties of casual labour.[147]

Although the enclosure of commons and wastes and human over-exploitation had undermined the bounty of English natural resources by our period of focus, the labouring population remained adept at grasping whatever opportunities the local economy had to offer.[148] Ashdown Forest in Sussex long provided support for a mobile population of working families who eked out a subsistence along its edge, combining farm work with the bounty of the woodland. Inhabitants worked with wood, cut turf, fern, gorse, bracken, heather, and dug clay. But they also migrated for the cereal harvest and fruit and hop picking, returning to Ashdown for the winter.[149] The nineteenth-century inhabitants of the village of Ashwell in Hertfordshire got their living not just by agricultural labour but by straw-plaiting, marketed at nearby Hitchin, and, in the 1860s and 1870s, through digging for coprolite, fossilized prehistoric animal remains which were treated and used as fertilizer.[150] This kind of combination of economic multiplicity and adaptation is demonstrated by the manner in which Headington Quarry's brickmakers, stoneworkers, dealers and laundresses sustained a living reliant on their proximity to Oxford.[151] A need to impose order as a means of explanation should not interfere with the dominant message of occupational variation and local opportunism – themes that we will return to in a later chapter.

3 Working Women and Children

It would be very misleading to convey the impression that rural work was limited to males.[1] Farmers were female as well as male, and daughters as well as sons were employed on family farms.[2] Local studies invariably contain examples of women who managed farms after the death of a husband, indicating significant involvement at an earlier stage.[3] The census of 1871 recorded 24 000 female farmers and graziers, 187 000 wives of farmers and graziers, and 92 000 daughters and other relatives of farmers. In other words, over 300 000 women either possessed or worked farms, or 'assist[ed] in the occupation' of a close male relation.[4]

3 Fieldworkers, 1860s

A group of female farm workers, from the collection of the collector of images of working women, the Victorian poet Arthur Munby

The crafts and trades included women as well as men. In 1901, a tenth of employed rural females worked as tailors, dressmakers, or in allied trades. There were as many female general shopkeepers as there were male in the rural districts in the early twentieth century.[5] We can explore this at the microlevel in local studies. In the Kent village of Boughton in 1851, women worked as laundresses, seamstresses, milliners and dressmakers, and there was a tailor, a grocer and draper, a milliner, a shoe-binder, and a female blacksmith who employed two male workers.[6] The women of Corsley in Wiltshire in the 1900s found employment as laundresses, and in charring, sewing, dealing, dressmaking and gloving. Indeed, gloving occupied a 'large proportion' of women in the Corsley area who took in work from local factories. As with the men, the category 'craft and trade' comprised employers and the self-employed, as well as workers. Laundresses in Corsley included women who took in 'sufficient washing to oblige them to employ other women to help them'. A laundress who managed to take in gross earnings of 12s per week had to pay a worker 3s and deduct costs of 1s 6d, leaving her with an income of 7s 6d ('For this she has to work hard'). Corsley dressmakers consisted of both the self-employed, who, at 3s 6d per skirt or blouse, managed incomes varying from 7s to £1 a week, and their day-workers who were paid 1s per day plus food.[7]

An added, but semi-visible, role of women in the 'male' crafts and trades is reflected in the almost 200 000 'wives of' innkeepers, publicans, beer-sellers, shopkeepers (undefined), shoemakers and butchers enumerated in the census of 1871. Over 90 000 women had their occupation defined as 'wife of shoemaker', presumably in recognition of the part that they played in their husbands' businesses.[8] Mrs E. Clark, daughter of a shoemaker, said that her mother did all the cooking for her father's five apprentices as well as embroidering flowers around the buttonholes on the women's shoes.[9] Fanny Rigden recalled that her father, a cabinetmaker, decorator and uphol-sterer, 'used to go about gentlemen's houses with my mother, she used the machine, he cut the material out, and my mother used to put it together'. Rigden also made coffins; but his wife did the linings.[10]

* * *

According to the census definition of 'occupation', agriculture was one of the largest categories of employment for women in England: about 25 per cent over the period 1851–91, dropping from 27 per cent at the beginning of the period to 16 per cent at its end.[11] The national patterns of male agri-cultural labour and farm service, discussed earlier in relation to the census of 1871, reveal differences for women. Although we are dealing with considerably smaller numbers – 30 500 labourers and 18 500 servants – a larger proportion of the recorded female agricultural workforce was employed as farm servants than that of the males, and the distinction between the south-east and north-west is less pronounced. (See Map 3.1.) Nearly 40 per cent of female agricultural workers were classified as farm servants (compared to 13 per cent for males), and the proportion that lived in the counties of the north-west was just under 60 per cent (compared to 85 per cent for male farm servants). However, the age profiles are similar to those of the men. Farm service was a life-stage occupation for women. 45 per cent of female farm servants in England and Wales were less than 20 years old, compared to 20 per cent of female agricultural labourers.[12]

The type of work that female farm servants carried out is discussed less than that of the men.[13] It is likely that there was some overlap between domestic activity and farm service, particularly on the smaller properties. Elizabeth Armstrong, who worked on a Cumberland farm, described her duties as including domestic as well as agricultural work: 'you had to start on your housework as well after you got in, whereas the men were finished, once they got their horses groomed and fed'. She would start at 6 a.m., milking, and then, after breakfast, would clean the dairy and wash the breakfast dishes; she milked again at the end of the day. In between, there were vegetables to prepare for the meals, the pigs to be cared for, and food to be taken to the men in the fields. However, she was also expected to help in fieldwork: 'Whatever season was on, I had to help with it. Pick potatoes and help with the harvest and such as that. Thin turnips . . . you were on call whenever the men decided they wanted a bit of help, maybe have to go and help move some sheep out of a field . . . help if the cows were calving or anything that was on a farm . . . scaling manure – putting it all over the field.'[14]

Women's work involved two economies: the formal market economy, with the wage at its centre, ruled by men, and the informal economy, non-wage-based, located in the family and dominated by the labour of women and children.[15] The census recorded participation in the formal economy, but notoriously failed to recognize those who worked part-time or whose labour became conveniently subsumed under that of the household head. While the census of 1901 gave the number of women (excluding farmers' female relatives) engaged in agriculture as 12 000, farmers' returns to the agricultural output survey of 1906 indicate a figure of 68 000.[16] A revealing comparison between the Gloucestershire census returns and farm accounts shows that the mixed arable and pasture areas offered work for women that was not recorded in the census: harvest work, hoeing, singling, weeding, topping, manure-spreading, reaping and threshing. The census

Map 3.1 Farm servants as a percentage of female farm workers, 1871

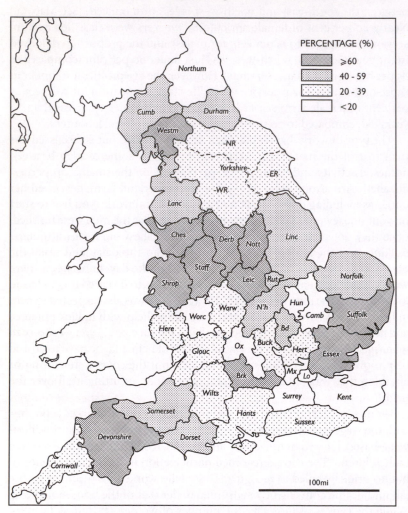

Source: My calculations from census of 1871: *Parliamentary Papers*, 1873, lxxi, part 1.
Female farm workers are defined here as the total number of agricultural labourers
and farm servants. The intention is to compare the relative strengths of these two
types of female farm labour. Family labour is not included in this calculation.

ignored most of these women, yet Celia Miller found that female labourers performed a third of the day-work in some Gloucestershire farms.[17] Unpublished research on nineteenth-century Somerset farms has detected a comparable mismatch between the census and actual female farm work.[18] Interestingly, Miller found that the employment pattern of Gloucestershire women was similar to that of the men: regular work for one group, casual labour for the rest. The constants had 'the same allocation of work as the regular male day-labourers, most of whom worked for between 150 and 250 days per year plus piecework'.[19]

* * *

Domestic service was a principal occupation for women. At any point between 1851 and 1931, between 1.1 and 1.8 million women earned their living in this way.[20] These were the general servants, maids, domestic servants, cooks, housekeepers and household nurses. Edward Higgs's revised census figures for women's work reduce these numbers to between 500 000 and 750 000 during the nineteenth century, but still indicate that around 20 per cent of employed women earned their living as domestic servants during that period.[21] Possibly a third of occupied females in 1891, according to another estimate, were domestic servants. A Board of Trade report in 1899 described domestic service as 'not only the largest women's industry, but the largest single industry for either men or women'.[22] Indeed, service was an important, if declining, occupation for young women right up until the Second World War.[23]

There was regional variation. In rural Hampshire in 1891, over 40 000 women over the age of ten were employed as domestic servants, more than for any other occupational category (male or female) and twice the number of male agricultural labourers and farm servants.[24] Michael Drake has demonstrated that the percentages of 15- to 19-year-old women employed as servants in the Yorkshire registration districts varied from a low of 7 to a high of 52; but these extremes were (respectively) in the industrial area of Keighley and the town of York. The bulk of districts had over 20 per cent so employed; in the East and North Ridings the totals were 40 per cent and over.[25]

Like farm service, domestic service was characterized by its mobility, relative youth, and the life-stage nature of this employment: the bulk of women employed as servants expected to move on to marriage or some other form of employment. We can see some of these elements in the statistics provided by the 1899 survey. Some 65 per cent of domestic servants in England and Wales were under 25 years old. And the bulk of those women surveyed had been in service for less than five years in the household making the return.[26] It is comparatively rare for the same domestic servant to appear in the same household in consecutive ten-yearly censuses.

Young women also moved out of their parish to take up service. All the single female emigrants from the Kent communities of Dunkirk and Hernhill, located in the census of 1851 in surrounding parishes, were house servants, maids, housekeepers and general servants. Although the stereotype is of service in the large household of the gentry or prosperous upper middle class, the majority of servants in studies of rural Kent and Rutland were in the households of farmers and the trades and crafts.[27] The 'typical' servant household was not one of a hierarchy and multiplicity of servants, but of one or two general or household servants. Nearly 80 per cent of the Kent servants were in households with from one to three servants; and 40 per cent were in houses where they were the only servant.

Service could be a rather isolating experience. In the words of a woman who had worked as a 'general', the only servant in a farming household, 'it was lonely to be in service'. She worked from 6 a.m. to 8 p.m., every day, with her only breaks on Thursday afternoons (2 p.m. to 6 p.m.) and Sunday evenings (6 p.m. to 8 p.m.). There was nowhere for her to go during her leisure hours: only 'roaming the country roads' or to church. Her daily duties involved cleaning, lighting the fires, helping to prepare breakfast, lunch and supper, caring for a baby (and then a young child), washing its clothes, doing the family ironing (their washing was sent out to a local woman), taking the child for a walk every afternoon. They were 'nice people to work for', but life was very restrictive. She had to wear appropriate clothing: a black dress when she took the child out, a white apron and cap for serving, a blue apron for scrubbing. She had to be in by certain times, and was not to talk to 'anyone' – that is, male farm workers – while walking the child. Her wage was 3s 6d per week.[28] An Essex cowman's daughter, who also worked as a general servant, thought that the experience would have been better where there was more than one servant. She spent every evening on her own.[29] Elizabeth Armstrong was a servant at an isolated Cumberland farm about the time of the First World War: 'I was never from that place for two and a half years apart from my half-term holiday. And I never spoke to anybody or anything at that place . . . I often think it's a wonder I didn't go crackers.'[30]

Village studies of female and male occupations indicate that there was roughly the same proportion of women listed as servants as there was men occupied as agricultural labourers or labourers. Although young women from the families of farmers and those in the trades and crafts worked in other households as servants, service was primarily associated with the

children of rural labourers. Nearly 90 per cent of unmarried women aged
15 to 24 who were assigned an occupation in the census of 1851 in the Blean
in Kent were listed as servants of some type.[31] The oral accounts of those
who grew up in the late nineteenth and early twentieth centuries are insistent on this. 'That's all the girls had to do, go in service. Nothing else.' 'That's
all there was for girls then.' 'When I was young there was nothing for girls
to do except go into service.' '[P]ractically any girl that had got any go at all
was in service.'[32]

* * *

There is historiographical disagreement over the role of women in the nineteenth-century rural workforce.[33] However, contemporary commentators
did not share the uncertainties of future historians. One of the commissioners examining the employment of children and women in agriculture
took it as axiomatic that by the 1860s there was a firm movement away
from the use of women in fieldwork, a disinclination shared by employer
and potential employee. Legislation was superfluous because the 'employment of women in the fields is gradually dying out'.[34] This axiom was
repeated in the 1890s: 'it looks as if the employment of women in agriculture is, at no distant date, likely to be a thing of the past'. Lancashire labourers were reputed to have said, 'we keep our women at home, which is their
proper sphere'.[35]

There is certainly no denying the ideological imperative in this direction.
'The principal objection to field work for women is the loss of refinement
which almost necessarily ensues. "It is most destructive to the female character" ... "It tends to tarnish the purity of their minds and feelings and to
make them 'mannishly' coarse" ... besides this, field work by married
women causes a "loss of evening comfort to the husband"... and too often
renders the woman altogether unfit for domestic duties.'[36] Nineteenth-
century parliamentary reports, newspapers and periodicals, novels, poetry,
art, rural memoirs all attested that women's fieldwork was the antithesis of
Victorian femininity. Karen Sayer has demonstrated cadences within the
condemnations. Many farmers, and the labourers themselves, valued
women's fieldwork. The parliamentary reports of the 1840s were more
tolerant than those of the 1860s, and, even in the latter, individual reporters
and regional findings showed greater ambivalence in their attitudes than
the overall tenor of the findings. While women's role in the agricultural
gangs was anathema, there was acceptance, indeed idealization, of dairy
work and harvesting throughout Victorian literature and art – the milkmaid represented nature and femininity. Supporters of the National

Agricultural Labourers' Union reinforced such messages in the 1870s. The allegation that women's work depressed men's wages was an important element in their argument, but the languages of domesticity were plain: a 'woman's place was in her home and her proper work was to keep it comfortable and happy'.[37]

It could be argued that from a labouring perspective the move to 'housewifery' was a conscious strategy, a way of making do born of the awareness that it was more cost-effective to focus on the home rather than the employment market. Married women had to consider the effects of their absence. With a young child in the house, and without older children to assume child-care responsibilities, it must have made more sense to stay at home with the child. If a son or daughter was working and living at home, the better strategy was probably to devote time to aspects of household survival other than simple wage labour. The cost of child care or clothing was often more than the potential wages involved in outside paid work. It was a common nineteenth-century complaint that 'Between the woman that works and the woman that doesn't there is only 6d. to choose at the year's end, and she that stays at home has it.'[38] The Assistant Commissioner, Frederick H. Norman, claimed that 'almost everywhere' in his counties there was 'an increasing disinclination to field work on the part of women'. Women told him that the money they could earn 'by going into the fields is insufficient to compensate . . . for the necessary loss which is occasioned by . . . absence from home'.[39]

We should not accept this claim uncritically. Discussions tend to lose sight of the fact that it was frequently the labourers' social superiors who were making this decision for them, rather than workers themselves. When the occasional rural worker spoke, he or she could be referring to uneconomic, part-time women's work (and the ill-paid labour of very young children) rather than women's (and children's) work *per se*. When labouring women did advocate relinquishing the fields, it was not just to prepare food and mend clothes but also to earn money by sewing, washing or charring for others. Where it did occur, then, the phenomenon was not so much a decline in women's work as a redirection of energies.[40]

In any case, it was rarely an uncomplicated choice between outside work and inside housework and/or homework. The reality was that rural working women faced a continual battle to make do, and individuals adopted changing strategies in their economies of makeshift. A Norfolk women, interviewed in 1867, explained that by taking in needlework she found that she could keep an eye on the household, look after the children, and monitor their consumption of food. (She also suggested that if women stayed out of the fields there would be more work for their husbands.) Her strategy was to get her daughters (eight in all) into service, and found that prospective employers were more favourably disposed to girls who had not been out in the fields. Yet she had worked at the harvest and had allowed her daughters to assist their father in fieldwork.[41]

While not minimizing the evidence for the decline of women's agricultural labour, it is also necessary to problematize any notions of a simple transformation. The mere fact that the demise of female fieldwork was taken for granted in two surveys 25 years apart suggests that its decline was not as rapid as implied by its detractors. We shall probably never have a clear picture. As will be stressed throughout this book, there were important regional variations. Alfred Austin, Assistant Commissioner for the Reports on the Employment of Women and Children in Agriculture in 1843, observed that the 'kinds of agricultural labour in which women are engaged appear to depend on the habits of narrow localities'.[42] Edward Stanhope's report to the Parliamentary Commission of 1867 stated: 'Women are engaged in farm labour in all the counties visited by me, but the nature and extent of their employment varies in almost every parish, and frequently on adjoining farms.'[43]

The problem is that the impressions of the agricultural surveyors do not always tally with the available statistics. The census of 1871 permits a tabular snapshot of female employment, with female agricultural labourers, farm servants and family labour plotted as a percentage of the total male and female agricultural workforce. (See Map 3.2.) The top ten counties in terms of female agricultural employment – Derbyshire (41 per cent), Durham (41), Westmorland (41), Cumberland (39), Cornwall (38), Northumberland (38), West Riding (38), Lancashire (37), North Riding (34), Cheshire (32), Staffordshire (30) – were in the north, Midlands, and the west.[44] They tend to correlate to the patterns of family labour mapped in the previous chapter. (See Map 2.1.) While some of the top ranking counties in the census do correspond to the commissioners' observations in the 1860s – Cumberland and Northumberland – others do not. Dorset, which figured as a county of regular women's employment in the 'Second Report of the Commissioners on the Employment of Children, Young Persons, and Women in Agriculture', had 20 per cent of its agricultural workforce comprised of women in 1871, below the national average of 25 per cent. Hampshire, described by the commissioners as a county where women's agricultural labour was 'universal' in the 1860s, was ranked (at 14 per cent) towards the bottom in the table of the female rural workforce in 1871.[45] These discrepancies are probably accounted for by an underestimation of the role of women in small-farming family labour – a mistake made by the commissioners as well as many future historians.

Map 3.2 Female labour as a percentage of the agricultural workforce, 1871

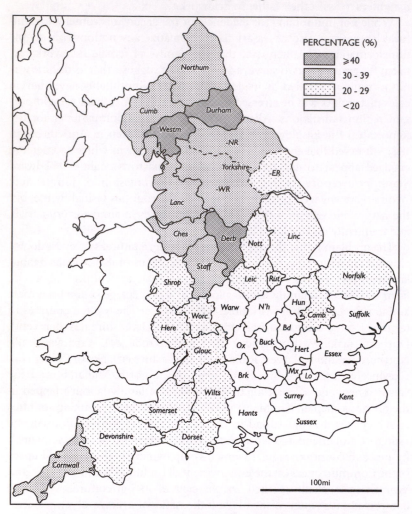

Source: My calculations from census of 1871: *Parliamentary Papers*, 1873, lxxi, part 1. The agricultural workforce (male and female) consists of the total of family labour, agricultural labourers, and farm servants. Farmers are not included in the calculation.

We can make some generalizations. There were areas of female strength. The role of women in Northumberland was clearly crucial; 'their labour is considered essential for the cultivation of the soil'. In north Northumberland in the 1890s, women were said to be 'very extensively employed', outnumbering men on many farms. Farmers were quite open about the cost-effectiveness of female labour in the north-east, providing 'work almost as effective as the men's at nearly half the price'. Women were hired in their own right as byrewomen (in charge of cattle), as cottars (farm servants), but mainly as the wives and daughters of hinds (ploughmen or spade men), hired by the year and moving annually from farm to farm. Indeed, the availability of female labour in a hind's family was a marketable commodity when it came to negotiating his contract. Hinds who did not have the requisite wives or daughters had traditionally hired women – bondagers – to provide the required female labour. Bondagers boarded with the hind and were paid by him; for obvious reasons both the term and the practice were dying out by the 1890s.[46] In the 1890s, women still made up a quarter of all farm workers in Northumberland, and one-eighth of the nation's female farm workers.[47] Mary Bruce, who worked as a farm worker just after the First World War, did pretty much anything on the farm, including mucking out the byres and working with horses (which astonished her interviewer).[48]

In Cumberland, another high-ranking county of female rural employment, commentators in the 1860s noted both the decline and the prevalence of female agricultural labour. While it was said that the days were gone when 'half the carts in the county of Cumberland were driven by females', there was agreement that in some districts farmers relied on women's labour. The messages could be somewhat confused. Though the claims are not necessarily mutually exclusive, some farmers felt compelled to employ women, given the high wages and alternative job prospects for male labour. Others claimed that they could not get women to work for them for the same reasons. But it does seem that the wives of brickworkers and railway labourers were employed in fieldwork, that many women were forced into agricultural labour after the decline of hand-loom weaving in that part of the country, and that farmer after farmer observed that 'If it were not for women it would be impossible to carry on farming in this county.' Women formed a reserve army of labour, drawn on for spreading dung, weeding, thinning, and harvesting turnips and potatoes. The farmer of a 600-acre estate rented from the Earl of Lonsdale employed 8 male and 2 female farm servants on a regular basis, but at peak times of labour demand brought in as many as 60 women and 20 to 30 children to work his fields.[49] A 2000-acre farm on the Scottish border did not bother with reaping machines because there were enough local women to bring in the harvest. In nearby Longtown, women either went into domestic service or lived by fieldwork.[50] Women also worked in the agricultural gangs, more of which later. It was a measure of the importance of women's agricultural work in Cumberland in the 1860s that they were able to strike successfully for higher wages.[51]

The contradiction between the quantitative and qualitative data on Dorset is relatively easy to explain. Female agricultural labour was said to be common in Dorset, partly because of the practice of hiring whole families to work the large farms, partly because of the presence of small peasant holdings, but also because of the seasonal and depressed nature of men's work. Much of the work done by women (apart from the harvest) was winter work – 'among the turnips, on the threshing machines, or in the barns' – and therefore unlikely to be recorded in the census.[52] Work on the threshing machines indicates the ability of women to adapt to new farming practices – though, as with much women's work in the nineteenth century, they did not escape middle-class scrutiny. 'The great objection to be made to all such employment is, that it places them during the whole day's work in close company with men ... the women who constantly work with threshing machines, following them as they go from farm to farm, are generally amongst the most degraded of their class, although in physical condition they are more than half men.'[53]

The assistant commissioner for the rather disparate counties of Surrey, Wiltshire, Warwickshire, Worcestershire and Herefordshire drew a useful distinction between ordinary employments for women and special employments. The former consisted of weeding, stone-picking, manure-spreading, potato- and bean-planting, haying, harvesting, acorn-picking, potato-gathering, and winter work on the threshing machine and with turnips and mangold-wurzels. Special employments included bark-stripping (April–May), hop-tying (May–June) and hop-picking (September). Some special employments were even more localized: carrot-washing and work in the medical herb gardens in Surrey, and opportunities in Worcestershire in Evesham's fruit and vegetable gardens.[54]

It is likely, then, that the most appropriate way to examine the rural work of women is at an inter-county level. The county, an administrative unit, provides little purchase on this evasive topic. As intimated, the fruit and hop economies of parts of Kent and elsewhere ensured an ongoing role for women in the cycle of employment; 'in the hop-growing parishes, almost any woman can work (if she will) during a considerable part of the year'.[55] Indeed, these economies figure strongly in accounts of married women's work in the early twentieth century. When M. F. Davies visited north Worcestershire in the 1900s, examining married women's work, she noted the opportunities offered by hops and fruit. Women could work for half or three-quarters of the year; many worked three or four ten-hour days a week as well as carrying out normal household responsibilities. Attitudes to work were at variance with the culture betrayed in nineteenth-century surveys. Although Davies admitted that women's work was decreasing, she wrote that 'Public opinion approves of wage earning by married women; and the woman who abstains from working in the fields is taunted – even if she has young children – with being lazy.'[56] September hop-picking became part of the labouring culture of these parts of rural England. Kent schools closed and the women and children of dockland and working-class London descended upon the hop-grounds, and the men joined them on weekends.[57] Hop-gardens also offered other work. Men did hop-poling with help from their families. Women tied hops.[58] The *Morning Chronicle* survey of the rural districts in 1850 was well aware of the importance of hops in the economies of families in the southern counties:

> the hop-picking season is generally looked forward to by many of them with considerable anxiety, as being the turning-point as regards their means for the year. It interposes like a screen between many of them and the workhouse . . . It is seldom, indeed, that you find them relying upon this alone for obtaining the necessaries of life. But they do almost universally rely upon it for supplying them with the means of meeting all the extra expenses to which they have been put, or may still be put, during the remainder of the year, such as for medical attendance, shoes, change of raiment, &c.[59]

* * *

Of course, the work of rural women was not confined to agriculture. The Poor Law Report of 1834 provides a convenient snapshot of the alternatives at the start of our period of interest. There was lace-making and plaiting straw in Bedfordshire and Buckinghamshire, mine-work and fish-curing in Cornwall, silk-factory work in Berkshire, Essex and Suffolk, button-making and gloving in Dorset, stocking-making in Gloucestershire and Leicestershire, lace-making in Northamptonshire, gloving in Oxfordshire, Somerset and Worcestershire, knitting in Rutland, lace and cotton work in Staffordshire, and weaving and employment in the woollen and cotton industries in Yorkshire.[60] Nicola Verdon has demonstrated a national pattern in 1834 where the counties of high incidence in rural industrial work for women and children record lower participation in agricultural labour.[61] They tend to correspond to the lighter shaded and white areas of Maps 2.1 and 3.2.

As hinted earlier, we should not equate the numerous comments about the demise of women's agricultural labour with a general decline in women's work. The Royal Commission on Labour of 1893–94 reported that women 'work very little on the land in Nottinghamshire', yet also stressed alternatives. Village women worked in the Nottingham hosiery manufactures and the Mansfield shoe trade. Formerly, they had been extensively involved in lace-making: 'The prevalence of this work in the old times probably explains why the women of district have never, or at least for many years, worked on the land to any considerable extent.'[62] Leicestershire women in the villages around Leicester, Hinckley and Lutterworth were employed in the 1860s at seaming and stocking-making.[63]

In areas where homework was available, the percentage of women workers was always likely to be substantial. In the Oxfordshire glove-making parish of Eynsham in 1851, 44 per cent of married women were in paid employment (many of them were married to agricultural labourers).[64] In the village of Headington Quarry, near Oxford, laundry work rivalled brickmaking, and building and stonework as the major local industry. By 1891, laundresses, who took in washing from Oxford's colleges, hotels, churches, dons and students, formed the largest single occupational group in Headington, male or female. Headington's 55 laundresses made up 16 per cent of all those employed and nearly 60 per cent of occupied women. Most were married women and daughters still at home, but over 20 per cent were widows. Raphael Samuel has observed that this laundry work was more than a mere supplement to male wages; for some households, it was the 'only means of support'.[65]

Davies described gloving in the villages around Westbury in Wiltshire in the 1900s as a 'new industry', so it survived into the twentieth century. It was, she wrote, 'a purely parasitic industry' in that it did not provide a living wage for an independent, single woman but rather low-wage supplementary subsistence to married women and children. Those women who worked at gloving averaged a mere 2s per week; 'Yet it is the prospect of gaining these tiny sums that induces the woman to take up this work. They need to eke out a husband's low wage . . . or they desire to have a shilling or two of their very own, as they feel their personal earnings to be.'[66] In the glove-making areas of southern Somerset in the 1860s – around Milborne Port, Yeovil and south of Taunton, along the Dorset border – labourers' wives and daughters were widely employed in this form of home-manufacture. 'Where it prevails, scarcely a woman is to be found engaged in outdoor work; it is difficult to combine the two, as a softness of hand and delicacy of touch is required for sewing gloves that soon disappears in manual labour, and gloving is naturally most often preferred as the more remunerative employment.'[67] Women in the village of Montacute worked at gloving (the men worked as farm labourers or in the quarries). Nearly 80 per cent of Montacute women worked according to the census of 1851, and in 1891 the proportion of working women was still over 60 per cent.[68] In Dorset, women in Pimperne and Stourpaine who were not engaged in agricultural work either took in washing from nearby Blandford or worked at knitting or gloving.[69] In the same area in the 1840s, in villages in a triangle from Blandford to Shaftesbury to Sturminster, women and children had worked at wire-button-making for shirts but were under serious threat from the competition of the pearl button.[70] Across the border in the Devonshire agricultural and lace-making market town of Colyton, some 75 per cent of the wives of labourers were employed, principally as lace-makers.[71]

The complementary pattern of male farm work and female industrial home labour can be found in other parts of the country. In the lace-making and straw-plaiting villages of Bedfordshire, the men worked as agricultural labourers and their wives as lace-makers or straw-plaiters.[72] Just over 50 per cent of females of the age of 15 and above were assessed as occupied by the census enumerators in lace-making Ridgmont.[73] The wives and daughters of farm workers in the Cambridgeshire fenland town of Littleport worked as either factory workers or outworkers in the shirt-manufacturing industry; at least 40 per cent of adult women had a stated occupation when the census of 1891 was taken.[74] Women near the Suffolk town of Bury St Edmunds were 'hardly ever employed' in agriculture, but they did outwork for clothing factories.[75] In the Suffolk village of Brandon in 1891, the wives of agricultural labourers worked in the local fur industry.[76]

In Essex, the decline of the cloth trade led to a reduction in the employment of women and children in spinning and weaving. However, a compensatory shift to silk and lace, straw-plaiting, and outwork for the clothing and footwear industries replaced the decline of cloth. As Pamela Sharpe has put it, deindustrialization was replaced by reindustrialization. These industries were centred in the towns, but much of the outwork occurred in the village hinterland, which also supplied labour for the mills.[77] Essex women worked at straw-plaiting in their own cottages rather than going out to work in the fields, and, in the Haverhill area on the Cambridgeshire/Suffolk/Essex border, carried out slopwork for the corduroy manufacturers and ready-made-clothing dealers in the town.[78] Davies wrote in the early 1900s of a viable outwork clothing industry in the marsh villages of the Essex coast, near Colchester. Here, the wives of sailors, fishermen and farm workers sewed garments for the Colchester clothing industry, which, in turn, filled contracts for large firms in the Midlands and London.[79]

Nigel Goose's Hertfordshire studies are particularly interesting in relation to women's work because they deal with an area where there were high
rates of female employment because of the straw-plaiting and hat industries. Nearly 70 per cent of women in the rural parishes of the St Albans
region were employed according to the census of 1851: that is, some 50 per
cent of married women, nearly 80 per cent of widows, and close to 90 per
cent of single women. In the large village of Harpenden, around 75 per cent
of married women were in employment. The figures for a comparable
hinterland of villages around the market towns of Great Berkhamsted and
Tring were similar. It is a remarkable record of female participation in the
formal workforce – albeit a highly localized and economically vulnerable
one.[80]

* * *

Children also played an important role in rural work. Assistant
Commissioner Stanhope outlined the nature of child labour in agricultural
districts: 'The labour of children is of two sorts; (1) where they are hired
directly by the occupier of the farm, and (2) where they are employed by
their parents on gardens or allotments, in assisting in gleaning or other
family work, in collecting fuel or woo[d], and in gathering blackberries or
mushrooms in the lanes.'[81] H. Seymour Tremenheere's report claimed that,
even in the counties where low numbers of children were employed,
restrictions on the age of field labour would 'in many cases inflict privation
on a labouring man and his family'. And in areas where farmers drew on
the labour of the very young, interference with employment practices
would cause considerable hardship: 'The earnings of these children are, in
numerous cases, an important addition to the family income. In others the
labour of such children is, in a large mass of instances, indispensable to the
parents, quite irrespective of the question of earnings.'[82]

Recorded absences in school records demonstrate the seasonal demands
for the labour of school-age children during the late nineteenth century.
Young hands either worked directly for wages or helped a parent with
piece-work: bark-stripping and hop-tying in April and May; pea-picking,
haymaking and fruit-picking in June and July; harvesting in August; fruit-
picking and hopping in September; the harvest of vegetables in October
and November; fieldwork, bird-scaring, wood-cutting and hop-pole shav-
ing during the winter.[83] A Devon school log book noted that 'The poorer
parents with long families think it hard if they cannot keep their elder children two or three days in the week to earn a little to support the family
generally.'[84] A Kent teacher complained that the upper-standard children

were away from their studies working in the fields, while 'Those children in the lower standards who are not at school are kept away to nurse the younger ones while the mothers are at work in the fields.'[85] Oxfordshire boys and girls were frequently away from their classrooms during the period from April to early July, stripping osiers for the basket-making industry. They returned to school briefly just before it disbanded for the harvest break.[86] Boys were employed in an extremely wide range of tasks – indeed most of the jobs done by men and women. The work of girls tended to reflect that of women. Thus, the skills of one generation were handed on to another.

The peak period for children's labour in many rural areas was from May to September, so arguing for a lack of jobs for children from a census taken in March or April is therefore somewhat beside the point. But Hugh Cunningham does demonstrate that when we write of child employment (or unemployment) during the nineteenth century, we are effectively writing about children aged ten and over. Nearly 5500 agricultural labourers were aged from five to nine, and nearly the same number of girls of that age group was a worker in the straw-plait and lace industries in 1851. Nevertheless, they were minorities. Only 2 per cent of boys and 1.4 per cent of girls aged from five to nine were listed as employed in that census: the comparable figures for those aged from ten to fourteen were 37 per cent and 20 per cent respectively. The main category of employment for the older boys was agricultural work; that of the girls, domestic service.[87] As a Kent farmer stated when explaining that it was not necessary to curb juvenile labour:

> in agriculture the children will not be of much use under 10 years of age, neither will they be of much use if they are kept without work much over that age, for it is by early and good training that the habits of industry are formed. Between 10 and 13 or 14 is a time of life when the children are unable to obtain a situation away from home, a time when they are a heavy and increasing expense to their parents, and a time when they require better living than perhaps the wages of their parents can afford, without the assistance of some earnings from their children.[88]

By the 1900s, the cumulative effects of Parliamentary legislation had forced the threshold of the effective working age of children upwards from ten.[89] In the labouring households of the villages and hamlets of Kent, the rule was that as soon as the child turned 14 it was agricultural labour for the boys and domestic service for the girls, a pattern that remained into the 1930s. The attitude was 'Get out and get on with it.'[90] It is clear from the interviews with the generation born in the 1890s and the 1900s that the little money they earned was not seen as their own. A 14-year-old girl who worked with her father in the brickfields in Buckinghamshire in 1903, recalled many years later that she was paid 9s a week, 8s 6d of which she handed to her mother.[91] Most young workers saw themselves as earning for the family economy, though they did not phrase it precisely in those terms. A brickmoulder's son put it quite simply: 'Us being a large family, as soon as I was able I left school for work. The four shillings I earned the first year would go into the pool.'[92]

The second type of child labour outlined by Stanhope in 1867 was unwaged work. As Anna Davin has put it, the labouring household was 'an economic unit in which all members but the very youngest played a part, contributing unpaid labour and any earnings'.[93] Children performed a myriad of unwaged tasks that contributed to making do. They gathered fuel, chopped wood and roots, fetched water from the well, and collected rabbit food or acorns for the pig. Both boys and girls helped around the house, caring for younger children, making sure that the fire was lit and there was a pot of tea for their mother when she returned from work in the late afternoon. Girls, especially, were kept home from school on washing days, to help with domestic chores or to mind the very young to free their mothers for fieldwork. Children ran errands. They shopped or performed a reconnaissance of the shops in the nearest town on Saturday mornings, seeking out the cheapest bargains so that their parents need not waste time looking when they went shopping later that night.[94] In short, children were 'their mothers' auxiliaries', 'caretakers' and 'little mothers'.[95]

Children also went gleaning with their mothers. A study of gleaning has found that it was worth from £1 to £3 a year for labouring families in the period before 1850, or 3 to 14 per cent of those families' average income. An 1838 survey of the earnings of agricultural labourers in Norfolk and Suffolk was at the bottom end of the margin: a consistent 3 per cent of annual earnings, an average annual value of just over £1. However, a pound was a significant amount in that penny economy. In the corn lands, where there was little prospect of other subsidiary earnings or means of gathering free food, the gleanings must have been extremely important for the family economy.[96]

Children in the Morecambe Bay area in north Lancashire worked for their families, collecting cockles on the sands. The seafood was bought by middlemen who then on-sold to fishmongers in the large manufacturing towns. They also found work potato planting and picking, again for a large urban market.[97] From late April to June, whole families were employed on the osier beds of the River Dove on the boundary of Derbyshire and Staffordshire. As one employer explained, 'in the peeling season I employ all the hands I can get, women and children, mothers bring their babies in cradles with them, whole families work together, the mother breaks the peel (draws the willow through a break), and the children peel'.[98] Cunningham has demonstrated that the economies of child labour were local economies.[99] Tremenheere's dissenting report on the employment of children made this very point when arguing that the 'labourers' point of view' be taken into account when determining legislation on the labour of children under ten years of age. The Commissioner claimed that where the wages of agricultural labourers were high there was less pressure on the children of those households to work.[100]

Although Tremenheere's identification of high-wage counties does not correspond to what we know of wage levels in the 1860s, his point about inter- and intra-county variation in child labour demand is entirely valid.[101] The large farms of Lincolnshire employed boys as young as eight years old 'in bird scaring, tenting (looking after cows, sheep, pigs, or horses), weeding, picking twitch or stones, bean-dropping, singling turnips'. The small farmers of the fens, the Isle of Axholme, and the marshes were dependent on the labour of their children 'at the earliest age that they can be of service to them'. 'At certain seasons (at potato-setting and potato harvest) almost all the female and juvenile population is engaged in fieldwork.'[102] The women and children of Canford Heath in Dorset worked their smallholdings while husbands and fathers went out to work for wages.[103] In the north, in Cumberland, gangs of from 20 to 40 women, girls and boys thinned turnips and were employed in other farm work from March through to November.[104] Those employed in the Norfolk agricultural gangs in the 1860s seem to have been mainly children and teens.[105]

As a pastoral farming region, Somerset was acknowledged to provide less opportunity for the employment of children. Nevertheless, farmers used young workers as a reserve army of labour in certain parts of the county, and their own families drew upon their work as a means of getting by. One large employer in Taunton Vale said in the 1860s that when he needed workers in the turnip fields he sent a man out to round up all the children in the surrounding villages. The market-gardens of the Mendip hills grew peas and potatoes for the London market, employing 'nearly every child in the neighbourhood, as well as every woman' during peak weeks of labour demand. There was further work for women and children in the withy peeling on Sedgemoor in spring, and the whortleberry harvest on the Exmoor hills. The rector of Hawkridge observed that boys and girls were employed in the four main harvests: turf (May), whortleberry (June), hay (July) and corn (September). All such employment was intermittent.[106]

Dorset, correctly identified as a low-wage area, provides another interesting example of the manner in which different pressures, in varying economies and ecologies, contributed to the same result: 'every labourer [was] anxious to send his children out'.[107] The practice in the large arable farms was for farmers to engage yearly labour and to expect the families of the hired man to work as well. The small farms of the Vale of Blackmoor depended on family labour and intermittent, low-waged, hired workers. Gloving was an important, though 'very unremunerative' alternative to fieldwork for the wives and children of agricultural labourers here and elsewhere in Dorset, but it also involved 'younger members of the family being kept at home from a very early age, being put to work as soon as they can hold a needle'.[108]

* * *

Some of the arguments surrounding the work of children are the same as those about women's work. The Commission of 1867 tabled evidence that the social economies of some labouring homes were false economies, and investigators located cases such as that of the Devonshire eight-year-old whose monthly income fell short of the cost of the pair of boots that she wore out while assisting her mother at stone-picking.[109] Some labourers' wives did indeed consider that the contribution of a child of less than ten years old was less than it cost to keep them at work; 'I think it is money in pocket for a parent to keep small boys at home.'[110] However, E. C. Tufnell's condemnation of bad budgeting – 'Labourers are bad calculators' – actually implied that many rural workers did not share the reservations expressed above: 'many of them imagine that any addition, however small, to the earnings of the family, is of importance; not observing that outgoings in clothes or food often exceed the value of the child's labour'.[111] Furthermore, his strictures do not appear to have been applicable to the contributions of those children *over* the age of ten.

A distinction should be made between the work of boys and girls. The Commissioners of the 1860s were united in their overall picture of the relative rarity of girls engaged in fieldwork compared to the boys. 'Young girls are not much employed in these counties', Stanhope observed of Kent, Dorset and Shropshire. Although class-blinkered condemners of young women's work in the fields alleged its degrading effects – 'it is ruination to young girls' – we should not merely assume that their social inferiors shared these sentiments.[112] While some may have agreed that fieldwork was undesirable, it is likely that more materialistic considerations came into play, and we should recall earlier discussions about the roles of alternatives such as home employment (glove-making, for instance) and domestic service.

If we are looking for trends over our period, then the dominant one was the upward movement of the age of waged work for children. This change represented a redirection of child labour rather than its cessation. It was what Michael Lavalette has termed the shift to 'out of school work', *c.* 1880–1918, when the work of children did not stop completely but, accommodating to the needs of school attendance, became (like much of rural women's work) informal, unstructured, seasonal and casual.[113]

For most of the period, schooling had to vie with the paid work or child-minding capabilities of children. Education was an extravagance for many labouring families.[114] According to both the logic of the self-interest of labourers and the vested interest of farmers, school not only imparted useless knowledge for those destined to be farm workers but kept them away from the useful skills learned at the side of parents and older siblings in the fields.[115] It was an attitude found as late as 1912 in the comments of even the most sympathetic observer: 'I will not tolerate the word "ignorant" as applied to agricultural people – knowing and caring little or nothing for books and studious pursuits, but well-versed in the trade of the countryside; pigs and horses, and cattle, cocks and hens, ploughing, sowing, reaping and threshing – that is the proficiency you want in the village.'[116]

School may have had a role as a 'nursery' for the children of the very young, while mothers worked, but the same children were removed when they were older and when work was available.[117] The literacy of the children of small farmers, called upon to contribute to family labour, was notoriously low.[118] Nearly 90 per cent of the sons of agricultural labourers in a small rural Kent community were not at school when the census was taken in 1851. And around 40 per cent of farm workers from the same area were not able to sign their own names when they married in the 1870s and 1880s.[119] Of course, England would achieve mass literacy at the end of the nineteenth century. Those Kent children were at school in the 1890s – most of them – and the majority of those marrying could sign their names. Yet, until then, literacy (as we think of it) did not hold high priority for many rural working people. Male literacy suffered where there was agricultural labour available for boys; low levels of female proficiency corresponded to relatively high levels of employment for girls in rural industry. Both suffered where, and when, wage-rates were depressed. The educational advances of rural women may well have been a result of their decreased employment as children, and where there were prospects of employment for school-trained domestic servants.[120] Literacy and the family economy were closely intertwined.

* * *

Before the more rigid sexual division of labour in modern industrialized societies, there was both greater flexibility in the sexual division of labour (though with a gendering of tasks) and local variation.[121] We have seen such diversity at the county level. Nicola Verdon's analysis of farm accounts from different parts of the country showed very different trends and patterns in women's farm labour in the first half of the nineteenth century. In Norfolk, their labour became seasonally constricted and replaced by that of children. In Yorkshire, they performed over a third of the annual labour hours.[122] However, farms from both counties demonstrated declines in female labour after 1850.[123] In Derbyshire, where there was enclosure and an increase in sheep-farming, the result is likely to have been a restriction of women's farm work to the rather limited opportunities for casual labour during a short hay harvest.[124] In Hertfordshire and Bedfordshire, straw-plaiting rather than farm work was the main form of employment for rural women.[125] In the Berkhamsted area of Hertfordshire, there were just three female agricultural workers out of a female population of more than 6000 in 1851; and only six in the St Albans region out of over 4000 women with a designated occupation.[126] By the time the straw-plaiting and lace-making industries declined later in the nineteenth century, the women in these counties had become unaccustomed to farm work.[127] Farm work provided a particularly irregular living for women, and it cannot be mere coincidence that female unemployment in the 15- to 19-year-old age group was highest in many of the primarily agricultural counties and lowest in those regions able to offer lace-making and straw-plaiting.[128] Census employment rates for girls in 1851 ranged from Bedfordshire's 51 per cent to Durham, Kent and Middlesex's less than 8 per cent.[129]

Yet we also need to sharpen the focus within the county. Helen Speechley's detailed study of female and child day-labourers in nine-teenth-century Somerset found that while, on average, women and children formed 20 per cent and 14 per cent respectively of the annual day-labour force, the rates on individual farms varied divergently.[130] Women in the west of England in the early 1840s were 'accustomed to reap' in one village, while in another the practice was unheard of. Women led horses in some parts of Somerset and Devon but not elsewhere in the area, or in other parishes in these two counties.[131] In Gloucestershire, agricultural work for women survived in the mixed farming areas, but was marginal in the grasslands.[132] Local economies governed strategies for survival and account for varying employment patterns. In the Hampshire market town of Alton in 1891, a third of women worked – but primarily as young, single domestic servants and married paper-mill workers.[133] The surveys of rural labour in the 1890s contrasted the lack of female rural employment in the Woburn district of Bedfordshire (with its decayed lace and straw industries) with the numerous opportunities around Huntingdonshire's St Neots, where women worked regularly in the market-gardens, and where the wives and daughters of farm labourers earned up to 12s per week in the town's paper-mills.[134] If the work of women and children is taken seriously, the economic history of nine-teenth-century England is a history of perpetually shifting localization.[135]

4 *Household Strategies*

Len Austin recalled that his farm-worker father got 15s a week in wages before the First World War, well below the estimated 18s 4d (rural) and 21s 8d (urban) required to keep a man, a woman and three children in 'physical efficiency'.[1] It is clear from the adult male wage rates discussed in Chapter 2

4 P. H. Emerson, *Osier Peeling* (1888)

A reminder both of the role of young women in the rural workforce, and the importance of rural industries. From P. H. Emerson, *Pictures of East Anglian Life* (London, 1888)

that there must have been large sections of the labouring population where the nominal income of the household's principal male wage-earner was insufficient to support a family. The budgets of over a hundred agricultural families in the 1860s show family incomes of from £42 to £37 a year compared to male wages of £34 and £28 respectively, conditional on whether the family concerned was in a high- or a low-wage agricultural area. This extra £8 or £9 a year, 20 to 25 per cent of the household income, came from the efforts of women and children.[2] It was estimated in the 1860s that adult female fieldworkers in Berkshire and Oxfordshire were contributing between £6 and over £8 a year into the family economy.[3] As a Berkshire farm labourer's wife put it, 'The best wife for a labourer is the woman who has worked out.'[4]

The percentages varied according to time, place, the internal family structure and the wage levels of male workers. A survey of over 500 labouring families in rural Norfolk and Suffolk in the 1830s found that only about half the income of an average family came from the husband's day-work and piece-work, about a third from the earnings of the wife and children (including gleaning), and 15 per cent in harvest wages, which presumably would also include (as may have the husband's piece-work earnings) the labour contribution of women and children.[5] One of the contributors to the Report on the Employment of Women and Children in Agriculture in the 1840s said that in his districts in the west of England there were few families of agricultural workers where 'the wife or one child or more are not employed in farm-labour'.[6] P. H. Mann's study of the Bedfordshire village of Ridgmont discovered that of the families of wage-earners who were *above* the poverty level, a 'vast proportion' were 'dependent' on the earnings of women and, especially, children. If these families had been dependent on the head of the household alone, over a quarter of them would have been 'in poverty'.[7] Almost two-thirds of married men in Ridgmont, employed or self-employed as labourers or in the crafts and trades, had wives and/or children listed with occupations in the census of 1891, principally as agricultural labourers and lace-makers.[8]

* * *

'Looking back, I think it was the fen women who had the worst time of it when I was a child', the mole-catcher Arthur Randell wrote many years later, 'They had to make the wages which their husbands brought home stretch as far as possible to provide food, clothes, and fuel; every penny had to be looked at before it was spent.' He recalled mothers walking the banks of the Ouse for firewood, and searching the low-tide shore for coal.[9] Labour history should be as much about budgeting as the male wage and organized labour.[10] There are thousands of budgets to choose from, but let us take just one example from the small Berkshire village of East Challow (population: 391) in the 1860s. Mrs Charles Payne (as she was identified) had four children, all under the age of ten and at school, and her husband, a 'fogger' (dairyman), worked seven days a week, for most of the year, for 13s per week. He earned extra for milking and harvest, and Mrs Payne, despite the youth of her children, managed to work for six months of the year as well as assisting at harvest. She estimated their annual income as follows:

Husband, 13s a week for 49 weeks:	£31 17s
Wife, besides harvest:	£3 12s
Husband and wife in harvest (including milking pay):	£3 3s
Total:	£38 12s

In other words, this provided average earnings of 14s 10d per week. The problem for the family, however, was that their weekly expenses were more than that. Mrs Payne itemized their costs:

	s	d
Rent of cottage with one bedroom	1	4
School fees	0	3
Clothing club	0	4
Bread	5	6
Flour	0	7
Suet	0	$3^1/_2$
Cheese, 1lb	0	9
Tea and sugar	1	8
Bacon, $2^1/_2$ lb	2	1
Lard, 1lb	0	11
Candles, $1^1/_2$ lb	0	$10^1/_2$
Coals, 1cwt (from the coal club)	1	1
Washing materials	0	$3^1/_2$
Total:	15s	$11^1/_2$ d

The shortfall, averaged over the week, was just over a shilling, or close to £3 a year. The surveyor calculated that the household could have found this if Mrs Payne had been able to get work during the remaining six winter months at even half the rates she enjoyed in summer.[11]

In the words of David Vincent, 'Any understanding of the strategies which were adopted to cope with poverty, and the costs which they entailed, has to begin with those around whom everything seemed to revolve.'[12] Being what one northern farm worker described as an excellent 'food contriver' was a valuable skill for motherhood.[13] The aim was to fill stomachs rather than to provide nutrition and variety. Household budgets drawn up in the various nineteenth-century surveys show that from 40 to 60 per cent of the male wage went on bread or flour. In the mid-nineteenth century, a family of two adults and four children would be spending about 5s a week on flour out of an adult male wage of around 13s. Although some women baked their own bread, many purchased it because of the lack of cooking facilities, the cost of fuel, and the amount of time involved in baking for a large family.[14] Surveys of the work of women and children in the mid-nineteenth century refer, in passing, to underfed labourers. Even those in regular employment in Dorset had to make do with diets 'almost entirely of bread, potatoes, and cheese'. Staffordshire and Shropshire labourers also lived on bread, potatoes and cheese.[15] It is likely that those who lived in as farm servants enjoyed better diets. In Cheshire, the farmers had meat and potatoes for dinner and bacon and potatoes for supper, but 'hardly any labourers eat meat at home, though some few can afford a little occasionally on Sunday.' 'Potatoes with butter-milk, if they can get it, is the ordinary food.'[16]

By the end of the century, the dietaries indicate that the percentage spent on bread or flour dropped as diets became more varied, but bread was still the basic food item in labouring households.[17] B. S. Rowntree and M. Kendall wrote in 1913 that in the south of England bread was 'the main-stay'.[18] Christopher Holdenby observed that there were 'thousands of cottages where they do not always see fresh meat once a week'. 'I have known men, subject to all weather conditions, go from morning to evening on a bread-and-butter pudding.'[19] The oral histories also mention the ubiquity of bread. 'But my father even then only had a piece of bread and butter or marge and my father used to go all day with a piece of bread and cheese and an onion.'[20] 'Bread was the major, the basic diet, bread was, bread and potatoes, no question of that.'[21] This must go some way to explaining the height differentials of the period. Data published by the Anthropometric Committee of the British Association for the Advancement of Science in the 1880s showed that 14-year-old boys from the professional classes were over three inches taller on average than the children of rural labourers.[22] This dietary context must also surely account for the obsession with food in the written and oral memoirs of the labouring classes; even a rare spiritual autobiography begins with an account of the scarcity of bread.[23]

Of course, bread was not the only food item. Vegetables were grown in cottage gardens and allotments; informants spoke of fathers digging their own plots after a day's labour. 'All sorts of vegetables, potatoes – mostly potatoes to save for the winter, you see, to spare buying potatoes, turnips, and in the spring beans and peas, carrots, onions.'[24] There are memories of jams, pickles, puddings (much of their food was boiled rather than baked), soups, stews, meat (mainly offal) and fish.[25] Some labouring households raised rabbits or poultry. Some kept pigs. Oral histories recount the psychic trauma of killing and eating a household friend and the guilt engendered by the sheer delight of that consuming:

> The pig was my job. Feed the pig in the morning . . . you got quite friendly with him. Some funny thing to have as a pet, a pig, but you'd scratch his back and he'd love it and he'd be honk, honk and grunting fine. Then it would come for the time for the killing . . . The butcher would get a knife and shave the hair from the neck where he's going to slit his throat. Now of course this was a bit like how I used to scratch him and old pig is honking again, he's quite enjoying it . . . I was furious and sad. I used to swear I would never touch a bit of it . . . But it was the smell of the cooking . . . Nobody in this wide world could make liver and faggots like my mother. Oh, they were delicious.[26]

A recent study has estimated that from a quarter to a half of nineteenth-century rural working households kept a pig – but it is only a guess.[27]

Poaching was also rife in the rural areas, a 'social crime' enjoying the sympathy of large sections of the labouring population.[28] Men poached to supplement their diet or their modest incomes. It was part of the family economy in Headington Quarry near Oxford, for men combined it with their work in the building, brickmaking and stoneworking trades, labouring by day and poaching by night, or taking a rabbit or two on their way to and from work.[29] It is astonishing how commonly oral histories refer to poaching, almost as if the game fell into their hands. '[S]ome of us were good poachers you know, which is another side of life . . . you sometimes won a pheasant accidentally and you won a fish . . . and in lots of little ways you could set a snare yourself and catch a rabbit or a hare or you could catch a few pigeons, and that was the way people lived in those days.'[30] 'You'd better shut it off and then I'll tell you a tale. Yes, he [her father] – everybody in the village poached you see, except the parson and the policeman, in Casterton.' The Cumbrian woman who provided this oral history said that it was 'wonder we didn't grow fur'.[31] The family of the Kent labourer Len Austin sold poached rabbits but also relied on them for meat – 'if we didn't get rabbit we didn't get nothing else'.[32] Clifford Hills said that his father would go out with a paraffin lamp to dazzle pheasants while they roosted, knocking them down with a long stick. This Essex agricultural labourer sold poached rabbits to 'men who were a little better off than him' (bricklayers, threshing-machine operatives, shopkeepers and publicans).[33] The subject of poaching always produced amusing anecdotes of policemen on the take, of rabbits stashed in trousers to avoid detection, and wondrous tales of men who could see a hare or rabbit a mile away and catch it with their hands – 'It seemed he could smell a rabbit.'[34]

However, the overriding impression is of the enforced vegetarianism of labouring households in both the nineteenth and early twentieth centuries: 'It was all vegetables . . . vegetables and cabbage and potatoes was your limit.'[35] A man born in a Staffordshire industrial village in 1887 expressed it even more graphically: 'When I was born I got starved to death well, and I've never got bloody warm since.'[36] Hence the fixation of labouring emigrants with the abundance and gastronomic bounty of the New World. Letters from Australia and New Zealand observed that dogs got more to eat there than labourers did in Kent; 'there is no sitting under the hedge gnawing a piece of bread and an onion, and talking over the bad times'. 'Working people don't eat sheep's and bullock's heads or liver here. They have the best joints, as well as the rich.'[37] Sussex labourers in Canada and the US wrote of 'this Palestine land'. 'Whilst this letter is writing, my wife is eating preserved peaches and bread, and washing them down with good whiskey and water.' 'The labouring people live by the best of provisions; there is no such thing as a poor industrious man in New York.'[38] '[T]his is the country to live in and yours the country to starve in', Henry Craig wrote in his letter from Ohio in 1850. Apple and peach trees were 'almost breaking down with fruit', and the wild grapes were as big 'as marbles'. The beef was 'bigger and better' than at home. There was plenty of game, 'which anybody is welcome to shoot'.[39]

We should be wary of English childhood memories of cottage-garden self-sufficiency, mother's faggots and rabbit stew. It is true that garden-grown potatoes and greens meant less money spent in the weekly budget. Rowntree and Kendall found in their study of rural labouring families in 1913 that a majority supplemented the food purchased with produce from their own gardens. However, they cautioned against overrating the value of the garden. On average, about a twelfth of the food consumed by these families was home-grown.[40] Len Austin pointed out that an average garden would not have kept a decent-sized family for long. At most, it was a help; people still had to buy or otherwise procure the bulk of their vegetables. 'Used to have to buy potatoes or pinch them.' He also pointed out that farm workers with yearly contracts, waggoners, stockmen and the like, were not in one place long enough to establish a working garden.[41]

The exception to this was in those areas where the allotment system took hold from the 1830s. Joseph Ashby and Bolton King examined one such region in the Midlands in a pioneering piece of rural sociology. Labourers here with allotments could choose from a selection of potential crops: wheat, barley, beans, potatoes, parsnips, mangolds, turnips, carrots and peas. They could keep pigs or, more rarely, a cow. Ashby and King found that the allotment system catered 'mainly for home consumption'. They calculated the amount of wheat per acre that would keep a family in bread for a year but observed that some of the produce was sold. Sold or consumed, it was an important contribution to the family budget in such rural labouring homes. Ashby and King's figures imply that some 16 per cent of the 'average [annual] income of a labourer's family' (assuming regular work) came from the profit of the allotment, almost the same amount spent by that 'average' family on bread and flour.[42] Jeremy Burchardt's recent history of allotments shows that these quarter- and half-acre plots concentrated on the staple crops of potatoes and wheat, and could contribute £5 or £10 to the family budget.[43] Although there was one allotment for every three agricultural labourers by the 1870s, this crude national average masks considerable regional variation. However, they appear to have been widespread by the end of the century. The Land Enquiry Committee of 1913 estimated that two-thirds of rural parishes had allotments.[44]

Rural mothers and wives had to 'make something out of nothing', in Emily Wade's apposite phrase.[45] Village women would walk to the nearest town because that was where the bargains could be found.[46] It was the wife and mother's task to purchase, procure, distribute, calculate and decide on priorities. Food was not the only demand on the family purse. Economies could be made through making or repairing items that would normally have to be bought: mats made out of rags, beds filled with chaff, hop-sacking curtains, clothes cut down in size (or worn large), home-made shirts, frocks, nightgowns, quilts and sheets.[47] Budgeting was a fine art.

We should also include theft in the economy of makeshifts. John Archer has noted the prevalence of crime in the rural areas of nineteenth-century East Anglia, particularly in times of economic distress: 'If there was a criminal class ... it was the entire labouring community.'[48] A labourer told a *Morning Chronicle* journalist that it was impossible to survive on the wages paid in the late 1840s and early 1850s: 'The truth is master, we are often driven to do many things those times that we wouldn't do if we could help it. It is very hard for us to starve, and we sometimes pull some turnips, or perhaps potatoes, out of some of the fields, unbeknown to the farmers.'[49] These were crimes of subsistence – theft of food and fuel. Wood thefts in nineteenth-century Herefordshire peaked during the cold winter months, indicating that it was used primarily for fuel, a potentially large item of domestic expenditure. Moreover, the fact that almost a half of convicted Herefordshire wood thieves were women further suggests that the bulk of the crimes were prompted by poverty.[50] Len Austin was candid about the situation in many labouring homes in the first part of the twentieth century: 'If you couldn't get it you'd pinch it. Well, I don't care what anyone says, if they speak the truth they did, they pinched all they could, they had to or else they'd starve.'[51]

* * *

An increasingly favoured method of coping was through low-level savings and insurance. There were various self-help schemes. Many labouring households belonged to coal clubs – often run from pubs – in which subscribers paid so much a week and coal was bought in bulk and shared out among contributors. Boot or shoe and clothing clubs consisted of time payments for specific items of clothing. Services were also provided by legally enrolled benefit or friendly societies – and a host of unregistered clubs and societies – that, for a weekly payment, provided insurance for sickness or death.[52]

There is some disagreement over the impact of these examples of mutual aid. One of the most recent estimates is that in 1900 up to two-thirds of British working men belonged to such societies.[53] Ashby and King found in their 56 Midland villages that statistically every family 'of the tradesmen and working classes' were members either of the larger lodges (Oddfellows, Foresters) or the smaller local clubs, although they were not able to adjust for multiple memberships.[54] A recent local study has argued that the evidence of surviving lists for the East Riding of Yorkshire shows that up to 80 per cent of new members to societies were agricultural workers, mainly young male farm servants.[55] Other evidence is more pessimistic. Martin Gorsky's survey of friendly-society distribution patterns in the early decades of the nineteenth century demonstrates a bias in favour of the mining and manufacturing counties and against predominantly agricultural regions, though areas of rural industry had stronger membership.[56]

We know the occupations of over a thousand associates of six Cumberland and Westmorland societies, and while farm servants comprised 15 per cent of subscribers, and agricultural labourers/labourers 28 per cent, the greatest representation came from the trades and crafts, comprising 54 per cent of the membership.[57] The Hampshire Friendly Society had just over 11 000 members in 1891 (including females) but there were around 160 000 men and women engaged as agricultural labourers and farm servants, domestic servants, and in the trades and crafts in rural Hampshire at that time, so the percentage enrolled in this society is not likely to have been very large.[58] The message of the Royal Commission on Labour in the 1890s was relatively clear. They recognized both a generational split (younger men were more likely to enrol in the registered societies) and regional variation (commissioners found Berkshire villages where 95 per cent of farm workers were in a friendly society, and others, in the same district, where less than a third had joined a club). But they maintained that the bulk of agricultural labourers were members of a benefit society.[59] Although we shall probably never know the exact proportions of rural workers who were members of particular clubs and friendly societies, and it is likely that the percentages were higher in the 1890s than the 1830s, membership of some scheme was widespread in labouring culture. There is little doubting the role of these societies in the family economy.[60]

* * *

Recent work on poverty and charity has suggested that poor relief should also be seen as a strategy for survival, and that we should not too readily assume any sense of shame on the part of the receiver. When Ashby and King drew up their chart of the 'average' income of a labouring family *where the man was in full employment and had an allotment*, they still included a small amount (almost £1) derived from charity and gleaning.[61] Charity was a 'neighbourhood resource'.[62] Even though the policy of the New Poor Law was to discourage such strategies, calling upon poor relief was an important part of rural working life. As Charles Booth wrote in 1894 in his survey of the aged poor, 'there are a few parishes where out relief is considered a disgrace, but in most places no stigma attaches to its acceptance by the old. It is regarded as a matter of course, and often claimed very much as a right.'[63]

The social investigators of the early twentieth century established the labouring life-cycle of poverty. Many labouring families could expect a period of deeper poverty before their children were old enough to make a substantial contribution to the family economy. As Mann wrote in 1904 of Bedfordshire rural workers:

> it appears clear that a man earning the average rate of wages, and the head of a household, must descend below the primary poverty line so soon as he has two children, unless he is able to supplement his income by an allotment, by fattening and breeding pigs, or by other means. It is also clear that he will remain below the poverty line until the eldest child leaves school and begins to earn money, and that, even if he has no more than two children [an unlikely assumption], his only chance to save will be in his later life when the children are

grown-up, and are earning money or have left home. This is the most favourable case: if there are more children the period of poverty is longer and the chance of saving less. In any case during life it is a weary and continual round of poverty. During childhood, poverty conditions are almost inevitable. As a boy grows up, there are a few years intermission till, as a young man, he has two children; then poverty again till these children grow up, and, finally, at best, a penurious old age, barely lifted above the poverty line.[64]

Mann was describing the phenomenon set out in graphical form by Seebohm Rowntree.[65] (See Figure 4.1.)

This wave-like cycle can be approached from the standpoint of the life-stage of the labouring household or the age of the individual, although the basic pattern of oscillation around the poverty line is the same. The hypothetical family entered poverty with the birth of young children, surfaced as the children began to earn, and then sank again after the children left home and married (to begin their own poverty cycles) and as the parents' labouring potential began to diminish with age. In other words, from infancy to the early teens was a time of poverty. From the mid-teens to mid-twenties was a period of respite from poverty as earning capacity increased. The later twenties and thirties saw a return to poverty with the impact of married reproduction. The forties and fifties was an age of relative prosperity, as the children contributed to the family income. Finally, there was another descent in the sixties. Life was not quite as tidy as this graph implied: it was not unusual for labouring households to contain both wage-contributing children *and* dependent infants. Nor were the age cut-offs as distinct as those of Rowntree's matrix were. Couples were marrying in their late teens, early twenties, and during their thirties and forties. Women gave birth to their last child when they were in their forties in many labouring

Figure 4.1 The family poverty cycle

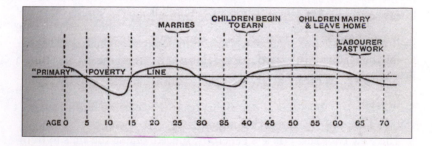

Source: B. S. Rowntree, *Poverty: A Study of Town Life* (London, 1902), p. 137.

households; such parents would be in their fifties or sixties by the time their children entered their wage-earning teens. But even if the cycles may have been rather more complicated than the investigators of poverty allowed, the value lies with the concept itself. Experience of poverty was not static, but varied over the life-course of the labouring family.

The Old Poor Law of the period before 1834 provided a wide range of welfare payments to help with such exigencies, and there was a range of personal and customary parish charities as supplements or alternatives.[66] The overseers' books record payments for food, clothing, tools, furniture, rent, fuel, even tobacco. Doctors' bills were paid. Women were hired to nurse, and care and wash for the elderly, the infirm and the heavily pregnant. Parishes paid for funeral costs, including payments for beer. They provided unemployment relief during the winter.[67] We shall see in a later chapter that the poor could be assertive in either claiming or negotiating this part of their living. The remarkable Essex-pauper letters show Essex workers, scattered throughout the south-east, requesting help during times of almost weekly crisis: payments for unemployment, the expenses of sickness and death, to reclaim clothing with the pawnbroker, to prevent furniture being seized to cover non-payment of rent.[68]

It is likely that there was considerable local variation in the generosity of the administration of the Poor Law – 'variety of experiences within a strong framework of stringency' is Pat Thane's description of provisions for the elderly during this period.[69] Steven King has argued for a contrast between the harsher north and west and the more benevolent south and east.[70] However, many rural workers would have received such assistance during their lives. King's study of poor relief in seven urban and rural communities under the Old Poor Law calculated that in the first part of the nineteenth century about half of *all* households received some form of assistance during their family history (a third required relief 'often' or 'always').[71] The proportions of affected *labouring* households would have been much greater. Over 80 per cent of labouring households listed in the census of 1841 for the Kent parish of Hernhill (not counting newcomers to the parish) had received relief at some stage in the life-course of their households. Under the Old Poor Law, recourse to relief was a central means of getting a living for large numbers of labouring people, adding as much as £10 a year to the family economy.[72] George Boyer has argued that in the rural south one of the main functions of poor relief was to provide welfare for seasonally-unemployed agricultural labourers.[73]

The New Poor Law was less generous. Indeed, one of the aims in framing it had been to remove such security. However, people still approached it for help with the hardship that inevitably accompanied old age, sickness and injury, death, childbirth, widowhood and desertion.[74] Many had little option other than the relieving officer. If local studies provide any indication of wider trends, from 10 to 15 per cent of rural households would draw on poor relief during any given year in the 1850s and 1860s.[75] The likelihood that an individual family would need assistance increased over its life-cycle. A Faversham man could remember parents putting their children in the workhouse in the winter in the 1900s because they could not afford to keep them; when things picked up later in the year, they took them home.[76] Lynn Hollen Lees has estimated that, for most of the nineteenth century, 'a high proportion' of workers' families would have applied for poor-law aid at some stage during their lives, although later in the century such requests declined.[77]

* * *

In Seebohm Rowntree's representation of poverty, the graph dips below the poverty level at the age of 65: 'Labourer without work'. We can be a little sceptical about the precision of the age cut-off. A recent quantitative sample of the censuses of 1851 and 1881 has shown that more than 70 per cent of men aged 65 and over were employed.[78] Agricultural work provided varied opportunities for older workers: 10 per cent of male agricultural labourers in 1871 were over the age of 65.[79] However, it is true that the rural workers who are the subject of this study did age, and that this ageing involved both poor relief and the assistance of kin. As Booth put it, 'It is abundantly evident that in town and country alike the large majority of the aged when past work are dependent upon someone; either on their children, or on the Guardians, or on the charitable, or on all three.'[80]

It has been observed of a nineteenth-century American farming community in Illinois, that it was 'a rural community that adhered through the bonds of kinship – subtly turning neighbours into family, and anchoring community into something more firm than merely a desire to belong somewhere'.[81] A farm worker, who grew up and worked in a Kent hamlet early this century, implied something similar when he discussed the implications of moving away from this kind of network:

> Horsemen used to move nearly every year. Stockmen and horsemen. But labourers didn't used to move so much. They moved more for, well, little better conditions of work. Not much more wages. Perhaps the boss was a little better where they went to, that's all, a little more lenient, but wages no more different perhaps. It's just that the ground was better to work, you see it was all hard work, so if you've got very stiff clay old ground over there and you could get a job on a farm with better soil, well you went if you could. If the conditions were suitable. Well

you might want to go somewheres where you'd got a few relatives. You see that's what it was. If you got the sack this week, you've got to get where you could, so you had to go and break all your ties with relatives or clubs or whatever you belonged to and go wherever you could get a job. That meant you was in a foreign land straight away didn't it. It all depends where you had to go, perhaps it would be four or five miles away and you didn't know anyone there perhaps at all. You had to start afresh. Kids all had to start a fresh school. It was all fresh you see.

He clearly saw kin as well as those community welfare agencies, the clubs, as factors in getting a living.[82]

Although some histories of English social welfare have minimized the role of the family in the support of the disadvantaged, particularly in the care of the elderly, this interpretation has been challenged by work that has discovered the very kinship links that were supposedly lacking in rural England.[83] Assumptions about the dominance of the nuclear household and the lack of kinship links were based on snapshot surveys provided by the census, but when life-courses and local contexts are considered it becomes clear that supposedly isolated households went through an extended phase or were close to numerous kin. Evidence is emerging of nineteenth-century agricultural villages and rural industrial communities where 70 to 80 per cent of households were related to at least one other in the village or in an adjoining settlement.[84] In such places, kinship was part of neighbourhood, and any separation between family and community would have made little sense. It certainly seems that the predominant pattern – whether the village was one of agricultural labourers, framework- knitters or coal miners – was for the elderly to live with their married or unmarried children or grand-children, or, if they lived independently with a spouse, to do so in a kin-based environment.[85] As Sonya Rose has expressed it, co-residence was a strategy that families employed 'to ease the struggle for subsistence'.[86]

Booth's village surveys of the elderly in the 1890s provide numerous case-studies of varied family assistance. We meet the widows of the Leicestershire village of Marsden, for example. One, a bed-ridden woman in her nineties, lived with a daughter and was helped by another daughter from a nearby village. Another, aged 80 and without children, received 2s 6d a week from the parish, earned a little 'by seaming', and was regularly given food by a niece. A 79-year-old, a former domestic servant, did needlework for 2s a week, and was supported by her miner sons and a granddaughter who lived with her. Another, aged 67, lived with her son (also a miner), next door to her married daughter. This woman earned about 2s a week by sewing. These are a few examples from a small agricultural/mining/hosiery parish of 500 people, but they typified patterns of existence throughout rural England.[87]

Households adapted to meet the demands of family and kinship. Survival in rural working lives was seldom a simple choice between family and what we would now term social welfare, but rather a long-term strategy of constant negotiation that drew upon all available resources.[88] Booth's calculations of the sources of maintenance of over 9000 village men and women over the age of 65 produced rather meaningless percentages of types of sustenance, precisely because of the constant overlap of the various categories. However, he did demonstrate that 32 per cent of the substantial sample drew on charity or parish support, 25 per cent were helped by family, and 25 per cent depended entirely on their own earnings (or those of a husband).[89]

Families could also turn to one another for assistance, as Ellen Ross has shown for London during the same period.[90] Vincent has argued that networks of neighbourhood-sharing may have been more attenuated in rural areas because of the scattered nature of some of the settlements and the size of their populations.[91] Yet Booth thought almost the opposite. Support for the poor and elderly was more likely in the villages than in the towns: 'Neighbourly relations are stronger.'[92] One of the Marsden widows survived through a combination of the money she earned by needlework and nursing and the informal assistance of fellow villagers: 'She is much helped by kind neighbours, one of whom gives her a dinner daily. Her rent is often remitted.'[93] Even something as straightforward as keeping a pig depended on a certain amount of neighbourhood reciprocity. The brick-moulders would usually keep a couple of pigs that they fed on scraps donated by their neighbours. In return, they sold the meat cheap when the pig was killed.[94] Indeed, an observer of village life in nineteenth-century Suffolk sided with Booth rather than Vincent. He thought the mutuality of poor women 'truly admirable':

> the trouble they take, the anxiety they endure, and the sacrifices they make, are unparalleled among the middle classes. The tradesman's wife relieves poverty by a *pecuniary* donation; the laborer's wife gives *personal* aid. They often nurse their neighbours in sickness without fee or reward, and help to feed the children out of their scanty means. Suffering and privation, though it breeds harshness towards their superiors, strengthen their sympathies towards their neighbours, and those best acquainted with the working classes in villages agree that the sympathy of the poor is the best alleviator of the sufferings of the poor.[95]

* * *

It is also significant that Rowntree's survey of rural poverty began with mention of the fact that substantial numbers of agricultural labourers were coping with conditions in England and Wales both by moving to the towns and by leaving for overseas.[96] Some two hundred people from Corsley emigrated to Canada during the demise of local cloth-making from the late 1820s.[97] Clearly, migration was an essential part of rural life in the nineteenth and early twentieth centuries. Between 1841 and 1911 there was a net loss of 4.5 million people from the rural areas. This rural–urban migration was destined for the coalfields, the large industrial cities, and London, all of which expanded substantially during this period.[98] A Poor Law scheme in the 1830s, aimed at unemployed labour in the south, 'encouraged' some five thousand people from Suffolk, Norfolk, Buckinghamshire and Bedfordshire to move to the textile factories of Lancashire and Yorkshire.[99] Bradford's wool mills were seen as a magnet for poverty-stricken agricultural labourers, and when a journalist from the *Morning Chronicle* visited one in 1849–51, he noticed the varying regional accents of the wool-combers.[100] Internal migration always outweighed emigration. Dudley Baines has estimated that in every decade of the second half of the nineteenth century the rural counties lost 10 per cent of their population to other counties and only about 3 per cent overseas.[101] The people of the rural south-east moved to London rather than out of England; on average, a third of a million people from these counties were living in London at any one time in the late nineteenth century.[102]

Those who emigrated overseas did so either directly or by moving first to the towns and then emigrating later – what are termed 'stage migrants'. The English and Welsh were leaving at the rate of around a hundred thousand a year throughout the second half of the nineteenth century. A total of 4.2 million left during the period 1861–1900, and a substantial number of these people were originally from rural communities. Of net emigration during this period, 54 per cent of emigrants were either stage migrants or from rural areas. Only 45 per cent of migrants were actually urban-born.[103] The USA (56 per cent), Canada (13 per cent) and Australasia (20 per cent) were the favourite non-European destinations for British emigrants during this period.[104] About 40 per cent of these people returned.[105]

This longer-distance migration has to be seen in the context of more generalized shorter-range movement, for rural workers were highly mobile. Studies of village and hamlet communities show that from 40 to 60 per cent of the population left their parishes in any given ten years – not including those who died. So these were not static and isolated communities.[106] Data from a national sample of the 1851 census indicates that over half of the rural population were 'life-time migrants', living more than two kilometres from their place of birth.[107] However, the majority of movement was within walking distance. An analysis of all 834 migrants from a small

Devon community, locatable in the recently computerized national census of 1881, discovered them as far north as Northumberland and Yorkshire, but the majority (nearly 70 per cent) were less than five miles away from their place of birth. A total of 85 per cent lived less than 20 miles from their village of origin.[108] Dennis Mills's database of 18 000 individuals in nearly 40 villages in the Midlands, south-east, and the west in 1851, found that 45 per cent were born outside the village in which they lived and that over 40 per cent of these outsiders came from less than five miles from their place of residence.[109] A study of migration distances recorded in 16 000 life histories during the period 1840–1920 found that more than 60 per cent of moves were less than ten kilometres.[110]

There is a case to be made for seeing migration as another component of strategies of family survival.[111] Letters from Sussex labouring families in Canada in the 1830s write of things that they did not enjoy at home: food, good wages, land, employment, abundance of game, and more humane relations between master and man. 'We . . . like this country much better than old England.'[112] 'I am a great deal contenter, than in England, and can make a good living. I can live better with working one day, than in England in seven.'[113] Yet if emigration was a coping mechanism, it has to be said that it could be a tough stratagem. The Sussex letters record the horrors of the sea journey, and the ravages of cholera at the other end. 'I lost my poor little Mary for the first', wrote a labourer to his brother in his home village of Lurgashall, 'then my poor dearest wife, then my two youngest, and little Edmund, all in the space of eight days. And what was more hard for me I was obliged to wrap them up in the rinds of trees and dig holes and put them in myself . . . There was 32 of us that came up into the woods together, and there is twelve of the 32 dead.'[114] An elderly woman, a weaver's daughter, only a child when she lost both her parents to cholera upon arrival in Canada in 1832, kept silent about this experience until she wrote it down for her own children in the 1890s: 'my history was so sad so filled with sad events on every hand that I avoided refering to it'.[115]

After the introduction of the New Poor Law in 1834, parishes assisted thousands of poor people to new lives in the British colonies. Of 9500 emigrants aided by Poor Law Unions between 1837 and 1847 (over half of whom were from the two counties of Kent and Sussex), 4800 went to Canada, and 4000 to Australia.[116] Gary Howells has shown that there was nothing passive about this process as far as the poor were concerned. Eager for better conditions, they actively used emigration as a strategy for improvement, sometimes putting considerable pressure on the local authorities. Nor were they afraid of direct communication with the Poor Law Commissioners:

Gentlemen,

I take the liberty of writing to you these few lines to inform you that we are Disposed to Emigrate to America for we are Labouring under the Galling yoke of Oppression and poverty frome want of imployment and when imployed Receiving such small Remuneration for our Labour that we our wives and children are in a state of Half Starvation therefore we are unable to Extricate ourselves from this state the Officers of the parish are Willing that we should Emigrate but they Do not Seem willing to raise the Money for the purpose therefore we your Humble petitioners wish you to inform us by what means we can go if you please pray excuse my Bad way of expressing Myself for I have Writ as Well as my Weak Capacity will allow.

These humble petitioners were William Jessop and others from the parish of Besthorpe, Norfolk, 1837, but there were many others using similar strategies.[117] George Fewins, a carpenter from Cheriton Bishop, Devon, who had left his wife and children 'for poverty', wrote from Missouri to his former parish in 1850–51, arguing that it would be cheaper for the parish to send his family to America than to maintain them in England. Fewins attempted to get the overseers to pay for his family to join him, and, when they refused, raised the stakes: 'I love my Wife and Children but if you love to keep them thair and main tain them you can du so and be dam . . . you Can Just kiss my Ass. I am now in America living in the land of the free.'[118]

The agricultural unions encouraged emigration in the 1870s as a way of reducing competition for work.[119] The landlords, employers and parish authorities supported it as a way of reducing the pressure of unemployed labour, and rural workers themselves saw emigration as a means of improving their situation. This is not the place to embark on the complexities of the emigration statistics – and there is some disagreement about the role of agricultural workers in British emigration – but it is clear that the flight of farm workers went in waves, peaking in the 1880s when 15 per cent of British emigrants were agricultural workers. There must also have been many others among the designated 'labourers' who made up a third of adult male emigrants in that decade.[120] Rural workers were probably underrepresented among those who left for the US, but figured more strongly among those assisted migrants bound for Australia.[121] In the 1850s and 1860s, Australia and New Zealand took around 20 to 30 per cent of emigrants from the British Isles but over 80 per cent of migrating agricultural labourers and from 60 to over 70 per cent of departing domestic servants.[122] Apart from an important contingent of Londoners, the 4000 young women who arrived in Canterbury, New Zealand, as assisted immigrants in the 1850s and 1860s, were predominantly domestic servants and farm workers from the south-east and south-west.[123] The wave of assisted immigration to New

Zealand in the 1870s, driven by rural discontent and agricultural-trade-union activity, drew on agricultural labourers and their families in most south-west and south-east counties.[124] Of 20 000 adult males who had arrived in the colony by 1875, over a third were farm labourers.[125]

There are fascinating micro-localities of migration to New Zealand, reflecting the diverse rural worlds discussed in chapter 1: the farm workers, glove-makers, and quarry-workers of Milton-under-Wychwood (Oxfordshire), the rural workers of the north Lincolnshire wolds and marshlands, the union-mobilized agricultural labourers and the brickmakers of Kent, and the miners, farm workers and dairymaids of Cornwall.[126] We even have a farm labourer and lace-maker from Ridgmont, Bedfordshire.[127] Many moved up the bottom rungs of the farming ladder, labouring first on the large properties, and gradually establishing themselves as small farmers in the South Island, or worked as bushmen, eventually establishing subsistence farms in the forest areas of the North Island. Thus Kent and Lincolnshire agricultural labourers became bushmen farmers in Taranaki; Bedfordshire farm workers settled in Karamea; and Oxfordshire labourers established farming communities south of Waipawa. In time, these former English rural workers formed the Moa Farmers' Club and the Woodville Small Farm Association![128] Clearly, these represented successful attempts at getting a living.

Sometimes, ready-formed, partial nucleuses of settlers from individual villages were transplanted to form fresh settlements in the New World. Edward Macarthur, member of a leading colonial family in New South Wales, referred to this process as similar to the planting of new woodland: 'each destined colonist should as surely have a known place assigned to him . . . as every tree previous to its removal from its native soil has a spot prepared for its reception'. In the 1830s, agricultural labourers and their families from several border villages in Cranborne Chase (Dorset–Wiltshire), and from Benenden (Kent) and Beckley (Sussex) were brought out to inhabit the planned 'English village' of Camden. The new settlers were said to have written home that they lived like 'little gentle folks' in their new environment, with its neat grid of squares and streets imposed on a very un-English Australian landscape. Some of these labourers had also become small farmers by the 1850s.[129] Organized migration to New Plymouth in New Zealand in the 1840s drew on small town and village communities of miners, agricultural labourers (the largest occupational category), and craftsmen (10 per cent were carpenters). They came in family groups with kinship connections: less than 5 per cent of the more than a thousand steerage passengers were without kin among this wave of emigrants. The main recruiting counties were Cornwall, Devon and

Dorset – with over a quarter of emigrants coming from just seven villages and market towns: Helston and Illogan (Cornwall); Boyton, Holsworthy, and Clawton (Devon–Cornwall border); Aveton Gifford (Devon); and Netherby (Dorset).[130]

A particularly useful study of emigration from the village of Melbourn in Cambridgeshire to Melbourne in Australia has shown that more than 70 per cent were agricultural labourers or labourers, and over 20 per cent employed in the village crafts. The Melbourn study implies that the migration of rural labour from England was more complex than a mere instinctual reaction to economic desperation. It is likely that the Melbourn migrants embarked on a strategy of betterment, seeking out fresh opportunities in Australia that were based on informed decisions about the offered alternative. They lived close to one another in the home village, travelled out in family groups in the 1840s and 1850s, and provided friendship and kinship support networks in a new country for later arrivals.[131] Another large group of agricultural labourers left nearby Fowlmere in the 1850s after the enclosure of their commons, also to join kin.[132]

Ironically, while English labourers left England in search of better conditions, Irish workers included work in England as part of their strategy for survival. The various parliamentary surveys of rural conditions are full of references to Irish migratory labour (often from English towns): in Cumberland, Derbyshire, Gloucestershire, Herefordshire, Lancashire, Leicestershire, Lincolnshire, Northumberland, Shropshire, Staffordshire, Warwickshire and Yorkshire.[133] 'The Irish, who, besides coming in very large numbers at harvest time, stay during a great part of the year in some places where labour is scarce, receive about two-thirds of the wages paid to the English, and are very ill-lodged.'[134] In the mid-nineteenth century, Irish gangs started in the south with the early harvest in Middlesex, and then worked their way north or west to take advantage of later harvests. By the end of the century, most confined their migratory labour to the Midlands and the north.[135] Farms in Lancashire had special buildings to house their Irish seasonal workers.[136]

* * *

Scholars have cautioned against careless use of the term 'household strategies', of assuming unity of purpose when there could be internal struggle and resentment over the allocation of precious resources.[137] So it is worth ending the chapter on this register. Some women thought that boys had it easier around the house; one woman remembered girls washing up or knitting while their brothers swapped comics.[138] As we have seen, children handed over pay packets, or worked for the family rather than for themselves. Li-Ming Hu has located muted retrospective resentment in the oral histories when rural workers talked of lost opportunities during their young lives.[139]

The enforced vegetarianism of rural workers was predominantly that of the women and children. Laura Oren has warned against assuming that all members of a family shared the same standard of living, for it was common practice for wage-earning males to enjoy a better diet than other members of the family. If meat was consumed, the chances were that it went to the father and the working sons.[140] As the wife of a Berkshire labourer explained in the 1860s, the little bacon that they bought was for her husband. 'When my husband is up at 3 o'clock for grass mowing and doesn't get home till 8 he requires more than the little necessaries he generally gets.'[141] Elizabeth Armstrong, the daughter of a collier/farm worker, recalled that she only had meat once a week but her father had it more often. When margarine replaced butter, 'Mother got it because it was cheap. But my father hadn't to eat it. He had to have the best of everything because of his hard work and we had to make do . . . I hated margarine and I do today.'[142] Oren has argued that at the very time that women needed additional calories – during their pregnancies and breast-feeding – they would have been most likely to have been sacrificing them for working husbands. In such households, a 'wife served as a buffer for her husband', absorbing 'the blows of an insecure existence'.[143] Clifford Hills was convinced, in retrospect, that his mother actually died of starvation because of such sacrifices; when her sons were bringing in money she spent it on better food for them, 'still going without herself'.[144]

Furthermore, men had the relative luxury of 'pocket money' for smoking and drinking; whereas the woman would go without to balance the budget. As late as the 1930s, agricultural workers in the UK were spending over 60 per cent more on the clothing of the head of the household than they were on that of his wife.[145]

Hugh Cunningham has suggested that the nineteenth-century male breadwinner 'norm' was a norm only at the stage of the life-cycle when children were young, normally when the man was in his twenties, and that not only were children's earnings vital to household survival in working-class families at all other stages of the life cycle, but the contributions of children were more important than those of women.[146] Although the data that he uses shows a far clearer dependence on the male wage-earner in the households of agricultural labourers, it indicates that when the household head was in his forties, some 30 per cent of the family income was being provided by the contributions of women and children, predominantly those of the latter. It is also noteworthy that even when the man was in his twenties, women and children were contributing 10 per cent of the family income – a higher percentage than for any group (mining, factory, trades) other than outworkers. This 10 per cent was divided equally between women and children.[147] Such findings mesh comfortably with the Rowntree theory of life-cycle poverty discussed earlier. Histories of farm workers which stress the role of the adult male wage-earner to the neglect of the contributions that women and children made to 'the adaptive family economy', and do not take into account the sheer range of strategies involved in household survival, are very partial histories.[148]

5 Life and Death

In her highly nostalgic account of rural life in 'Lark Rise' during the 1880s, Flora Thompson wrote of cottages where 'children swarmed, eight, ten, or even more in some families', but where the 'general health of the hamlet was excellent'. There was a local saying, 'Nobody ever dies at Lark Rise.'[1] However, the real 'Lark Rise' was the hamlet of Juniper Hill in the Oxfordshire parish of Cottisham, and Flora Thompson was Flora Timms, the daughter of a Buckinghamshire stone mason. The historian Barbara English traced the family in the local records and discovered that Timms

5 Frank Bramley, *For of Such is the Kingdom of Heaven* (1891)

A moving image of young death. Painted in a Cornish fishing village, this is most likely a depiction of the funeral of a middle-class child. Labouring children appear in the right-hand margin of the painting

had indeed come from a large family (ten children between 1875 and 1898), but had glossed over death in her own household and community. Four of her nine brothers and sisters died under the age of three. Childhood death was commonplace in the parish of Cottisham.[2] If Thompson's *Lark Rise* 'constructed a past which never really existed',[3] Timms's Juniper Hill more accurately represents Victorian rural life and death. The people of rural England lived into the 1920s with such large families and young deaths.

Flora Timms and her contemporaries lived in an important period of English social history. Some simple statistics capture this social shift. Just over 50 per cent of marriages in the 1870s produced six or more children, but by the 1920s only 7 per cent of families were that size.[4] In early Victorian England, 25 per cent or more of children were dead by the age of five; in 1921, the rates were a little over 10 per cent.[5] The expectation of life at birth in 1826–50 (influenced by those child mortality rates) was 40 years; in 1901–25 it was 53 years.[6] This demographic transition, a dual decline in British fertility and mortality in the late nineteenth and early twentieth centuries, was one of the great transformations of the modern world. However, the role of the rural regions and rural workers in these changes is less clear. Nineteenth-century mortality figures are notoriously skewed towards the urban. Demographic histories do not always extricate the rural in their accounts of the transition. And histories of rural workers are rarely concerned with fertility and mortality. The aim of this chapter is to focus on the role of rural workers in England's dual transitions.

* * *

The broad parameters of the dominant interpretation of England's fertility transition are clear. The pattern was one of population increase, triggered in the eighteenth century as family sizes increased, and then family limitation in the second half of the nineteenth century: population continued its upward trend but the size of families began to decrease. When Etienne van de Walle and John Knodel summarized the dynamics of Europe's demographic revolution, they wrote of a 'radical change in the reproductive behaviour of couples and societies'. In England, it began at the end of the nineteenth century and involved all parts of the nation. They emphasized the absence of deliberate fertility control before the transition, the sudden adoption of birth control, the rapidity of the process, and the creation of a new mentality.[7]

There is virtual agreement that a drop in female marriage ages and the proportion of women not marrying were the driving forces behind England's population explosion in the eighteenth century, but their role thereafter is obscure. There is an orthodoxy that marital fertility was remarkably uniform in England from the sixteenth to the nineteenth centuries, varying little over time or between regions. It is also argued that although English fertility was of a modest level compared to other natural fertility regimes, it was indeed natural fertility, with little or no evidence of family limitation until the late nineteenth century.[8] The impression conveyed is of rather sudden change from the 1870s, when natural fertility gave way to family limitation.[9] This initial reduction in English marital fertility was achieved by means of 'stopping', the cessation of childbirth before the end of the woman's fertility, rather than by 'spacing', the deliberate lengthening of the intervals between births.[10] Finally, there is the issue of which social group initiated the transition in Britain. The old interpretation of the social diffusion of fertility limitation from the middle classes down has been challenged, but critics have yet to present a widely subscribed academic alternative: 'The picture is still confused on these matters.'[11]

There are several parts to the received interpretation: the role of marriage in population patterns; the type of fertility before the transition; the character of fertility control during the transition; its social configuration; and the speed and extent of the transformation. Can we use the rural evidence to challenge a number of these orthodoxies?

England was situated in what has been termed the north-west European marriage pattern, characterized by relatively high ages at marriage and a substantial proportion of the population who never married (10 per cent in the first half of the nineteenth century). The delayed marriages of the north-west pattern were linked to the widespread practice of service, where, as we have seen, unmarried women and men spent their teens and early twenties in other households as farm or domestic servants.[12] However, the stability of this demographic regime had been disrupted by the beginning of our period of interest. The eighteenth century saw a substantial increase in population, driven, historians argue, by a drop in female marriage ages.[13] The work of the Cambridge Group suggests that female ages at first marriage decreased from an average of 26 years for the early eighteenth century to 23.5 at the beginning of the nineteenth century, and that the result was an increase in the period of women's total, potential, marital fertility by 20 per cent or more.[14] This fall in marriage ages, it is claimed, was linked to the demise of farm service.[15]

The rural data complicates the picture somewhat. Robert Woods has suggested that the older demographic pattern may well have survived in some rural areas. The nineteenth-century pattern of living-in farm servants in the pastoral north and west and living-out wage-labourers in the arable south and east mirrored national female marriage patterns. In rural

England, those areas with higher ratios of farm servants to labourers roughly corresponded to the areas of lower nuptiality – and vice versa.[16] Woods and Andy Hinde have demonstrated the contrasting marriage communities of arable Mitford (Norfolk) and pastoral Atcham (Shropshire), where the latter's higher marriage ages, to the end of the nineteenth century, are explained by the continuing importance of farm servants.[17] In other words, the nineteenth century was characterized by regional variations in marriage behaviour and therefore fertility.

In fact, it is tempting to argue that the rural communities provide evidence of the extremes of population trends. It is likely, for example, that marriage ages in many rural areas were even lower than the Cambridge Group's means referred to earlier. Women who married labourers and agricultural labourers in three Kent parishes in the period 1800–34 averaged 22 years of age, figures reflected in several other local studies.[18] Some 50 per cent of early nineteenth-century labouring brides in the Kent study were aged 20 years or younger. The implications of these marriage ages can be seen in the family sizes of this cohort of women: two-thirds had seven or more children.[19]

As mentioned earlier, most demographers have argued that English fertility was 'natural fertility', until the onset of family limitation in the late nineteenth century. But some have become increasingly sceptical of the usefulness of the natural fertility model. David Levine recently described it as 'at best a tendentious abstraction'.[20] It is a somewhat crude standard that sets up a rigid polarity between so-called natural fertility (an absence of deliberate birth control) and controlled fertility (deliberate birth control), with the latter defined purely in terms of parity-dependent control (stopping). There is no place for *controlled* natural fertility in the logic of the traditional model. It is blind to the possibility that in natural fertility regimes fertility may well indeed have been controlled by coitus interruptus.[21]

In reality, the fertility regime of much of the nineteenth century does not quite correlate either to 'natural' fertility or to 'fertility control'. It is difficult to distinguish intent in birth spacing, to separate spacing due to breast-feeding, deliberate abstinence or coitus interruptus, or combinations of all three. But clearly a variety of checks were in place, some of them calculated and some of them involuntary responses to social, institutional or economic imperatives. Family reconstitutions provide some clues to behaviour in what have traditionally been assumed to be 'natural fertility' regimes.[22] (See Table 5.1.)

These reconstitutions permit the separation of data for obviously family-limiting couples from that of those who could be defined as practising natural fertility. They show that even among the 'natural fertility' group

Table 5.1 Fertility contrasts in Kent rural couples, 1800–1880

Cohort	No. of couples	Never started	Spacing only	Stopping only	Both spacing and stopping	Neither stopping nor spacing
Family limiting group	59	27% [16]	8% [5]	25% [15]	36% [21]	3% [2]
'Natural fertility' group	171	5% [9]	44% [75]	4% [7]	9% [16]	37% [64]

Source: Based on a reworking of my family reconstitutions for the Kent parishes of Hernhill, Dunkirk and Boughton: see B. Reay, Microhistories: Demography, Society and Culture in Rural England, 1800–1930 (Cambridge, 1996), pp. xix–xxi for the procedure. Family limiting group = completed families (marriage intact until woman aged 45) with 0–3 children. 'Natural fertility' group = married when the woman was aged 20–24 and with marriage still intact at age 35. Spacing = experienced at least one birth interval greater than 36 months. Stopping = experienced 5 years without a birth.

(couples married when the woman was aged 20–24), almost 60 per cent had practised some form of family limitation in the early stage of the marriage. The most prevalent form of control (44 per cent) was spacing, but some couples employed stopping. The difference between this cohort and the family-limiting group, as we shall see later, is that a large percentage of the 'natural fertility' couples (37 per cent) was not practising any detectable birth control whatsoever, but it is significant that there is evidence of spacing in this early-marrying group.

* * *

What about the patterns of fertility control, once the transition was in place? At a national level, Simon Szreter found different family control patterns among those with the lowest fertility in the 1911 census. For the majority, there was a positive correlation between age at marriage and low levels of completed fertility: those controlling fertility after marriage tended to wait longer to get married. But there were also fertility-controllers who combined *extremely high* age at marriage with family limitation, and birth-controllers who married *young*.[23] As Szreter explains, 'If such variation in patterns of family formation exists just within that part of the population represented by these few elite occupational groups, this is strong testimony in favour of a wide variety of family-building forms changing alongside each other across the diverse social groups and communities of the nation, rather than the diffusion of a single new norm or the operation of a single process.'[24] It is also becoming evident that the fertility transition was not synonymous with stopping, the cessation of childbirth once the required number of children had been achieved.[25] The professions practised both spacing and stopping in the early twentieth century.[26] Northern textile-workers were spacing births in the early years of marriage, including, possibly, first births.[27] Szreter has mounted an impressive argument which turns former assumptions on their head: 'spacing from early on in marriage, rather than stopping, was *the* predominant form which family limitation took throughout most of British society by the Edwardian period'.[28]

We have already seen that at least some agricultural labourers were practising both stopping and spacing controls, and that it is possible to isolate all the families that may have been employing more aggressive family control during the period 1800–80. (See Table 5.1.) Of those completed families with 0–3 children in the Kent rural reconstitutions, 25 per cent were practising stopping, 8 per cent were spacing only, and 36 per cent were employing what appeared to be a combination of both spacing and stopping. In other words, a substantial percentage – just over 60 per cent – were using stopping at some stage in their fertility histories; and another significant number, over 40 per cent, spaced their births. Another large proportion, those with no children – almost 30 per cent – never started at all. The controllers had larger percentages of stoppers and those who employed a mix of both methods. (The 'natural fertility' group had few pure stoppers and a greater percentage of spacers.) The family controllers came from all social groups – labourers, farmers, crafts and trades – and no one occupation favoured a particular method.[29]

A final noticeable characteristic of the controllers is that the women's marriage ages were higher than those of the general population in that part of Kent: an average of 27 to 28 compared to 22 to 23. This suggests the continued importance of delayed marriage as a means of fertility control. Indeed, Szreter has argued for the 'continuing central significance for the timing of marriage as an integral part of the populace's family planning tactics': marriage age and proportion never marrying were not immediately replaced as checks to population in every part of the country.[30] Farming couples in some Kent parishes were marrying far later than the other main occupational groups during the period 1850–80, presumably in response to agricultural crisis, and had thereby reduced their completed family size to just over four, compared to the average of six for the earlier-marrying labouring population. Farmers' wives reduced their potential child-bearing span by an average of more than five years. Age at marriage could have been as important in reducing this group's fertility in the nineteenth century as it had been in increasing that of its ancestors in the eighteenth.[31]

* * *

There is considerable debate about the social origins of fertility control. For this writer, the most persuasive interpretation is that of 'multiple fertility declines'.[32] Szreter's reworking of the fertility data in the census of 1911 demonstrates considerable variation in occupational fertility in the families of those married during the period 1881–85 (when the woman was aged 20–24). The mean completed fertility levels varied from 3.2 for barristers to 7.6 for coalminers. Urban and rural figures are not disaggregated in these figures, but they provide some indication of the fertility levels of various rural workers at the turn of the century. Thus agricultural and general labourers and shepherds were among the most fertile sections of the population, with means of 6.7 and 6.8. Farmers, at 5.7, were towards the middle range of the fertility scale. However, the crafts and trades showed remarkable range: 4 (drapers, ironmongers, grocers, publicans, woollen-weavers, clothiers, various dealers, bakers); 5 (builders, gardeners, cotton-weavers and spinners, general shopkeepers, timber merchants, milk-sellers, brewers, greengrocers, plumbers, carpenters, saddlers, wheelwrights, millers, tailors and market-gardeners); and 6 (painters, cabinetmakers, boot and shoe makers, sawyers, blacksmiths, masons, hawkers, coopers, china and pottery manufacturers, stoneworkers, tanners, plasterers, bricklayers). This diversity depended on whether those concerned were employer or employee; masons and bricklayers had slightly lower family sizes than their labourers did.[33]

Diversity was also almost certainly correlated to local labour contexts, for there is compelling, though ultimately inconclusive, evidence that fertility was closely tied to the work practices of men (Szreter hints at machismo culture operating against fertility control), and to employment opportunities for women and children.[34] Michael Anderson suggested many years ago that there was a direct link between the numbers of women in domestic service and marriage chances and marital fertility.[35] There are various scenarios in what has been mooted as the connection between fertility decline and the perceived costs of child-rearing. Where the male wage was high and women's wage opportunities limited – as in mining areas – the male breadwinner/female home-keeper culture was reinforced, and fertility was high. Where there was good employment for women and limited child-earning potential – the textile areas after the Factory and Education acts – it made more economic sense to maximize a couple's earnings and limit child-bearing, and fertility was low. Where the male breadwinner wage was less secure, but compensated for by opportunities for household labour in the form of outwork for women and children (the sweated trades), the economic imperative may have been to encourage fertility rather than to reduce it.

Much of this argument seems more applicable to urban economies, but similar logic can be directed at the social economies of rural workers. The relative fertility of agricultural labourers may have reflected the perpetually depressed male wage and their household dependence on the seasonal and casual work of women and children; 'early marriage and high fertility made economic sense'.[36] There is certainly need for interpretive caution, and one can empathize with Bridget Hill's frustration with demographers' arguments about the relationship between wage-rates and the marriage ages of women: 'So it would seem both increased *and* decreased real earnings could lead to early marriages!' This does not mean that the logic of such linkages is wrong: *both* economic scenarios *could* lead to early marriages. But, as Hill also pointed out, the ultimate working-out of these issues was governed by local economic and cultural needs and practices.[37]

* * *

By the 1890s, 'there is clear evidence of widespread family limitation'. Perhaps 30 to 40 per cent of married women were practising fertility control. By 1911, 'the progress of the fertility transition is unmistakable and irreversible'.[38] Recent work based on data from the 1911 'fertility' census has demonstrated a sharp reduction in marital fertility rates from 1891 to 1911, both in the agricultural sample and among agricultural labourers, dropping some 30 per cent from a 'natural fertility' high. Celibacy rates were also relatively high among these rural cohorts: 15 per cent of men and almost 20 per cent of women in their late forties and early fifties had never married.[39]

Although all groups participated in what would become known as fertility decline, there was significant social and regional variation. The agricultural sample from 1891 contained rural areas that experienced little decline in marital fertility (the agricultural area around Banbury, Oxfordshire, and the moorland farming district near Shap in Westmorland), as well as those where it declined rapidly (the villages and small market-towns in the Colyton area of Devon, and around Elmdon in Essex).[40] Changes in averages over the century mask rather more nuanced distributional shifts and adjustments in fertility.[41] Aggregated runs also conceal district fluctuations.[42] National figures of declining fertility indicate that agricultural labourers were among those least likely to be reducing their fertility (see above). Yet there is local evidence of village communities of rural workers where the most significant fall in family size occurred in the period immediately following the institution of the New Poor Law of 1834, notoriously framed to discourage support for large families among the poor.[43] Arguably, then, the transition had begun several generations earlier than the 1890s. Its origins lay with the gradual adjustments of a small, gradually increasing, number of couples who were controlling their fertility.[44] Even in our high-fertility, Kent labouring communities, the percentage of families with no more than three children rose from 11 per cent for those married in 1800–34 to 24 per cent for the cohort of 1835–49.[45] This suggests that the orthodox preoccupation with changes in mentality and behaviour in the 1890s is no longer tenable.

Doubtless, many rural women practised what a Kent informant described as the 'push him off' method of birth control.[46] One fenland villager recalled working late into the evening, mending clothes, so that her husband would be asleep when she came to bed: 'My mother had fourteen children and I didn't want that.'[47] Perhaps some observed the folk adage collected in Oxfordshire in the early twentieth century:

> When you've got one [child] you may run,
> When you've got two you may goo,
> But when you've got three you must stop where you be.[48]

But rather than a rapid break from natural fertility to 'family limitation', there was a series of adjustments within the 'natural fertility' regime (if we can persist in so terming it) until family limitation began to dominate. No change in *mentality* need have occurred.[49] All that was required was an increasing number of couples showing a willingness to control the size of their family through the methods used for centuries and which would continue to be employed, oral history indicates, into the twentieth century: abortion, about which we have little firm statistical information, coitus interruptus or withdrawal, and abstinence, or what Szreter terms 'attempted abstinence or coital spacing' and which he proposes as the most common form of fertility restriction throughout our period of interest. Contraceptive devices were rarely used in the nineteenth century.[50] Kate Fisher's oral histories of the birth-control practices of urban workers in Wales and Oxford found that rather than deciding on an optimum family size, and then controlling their fertility, couples used contraception (mainly withdrawal but also condoms) in a vague, unplanned manner 'to delay the next birth or to have fewer or no more children – a goal that might emerge at any stage of marriage and that was not necessarily maintained'.[51] Their rural counterparts are unlikely to have been more calculating or rigorous. 'Fertility control' did not emerge fully-formed in the 1890s.[52]

* * *

A study of a group of rural parishes in nineteenth-century Kent calculated that up to a third of married households were broken by the death of one of the partners before the woman reached the age of 45. This simple marriage disruption decreased the number of children per family by between two and three from the average number of children that would have resulted had the marriage been permitted to run its normal course of fertility.[53] Early childhood mortality removed an average of a further one child per couple.[54] Therefore, it would be surprising if mortality had no role to play in the population changes described earlier. The latest estimate is that two-thirds of the population increase in the eighteenth century was due to a rise in fertility governed by the fall in marriage age, and a third due to decreasing mortality, particularly maternal mortality and the stillbirth rate.[55] Historians and demographers have long debated the problematic relationship between declining fertility and infant and child mortality. Does a controlled, declining family size ensure better care and therefore higher survival rates of children? Or, reversing the relationship, do increased rates of survival encourage family limitation?[56]

Yet health and mortality in the rural areas of nineteenth- and early twentieth-century England are relatively neglected topics. Most of the focus has been on the towns.[57] National annual infant mortality rates, IMR (those dying before the age of one), fluctuated around a consistent 150 per 1000 births from the 1830s through the 1890s, and then began a sharp decline. In 1911, the national rate was 110/1000. Early childhood mortality, ECMR (those dying in the age group one to four), was at a comparable level to infant mortality in mid-century but began to fall in the 1870s, earlier than infant mortality.[58] Rural rates were lower than in urban areas, and (like early childhood mortality) fell earlier than the national decline in infant mortality.[59] When IMR and ECMR are combined as childhood mortality rates, CMR (all those dying before the age of five), the rates are compounded in a noticeable peak in the 1850s and 1860s (around the 290/1000 level), and then decline, apart from a revived high in the towns in the 1890s due to the ravages of infant diarrhoea. Rural CMRs were lower than the national ones, maintained constancy from the beginning of the century (on or about 250), and did not experience the same mid-century peak, though they too declined from the 1850s.[60]

Although academic commentators agree on the universal decline in 1901, they have disputed the significance of nineteenth-century national trends. There is notable regional variation in mortality turning points when the various counties are plotted from 1861 to 1911: 80 per cent of them experienced their highest infant mortality rates in either 1861 or 1871.[61] (See Figure 5.1.) The sheer range of mortality experience in nineteenth-century England is indisputable, and illustrated dramatically in Woods's colour-coded maps of infant mortality in the 614 districts of England and Wales.[62] Infant mortality rates ranged from 240 in Liverpool and Birmingham to north Devon's 100.[63] As intimated earlier, urban and rural experiences differed: Woods describes this as a strong, though not exclusive, urban–rural variation.[64] The respective lines plotted on the graphs of infant mortality for London, the large towns, the small towns, and England and Wales, always maintain a higher discreet distance from those of the 'rural residual', even when they converge towards one another after 1901.[65]

If we widen the discussion of urban–rural differentials to include childhood mortality rates and expectation of life at birth, the theme remains one of urban penalization. The large towns peaked in the 1850s with CMRs of 358, when the

Figure 5.1 Regional patterns of infant mortality, 1862–1921

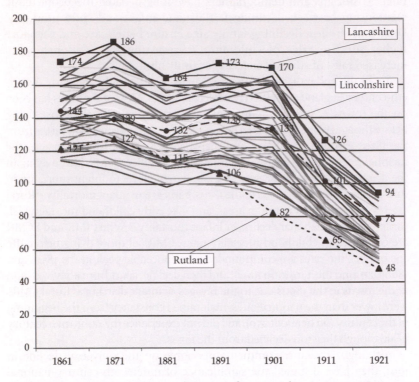

Source: C. H. Lee, 'Regional Inequalities in Infant Mortality in Britain, 1861–1971: Patterns and Hypotheses', *Population Studies*, 45 (1991), pp. 55–65. My calculations for London and the English counties are from Lee's table on p. 57: 15 experienced their highest infant mortality rates in 1861, 19 in 1871, none in 1891, and 4 in 1901.

rate for the combined rural areas was 255.[66] To return to the life-expectancy figures with which we started the chapter, the 40-year estimate for the nation in 1826–50 disguised life-expectancy at birth of a mere 32 years in large towns like Manchester and a contrasting 44 years in the combined rural areas.[67] In 1841, the rates for rural Surrey were 45 compared to 28 in central Liverpool.[68] The same trend occurs if the experience of the agricultural labourer is used as a proxy for the rural. In 1911, the national infant-mortality levels in the families of agricultural labourers were lower than any of the Registrar General's 'social classes' other than that of the professionals.[69]

* * *

However, national and broad regional trends could disguise interesting local variations, particularly given environmental impact on morbidity and mortality. It is also important to note that many of the high-mortality mining areas were situated in rural sectors.[70] Furthermore, there is a demographic blind spot in the first half of the nineteenth century, the period between the end of the Cambridge Group's population project and the commencement of the statistics generated by civil registration.[71] Therefore, it is particularly noteworthy that local studies, as diverse as agricultural parishes in Kent and industrial parishes in Lancashire, Staffordshire and Yorkshire, demonstrate rises in infant mortality during that half-century.[72] Infant mortality in the Blean in Kent moved in the opposite direction to the national rural trend, increasing by 60 per cent from 1800 to 1880. Childhood mortality rates increased by 50 per cent.[73]

These microhistories can also reveal tiny rural pockets of death. One hamlet in the Blean had a CMR of 333 for the period 1840–80, a rate that would not have been out of place in nineteenth-century Liverpool.[74] The CMR in the villages and towns of the Staffordshire Potteries in the 1830s and 1840s was 323 for boys and 235 for girls.[75] The industrial textile village of Armley, on the outskirts of Leeds, had an IMR of nearly 250 in the 1830s.[76] The expanding Leicestershire framework-knitting village, Shepshed, had an IMR of 208 for the period 1825–49.[77] The heavily polluted, worsted spinning and weaving Yorkshire community of Haworth (population: 2400) had an infant mortality rate of 223/1000 in the 1830s and 1840s, with over 40 per cent of children dying before they reached the age of six. A health inspector observed that such mortality levels corresponded to those of 'some of the most unhealthy of the London districts'.[78] Steve King discovered spatial concentrations of infant mortality in the proto-industrial village of Caverley-cum-Farsley in the West Riding, and presumably other instances will emerge when more detailed local studies are undertaken.[79]

Woods is insufficiently attuned to such inter-rural contrasts, although they by no means conflict with his general argument for geographical variation. Certainly he is aware of the 'case of high infant mortality in certain rural districts', referring directly to Norfolk, Cambridgeshire, Lincolnshire and parts of Yorkshire, but confines his interest to a one-sentence paragraph.[80] It would be unfortunate if rural mortality patterns were subsumed under one national 'rural' or 'residual rural' measurement, for variations within the combined category were as wide-ranging as the differences between London and the large and small towns that Woods has been so careful to separate from the national estimates.[81] We need to allow for striking contrasts in rural infant- and child-mortality experiences and for both high and low mortality regimes in English villages.[82]

Doubtless, the industrial villages, with populations stretching over the 2500 level, merging city and countryside, and exposing their inhabitants to the dangers associated with work and environment, were candidates for higher mortality. Levine has suggested overcrowding and poor water and sanitation as the probable cause of the high infant-mortality rates in proto-industrial communities.[83] The framework-knitting and lace-manufacturing village of Arnold (not far from Nottingham) was said to be in a sorry state of pollution in the 1850s. The brook was a 'common conduit of filth from the whole length of Arnold'. Wells were corrupted by offal, animal skins, and dead kittens and puppies – 'I have seen hair in my own tea cup'. Numerous dung-heaps, positioned near walkways and homes, contained human excrement as well as slops and ashes: 'In the churchyard it is impossible, for many square yards near the entrance, to place the feet without treading in deposits of human ordure.' Not surprisingly, infant-mortality levels were double the national average.[84] Mining villages must have been dangerous places to live in. The early nineteenth-century journal of the rector of the Somerset coalmining and farming community of Camerton is full of gruesome accounts of mining accidents and deaths, as well as qualitative evidence for the frequent illness and mortality associated with the living conditions of the inhabitants.[85]

But there were also 'traditional' rural hamlets with poor sanitation, polluted watercourses and wells, manure pits, seeping cesspools, stinking privies, pigsties close to houses, and badly drained stables and sheds, ideal environments for the flyborne endemic diarrhoea, traceable in the August and September peaks in infant burials.[86] The Reports to the General Board of Health on sanitary conditions in England's towns and villages in the 1840s and 1850s exposed many such examples of rural danger. A medical specialist from the Lake District area of Cumberland contrasted the natural beauty of the region with the reality of life in its villages:

> The village of Braithwaite ... contains, in proportion to its population, more dirt, disease, and death than any decent town. It is one of the most romantic and filthy villages in England ... There are lanes, alleys, and courts, in almost all small towns and villages, in which the mortality is higher than that of the average of great towns. Nay, in hamlets and isolated farmhouses in this, as in many other country districts, there is often more sickness in proportion to the population than in cities; and I could point out within a circuit of a few miles, localities, in which, during the last few years, scrofula, small-pox, measles, and typhus fever have left their ravages, and which, with proper care and cleanliness, might, I firmly believe, have escaped.[87]

The report on the small Herefordshire agricultural town of Bromyard claimed annual mortality rates comparable to Hull and London's Rotherhithe, and attributed this state of affairs to the 'defective sanitary arrangements' of the place.[88] Because of local water-storage and irrigation practices, the Wiltshire villagers of Crockerton and Longbridge Deverill suffered both from malaria and an outbreak of cholera in 1849.[89] The report on the Lincolnshire fenland parish of Holbeach presented a gloomy picture of a demoralized, and opium-addicted population, also suffering from malaria and rheumatic complaints, only intermittently employed in agricultural day-labour, and having to walk long distances from the town to work on the farms. The infant-mortality rates in the parish were between 300 and 460/1000.[90] Even the *health resort* of Burnham was prone to 'fevers and ague'. This tiny town and its nearby villages were situated on the low-lying coastal marshland area of north Somerset, the ideal environment for the malarial mosquito.[91]

* * *

Infant-mortality levels may well have been linked to women's work and breast-feeding practices. It is clear that exclusively breast-fed infants had a better chance of survival than those who were fed with supplementary food or who (worst of all) were only bottle-fed.[92] The long-tubed bottles favoured by working-class populations in the nineteenth century were notoriously unhygienic. The Medical Officers for the urban and rural authorities of Faversham (Kent) attributed the extensive mortality of the 1880s to bacteria and decomposing milk in these bottles, and to the prevalence of hand-feeding; 'many of the infants in this locality are fed from bottles, and often left for hours while the mothers are at work in the brick-fields & factories &c'. '[D]iarrhoea and many other intestinal diseases . . . decimate infant life.'[93] Surveyors of the high-mortality, marshland areas of mid-nineteenth-century England demonized women's agricultural work, blaming maternal absence, inadequate childminding, interrupted breas-feeding, polluted food substitutes, extensive use of narcotics, and a neglect which bordered on 'deliberate starvation' for the 'monstrous infantine death-rate of the examined agricultural districts'.[94] However, the correlation between women working and breast-feeding practice depended on local work contexts. Valerie Fildes suggests that labour in the potteries and mills did not encourage breast-feeding, whereas those involved in homework were able to accommodate the regime.[95] It is often assumed that rural women left their infants to work in the fields, yet oral histories refer to breast-feeding as being the most convenient option for such work.[96] Demographers hold that 'natural fertility' indicates breast-feeding durations of at least a year in premodern England, though there is little evidence to support this claim into the nineteenth century, and no accurate information on the duration of breast-feeding or the mix or extent of artificial feeding practices in the rural areas. The empirical evidence so skilfully mined by Fildes is for the towns in the 1900s.[97]

Mary Dobson has usefully drawn a distinction between two different mortality environments in early modern south-east England, the former associated with the low-lying marshland areas, and the latter with the uplands. 'The contours of death and the contours of health were separated by an elevation of little more than 400 or 500 feet, a distance of little over ten miles in parts. Their geographical proximity was close. Their epidemiological histories were worlds apart.'[98] Although the levels of mortality in the marshland areas were somewhat more muted by the nineteenth century, and conditions in Romney Marsh had improved, geographical and ecological contrasts between upland and lowland remained, reflected in infant-mortality rates: the Sussex Downs versus the coast; the Weald of Kent versus the north Kent marshes; the Essex uplands versus the Thames estuary and the Essex marshlands. IMRs in the south-east in the early nineteenth century varied from the lows of 74 in Ardingly (Sussex) and 121 in Penshurst (Kent) to the highs of 370 in Burnham (Kent) and 451 in Southchurch (Essex): a clear contrast between the rural inland/upland and the coastal and marshland parishes. Life-expectancy at birth in the marshes was 31 years compared to 44 in the non-marsh areas.[99] In 1861, infant-mortality levels were still disproportionately high along the estuaries of the Thames and the Medway and the Isle of Sheppey in north Kent, in the fens, in patches in Norfolk, as well as along the Ouse and Humber.[100]

Dobson has argued that much of the ill health of these regions is explained by malaria (often described as marsh-fever or ague and present in England into the twentieth century), and that the heavy dosing of opium to alleviate suffering, as well as the debilitating effects of the disease on both mother and child, doubtless contributed to infant mortality.[101] As already intimated, medical commentators on the high infant-mortality of the fens and marshes in the 1860s had a slightly different emphasis. For them, the draining of the marshes in the nineteenth century had considerably reduced the problem of malaria but the resultant conversion to arable land had produced a new evil: an increase in women's work. In other words, infant mortality remained high but due to new causes. The evil was no longer malaria but 'a more fatal enemy . . . the employment of mothers in the field' resulting in maternal neglect, overexertion (there was much discussion of premature births), bottle- or hand-feeding of infants instead of breast-feeding, and habitual opium usage, a taste acquired during the malarial times but redirected to pacify children. The problem with such accounts is that their hysteria and moral condemnation tell us more about the cultural assumptions of the commentators than they do about labouring motherhood.[102]

Like infants, the very young (those aged one to four) were vulnerable to the diarrhoeal infections of the warm weather and to the respiratory ailments of the late winter and spring. They were also susceptible to the diseases that particularly hit children – whooping cough, scarlet fever, measles and (to a lesser extent) diphtheria. Indeed, Anne Hardy has argued that measles mortality helped to sustain childhood death in the decades up to 1900.[103] Mortality was often the result of secondary pneumonia (rather than the disease itself), and this was more likely in the colder months.[104] The main diseases that killed older children (those aged from 5 to 14) were diphtheria, scarlet fever and measles, all major killers in nineteenth-century England.[105] The incidence of diphtheria and scarlet fever was highest among children of school age, and it is tempting to relate the impact of such infectious diseases in the late-nineteenth-century rural areas to the rise in school attendance. Compulsory schooling, with the increasing likelihood that young children would be together in close proximity for long periods, must have provided the ideal environment for contagion.[106] Demographers have established the close relationship between the mortality rates of these diseases and population density; crowding in the urban areas increased the levels of early-childhood mortality.[107] It is arguable that rural schools provided similar conditions. The classroom could convert isolated outbreaks into epidemics.

Infant and child mortality are usually treated as proxies for wider standards of living. As Richard Vann and David Eversley have put it, 'quality and quantity of life come close together'.[108] However, it is important not to confuse mortality with morbidity: childhood death was but a rough guide to more general conditions of health. School log books provide a survey of the communicable diseases of the latter part of the nineteenth century, the ailments which kept rural children away from school without necessarily killing them: mumps, skin disease, sore throats, chicken-pox, coughs, colds, bronchitis and influenza. They also list the impacts of diphtheria and measles. The pattern in rural Kent was one of background low-level sickness, punctuated by epidemics two or three times a decade from the 1870s until the end of the century.[109] The gap between morbidity and mortality is indicated in the figures for one rural district that recorded the impact of a particularly virulent strain of measles, allegedly brought into the area by hop-pickers; there were five deaths out of over five hundred cases.[110] James Riley has described this period in Europe as 'a transition from an age of death to an age of sickness'. Rural England was part of this age.[111]

Children and adults had different patterns of mortality. Young deaths peaked in the late summer and autumn months, because of the diarrhoeal infections of the warmer weather, and in the late winter and spring owing to respiratory ailments. The more muted seasonality of adult mortality, applicable to many parts of north-west Europe over long periods of time, reflected winter and spring respiratory death.[112] But age-specific mortality was slightly more complicated than this. The elderly (those over 60) shared the pattern of the very young: the twin peaks of diarrhoea/dysentery fatality, and diseases of the lung/respiratory system.[113] Phthisis or pulmonary tuberculosis (consumption) was particularly concentrated in the young-adult age group in its mortality pattern (those aged 15 to 54). It lacked the seasonality of other diseases, and does not appear to have shared their urban bias to the same degree. Phthisis provides further demonstration of a theme to which we keep returning: the variability of the rural experience. Rural districts contained both the highest and the lowest tuberculosis-mortality rates.[114]

Typhus fever, transmitted by the body louse and at its height in winter (in contrast to typhoid, a summer ailment spread by contaminated water and the fly), was another common ailment. It was a product of crowded living conditions, and therefore favoured the kind of borderland urban/rural settlements referred to earlier. Baildon, in Yorkshire, a large village and several hamlets not far from Bradford, with a population of about three thousand at mid-century, suffered from intermittent outbreaks of typhus among its home-based wool-combers, weavers and sorters.[115] The female silk-factory workers and the male agricultural labourers of the populous Devon town of Ottery St Mary likewise experienced typhus.[116] But so also did the little agricultural parish of Mileham, in the fenland area of west Norfolk. Its population of just over five hundred suffered not just from typhus but also from a severe outbreak of cholera in the late 1840s. Apart from general unsanitary conditions and problems with drainage in this malarial, marshland region, the health inspector noted that the cottages of the agricultural labourers in Mileham were crowded, 'and were much more so until a few months since, when an all-wise but inscrutable Providence removed some of the occupants'.[117] Typhus was also common in the villages and hamlets around the town of Banbury, Oxfordshire.[118]

As already intimated, the rural areas were not exempt from the depredations of cholera in the 1840s, though it was the towns that were most affected. The village of Wrekenton (Durham) had a population of less than a thousand, yet lost 'one out of seven of the entire population'.[119] Victims in the cholera epidemic included the families of the agricultural labourers of fenland Mileham (Norfolk) and March (Cambridgeshire), the agricultural and cloth workers of Wotton-under-Edge (Gloucestershire), and the pit-men, farm labourers and fisher-folk of the tiny villages and hamlets near and around Warkworth (Northumberland).[120]

* * *

National figures for the middle of the nineteenth and early twentieth centuries point to the longevity of the rural labourer in comparison to other workers. At age 20 in 1850, a rural labourer could expect another 45 years of life compared to 38 for miners and 41 for urban labourers.[121] The usual argument is that this is support for place rather than class or occupation as a determiner of nineteenth- and early twentieth-century mortality, that class differentials in mortality were constantly overridden by environmental factors.[122] However, mortality rates do not guarantee lives free from ill health and pain. Riley's thesis of a transition from death to sickness in the late nineteenth century – 'sick rather than dead' – anticipates my argument. The improvement in people's health, in the sense that their mortality declined, actually meant that sickness increased: 'In Britain's health transition, life spans first became longer and more occupied with sickness, marked by somewhat fewer episodes that lasted much longer.'[123]

A report from a Canterbury hospital that treated rural workers wrote in 1841 of the 'prevalence of chronic diseases' in Kent. 'In this part of the country, where the working classes are chiefly field labourers, atmospheric changes, and constant exposure to cold and wet . . . determine the character of the resulting diseases: thus we have, in abundance, inflammatory affections of the pleura, the lungs, and the air-passages; obstinate rheumatisms of muscular parts; and neuralgic affections from cold, sometimes amounting to complete paralysis.'[124] As we have seen, malaria was a common ailment in some areas of rural England. The disease did not kill large numbers of adults, but it contributed to general debility. Fever, 'continued', 'intermittent' and 'remittent', 'more prevalent in spring and autumn than at other seasons of the year', was one of the main complaints of patients in the Kent and Canterbury Hospital in the late 1830s.[125] In the Peterborough Infirmary, which treated cases from the fens of Lincolnshire and Cambridgeshire, the main adult illnesses in the 1840s and 1850s were (in descending order) ague, diarrhoea, influenza, fever and cholera. (See Figure 5.2.) Cholera was the greatest killer. Only one death

Figure 5.2 Seasonality of adult illness in the fens, 1845–1859

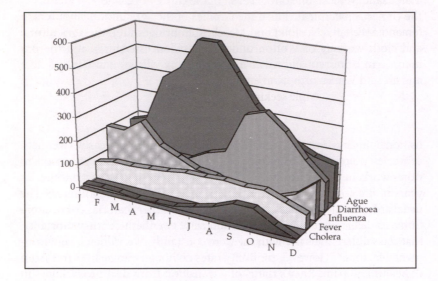

Source: Records of the Peterborough Infirmary, in *Parliamentary Papers*, 1864, xxviii, Appendix 13, pp. 452–3: 'Report by Dr. George Whitley as to the Quantity of Ague and Other Malarious Diseases Now Prevailing in the Principal Marsh Districts of England'.

occurred out of nearly four thousand cases of the ague.[126] Rheumatic pain – the result of cold and damp living and working conditions – must have been commonplace in the rural areas. The average age of Canterbury hospital patients suffering from chronic rheumatism was 47 for males and 49 for females, but they included people in their twenties experiencing acute pain. As with malaria, quinine and opium were employed to alleviate the suffering.[127]

Winter was a difficult period for populations that depended heavily upon agricultural labour: work was lost through wet weather and snow, or simply because there was little to be done at that time of the year. Household resources dwindled, and, as families tightened their belts, they must have been particularly vulnerable to the effects of illness. Oral accounts speak of winter desperation, and of recognition that those were the difficult months to get through. 'After Christmas . . . yes, winter time . . . I think that was the worst time.' Dorothy Tong recalled that her mother used to say, 'the falling of the leaf is going to tell whether he's going to live'.

If a sick or elderly person could survive the period after November, then they would be all right.[128]

Poor Law Union records chronicle the sicknesses and injuries which forced families and individuals to seek poor relief: continuing fevers, consumption, injuries of the arm or leg, fractures, burns, shoulder or side injuries, ruptures, infections, abscesses, leg ulcers, sprains and cuts.[129] The records of the friendly societies take the picture into the early twentieth century. Working people seeking sickness benefits from three friendly societies in 1896–1919, including a branch in rural Northamptonshire, suffered – in descending proportions of cases – from accidents, influenza, bronchitis, rheumatism, lumbago, gastritis, carbuncles, tonsillitis and skin ulcers.[130] A Wiltshire doctor commented on the strains experienced by dairy-farm workers in the 1840s. He was 'not unfrequently applied to for advice by women suffering from symptoms of over-work, generally attributable to their being employed in the dairy . . . pains in the back and limbs, overpowering sense of fatigue . . . want of appetite, feverishness'.[131] Such routine ailments cannot compete with the drama of epidemics in medical historiography, yet they affected the lives of large numbers of people and must have been particularly worrying for a population that earned its living by labour.

* * *

My argument in this chapter has been that the broad contours of national fertility and mortality disguise as much as they reveal. Moreover, this is true even of the disaggregated rural rates. While some recent demographic studies have attempted to overcome the simple urban–rural classification of fertility and mortality, they remain more attuned to urban, environmental complexities than rural gradations.[132] In some Kent parishes, not notorious for their high mortality, the risks of a woman dying during or immediately after childbirth (maternal mortality) were higher in the nineteenth century than the national average. In Boughton-under-Blean, they were as high at the start of the twentieth century as they had been nationally in the seventeenth century.[133] In the Cambridgeshire market-town of March, a fenland community with notoriously high infant-mortality rates, rural workers in the 1840s were subject to 'almost every indigenous and imported epidemic disease that has prevailed in this country'. With malaria, typhus, typhoid, measles, smallpox, influenza, diarrhoea, cholera, bronchitis and phthisis, March's inspector concluded that conditions there were worse than any he had encountered.[134] In the 1890s, a report from the Cambridgeshire fens around March said that although

health had improved, 'the rural population living in the Fens is very subject
to a peculiar form of pneumonia, characterised as low or typhoidal pneumonia, which is generally fatal in four or five days. More deaths arise from
this than any other cause, but rheumatism is prevalent, and intermittent
fever from damp has not altogether disappeared. The long-continued habit
of opium-eating still prevails.'[135] On the other hand, there is the appropriately named Hartland, a healthy, upland Devon parish, with IMRs in the
nineteenth century of around 70/1000.[136] The contours of the life and death
of rural workers were experienced at such microlevels.

6 Leisure

The diary of Robert Sharp from the Yorkshire agricultural village of South Cave reveals a fascinating case-study of rural leisure in the north of England during the 1820s and 1830s. We can begin the festive year at Christmas, for the schoolmaster, Sharp, refers to women and children 'running about Gooding' on 23 December, begging for pennies and provisions.[1] On the

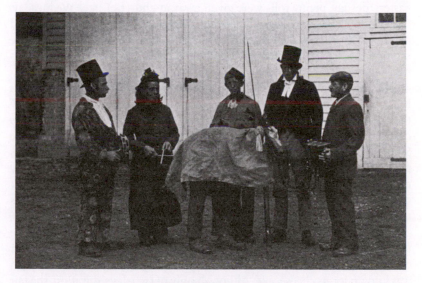

6 The hooden horse, 1905

We know something of the context of this photograph. The hooden horse was a Kent Christmas ritual, but this image was taken in June. Although the performers were a team of horsemen from a farm in St Nicholas-at-Wade, the setting was actually another farm in Sarre. They did not have the appropriate broom for the cross-dressed character, Mollie, so gave him a triangle to hold instead. Even his presence was a fiction: the collector was told that Mollie 'was revived and brought into the group for my benefit'. See P. Maylam, *The Hooden Horse, an East Kent Christmas Custom* (Canterbury, 1909)

25th, singers and dancers descended upon the houses of the local minister and the more substantial residents – sometimes at very unseasonable hours – seeking gifts of food or money.[2] Sharp complained that singers were at his window at 1 a.m., expecting to be rewarded for waking people up. At about 5 or 6 a.m., 'lads and lasses' came around for their Christmas boxes.[3] As in other places in the north, performers of dance and drama continued the quest for largesse during December and January, sometimes coercively. The South Cave ploughlads collected as much as £9, which they spent on a dinner and drink.[4]

He recalled other moments of recreation – pancakes on Shrove Tuesday in February – but the next principal date in the leisure calendar was Easter. Sharp never provided the thick description demanded by modern ethnographers; however, he does refer to a mix of dole-giving, anticipation of the change of seasons, and feasting and merrymaking. On Easter Sunday, it was the custom for children to wear new clothes, if they could afford them. On Easter Tuesday, penny rolls were given away at church. Easter Wednesday, 'Tansy Day', was marked by dancing and consumption of tansy cake and pudding. Sharp noted fiddling and dancing into the night in 1837. He thought that Easter customs were in decline: both Tansy Day and the wearing of new clothes were falling into disuse.[5]

The next festive moment in the calendar was Oak Apple or Royal Oak Day, commemorating the restoration of the monarchy in 1660. Sharp knew the origins of the celebration, but observed that many who stuck oak leaves or branches in their hats, or who wore garlands, knew nothing about the Stuarts. They merely thought of 29 May as Royal Oak Day. He also made his political sympathies abundantly clear: 'This is what is called or sadly miscalled King Charles' martyrdom. I don't know what pretence there is for calling such a Tyrant as Charles was, a Martyr, except he was a Martyr to his tyrannous arbitrary and unjust proceedings.'[6]

Whitsun, beginning on the seventh Sunday after Easter, and therefore falling at any time in May and June, was an important date on the calendar of rural workers. Cave fair, held on Trinity Monday and Tuesday every year, was known for its cheesecake. Although only of two days' duration, the fair could drift into a third day, and practically a whole week was taken up with arriving, packing and unpacking stalls, and preparing. It was also a great market for pots, presumably to accommodate the cheesecake and other produce. People dressed in their finery and spruced up their homes. Visitors and relatives descended upon the inhabitants of the small village, and the population of South Cave and its surrounding villages doubled overnight. The structure of the fair days reflected a duality of work and play, with the Monday concerned principally with the sale of cattle and the

Tuesday taken up with pleasure. Sharp's diary entries mention performances of melodrama, horse, ass and foot racing, running wheelbarrows, orange bobbing, street music and copious consumption of drink.[7]

The next date on Sharp's calendar was Midsummer. This was the time of the Beverley fair, attended by many of the locals; 'it is amongst other things a fair for Pigs, and several poor people who can raise as much money generally buy a Pig, to feed for the Winter'.[8] The South Cave club feast, the annual celebration of the local benefit or friendly society, was also in July, always held on the Thursday after Old Midsummer Day (6 July). An entry for 12 July 1827 gives some indication of the tenor of these events: 'Club feast day, it was at Newlove's [The Bear public house] where they had a Booth fixed in the yard, and the Members all dined together, at two tables set the whole length[;] there were about 120 members, a very good plain dinner, and good order kept, Mattw. Smith towards night got very drunk and some Boys got some Soot, Tallow & Reds, and daubed his face all over, making him look wilder than an American Savage.'[9]

November festivities began with 5 November. 'Yesterday the fifth of Novr. was kept as usual with the ringing of Bells, Bonfires and Hare feasts at the Public houses. I attended none of them', Sharp wrote in 1829. He recorded hare feasts in the public houses most years in the 1820s and 1830s.[10] Then there were the amusements associated with Old Martinmas (23 November), when servants finished their contracts and faced new hirings: 'This is Martinmas Day, the Servants with us receive their wages and are their own Masters for one short week.' Some went to the Hull market. In effect, servants enjoyed several weeks of respite from their labour, for hiring or statute fairs were held in South Cave on the two consecutive Thursdays leading up to Old Martinmas. The beer-shops and public houses were certainly busy. Sharp remarked of one such occasion that there was not much hiring but plenty of dancing. In 1829, the revelry in the public house lasted for most of the night: 'if the house were mine I should be afraid of them dancing it down'.[11]

* * *

Now consider this description of the rather thin social life of the scattered Wiltshire hamlets and villages of the parish of Corsley in the 1900s. Men played and watched football in the winter, and cricket in the summer. (The women, of course, never played, though they sometimes watched.) On Sundays, people went out walking and congregated on the streets in their best clothes. Although wives and daughters were present over Christmas, when Maude Davies carried out her observations, the pubs in Corsley drew

mainly on a male clientele. A gramophone and singing provided entertainment, and patrons played darts and bagatelle. Church and chapel –
Wesleyan and Baptist – were important sites in Corsley, but social life was
centred in the home and the pub. Davies distinguished between the leisure
of the summer months, when the days were longer and people were active,
and the quiet and darkness of the winter, when families stayed in their
cottages and went to bed early. She thought that the younger men tended to
gravitate to the pubs, while the married men often spent their evenings at
home with their families.[12]

There are elements of agreement between the accounts of South Cave in
the 1820s and Corsley in the 1900s – the centrality of the pub and alcohol –
but the contrasts are more noticeable. One is immediately taken with the
relative lack of choice in the early twentieth-century communities.
Moreover, the situation in rural Wiltshire contrasted with the recreational
prospects in urban areas, for the increased national leisure opportunities of
the late nineteenth and early twentieth centuries were unequally experienced. The regularization of work and play experienced by factory workers
did not apply to many agricultural labourers, who still worked long hours,
including Saturdays and even Sundays, or who, alternatively, had to
contend with periods of inactivity and loss of income.[13] The
Northumberland farm worker, Andrew Patten, considered it impossible for
agricultural workers to participate in cricket and football until they gained
the Saturday half-day; until then, well into the twentieth century, they were
working from 6 a.m. to 6 p.m. There was simply no space for sports.[14]

Many of the new mass leisure forms, music hall, horse racing, football
and, later, cinema, were concentrated in the towns.[15] This did not mean that
rural dwellers had no access. Nineteenth-century autobiographies describe
the travelling players, medical charlatans, entertainers and exhibitors of
curiosities who reached a rural audience in one-off performances in village
pubs or barns, or by plying the fairs in the towns.[16] Rural workers the length
of the Midlands and the north were exposed to wonders exhibited from the
back of travelling caravans: the eight-foot-tall, black giantess, who was
really a blacked-up, white male of normal stature ('Sometimes a drunken
fellow would attempt to take indecent liberties with me'); the pig-faced
lady, who was really a shaved bear strapped in a chair (in this case a
drunken villager got far more than he bargained for); and the 'illustrious
Wang Fong, the Chinese Enchanter', who was the same person as the fake
giantess![17] They could see a dramatic rendition of the Battle of Waterloo,
with one actor (the same man as the giantess and Chinese enchanter) playing 'the whole French Army', or *Richard the Third* performed in twenty
minutes flat.[18] The strolling player, Christopher Thomson, earned a very

precarious living in the late 1820s, 'village hunting' in Nottinghamshire and Derbyshire, performing plays in at least a dozen venues one summer.[19] It is a history yet to be written. Ruth Robinson remembered 'blood and thunder' drama in a tent at the back of a public house in Eastwood, Nottinghamshire, when she was a young girl in the 1890s or 1900s.[20] The farm labourer Fred Kitchen compared the impact of his first experience of the theatre to that of his first kiss.[21] At the end of the period, oral histories contain startled memories of first encounters with film as innocents in the front row: 'to my dying day . . . I shall see these camels nearly coming onto my face'.[22] However, the point remains that those who lived in the cities and large towns had greater choice. Consequently, the developing youth culture and increased spending power associated with the labour of new wage-earners was disproportionately an urban affair.[23] The experience of the young in rural areas, according to several commentators at the time, was more likely to be one of boredom.[24]

Moreover, the history of rural leisure in Victorian and Edwardian England forms something of a historiographical vacuum between the agreed richness of the early modern period (with its feasts, fairs, wakes and ales) and the urban/industrial focus of the organized sports of the later nineteenth century.[25] Hugh Cunningham's skilful survey in *The Cambridge Social History of Britain, 1750–1950* contains a mere two pages on rural popular culture as he moves quickly from a discussion of hours of work, reforms of leisure, and the elements of artisan culture to focus on *urban* leisure and popular culture. The rural sector is almost an interlude in his analysis. His theme is of 'the pervasive poverty of the rural leisure culture'.[26] But was the recreational culture of rural workers in the long nineteenth century really so deficient?

* * *

Although we do not have the space to discuss every celebration, the festive calendar outlined by the Yorkshireman Sharp held for much of our period of interest. Christmas, vastly different from its modern commercialized form, was consistently a time for largesse. In Burwash, Sussex, the singers were outside the vicar's window at 3 a.m. on Christmas morning in 1880.[27] Indeed, the day seemed a focus for a series of dole-seeking activity that could stretch through the economic harshness of the English winter. As with 'Gooding' in South Cave, 'mumping' or 'Thomasing' began around St Thomas's Day (21 December); these various forms were widespread in most counties during the nineteenth century, fading in the early twentieth century.[28] Church doles were often dispensed about this time in the year:

the Burwash dole of flour or grain to the poor occurred on 21 December.[29] The ploughboys were active in parts of East Anglia and in the Midlands and the north, as we saw in South Cave.[30] 'Plough bullocks' were still 'occasionally seen' in Derbyshire in the 1840s, young farm workers, dressed in ribboned clothing and yoked to a plough, going from house to house, collecting money. They had a band, and were accompanied by a performer, the Fool, dressed in a calf's skin and tail, and another, Bessy, 'a young man in female attire'. 'When anything is given, a cry of largess is raised, and a dance performed around the plough; but if a refusal to their application for money is made, they not unfrequently plough up the pathway, door stone, or any other portion of the premises they happen to be near.'[31] In the fens, molly dancers, labourers in female dress, performed the morris in return for drink or money.[32] In north-east Kent, the Christmas dole-seeking performance of nineteenth-century farm servants consisted of the hooden horse, a horse's head carved from a block of wood, with moveable, clacking jaws, operated by a man, semi-concealed under a sacking horse's body. The performers that accompanied the horse came from real farm teams of horsemen, and normally consisted of a waggoner, a rider, a couple of musicians and the cross-dressed 'Mollie' or 'Dolly'.[33] A contemporary attested to the fearsome potentials of the 'horse', that, 'in the dim winter's night, made even more indistinct by occasional cross rays of flickering light from the windows, becomes a monster of weird and awesome possibilities'.[34]

Easter, a long-standing folk and church festival, was another date on the South Cave calendar. Work stopped in Middleton, a weaving community of several thousand people, not far from Manchester. '[G]ood eating, good drinking, and new clothing were the order of the day.' Children would go from door to door on Good Friday, 'peace-egging'. On Easter Monday, it was the turn of young men, 'grotesquely dressed', some in female attire, who would go in companies led by a fiddler. 'At some places they would dance, at others they would recite quaint verses, and at the houses of the more sedate inhabitants, they would merely request a "peace-egg".'[35] On Easter Wednesday, Middleton held the 'White Apron Fair', 'an occasion for the young wives and mothers, with their children, and also for the young marriageable damsels, to walk out to display their finery and to get conducted by their husbands, or their sweethearts, to the ale-house, where they generally finished by a dance'.[36] These themes of ritualized begging, merriment, misrule, sports and fairs could be found elsewhere in England. Pace- or peace-egging was common in the agricultural villages and textile towns and hamlets of the Victorian north.[37]

It is intriguing that 1 May was not featured in Robert Sharp's diary. May was a time of renewal and growth, traditionally proclaimed in the iconography of greenery, garlands and maypoles.[38] By the nineteenth century, the symbolism of May seems to have centred on the garlands collected by children and coming increasingly under the tutelage of the schools as the century progressed.[39] What was yet another dole-seeking activity was brought under control and the spending of the proceeds channelled into acceptable activity. The diaries of George Dew, from Lower Heyford, Oxfordshire, record activities marking May Day in the 1860s and 1870s. 'May 1: It being May Day the children, as has been their custom from time beyond memory or record, dressed themselves in their best clothes, with all the fine pieces of coloured ribbands for adornment they could obtain, & marched around the village with their flower garlands & flags to gather as much money as possible in order to have a tea in the afternoon.' Accordingly, tea was held in the school and they then played in the rectory paddock.[40] The milieu that Dew described was in flux, and he sometimes noted the intervention of reformers. The vicar of Weston-on-the-Green put an end to children's Maying in his village.[41]

Perhaps the 29th replaced 1 May in South Cave. In any event, Oak Apple Day blurred May festivities with those of Whitsun, the next important date of the leisure calendar. In some parishes, 29 May was observed as the annual feast-day of the local club or benefit society. This was the case in the Somerset parish of Over Stowey in the 1800s. The village enjoyed a general holiday, with racing for the girls and the club parading 'with Colours flying, drums beating and a band of Musick'. 'After Church they returned in the same order and parade and we all dined at the Rose and Crown.' The parson, William Holland, who preached the club sermon, observed that 'Stowey was very gay this day'.[42] 29 May was also a club day, Shick Shack Day, in Souldern, in Oxfordshire. In 1874, it was characterized by 'excessive drinking'.[43] Historians have argued that Whitsun (late May/June) formed one of the front lines in the mid-nineteenth-century attempt to control popular leisure, what Cunningham has termed the repatronization of rural popular culture.[44] Friendly-society annual feasts merged with more traditional Whitsun festivities, and the societies fell under upper- and middle-class control.[45] In rural Oxfordshire, the vigorous Whitsun leisure culture of the early nineteenth-century Whit ales, characterized by consumption of drink, morris dancing and blood sports such as cockfighting and bull- and badger-baiting, was undermined by a mixture of outright suppression, the substitution of a shorter holiday to replace the extended drinking spree, and by the friendly societies' choice of Whitsun for their club days.[46] Alun Howkins has suggested that this impetus to control from above, the 'taming of Whitsun', was reflected in the orders and procedures laid out in the rules of the friendly societies, the dinners and church processions of the club days, and the sermons and speeches at club dinners and services that allowed vicars and gentry to impart their messages to the assembled members. Nevertheless, it would be a mistake to interpret impulses as actual behaviour. As Howkins himself admits, the need for rules enjoining sobriety and decorum implies that their opposite was a distinct possibility.[47] George Dew was certainly struck by the drunkenness of Oxfordshire Whitsun club days in the 1870s.[48]

There were four benefit clubs or friendly-society branches in Burwash when John Coker Egerton was the minister in this Sussex parish, and they all held their dinners or annual celebrations in May or June. The invariable pattern was for a procession to the pubs, rectory and principal houses, service and a sermon at the church, and then a dinner in the evening with singing, drinking, eating and speeches. Often, a band would perform and there could be a game of cricket. The participants varied. Egerton recorded the attendance of farmers and tradesmen some years, and then their noticeable absence during the farmers' dispute with the Agricultural Labourers Union in the 1870s. He usually gave the sermon and chaired the dinner.[49] Egerton was not as condemnatory of the club days as Dew, but he does refer to lapses of decorum, recording a man removed from one dinner for bad language, others being helped home afterwards, and, on another occasion, 'a good many men worse for liquor before dinner'.[50] Teams or sets of morris dancers performed at Whitsun club feasts, just as they had danced at the Whitsun ales, and their consumption of alcohol was legendary. In the 1870s, the Headington Quarry morris dancers started in Headington, the week before Whitsun, and progressed to other Oxfordshire and Buckinghamshire villages: Wheatley, the Miltons, Long Crendon, Oxford, back to Headington, and then to Kirtlington on the following Monday, 'dancing for a day in each & sleeping rough'. By Whit Monday, 'they were too drunk to know whether they were dancing or not!'[51] We should therefore probably think in terms of accommodation of tensions rather than an incorporation or repatronization of rural popular culture. This uneasy alliance is symbolized in the banners of the friendly society of the Cotswold village of Ebrington. The royal blue, silk banner of the 1850s, with its paintings of farm workers and clasped hands, and slogan 'Unity is Strength', was later joined by two smaller banners depicting the arms of Lord Ebrington and the Earl of Harrowby, the major landlords in that part of Gloucestershire. The banners are visible in a photograph taken around 1900.[52]

The bonfires of 5 November, the anniversary of the discovery of the Gunpowder Plot, and the next main date in the festive calendar, featured in diaries and memoirs throughout the nineteenth century. Egerton recorded Sussex village celebrations in 1873 that included the burning of the effigy of a local farmer who had previously been the object of charivaris for beating his wife.[53] Bonfire nights also appear in Edwin Grey's memories of Hertfordshire social life towards the end of the nineteenth century. Children of the various hamlets and clusters of cottages prepared their own fires, but the main event was held in the village green and consisted of grotesquely dressed and masked men parading with sticks and an effigy which they eventually burned. They went from house to house and pub to pub, shouting and singing, in an effort to solicit money.[54]

There were strong local variations in nineteenth-century English rural festivities. For many towns and villages in Lancashire, the West Riding of Yorkshire, and the Midlands, the 'great feast of the year' was 'rush-bearing', or wakes week.[55] Areas of arable farming, stock-rearing, and rural industry had different patterns of marriage seasonality and labour-hiring, and therefore of the festivity and ritual associated with these moments in people's lives.[56] In central Lincolnshire, May marriages and May fairs corresponded to the change-over in servants' hiring contracts.[57] Local interests continually dictated that national commemorations could be used to settle specific grievances, and would be invested with local rather than national significance. Thus, 5 November was used as an opportunity for mockery of unpopular local figures.[58] Oak Apple Day merged with the needs of benefit clubs, local May customs, and the traditional right to gather wood.[59] The various calendars of English folk-customs provide ample evidence of regional variety.[60]

* * *

Clearly, the public house was a constant site of popular recreation.[61] The self-help clubs and friendly societies were based in pubs; people congregated there after funerals; dances were held there; dealers used them as their bases to strike deals and carry out their trade; stolen goods were unloaded there; and they were the venues for a range of sports and games, invariably played for beer or money.[62] Given the cramped, cold and dark conditions of many labouring homes, it was natural for rural workers to gravitate towards the warmth, light and conviviality of the pub or the beerhouse. The following interaction with a Kent informant was typical of many oral histories:

> No, of course he [the informant's father] was like a lot of men at that time, especially family men, their evenings were spent out, they'd have their tea and perhaps stop indoors till about 7.00 then they'd go out till 10.00. That applied to most men at that time.
> Q: Where would he go?
> A: To the pub. That's the only, there was no amusements.[63]

As James Obelkevich once observed, if the beer-shop was the shortest route out of Manchester, it was also the quickest way out of the village.[64]

There was a double standard involved. Although women were not barred from drinking establishments (and many served there), pubs were male-dominated havens. Richard Jefferies referred to the rural pub as the poor man's club: 'it is his theatre, his music hall, picture gallery, and Crystal Palace'.[65] Before the hours were regulated in the twentieth century, pubs were open early and closed late. Oral histories from various parts of the country recall men at the pub on the way to work or as early as 6 a.m. on holidays. Nine-year-old Harry Matthews went to the pub at 7 a.m. on summer mornings to fetch his brickmaking father his first pint for the day. There are references to Kent workers drinking in village pubs as late as 2 a.m. or 3 a.m., with the constable also seated in the bar.[66]

Fairs were another site for rural leisure. Apart from their serious, economic function – cloth, wool, hides, sheep, cattle, horses, poultry, dairy products, the hiring of labourers and servants – fairs were transient moments of fun and festivity.[67] The Yorkshire farm labourer, Fred Kitchen, said that the hiring fair at Doncaster in the early 1900s drew servants from south Yorkshire, north Nottinghamshire, Lincolnshire and Derbyshire, and claimed that, even before speech gave the different dialect away, farmers could tell the district of origin from the dress and physical appearance of the farm servant. The pleasure of the day consisted of the journey from the farm as well as the offerings of the fair itself, for it was a group outing, with carts from the various farms stopping at the pubs en route: 'The covered wagon became a musical-box on wheels.'[68]

Although hiring fairs were held at Martinmas in south Yorkshire, they were held earlier in other parts of the country. In Cumbria, for example, the larger hiring fairs were at Whitsuntide.[69] The Northumberland farm worker, Mary Bruce, recalled that the hiring fairs in her district (Belford) were in March in the early twentieth century, presumably around Lady Day, and she was able to rattle off daily fairs held in the same week over a radius of ten miles or more.[70] In central Lincolnshire, the hiring fairs were held around Old May Day (13 May) which was treated as the pre-eminent holiday for servants. Even when their hiring role was no longer necessary, the Hainton, Horncastle and Louth fairs remained sites for pleasure.[71] Grey said that the Harpenden (Hertfordshire) statute or hiring fair had previously 'combined the business of hiring with that of pleasure, but now [in the 1870s] the affair was that of pleasure only'. Another hiring fair was held in nearby St Albans in October, drawing people from an arc of surrounding communities. 'The pleasure part of the fair was a great attraction, and many of the young men and women from this part of the parish, other than those

engaged in farm work, would walk over (being on a Saturday) to attend it.'
Grey remembered the booths, shooting galleries, roundabouts and swings
of Harpenden fair. The shows, held in September, 'were always well patron-
ized; the crude drawings and pictures exhibited outside the booths
presented most wonderful and astounding freaks of nature, etc.' He was
particularly taken with the performing fleas. A major attraction at St
Albans was the presence of a travelling theatre company.[72]

Sally Alexander's fascinating study of St Giles Fair, a major two-day
September holiday for the working people of villages around Oxford,
demonstrates that fairs were not necessarily casualties of the nineteenth
century; indeed, the scale of this fair was a product of the railway age. St
Giles Fair provided a rich range of leisure activity and exerted a noticeable
influence on the rural popular culture of the region: young servant-women
and their potential lovers flocked to the fair in their thousands. Alexander
describes its hawkers and stalls, providing entertainment as well as cheap
goods (the *Oxford Times* wrote in 1900 of Oxfordshire cottages with old
prints and gaudy china ornaments bought at St Giles Fair decades before),
circuses, waxworks, fine-art exhibitions, drinking booths, mechanical
exhibitions, menageries, roundabouts, boxing booths, dancing saloons,
freaks and peep shows. The fair brought modernity to the rural workers of
the 1870s and 1880s: 'the hall of scientific amusements', electric light,
mechanical organs, electric shock, the phonograph, steam-powered
roundabouts, and, later in the century, the cinematic images of the
bioscope.[73]

* * *

Both public house and fair were closely associated with the music and
song that were key elements in the culture of rural workers. Alfred
Williams was clear about the role of folk-songs in the culture of the upper
Thames valley, but his observations would have applied to much of rural
England. He wrote of the printed literature – poems, ballads, hymns, 'rude
rhymes' – disseminated at fairs and hawked from village to village. He was
alert to the cultural loops linking the printed ballad sung aloud and
purchased at the fair and then learned and relayed in a range of settings
and occasions. He distinguished between the songs sung by men at the
public house and those sung in the household by women. The harvest
home, church and friendly-society feasts, May games, morris dancing,
mumming, weddings, Christmas, were all occasions for song, but so also
were ploughing, work in the stables, fields and kitchen, milking, shearing,
weaving and straw-plaiting.[74]

We saw at the beginning of this book that the folk-song-collector Cecil Sharp complained of the corrupting influences of the printed ballad and music hall on village songs. The irony here was that there had long been an interaction between orality and the culture of print in the shaping of English working-class song. Readers memorized written texts and then recited them to non-reading hearers. Oral ballads were recorded in print, and then fed back to oral transmission: printed ballads were sung out loud, remembered, and then collected later as traditional or folk-ballads.[75] Although they seemed oblivious to such cultural loops, the vast majority of folk-songs collected by Cecil Sharp and others early in the twentieth century derived from printed ballads, and many came from ballads published before the beginning of the eighteenth century.[76]

It is clear that this sort of literature was an important part of the leisure culture of the young John Clare in rural Northamptonshire and, presumably, a formative influence on generations of rural labourers living into the middle of the nineteenth century. Apart from the Bible and Prayer Book, he remembered cheap romances, and ballads 'hawked about a sheet for a penny': 'these have memorys as common as Prayer books and Psalters with the peasentry such were the books that delighted me and I savd all the pence I got to buy them for they were the whole world of literature to me and I knew of no other I carried them in my pocket and read them at my leisure and they was the never weary food of winter evenings . . . and I even feel a love for them still'.[77] His poem, 'Dobson and Judie', refers to labouring cottages with ballads pinned or pasted to the walls:

> . . . Ballads, songs, and Cutts, that hide
> Both window-shutters, wall, and door,
> Which tell of many-a-murder'd bride
> And desperate Battles daubed oer.[78]

Clare's first poetry was in imitation of popular balladry, and he would later draw on the songs and stories he learned as a boy, building them into his verse.[79] Although rural-worker poets were a comparative rarity, exposure to song – whether in print or orally – was taken for granted. There are records of extensive individual repertoires. Clare's father, who could read a little but not write, was able to sing or recite over a hundred ballads, and was frequently called upon to sing at the public house.[80] The Sussex singer, Henry Burstow, claimed to have learned more than four hundred songs from his parents and a variety of rural working folk. In 1906, he sang all of them to his wife for her birthday – over a period of 41 consecutive evenings![81]

Henry Mayhew's account of the street sellers of print in London in the mid-nineteenth century shows the ways that vendors attempted to appeal to the widest possible audience, varying their patter to suit the clientele. A ballad-seller, who could sing the songs he sold and was able to remember others from past repertoires, told Mayhew that he could flatter a servant-girl into buying a ballad by pretending that he mistook her for her lady: that 'chloroforms her'.[82] Standard pieces were adapted to appeal to the occupational make-up of the town, village, neighbourhood or street in which the piece was being hawked. A good seller knew the attractions of individual titles, what type of murder would intrigue tradespeople, for example. Servants liked items such as the 'Rich Man and his Wife Quarrelling'. Stories about apprentices appealed to apprentices.[83] One patterer explained the specific appeal of accounts of gruesome murders, one involving the seduction of a clergyman's daughter by a young naval officer and her subsequent murder of her illegitimate child, the other a mother's slaying of her own son. The seller said that these sort of stories held particular fascination for women, who were his main customers. Young women liked the first murder best because of its seduction scene. 'This has had a great run. It sells all round the country places.' 'It draws tears to the women's eyes to think that a poor clergyman's daughter, who is remarkably beautiful, should murder her own child.' Mothers took more to the story about the murder of the son.[84] Although Mayhew was interviewing those involved in the London trade, many had peddled their wares further afield. Stories such as those just described, often with accompanying verse, could sell lucratively for decades and would be hawked all around the country: 'There's nothing beats a stunning good murder.'[85] One seller of gallows' literature told Mayhew that he had seen a group of Norfolk villagers sitting in a cottage while an old man read a broadsheet relating a recent execution:

> Now in a dismal cell I lie,
> For murder I'm condemn'd to die;
> Some may pity when they read,
> Opression drove me to the deed.

He said that in such villages it was not unknown for two poor families to club together to find the 1d needed for such a purchase.[86] Grey mentions ballad-singers crying out murder ballads in rural Hertfordshire during the 1870s.[87]

That song was still integral to rural labouring culture at the close of the nineteenth century is clear from memoirs, oral histories and the activities of the folk-song collectors discussed elsewhere in this book. When George Sturt heard rural workers singing in 1899, he commented both on their vulgarity ('for the most part not meant for ladies' ears') and on the fact that about half of the twenty or so he heard were self-mocking in a slapstick

way, relating the 'misfortunes of the singer'.[88] Flora Thompson described a
mix of old country ballads and newer music-hall songs performed nightly
at the public house in the Oxfordshire parish of Cottisham during the
1880s.[89] Albert Packman's father, a Kent agricultural labourer and bailiff,
used to sing both hymns and cockney songs learned from penny song-
sheets. Albert was puzzled by the way that Packman senior sang in cockney
slang, learned perhaps from the hop-pickers.[90]

The content of popular song was as varied as it had always been: a mix
of political and social observation, celebration of work, as well as the sexual
commentary that so shocked most collectors:[91]

> I put my hand all on her thigh
> Fair maid is a lily O
> I put my hand all on her thigh
> She says to me do you want to try?
> Come to me quietly
> Do not do no injury
> Gently Johnny my jingalo
>
> I put my hand all on her billy
> Fair maid is a lily O
> I put my hand all on her billy
> She says to me do you want to fill'ee?
> Come to me quietly
> Do not do no injury
> Gently Johnny my jingalo.[92]

Flora Thompson referred to the light-hearted parodying of well-known
hymns, songs about the politician William Gladstone ('God bless the
people's William'), and 'the filthiest of . . . stock rhymes'.[93]

Musical expression took other forms. The history of the rural brass band
has yet to be written, but it clearly dates from this period of supposed cultural
poverty.[94] Egerton's diaries mention their popularity in Sussex in the 1870s.[95]
The brass bands are probably linked to an older institution of popular culture,
the church bands, which they may well have replaced after the latter's demise.
The church bands or singers (they performed both functions) were an important part of the church's link to the community in the first half of the nineteenth century, performing in the gallery with a rudimentary orchestra – flute,
bassoon, bass viol, fiddle, clarinet – until their music was eased out by the
more compliant harmonium. Contemporary critics condemned the singers'
hard drinking and misbehaviour as well as their sawing and jarring instru-
ments, and untrained rustic voices. The music historian Vic Gammon refers
more sympathetically to a fully-developed rural popular musical style.[96]

The diaries and memoirs of the English clergy and parish officials are peppered with complaints and reported conflict with the singers. John Skinner, the rector of the coalmining village of Camerton, Somerset, struggled constantly with the independence of the church band and singers. They were habitués of the pub, and one Saturday night in 1821 got involved in a brawl so that some of them were not allowed to perform in church the next day because of their blackened eyes. Relations had deteriorated so much in 1822 that the band staged a walk-out during the service, and then went on strike. Skinner said that they had been 'in a state of constant intoxication' since the day before, and later discovered that they had returned to the ale-house after the altercation.[97] (He also battled with the hard drinking of the church bell-ringers who spent their fees in the pub; Skinner observed that the men would have been better served by giving their money to their families rather than spending it on drink and then going home 'and beating their wives to a jelly'.[98]) In Oxfordshire, Dew recalled in the 1870s that the Lower Heyford band and choir had been 'very immoral, & strangely disgraceful tales are told of some of the proceedings at their annual feast. I can well recollect some of the bad behaviour in the gallery during service time.'[99]

* * *

Then there were rural sports, demonstrating further instances of the reality of regional variation. The pubs and beer-houses of the Cleveland ironstone mining villages organized rabbit-coursing, dog and cockfights, prizefighting, and pitch and toss. They were notorious in the 1870s for their rough, masculine, woman-hating culture.[100] Sport – almost always underlain by gambling – was an everyday part of the lives of the male miners in the pit villages of Northumberland: cockfighting, pedestrianism, quoits, potshare bowling, rabbit-coursing, dog- and pigeon-racing, and football. Cockfighting was popular at the start of the nineteenth century; football reigned supreme as the twentieth century began.[101] Workers in the Staffordshire chain-making villages were involved in cockfighting (long after it had been outlawed), dogfighting, and pigeon-racing, well into the early decades of the twentieth century. They operated in groups of ten, known as camps, breeding, training and nurturing the animals for competition, killing the weaklings, fighting for a purse or a bet. 'It was wonderful, or wicked, I doh know which. Lot o' cruelty in it; lot o' cruelty in the cock fightin' an' dog-fightin', ar. And in the pigeon flyin', but in the pigeon flyin' it was cruelty to *yo*'.[102] In Cumbria, hunting, dog-racing, wrestling, athletics, folk football (played on a one-mile 'pitch'), rugby, soccer and cricket – with varying degrees of gender and social inclusion (the biases are pretty predictable) – provided a range of activities for rural workers and their families, either as spectators or participants. The savage but persistent sport of cockfighting resisted the interventions of reformers and legislators.[103]

Areas had their specialized forms of entertainment. The rural weavers of Saddleworth, Yorkshire, hunted hares with beagles. The Middleton hand-loom silk-workers were great pigeon-fanciers, gambling on the speed of their birds.[104] In Northumberland, we have seen, the local speciality was potshare bowling. The Cotswolds were famous for shin-kicking: 'The two contestants had iron plates on the toes of their boots and, holding each other by the shoulders with outstretched arms, kicked at each other's shins until one was obliged to give in.'[105] The villages and towns of the Stafford-shire Potteries favoured pugilism and dogfighting.[106] In the Lincolnshire communities around Haxey, in the Isle of Axholme, the local sport was throwing the hood, a form of folk football played on Old Christmas Day (6 January). The 'ball' was a 6 lb roll of canvas, and the object of the game, involving several hundred participants, was to convey the hood from an open field to the cellar of a public house. The game experienced various moments of lapse and revival but survived throughout the nineteenth century.[107] Shrove Tuesday football was played in the small country towns of Surrey, lingering on in Dorking into the early twentieth century.[108]

In Kent, the local game was goal-running, a rather-hard-to-explain sport that involved both running and capture, and a complex playing strategy: oral informants refer to the need for both runners and fighters in a successful team, the fighters to deal with the spectators. Syd Twist explained that it was an informal sport in the 1870s, timed to fit in with the work schedule of rural workers, a summer game, starting at 7 p.m. on Saturdays, after work. Although there had always been inter-village matches, a more organized league was formed round 1900, with codified rules, and large Whit Monday away competitions, again coinciding with the labouring leisure calendar. But for the rest of the summer it was a social game played between workers, with drinking in the pub after the match (all the local clubhouses were pubs). The various teams reflected local working economies. Oare, Ospringe and Faversham contained a mixture of farm workers, brickmakers, and workers from the explosives' factory. Teynham had a core of brickmakers. Whitstable had the fisher-men and dredgermen.[109]

Certain pastimes were ubiquitous. The quoits, skittles (the larger pubs had skittle-alleys), and shove-halfpenny that were played in Harpenden in the 1870s were played in and around pubs throughout the country.[110]

However, some prominent twentieth- and twenty-first-century sports were not as central to rural working-class life as modern enthusiasts might assume. Football is a good example. Although there is no written history of nineteenth-century village football, the impression is that the sport was principally an urban affair.[111] The rural working informants in the various oral-history collections are surprisingly silent on the subject. Indeed the Kent oral histories imply that it was more a sport of the towns before the First World War.[112] Cricket is also somewhat problematic. Although commonly referred to as a spectator sport in rural areas – the Burwash club and friendly-society annual dinners and festivities usually included a cricket match[113]– there are several indications that participation was socially selective. Agricultural labourers rarely had the time to play cricket, as many of the oral histories from this period point out. 'I don't remember any young men, of the *bona fide* agricultural labouring class, being members of the club, although some joined in at the practices, or in a little friendly game in the evenings.'[114] 'Well, . . . the only cricket . . . played in the village was by the local squire or farmer or big nob that could get some of the school masters or higher nobs round the village in his team.'[115] Harry Matthews, a Faversham brickmaker, said that cricket was 'more for the top class'.[116] William Brakespear explained the difficulties in getting a village cricket team going in Eynsham in the early twentieth century, cycling around the scattered Oxfordshire settlement on an old bicycle to organize a team. There was a first eleven, based at Eynsham Hall and composed of 'doctors – farmers – and people of that . . . renown', but Brakespear and his friends developed a second eleven out of a village team with home-made bats and stumps. (Cricketing clothes were out of the question.) He was later invited into the first eleven, but most of his memories of this time are of his realization that he did not belong socially with his team mates.[117]

Nationally, sporting patterns changed over the period. Everywhere, the codified mass-spectator sports of football and cricket dominated by the end of the nineteenth century.[118] But there was certainly no dearth of sporting choice in the period before then.

* * *

There are several reasons for not imposing modern assumptions on nineteenth-century contexts. Much of the 'leisure' in England's rural areas was enforced idleness; many men inhabited the public house in the absence of work rather than to refresh themselves before or after a hard day's labour. George Dunn, a former Staffordshire chain-maker, expressed this perfectly when reminiscing about life in the metalworking village of Quarry Bank:

'There was quite a lot o' play. When I say "play" I mean unemployment.'[119] Rural leisure was not at all firmly separated from work in the manner that we now take for granted, with the week divided into work and play, and with the latter an escape from the former. Oral histories refer to fathers spending their Sunday leisure time walking country lanes, assessing the ploughing skills of neighbours. Yorkshire horselads admired one another's horses. Labourers paraded work skills at competitions and fairs: 'best shepherd's sheep', hand-crafted crooks, stacking competitions and ploughing matches.[120] They were not actually working, but they had not escaped the culture of work. Many labouring men also spent their time outside of their hired labour working in gardens or allotments. The working-class garden was a unit of production rather than the leisure sanctuary that it was for the middle classes.[121]

Hopping is another good example of the mix of work and recreation. The families of Black Country nail-makers who came by train for the hop harvests of the 1890s, treated the working excursion as a 'cheap family outing'.[122] 'What the banks of the Riviera are to the children of the aristocracy, the banks of the Medway are to the children of the poor', was one commentator's rather ludicrous description of the holiday role of Kent hopping in 1892.[123] Many men would have had trouble grasping that there really were alternatives to work. Unemployment only reinforced its importance: its absence proclaiming its centrality. This was surely linked to the educational values of the time; rural working-class boys were educated to a life of labour. It was all they knew. For different reasons, both they and their social betters thought that any other kind of knowledge was superfluous.[124] It is little wonder, then, that an Essex man observed of his father (who had always done farm work) that work was all he thought about: 'He was no scholar you see. All his interest was in work. He was – he was more happy at work than he would be at pleasure.'[125] George Sturt observed in the 1890s that the conversation of his gardener was entirely work-related; 'his true interest is that which he shares with all the other villagers; interest in work, especially in work on their gardens, in their crops, and in the management of their ground . . . Almost all of Bettesworth's stories . . . have had a close bearing on his work.' 'Doubtless this kind of talk goes on, throughout the length and breadth of rural England.'[126] It was a preoccupational pleasure intimately related to the masculine identities of these workers, and reflected in the work-related detail provided in their oral histories.[127]

Boundaries between work and play were breached in other ways and for other groups. One historian of folk-song has referred to singing as an auxiliary of physical labour in the rural areas, for the context for singing was often work rather than play.[128] It was common for lace- and shirt-makers to sing as they worked with their fingers.[129] The Black Country folk-singer, George Dunn, recalled singing in the hop fields in the early 1900s, as he worked picking: 'Everybody was a-singin'. I sung better down th' opyard than ever I did in me life, in the fresh air. I was wonderful.'[130] Similarly, the culture of young male farm servants was work culture, whether we are referring to the hiring fair, the lore attached to their care of animals, their songs or their folk drama. Much of their social and cultural interaction took place at the site of their labour, even when their work had ceased for the day.[131] The stable was vital to their world. A Northumberland farm worker spoke of men congregating in the stables late at night after grooming the horses, polishing their harnesses and swapping gossip about 'what was happening on the other farms . . . you got all the news in the stables'. The female workers, the bondagers, would take it in turns to work on one another's mats in the winter evenings. It was a way of socializing and relaxing, while still performing a useful task.[132]

Finally, the margins of work and play were blurred by the customary dole-gathering discussed in the pages above. Over and over again, the ritualized performances of rural workers were in search of sustenance as well as distraction. When the former Lancashire farm servant, Charles Simpson, recalled the farm lads turning their jackets inside out and blacking their faces with soot to visit the farmhouses on Collop Monday in the 1900s, his recollection of this Shrovetide custom focused on the collops rather than the ritual: the cooked bacon that provided a 'jolly good feed'.[133] Though the ritual forms themselves are of immense interest, we should never lose sight of their basic material drive. For many, 'leisure' was yet another way of getting a living. Indeed, the ubiquity of the begging rituals of this period is unique in British history.[134] Midland morris dancers combined their dancing with migration south for the harvests, performing in London and villages on the way. They were said to make as much from their dancing as they did from their labour.[135]

* * *

I need to be clear about my argument in this chapter. In challenging the claim for the 'pervasive poverty of the rural leisure culture', I am not denying restrictions upon leisure opportunities in the rural areas and among certain groups. Rural workers were not an undifferentiated block. Young earners represented a peak in leisure opportunities because of their spending power, and preoccupation with sexual interaction and courtship. Though we have observed that the possibilities were better in the towns, young rural workers were theoretically in a position to take advantage of the new leisure forms of the late nineteenth and early twentieth centuries. With marriage, opportunities declined, especially for married women:

> Question: When your parents were not doing their work, how did they spend their time?
> Answer: They never had any.[136]

Leisure became more home-centred during marriage. Men still sought out the pub, but the allotment entered the realm of leisure for many married workers.

Leisure also followed the peaks and troughs of the poverty cycle.[137] When single children earned, the leisure-spending of parents (or male parent!) could increase; but with old age, and the absence of contributing children, the onset of potential poverty was accompanied by the revisiting of a lack of leisure opportunities. As Andrew Davies discovered of urban working-class leisure in the early twentieth century, poverty structured patterns of leisure and severely curtailed the range of available pleasures. 'We have no football team in our village', wrote a miner in the 1930s, 'If you want to go to a match it costs either 9d. or 1s. 6d., and then there's the gate money so you can see that it is a clear outing, more than we can af[f]ord.'[138] B. S. Rowntree and M. Kendall ended their survey of the budgets of rural labouring families in 1913 with the observation that the struggle to make ends meet had cultural as well as economic implications: 'It means that every natural longing for pleasure or variety should be ignored or set aside. It means, in short, a life without colour, space, or atmosphere, that stifles and hems in the labourer's soul as in too many cases his cottage does his body.'[139]

The restrictions of poverty (and gender) meant that other forms of leisure were important for rural workers. Davies discovered that in the cities informal activities, including sitting on the doorstep talking to neighbours, socializing in groups on the streets, or walking around, cost little or nothing.[140] The scale was reduced in the villages, but the basic principle applies. Oral histories discuss neighbours coming in for a cup of tea with their mother or a drink of home-made wine with their father, Sunday walks, singsongs at weddings and funerals or after others in the street dropped in to visit ('they used to go in and out of each others').[141] In Faversham and the surrounding Kent villages, families would go out walking on Sunday summer evenings. Young people promenaded the streets of Faversham much as they did in cities; 'they found sufficient entertainment walking up and down there, meeting people and talking to them'.[142]

As already hinted, the differential experience was also gendered.[143] Female servants in the rural areas frequently sent their earnings home rather than spending them. Many had little time for leisure, and the time that they had could be controlled by their employers. John Skinner did not like his servants socializing in the village.[144] Married rural women were definitely at a disadvantage in terms of their leisure prospects, with time away from paid (or unpaid) work outside the home being taken up with housework or care of the children inside the home, and with the various tasks involved in getting a living. 'Mother . . . never had any idle time.' 'Oh no, she'd no time. Washing and cooking for a flock of five.'[145]

Women were not excluded from all the pastimes covered in this chapter. They were involved in the dole-gathering and pleasure-making at Christmas, Easter, May and Whitsuntide. They helped with the preparations for rush-bearing. They were repositories of folk-song sought out by the genteel collectors of the period. They watched goal-running. They were there at the fairs and hopping. Indeed, spring and summer festivities recur in the nineteenth-century court dossiers outlining the social context of unmarried motherhood in rural Kent. Local friendly-society club days (May–July), Whitsun celebrations (May–June), hopping festivities (September), and unsupervised servant courtship at Christmas and New Year feature in young women's statements about the circumstances of their pregnancies. These were the occasions for dancing, flirting, 'walking out' and courtship games such as 'Kiss in the Ring'.[146] Yet Skinner's comment about drunken bell-ringers beating their wives to jelly is a grim reminder of the real gender fractures in the history of leisure. Notoriously, the pub and so many of the sports and leisure activities connected to it were male-dominated affairs. Football, the appropriately named cockfighting, and the multiple forms of baiting, hunting, throwing, combat and racing, were merely variants of masculine self-expression. The hooden-horse performers, molly dancers, ploughboys, church singers, brass bands, pace-eggers, bell-ringers, mummers, the makers of November bonfires, and the great majority of benefit clubs and morris dancers, were male. Like the molly dancers, the 'women' involved in the ritual drama and calendar customs of the nineteenth century were most likely to be cross-dressed men!

* * *

Nor am I neglecting change. While, on the face of it, the identified festive moments – Christmas, Easter, Whitsuntide, 5 November – appear consistent over the period, the extent of the underlying change is evident in a recent history of popular leisure in Victorian and Edwardian Cumbria. The household visiting and conviviality associated with Christmas had died out by the early twentieth century, making the event more a family affair. Easter remained a community festival in the north, throughout the period, though, as with many Victorian festivities, it became increasingly child-centred. The Whitsuntide hiring fairs survived into the twentieth century, long after their employment role had ceased, strengthened by a wider clientele brought in by the railways. Friendly-society processions continued to be held in Whitsuntide in what was, in effect, the region's 'annual summer break'. Rush-bearing declined, but was then revived by clergymen and gentry, so its popularity in the early twentieth century cannot be interpreted as strict continuity with an earlier period. 5 November occasioned a protracted struggle between the forces of order and bonfire revellers, though, as with Easter, the trend was for this public celebration to be confined more to the enjoyment of children. The picture, then, is of complex adaptation and change beneath a superficially similar calendar.[147]

Recent work on British folklore has demonstrated that the rituals of recreation were continually invented and reinvented.[148] Harvest celebrations appear to have been both suppressed and reintroduced in nineteenth-century Lincolnshire.[149] When Percy Maylam attempted to chart the distribution, history and intensity of survival of the east-Kent horsemen's ceremony of the hooden horse, the impression he gained was of a practice both in decline and in a patchy process of revival; in one case, the cross-dressed 'Mollie' was reintroduced purely for the benefit of his recording camera.[150] (See Plate 6.) The regionalized begging customs of St Thomas's Day (21 December), a doling day par excellence, seem to originate in the eighteenth century.[151] The folk drama, the mummers' play, probably dates from about the same time.[152] North Riding Plough Monday customs, involving the doling dance and drama of the ploughboys or stots (bullocks), faded in the 1870s, but were revived in the 1920s.[153] We started this book with George Butterworth's attempt in 1912 to discover morris dancing and music in Oxfordshire villages where the morris was in decline. His expedition was fruitless, partly because what he found did not meet his own standards and preconceptions, but he did discover that since its decline (possibly twenty, perhaps forty years before) the dance had been revived from time to time, most recently at the time of the coronation of George V in 1911.[154] In fact, the national history of the morris provides an example of a custom where the basic name continued, but its functions, meanings and modes of performance shifted. In the fifteenth century, the principal site of the English morris dance was the noble household, but during the eighteenth and nineteenth centuries it was used by rural workers as a way of raising money.[155] In the words of Ronald Hutton, the history of the morris is not of an 'unchanging and ancient rite', but rather 'one of a triumph of versatility'.[156]

In short, I am certainly not claiming that leisure in the villages of the 1900s was the same as that of the 1800s. After all, rural England had experienced a century of attempts to reform popular culture.[157] Sturt clearly had this process in mind when he commented on the role of the parson and the policeman in inhibiting popular culture. 'And I have wondered whether the turbulent English of Chaucer's time, – they who began building the Empire and inventing its Arts and Commerce – could ever have emerged from their barbarism, had they been so watched, so checked, as these people are.' Christmas mumming and public-house singing, Sturt thought, were the only avenues for their 'own spontaneous efforts at art', but even these had to be concealed from their social superiors. 'Here it is the Parson; there the Policeman.'[158]

As has been intimated from time to time in the pages above, interventions could be more genteel, including the repatronization referred to earlier. Recent students of folklore have traced some truly fascinating refashioning and reinvention of the ceremonies attached to the nineteenth-century morris and May – Butterworth's search for the Oxfordshire morris was part of a far wider process. From the 1840s onwards, lords of the manor and clergymen, their wives, and middle- and upper-class enthusiasts revived fading folk-dance and drama in an effort to recapture an imagined, lost and considerably tamed 'Merry England'. Enthusiasts imparted their notions of 'authentic' folk-dance and drama to local practitioners, and then the next generation discovered them as examples of an unchanging tradition. Cecil Sharp was collecting some 'traditional' dance that had been invented in the 1870s and 1880s.[159]

* * *

Another arguable change over the nineteenth century was the increased role of print in the leisure of rural workers. For much of our period of interest, oral culture was still important in the everyday lives of rural workers.[160] It was a milieu where literacies were mixed. Some could read and write. Others – a potentially large percentage hidden by historians' preoccupation with the ability to sign – could read but not write, and it is therefore inappropriate to describe them as illiterate. And, of course, a decreasing number (the true illiterates) were without either skill. It was common for individual labouring families to contain those very combinations of cultural skills.[161] Literate and illiterate lived side by side.[162] Such mixed literacies meant that rural workers had long had access to print, as we saw earlier in the discussion of the printed ballad. All that was required was a literate family member or neighbour. And there were complaints about the impact of print on the rural communities in the 1840s and 1850s. Egerton examined the reading material ordered at the shop by 'young Burwash' in 1857, 'a miserable commentary on our education certainly. Weekly pennyworths of tales made up of murders, & the like that is if one may judge by the horrible similarity of the woodcuts in all of them.'[163] A *Morning Chronicle* journalist assessed the stock of a Manchester wholesaler destined for bookshops in Manchester and the surrounding villages. He took this favouring of illustrated weekly penny novels as a guide to the taste of 'the poorer reading classes': a 'mass of literary garbage', 'utterly beneath criticism'.[164]

Signature literacy and illiteracy rates were highly variable by county, locality and occupation, but they converged towards the end of the nineteenth century.[165] (See Figure 6.1.) In the 1900s, 97 per cent of labouring grooms were able to write their names, whereas in the 1840s the figure had been just over 30 per cent.[166] Moreover, the literacy of the daughters of rural workers overtook that of their sons.[167] By 1900, the postal usage, low price

Figure 6.1 Signature illiteracies, 1845–1885 (males and females combined)

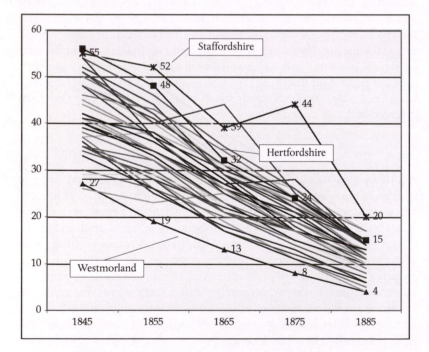

Source: Based on tables in W. B. Stephens, *Education, Literacy and Society, 1830–70: The Geography of Diversity in Provincial England* (Manchester, 1987), pp. 322–3.

and high circulation of newspapers, and signature literacy rates indicate that reading and writing played more of a role for working people, and that this included their leisure lives.[168] The flow of 'literary garbage' was even greater. Kitchen, a Yorkshire farm servant in the 1900s, referred to fellow-workers reading and talking about the newspapers, *Police News* and *Ally Sloper*: 'So we got sensation, entertainment, or jollification.'[169] The autobiograpies of rural workers reveal that the motivated were able to gain access to the world of the book.[170] Kitchen discovered a new interest in literature because of an attractive servant who was a member of the local library, and progressed from *Ally Sloper*. '[S]eated on the corn-bin, by the light of the stable lantern, I pored over Mrs Henry Wood and John Strange Winter.' He also read Eliot, Dickens, Thackeray and Emily Brontë.[171] Of course, such mental escape or entertainment was more likely to come from the newspaper or cheap print than serious literature. Sturt thought that the only emotional stimulus villagers got was through the scandal of their own lives or the 'sensational news in the papers'. Yet he did see the benefits of the 'yellow press'; 'thanks to the cheap press, ideas and information are finding their way into the cottages of the valley . . . Shackleton and the South Pole are probably household words in most of the cottages; it may be taken for granted that the wonders of flying machines are being eagerly watched'.[172]

The bridging of literacy and illiteracy continued after 1900, but with greater access to print. Young rural workers read to 'illiterate' parents. Wives read to husbands. Jonathon Rose has calculated that a half of the working-class interviewees in the famous University of Essex oral-history archive, covering life in Edwardian England, referred to reading aloud in their homes.[173] Frank Kemsley's dealer father 'used to come home from Canterbury market or from town with a little old paper he give a 1d. for, so that I could read out to him what happened in the Boer War'.[174] The fenman Arthur Randell also used to read the news to his illiterate father at the start of the Great War; the boy thought that the abbreviation 'Pte.' stood for 'Peter', until his father observed that an awful lot of soldiers had the same name![175] Harold Kay's father, a small farmer who was unable to read or write, used to get his wife to read the newspaper to him – and this was in the 1920s.[176]

* * *

There is also mounting evidence that religious institutions figured strongly in the recreational activities of nineteenth- and early twentieth-century rural inhabitants, particularly those of the children of rural workers.[177] Keith Snell and Paul Ell's recent quantification of the religious census of 1851 has shown a positive correlation between areas of rural child labour and Sunday-school attendance.[178] The Sunday school was the main source of education for many labouring children at mid-century; they could work during the week and attend school on Sundays.[179] For the potter Charles Shaw, Sunday school was a means of release from the cares of his young working existence. On Sundays he could wash and dress in clean clothes, oil his hair ('I have the memory of that scent yet') and escape the drudgery of his working week. 'To me, very soon, it was a life within my life. In the midst of a life of hardship and temptation, this inner life shed a brightness and a sweetness which always gave me an upward look and an upward aspiration . . . Whatever the weather on other days, Sunday always seemed to me a sun's day. It gave me the only gladsome morning of the week.'[180] The introduction of the Education Acts of the 1870s modified this pattern, but the Sunday school still figured strongly in the oral histories of rural activities at the turn of the century. Instruction, treats, concerts, penny readings, Bible class, temperance activities, hymn-singing, choir and choir outings, and other excursions arranged by church, chapel and Sunday school had a significant role in structuring children's leisure.[181]

Sturt was scathing, asking what the church had to offer the village girl in 1898: 'A meeting, next Tuesday, at the Vicarage, of the Girls' Friendly Society. Tea and cake: piano playing by the vicar's sister: an address by "Sister Emma": a church service: more tea, and a distribution of certificates to a few.'[182] However, the oral histories are rather more accepting. Bob Jaggard, the son of an Essex farm worker, spent every Sunday morning and afternoon at Sunday school, with a Methodist sermon in-between.[183] Young Louisa Watson, the daughter of a horseman, moved between Sunday school and church in much the same manner.[184] Sunday school was part of the Sunday routine in the homes of many of the rural labouring informants. 'Oh we used to go to church every Sunday – and Sunday school. But whether it was from the religious point, or whether it was – to form the habit – I don't know.'[185] While there are those who seldom attended, the experience of the child of a Kent-village wheelwright was not untypical: 'Sunday mornings we used to go to Sunday school, and then from there we were marched to church. You sat through the service. You went home to dinner. Back again in the afternoon to Sunday school again, and from there you went home to tea. Then dad made you go to church again in the evenings. So you had quite enough church on a Sunday.'[186] But there were fond memories of annual excursions and Sunday-school treats in the grounds of the local landowner; 'It was really smashing.'[187] The only time the Essex farm worker, Clifford Hills, ever went to the seaside as a child was on a Sunday-school outing.[188]

The Methodist-inspired teetotal movement provided recreational coun-
ters to the traditional popular culture of the Cornish mining villages of the
mid-nineteenth century.[189] So religious influences were not confined to
children. Bob Jaggard's family played sacred music and sang hymns ('it was
always sacred') rather than folk-songs; neighbours and visitors would join
in.[190] Emily Burgess, the daughter of a Kent farm worker, said that her
village, Old Wives Lees, 'was a place of two sets of people. Those that went
to the pub and those that went to chapel, and I belonged to a family that
went to chapel, and our interest in life was our home, our family and our
chapel and Sunday School.'[191] The Oxfordshire shepherd, Mont Abbot,
remembered hundreds of labouring and farming families walking across
the fields to revivalist meetings or camps on the edge of the Cotswold Hills,
near Chipping Norton. He recalled a brass band, a great deal of extempore
preaching, and hymn-singing: 'It was fun that was, Lidstone Camp. They'd
go boozing after. See, there was a pub opposite side of the road where they
had it. Oh, I don't mean ... the ... preachers and that.'[192] The fenland
labourer, Arthur Randell, said that both Methodist and non-Methodist in
the Norfolk village of St Mary Magdalen attended camp meetings; 'such
events were exciting affairs in days when few people had much to entertain
them'.[193] Obelkevich has written of religion as a form of entertainment,
suggesting that nineteenth-century Methodism offered alternatives to the
beer-house and village feast as well as the church – though, as Mont Abbot's
experience shows, the attractions were not necessarily mutually exclusive.[194] Whether providing the opportunity for genuine religious commit-
ment or a venue for enjoyable pastimes, church and chapel should be
considered seriously in the history of rural leisure.

* * *

While not wanting to minimize the role of religion in any way, we should
not always assume a straightforward religiosity. A Kent man claimed that
the 'young chaps' in his village went to the Salvation Army because of the
female officers; 'As soon as they sent men, they stopped going.'[195] An
Oxfordshire worker said that in one village the only labourers that went
near the church were the bell-ringers, but they left as soon as they had
carried out their much-loved duties: 'never stopped to church. Oh no, no,
no.'[196] Religious activities could also be a source of amusement. Frances
Harker was a 'little sister' for the church-based Women's Help Society, and
described six- and seven-year-old girls hand-sewing blue and red gingham
clothing destined for developing countries – 'Sew all the wretched things by
hand ... in the vicarage. There's no wonder there's disturbances out there

now.' When her brother was asked to recite a prayer that he was supposed
to have learned at religious instruction, he came out with, 'Oh Lord we
beseech thee, send my mother up a beech tree.'[197]

The annals of rural workers are full of such moments of seized pleasure.
We hear of young women, Northumberland bondagers, working to 9 p.m.,
then cycling four or five miles to a dance, returning early in the morning
and resuming work with only an hour's sleep.[198] There are Essex-childhood
memories of ginger cakes, home-made wine, and singing and dancing at a
village wake – 'We enjoyed people dying in those days.'[199] And there are the
never-forgotten delights of a young Kent servant's earliest sight of a real
shop window ('our little shops in Boughton High Street was tiny little
windows and these was massive'), first visit to a music hall, and first taste of
fish and chips.[200] The history of Victorian and Edwardian rural working-
class leisure is not a story of cultural poverty.

7 Protest

When Frederick Law Olmsted, the gentleman farmer and future designer of New York's Central Park, visited England in 1850, he encountered the rural worker. It was a somewhat superficial meeting. The young American was more at home with the countryside than its inhabitants: 'such a country! – green, dripping, glistening, gorgeous! We stood dumb-stricken by its loveliness ... sunny, leafy, blooming May – in an English lane; with hedges, English hedges, hawthorn hedges, all in blossom; homely old farm-houses, quaint stables, and haystacks; the old church spire over the distant trees; the mild sun beaming through the watery atmosphere, and all so quiet – the only sounds the hum of bees and the crisp grass-tearing

7 The Kent Rising, 1838, from a contemporary print
Note the facial characterization of the labourers

of a silken-skinned, real (unimported) Hereford cow over the hedge.' He was more comfortable with farmers than their employees, those he termed 'the lowest class of labourer'. He had problems in the rare moment he actually talked to farm workers: 'I could make nothing of two-thirds of their replies, and I doubted if they could understand me much better.' Yet, he listened in on their conversations and observed their interactions.[1]

In a section called 'Tap-room Politics', Olmsted captured the gist of a discussion among English and Welsh country men in a pub in Wrexham in 1850. They talked about possible war with France over Greece, and an ex-soldier conjured up the image of inevitable defeat, with Chartists, Frenchmen and radicals setting up an English republic 'where the poor man was as good as the rich'. 'The company all thought it very probable . . . A coarse joke about the queen's bundling off with her children produced much laughter; and the hope that the parsons and lawyers would have to go to work for a living, was much applauded.' Olmsted was impressed less by the demonstrated hostility to the ruling class and the possibility of anti-English sentiment than by a strong sense of detachment: 'It was strange what a complete indifference they all seemed to have about it, as if they would be mere spectators, *outsiders*, and not, in any way, personally interested. They spoke of the Government and the Chartists, and the landlords and the farmers, but not a word of themselves.' An acquaintance, a Methodist tea-seller, said that they had just witnessed a good example of 'the character of a large part of the labouring class about here'.[2]

Olmsted's overall verdict was negative. He encountered farm workers whose only topic of conversation was beer and 'girls', and who touched their forelocks in deference to him. He was shocked by their perceived stupidity, their 'dumb-beast lives'. Such men lived in a wide-ranging state of deprivation, a 'balance of degradation and supine misery'. 'The labourers in this part of England (Herefordshire, Monmouth, Gloucester, and Wiltshire) were the most degraded, poor, stupid, brutal, and licentious, that we saw in the kingdom . . . I did not see in Ireland or in Germany or in France, nor did I ever see among our negroes or Indians, or among the Chinese or Malays, men whose tastes were such mere instincts, or whose purpose of life and whose mode of life was so low, so like that of *domestic animals* altogether, as these farm labourers.' Thus, the rural workers' class superiors did not seem to include them in their conceptions of the nation. Olmsted spoke to men who could argue that the condition of the labouring population was responsible for the greatness and prosperity of England, and then exclude that same class from their 'judgment of national character'. It was as if the largest occupational group in the country was invisible.[3] It was a fleeting visit that confirmed the traveller's faith in the democratic superiority of his home country, but the American touched on some key aspects of the politics of the excluded.

* * *

The atmosphere of degradation and alienation that so troubled Olmsted was also apparent to others. Alexander Somerville met men in the 1840s and 1850s who were not afraid to speak their minds to him as a perceived social superior. But despite this willingness to engage verbally, the most outspoken did not seem able to hope for anything other than moving on in search of better conditions, or simply making do in vague expectation of some eventual retribution: 'Ah! I don't care; we must just go on. We be all like to have justice sometime; there ben't no noblemen in heaven, they say.'[4] One of the intriguing questions in rural history is the degree to which this quest for making do impinged on protest. Did what James Scott has termed the day-to-day imperative of household survival subvert not only attempts to challenge that situation but even to envisage any alternative to the status quo?[5] It was a problem assumed by writers of varying political persuasion. The novelist Elizabeth Gaskell wrote of farm workers who laboured 'on, from day to day, in the great solitude of steaming fields – never speaking or lifting up their poor, bent, downcast heads. The hard spadework robs their brain of life; the sameness of their toil deadens their imagination; they don't care to meet to talk over thoughts and speculations, even of the weakest, wildest kind, after their work is done; they go home brutishly tired, poor creatures! caring for nothing but food and rest.'[6] George Sturt referred to the 'instinctive fatalism' of the poor. 'Being born to poverty and the labouring life, they accept the position as if it were entirely natural.'[7]

As the rural sociologist Howard Newby has discussed more recently, the conditions that the rural worker faced seemed natural, a given. Subordination 'is an awesome and apparently irrevocable fact. It is *there* and possesses a reality in comparison with which all alternatives appear abstract and putative.'[8] A sense of resignation rather than active endorsement of the social order comes through in some of the oral histories of rural workers born in the 1900s. A horseman's son said that he did not blame anyone for his family's poverty, 'because it didn't occur to me, who could I blame. Only God!'[9] The Kent labourer, Len Austin, spoke of the narrowness of expectation produced by the poverty of options: 'People say why did you put up with it? Because you blasted had to.' 'Well you didn't expect nothing better in those days, you knew you wouldn't get anything better.'[10]

There were other obstacles to rural mobilization and political expression. The transportations and executions after the East Anglian agrarian riots of 1816 and Swing in 1830 were meant to deter, to strike terror into the hearts of potential protestors. The riots at Downham Market, Littleport and Ely in 1816 resulted in 7 executions and 32 transportations and imprisonments.[11] As one of the trial judges expressed it: 'The law of the land will always be too strong for its assailants, and those who defy the law will, in the end, be subdued by the law, and be *compelled* to submit to its justice or its mercy!'[12] The Swing riots of 1830 resulted in the execution of 19 and the transportation of 481.[13] Labour combinations were legal after 1824, but oaths of initiation were not, so the magistrates were able to prosecute the Dorset unionists in 1834, and six farm workers were transported as a lesson to others.[14] While the move against the labouring unionists backfired, prompting a campaign for their pardon and return to England, the combined lesson of the penalties from 1816 to 1834 would not have been without impact on the rural population. The failure of Chartism in the rural south-east may well be linked to this bitter history, reinforced by the horrors of the Hernhill rising of 1838. The Chartists' campaign in the villages of Kent and Sussex coincided with this massacre of nine agricultural labourers in a wood in Kent, the wounding of ten or so others, and the transportation or imprisonment of the surviving leaders.[15]

Furthermore, those who showed any interest in Chartism could be threatened with dismissal. A northern Chartist who spoke at meetings in the south said that the thinness at meetings was because 'men dare not attend, that they could not exercise their own thoughts for the loss of their work wd. be the consequence'.[16] When workers did join unions, they were likely to be faced with a lock-out. Kent employers dismissed labourers who joined the emerging union in 1872, and other farmers showed solidarity by refusing to employ the sacked men. The farmers also exerted pressure on their workers not to attend union meetings.[17] Some 10 000 men were locked out nationwide in 1874, when the farmers mounted their counter-attack on unionism.[18] In Northamptonshire in the early 1870s, farmers retaliated against the emerging unions by squeezing poor relief.[19] Intimidation by employers was a problem faced by combined labour throughout its history. Arthur Tweedy, who was born in 1900, said that northern agricultural workers were terrified of getting the sack; 'The few who had the courage to stand up for their rights and even mention the word "union" usually got instant dismissal.'[20]

Rural communities were notoriously parochial in their loyalties, cultures and interactions, and any effective protest movement on a scale wider than the immediate locality had to contend with these limitations.[21] The conscious federalism of the rural unionism of the 1870s was an attempt to overcome fragmented interests, but it is significant that the so-called

National Union had to contend with internal divisions and strong regional-ism.[22] The simple structures for mobilization did not exist in many of the rural areas. Workers rarely congregated in large numbers; they were dispersed in terms of both employment and residence. Their work patterns denied them the leisure opportunities that could reinforce the associational patterns contributing to political mobilization. It is no accident that the meetings held to form agricultural labour unions in the early 1870s were held at 7.00 or 7.30 in the evenings, after work.[23] Nor is it a mere coincidence that the larger farms and village communities of East Anglia – the closest equivalent to the concentrations of urban workers – were centres of rural protest and unionism.[24] Rural labourers also lacked the preconditions for politicization, assumed by so many radicals and modern-day historians. They were unable to vote until 1884; and, even then, there were still many effective barriers excluding large sectors of the supposedly eligible male population.[25] They were denied much of the organizational training and skills of public speaking taken for granted by the politically committed of the towns. The literacy levels of rural workers were also a constant source of complaint and comment.[26] Everything seemed against them. As a Norfolk agricultural labourer and unionist expressed it in the 1870s: 'They have been crushing us ever since we left Paradise. They got us down – feet, legs, hands, arms and shoulders. Our faces were crushed in the mud. We could not see.'[27]

It is tempting to take such obstacles at face value. This is what the Metropolitan Police seem to have done in the 1880s when they actively recruited agricultural labourers because of their perceived political acqui-escence.[28] This is what Alan Armstrong seems to have done in his history of English farm workers, where their political aspirations and consciousness are summarized in terms of their 'marked reluctance to engage in any clearly recognisable form of class conflict, whether institutionalised or otherwise'.[29] However, we know that rural workers did protest. Actually, the Norfolk agricultural labourer continued his statement about his down-trodden class: 'We have now just raised our heads, but they are resting still upon our hands. Our elbows are yet in the mud, but even in this position some of us are digging at law, others studying politics, others unions.'[30] Indeed, the historian is confronted with a long list of types of protest and insurrectionary moments. Nor should we be taken in by the forelock-tugging of Olmsted's labourers. An expert in the anthropology of resis-tance has warned against inferring ideological support, 'even from the most faithful compliance'.[31] Recall that Olmsted also witnessed expressions of class hostility. It was a culture that combined elements of both conserv-ative deference and radical resistance.[32] The rural historian Keith Snell has put a name to the animosity behind the public face of compliance: he calls it 'deferential bitterness'.[33] Rural workers were capable of both the hat-doffing that so infuriated Chartist missionaries, and, as we shall see, moments of genuinely chilling oppositional terror.[34]

* * *

Although most of those arrested for their involvement in the agrarian riots in East Anglia were agricultural labourers, the protest in Cambridgeshire, Norfolk, and Suffolk in 1816 is significant for the manner in which the workers of village and town combined to advance their demands. It was not a simple case of the experienced, urban, industrial workers influencing their unsophisticated, agrarian comrades: it was a contingent of Norfolk farm workers from surrounding villages that went into Downham Market and then combined with local labourers to create the Downham riots of 1816. Nine men and six women were sentenced to death for their part in this protest.[35] We see several forms of mobilization that we will encounter in future protests: the central core of mobile activists, the use of coercion to get others to join the group as the protest gathered momentum, and impressment of workers from the fields.[36] We see the techniques of political representation that recur in moments of resistance: the delegations of labourers chosen to negotiate terms with the magistrates and employers in a specially convened meeting, while the crowd demonstrates its force of numbers outside.[37] The demands and concerns of the various rioters were wide-ranging, including action against enclosure, the smashing of threshing machines and the mole ploughs used for drainage work, arson and combinations to force wages up, and demands for cheap bread and food.[38] The authorities were outnumbered, and played for time by granting concessions while they brought in forces to crush the labourers. Each temporary success increased the protestors' confidence. Concessions of fixed flour prices and a minimum wage at Brandon (Suffolk) encouraged agitation in Downham, sparking, in turn, the Littleport riot. (Interestingly, the Littleport labourers had been gathered at a benefit-club meeting in a public house.) A Littleport band then took the unrest on to the Ely fair. The protest was violent and coercive. The protestors demanded and seized bread, meal, food, beer and money – and rarely in the orderly manner that historians have attributed to food-rioting. Though they were violent and dramatic in both their impact and their ending, the riots of 1816 were a localized phenomenon, confined to a few towns and villages in East Anglia. The cry of 'Bread or Blood' that has given them their name was actually 'Bread or Blood in Brandon'.[39]

The riots of 1822 were also regionally-contained moments of demonstration, centred in Norfolk and Suffolk, though in different areas from those of the earlier unrest. The focus here was machine-breaking, and the instigators were agricultural labourers.[40] One group of Suffolk labourers assembled on the Hoo village green and passed a resolution 'that all threshing machines, whether in use or not, should be destroyed immediately; that all farmers who insisted on continuing the use of them should be burnt; as well as their property, and that all corn drills and mole ploughs should be demolished without loss of time'.[41] More than fifty machines were broken during two months of machine-breaking involving over forty parishes.[42]

The Swing rising of 1830, named after the mythical leader of the unrest, was the only movement of agricultural-labouring protest, apart from the unionism of the 1870s, to breach the invisible bounds of the locality. It is notable for its scale, its spread (across southern and eastern England), the range of the demands of its participants, and the pre-eminence of the agricultural labourers.[43] It seems likely that George Rudé and Eric Hobsbawm's classic account of Swing underestimated its sheer scale, both in terms of the tallies of acts of arson and machine-breaking and the number of parishes affected by the protest.[44] Swing was a series of sporadic, locally-based riots rather than a nationally co-ordinated rising, even if its scale may have encouraged some into the illusion of the latter. Labourers and craftsmen protested over agricultural machinery, low wages, high rents, tithes, poor relief, and Irish labour, as what Rudé and Hobsbawm have termed the 'multiformity' of their protest was replicated in neighbourhood after neighbourhood.[45]

The example of insubordination was contagious, far more so than in previous episodes of unrest, and relayed dramatically by the incendiarists' fires. Many acts of arson occurred on the tops of hills. There was a mood of anticipation among those not directly involved in overt action but indicative of wider grievances. We hear of conversations in beer-shops and public houses: 'Mr Parren [a local wood-dealer] had been buying wood and had done so many poor people out of their money that we should not wonder if his Stacks were not set on fire.' According to a Kent curate in 1834, the farm workers had discovered that 'agitation and burning' did for them 'which remonstration never could'; 'even now they commonly say "Ah them there riots and burnings did the poor a terrible deal of good"'. As in 1816 and 1822, there are indications of fleeting successes. Farmers surrendered their machinery for destruction or stopped using it. They raised wages and lowered rents – until the inevitable repression.[46] It is likely that the temporary success of the labourers was aided by their brief and somewhat unholy alliance with farmers over the issue of tithes: if tithes could be reduced, farmers could pay their workers higher wages. It was probably also fuelled by Reform agitation in the towns. One of the more articulate Swing transportees, Joseph Mason, a Hampshire worker peasant, was involved in a radical club of village craftsmen, small farmers and agricultural labourers, the Radical and Musical Society, which met at a tavern in the village of Sutton Scotney, and subscribed to William Cobbett's *Political Register*. Mason organized a petition to the King, endorsed by nearly two hundred rural workers from villages in the immediate area, a mere month or so before the outbreak of rioting in Hampshire, complaining of the condition of the labouring classes and advocating universal suffrage and annual parliaments.[47] The occurrence of Swing and Reform in 1830 would seem to be more than coincidental, though the impact of village and rural-town radicals on the agricultural labourers remains a somewhat illusive possibility.[48]

The tactics of mobilization and negotiation in Swing were forceful – its most recent historians have aptly termed it a combination of menace and restraint.[49] As in East Anglia in 1816, delegates representing rioting labourers met and parleyed with magistrates and farmers.[50] Bands of labourers went from village to village, farm to farm, pressing for an increase in wages. In the Faversham area of Kent the demand was for 2s 6d a day.[51] Hollingbourne labourers had cards in their hats which read, 'Starving at 1s. 6d. per day'.[52] The Swing protesters broke the machinery that they blamed for causing winter unemployment. Nearly four hundred machines in all were destroyed;[53] 35 were smashed in farms around Aldermaston in Berkshire in a matter of hours.[54] A Hampshire man told Somerville that it was the young, poorly-paid men who led the riots around Andover, and who coerced others to join. The aim of the protesters there had been to halt work by forcing ploughs to stop and breaking threshing machines. They also demanded money and drink, much in the manner that they sought largesse during times of festivity, though with greater force and menace. The man said that he was carrying £40 at one time.[55] Though the authorities talked in terms of extortion and pillage, it is likely that the rioters saw it as payment for labour done or work missed, or as a statement of support for their cause – the meanings must have varied. Historians are correct to focus on the similarity between this protest and the rituals of festive culture discussed in the previous chapter. It was as if customary practices were being applied to a different context: the quest for food, drink and money, the processing, the blowing of a horn to marshal the crowd.[56] One of the peaks in the pattern of disturbances was 23 November, St Clement's Day, and St Clement was the patron saint of blacksmiths, particularly adept in breaking machines.[57] Local leaders emerged, self-proclaimed military men such as 'Captain' Revell (note the festive allusion), 'General' Moore, any number of 'Captains', and the Norfolk man known simply, but ominously, as the 'Counsellor'. Though some were agricultural labourers, many were craftsmen.[58]

The next instance of widespread direct action on the part of the rural labourers occurred in the wake of the introduction of the New Poor Law of 1834, like Swing a series of locally-based protests, in this case against the perceived threat to the poor relief that had become such an important part of labouring survival. Bands of labourers, some with faces blackened, most carrying sticks, went from village to village in the Kentish Blean, protesting over the replacement of money relief by a system that issued bread and provisions tickets and only partial payment in cash. The protestors forced the relieving officers to pay recipients according to the old method, and intimidated them so much they increased the rates of relief. One man carried a stick on which was carved the words, 'Plenty or this'. Another had a card in his hat with the caption, 'We want no tickets, no bread'. They told the officials they would 'have their rights'. There are references to the blowing of a horn, and impressment of participants as in Swing, and the rioters were lead by a labourer, Major Murton, also known as 'The Judge'. Over forty men were arrested, half of whom had been involved in disturbances in three or more separate villages.[59]

Though the focus of protest in the mid- to late 1830s was the Poor Law and the persons and properties of those associated with it, the repertoire was far wider, including by-now-familiar targets, grievances and forms. One parish official from the Headington Poor Law Union complained in 1835 that Oxfordshire paupers 'came into his presence with only three words in their mouths . . . "Work Money or Fire" '.[60] Many of these events would have passed unrecorded. A Kent farmer casually recalled that other farmers in his parish had been forced to raise their wages in 1835 because of the collective action of their labourers, yet there is no record of any such combination in the newspapers or court records.[61] In the south, the 1830s saw rioting, arson, attempted unionism, animal-maiming, protest songs, individual acts of defiance, and patchy support for rural Chartism.[62] There were around a hundred incidents of anti-Poor-Law activity in Kent and Sussex in the second half of 1835 alone.[63] Norfolk, Suffolk and Essex saw attacks on workhouses, fires, threatening letters, riotous assemblies at the meetings of guardians, and attacks on the property or persons of poor-relief officials. Anne Digby has discovered over sixty such incidents from 1835–37.[64] Roger Wells has demonstrated that there was widespread unrest in the south in the 1830s, including the Hernhill rising of 1838 that can also be seen as protest against the Poor

Law.[65] Moreover, unlike Swing, opposition to the New Poor Law was a truly national protest. In the north, the populations of the weaving towns and outworking villages demonstrated, petitioned, rioted and employed intimidation and direct action against poor-law guardians in a loose but more organized opposition that was to feed directly into northern Chartism.[66]

* * *

Historians often distinguish between overt and covert actions, claiming that rural workers resorted to the latter after the defeat of more open forms of protest. But this separation is misleading. Arson is sometimes given as an example of the latter, but it provided an opportunity for both group strength and more targeted intimidation. Those who collected to watch a blaze, or who refused to help those putting it out, were exercising an overt form of collective protest.[67] Incendiarism was an extremely common tactic of coercion that occurred before, during and after the major moments of organized protest. In Kent, for example, incendiarism was used as a weapon in 1830 in the Swing rising, against threshing machines in the 1840s, by hop-workers and harvesters in the 1850s, to combat the introduction of steam machinery in the 1860s, and during the union unrest of the 1870s.[68]

John Archer has located almost two thousand cases of arson in Norfolk and Suffolk alone between 1815 and 1870.[69] There were over four hundred cases in Kent in the more limited period from 1834–59.[70] Wiltshire saw some three hundred fires from 1830–75.[71] It was the weapon of choice of farm workers: over 60 per cent of those convicted of incendiary offences in East Anglia, and over 70 per cent of those arrested in Kent, were agricultural labourers.[72] Fires appear constantly in the catalogue of rural protest.[73] When demand for labour was high, labourers used the strike as a means of wage negotiation: during periods of unemployment and underemployment, the favoured tactic was incendiarism.[74] Labourers used the threat of arson to force farmers towards employment and retention, and to try to arrest the reduction of wages.[75] Fires were applied against farm machinery: 'I understand that you have a wheat hoe . . . and we have a life hoe prepared for you.'[76] They were used to oppose the New Poor Law: 'If you do not put a stop to the [Poor-Law] union, we will burn you up, and we will wait till harvest is got in to do it completely.'[77] Incendiarism was an effective psychological weapon, all the more powerful given that offenders tended to live locally and the target was usually an employer.[78] It carried, as David Jones once expressed it, a menacing sense of internal danger.[79]

'Farmers, we are starven, we wol not stan this no longer', a young farm worker wrote to a former employer in 1844, 'this gang is 600 and 80. Rather than starv we are tormint to sit you on fire. You are roges and robbs the pore of their livin by imployan thrashmans sheans. [T]his primsas will sone tak plase fire if you do not olter. You must note be surprised if you see your primsas on fire, and stock al burnt, there will be six on fire in one time.'[80] Arson was often accompanied by yet another weapon of the weak, the threatening letter. It too was a powerful form of coercion, combining wider popular sanction with explicit personal threat. 'Blood and Vengeance against Your Life and Your property for taking away our labour with Your Threshing Machine', wrote a Berkshire labourer from a property near Reading in 1811, 'if You do not refrain . . . we will Thresh Your Ricks with Fire & Bathe Your Body in Blood. How will the People of Reading Gase to see Early Court all in a Blase.'[81] These missives of the rural worker, with their phonetic expression, random spelling and punctuation, regional flavour, and sometimes highly specific points of reference, provided short political messages of varied content. Those who were unable to write themselves might get someone else to pen the message.[82]

These letters could be most intimidating when they were the most deferential: 'Sir, We have inquired into your tithes, and we have determined to set fire to you in your bed if you do not lower them . . . Deem this as friendly [the letter signed off], and consider that we would not burn you up without notice.'[83] They could be scary in their religiosity: 'Gentlemen, these few lines are to inform you that God Almighty have brought our blood to a proper circulation, that have been in a very bad state a long time, and now without an alteration of the foresaid, we mean to circulate your blood with the leave of God.'[84] They could terrify with their specificity: 'all you farmers around, your houses and you must leave them for they shall be in flames but you G.F. shall be a dade man, prepear yourself to dic . . . you shall be shot like a dorg before long'.[85] There were threatening letters covering all the familiar grievances of the rural poor.

* * *

There had been earlier attempts at combination among the agricultural labourers – in Dorset in 1834 and in Kent and Sussex in 1835 – and a foretaste of the sort of opposition that unionism might expect from the employers and magistrates.[86] The Kent Agricultural Labourers' Protection Association campaigned for higher wages in the 1860s, anticipating later unionism in terms of personnel and use of the press.[87] Yet it is not until the 1870s that the trade unions can be taken seriously as part of the repertoire of labouring protest. Though this writer is instinctively wary of teleological views of historical process, it is easy to see why historians could be misled into seeing all the routes of rural protest as leading to the high point of the organized labour of the 1870s. Membership of the agricultural labourers' trade unions in 1874 numbered some hundred thousand, possibly as many as one hundred and fifty thousand, though the estimates are somewhat unreliable.[88] However, teleologies weaken when the rapid decline of the rural workers' unions is considered. The membership of the main union, the National Agricultural Labourers' Union, slipped from over eighty thousand in 1874 to 24 000 in 1879.[89] Like all the other rural protest movements we have considered, the so-termed 'Revolt of the Field' was strongest in the south and east, and weakest, or non existent, in the west and the north.[90]

The Warwickshire farm workers' union stated its objectives in 1872 as increasing wages, decreasing hours, improving housing, obtaining gardens or allotments, and encouraging emigration.[91] In 1873, at a meeting in Yeovil, in Somerset, the men had cards in their hats that read: 'THE FRANCHISE FOR AGRICULTURAL LABOURERS. 15s. a week all year round and no surrender.'[92] The Reverend John Coker Egerton witnessed a union meeting at Burwash, Sussex, in 1873, and provided his version of what was said in the yard of the public house: 'The Harristocrats & the Farmers the tyrants, the labourers the slaves: the Farmers rolling in luxury, on their pianos, & plate & carpets, 100 & 150 guinea hunters, waggonnettes, dog carts etc, the poor man's children crying for bread.'[93] It was hardly an impartial account, but Egerton captured the class potentials of the mobilization. The improvement of the conditions of labour was an old demand. Emigration, advocated as a way to reduce the surplus of labour and thus increase its value, had also long been a strategy of the poor, though more as a means to make ends meet. The unions' support for an extension of the franchise so that labourers could influence central policy was a new development for rural workers, although it had of course been a central part of the Chartist agenda. The provision of small plots of land for labourers, also a Chartist demand, continued as a theme in rural unionism into the 1890s.[94]

Although the unions fostered a sense of collective might, and of the interest of worker pitted against employer, the temperature of class hostility (if we can so term it) varied according to the fortunes of the movement. It is tempting to say that it was the actions of the employer rather than the worker that determined the levels of class-consciousness. When the unions achieved an increase in wages, which they frequently did in the early years of their existence, their language was more temperate. The leader of the Kent and Sussex Labourers' Union in 1874 'urged the labourers to give their employers no complaint against them. They should all work harder, if possible, and be more courteous than before, and he was sure that the great majority of the farmers of that district would meet the men fairly.'[95] Hostility was at its peak during the lock-outs, especially in 1878 when Kent farmers reduced the wages of between 600 and 700 labourers and refused to let them work until they agreed to the new terms; they also attempted to turn 80 families out of their cottages.[96]

Kent union activities were highly respectable. A meeting at Minster Sheppey in 1874 began with an open-air tea for members and their wives by the union meeting house, while the band of the Royal Artillery at Sheerness played dance music. Then a public meeting was held on top of the cliff at the sea shore. It was all very orderly, and farmers were in attendance.[97] The Kent and Sussex union celebrated union branch anniversaries much as workers observed their local club or benefit-society feasts.[98] In Burwash, local village branches, accompanied by a brass band, paraded to church as a group, sat quietly and then arranged for the sermon ('Let Brotherly Love Continue') to be printed in the union newspaper. The minister, Egerton, had to pick a diplomatic path between the interests of farmer and labourer.[99] In addition, the unions held very non-threatening views about the role of women. Unionists and speakers at their rallies argued that 'A woman's place was in her home and her proper work was to keep it comfortable and happy.'[100] The Kent union leadership refused formal support to women working in the hop-grounds who were demanding better conditions: they 'had no right in the fields . . . The place for the wife is at home and attending upon the wants of the family.'[101]

* * *

We have so far focused on dramatic forms of organized protest. However, these concentrated moments of resistance merely represented a multiplication of techniques applied on a more regular, random basis. We know of labouring petitions to parliament, union activity, and wage strikes in Kent, before and after Swing.[102] Labourers in Snape and Sudbourne, along the estuary of the River Alde in Suffolk, 'regularly extorted their [poor relief] allowances by threats of violence' in the 1830s.[103] Wage deputations and strikes were probably also a common tactic of negotiation – as in Wiltshire in 1850 – but only registered on the map of protest if the strike turned to violence or escalated beyond the village or farm.[104] Although it stressed the weakness of formal trade unionism in the 1890s, the Royal Commission on Labour discovered several instances of strike activity and forceful negotiation ('insubordination') on the part of individual work groups. In the village of Probus in Cornwall, for example, a gang working on a threshing machine forced a farmer to reinstate one of their number by stopping work.[105] Hop-pickers in Herefordshire and Kent commonly applied the tactic of striking; they knew when an employer was the most vulnerable and understood just how to squeeze them.[106] One commissioner said that even where there were no unions, 'agricultural labourers in an informal way . . . combine to regulate the price of their labour or their hours of work. Labourers often say that farmers regulate the price of labour at the market ordinary, and in the same way the price of piece-work is probably fixed by the men at the village public-house.'[107]

Opposition to enclosure could take the form of open rioting. Concerned officials wrote dramatically of anti-enclosure rioting at Otmoor, in Oxfordshire, in the 1830s: 'the whole labouring population rose in formidable array'.[108] When rioting did occur, the composition of the crowd included wide sections of the local community, and protest assumed a festive drama akin to the communal insubordination of Swing. At Hardown Hill in Dorset in 1811, a crowd of 90 assembled to the blowing of a horn, lined up and, on command, levelled recent enclosure banks and fences. Cider was distributed. A man played a violin while the protestors reclaimed their turf-cutting rights. Those arrested were small farmers and a few labourers.[109] Yet historians generally agree that riot was probably the least common way of opposing enclosure, even in the early modern period when that form of resistance was widespread.[110] A common means of opposition was to refuse to sign a petition for enclosure or to sign a counter-petition. The parliamentary records alone indicate that over a third of enclosures during the period 1730–1839 were opposed in this manner.[111] Such protest was not exactly hidden in the community, and involved organization and mobilization, but it also encompassed individual acts of non-compliance. Theft of field books, damage to property (destruction of markers, and fence-breaking), verbal or written threats and rumour were all used to counter intended enclosure. Demonstrated local opposition to an initiative could stall it before it even got to the stage of a formal petition.[112] Rioting was rare, but foot-dragging was commonplace.

The more visible modes of group protest were almost exclusive to the south-east areas of England. But the northern and western areas that seemed free of the organized group protests of the 1830s employed tactics of negotiation as a matter of course. The Yorkshireman, Fred Kitchen, was attuned to the micro-politics of labour, observing that the hiring negotiations were about the only time that 'master and man met as equal and separate units', so the man 'made the most of his time'.[113] Farm servants, more prevalent in the north and west, were used to such interactions.[114] The Royal Commission on Labour observed that the hirings undercut the need for unions in Northumberland in the 1890s: 'The hirings to some extent supply an element which is unknown in the southern and eastern counties, namely, the opportunity afforded to the employed of meeting together and discussing the rate of wage and conditions of labour, and though there is no actual combination of the men on these occasions, still they do really control the market place of wages.'[115] The farm worker Joseph Mayett's autobiography reveals his readiness to negotiate wages, conditions, employment and poor relief with his immediate social superiors, the farmers, overseers and magistrates. Mayett was well aware that farm servants had power to deal with an unsatisfactory employer by leaving when their time was up at Lady Day or Michaelmas. He described how he invented interest from another employer to force a farmer to hire him, and how a fellow-servant colluded in the deception; 'I began to be a little political.' He was not always successful in his actions, but the point is that he tried. There are several instances where Mayett left an employer when they failed to reach agreement over conditions. Perhaps his evaluations of respective employers ('like a madman'; 'I did not very well like my master for he was a very odd man') also helped him to cope with his situation; employees would have derived some satisfaction from grumbling together about an employer.[116] Moreover, if a farmer gained a bad reputation, it affected his ability to hire workers.[117]

Day-to-day methods of resistance, the weapons of the weak or hidden transcripts of resistance, were arguably the most common means of struggle.[118] These were the often subtle but sometimes savage ways in which the powerless asserted themselves in what John Walter has termed 'the infrapolitics of the subordinate . . . the quotidian and largely unremarked exchanges by which individuals attempted to blunt the exercise of power in the micro-politics of manor and parish and the opacity of the workplace'.[119] Individual acts of resistance were myriad in their strategies and forms.

At one extreme, the weaponry of the weak included terror. By poisoning, maiming, slashing, strangling or hanging, beating or drowning an animal, an employee could both inflict financial damage and send a horrific warning to the beast's owner. The next mutilation could be theirs. The practice of animal-maiming was an effective form of psychological warfare.[120]

However, tactics also involved gentler methods of rebuke. The singing that we saw was so integral to rural labouring leisure and work culture expressed political and social grievances as well as sexual longing:

> Here's first to those farmers who do sell the corn,
> And they are as big rogues as ever were born;
> They are never contented, but still they have none,
> If the land were to yield fifty bushels for one.[121]

> Those rich grinding kn[a]ves will have us poor slaves,
> And take fron the poor man what he earns;
> To hear them boast how they carry every course!
> And the poor man they treat like a worm.[122]

There were songs that anticipated Swing, and union songs in the 1870s and 1880s. There were songs about the evils of enclosure, farm machinery, the New Poor Law, unemployment and low wages.[123]

Two Sussex singers who sang 'We're All Jolly Fellows that Follow the Plough' at harvest celebrations told a collector of folk-songs that they were fully aware that it was heard differently at the same performance. Employers and their guests (often from the town) took it as a song about a 'carefree country experience'. But fellow workers interpreted it more ironically 'as an expression of all that was wrong in society': given the conditions of their work, they did not feel remotely 'jolly fellows'.[124] We should recall the scepticism about outward shows of deference, discussed earlier. This is what a prominent manager of aristocratic estates in the Midlands meant, when, at the height of Swing, he wrote of the cunning and insincerity of the poor, 'their *apparent* deference towards their superiors'.[125] Sometimes we can detect a defiance of the mind behind outward conformity to the rituals of deference. There is a hint of this in Fred Kitchen's canniness about the strategies of getting small things done, saying of a gentleman farmer that 'If you wanted a favour of him, all you had to do was to pump hard on the handles at each end of his name. If you omitted the handles you drew no water from his well.'[126] We can see it more blatantly in the case of the northern farm worker, Arthur Tweedy. When he asked his father why labouring folk had to call the squire 'Sir', his father replied, ' "Sir", my boy, is only the nickname for a fool.'[127] Tweedy's father was not a man who outwardly challenged. His son complained that he had allowed himself to be 'trampled down to a near starvation life as a farm worker', accepting his situation rather than trying to change it.[128] But, clearly, Tweedy senior rebelled internally.

At almost every turn, it is possible to locate examples of the 'arts of resistance'. The poor wrote letters to poor-law officials from villages and towns throughout the south-east, threatening to return home to put themselves on the parish and thereby incur greater costs to the local authorities than they would if they were paid to stay where they were: 'Jentlemen All i hope you Will not Be Angry of Me By Senden you these few Lines for i Bag the faver of you All that is i hope you Will Be So kind Jentlemen as to Grant me a Pare of Shooes for three of My Children . . . for i have thought Jentlemen Many times that i Should Come home.'[129] It was a widely known and work-able ploy. Even though the officials knew that the poor were playing the system against them, their vested interests forced them to comply.[130] Some of the letters were rather assertive: 'if you Sir and the Gentlemen Knew alltogeather My Situation they would Not So Delay in Affording Me Soum thing Moor than what they have Done.'[131] 'Gentlemen if you Do not send me some releif by Thursday next I Shall Consider your Silance to be a refusal to releive me and must Come with my family into the house.'[132] These letters merely represent the tip of the iceberg of actual negotiation: most interac-tion was carried out in person.[133]

Flight was yet another weapon of the weak. Emigration was used as a form of protest as well as a means of self-improvement. Getting out was an explicit critique of current conditions: praise of the New World was, by definition, condemnation of the Old. 'We are quite tired of this Country', some labourers from the Norfolk village of Besthorpe wrote in 1837, 'We Know we Cannot be Worse of than we are at all Events For the Farmers are imployint the Treshing Mechines and ofter Mechinery so that there are from 6 to 12 of able Men that are able to Work that cannot get Imployment.' Shortly afterwards, 12 men and women with children – about fifty in all – left to try their luck overseas.[134] Letters from union members who left for Australia and New Zealand in the 1870s continued this literature of critique. 'Give my fellow workmen my best wishes, and tell them to have blood in their ears, and do the same as I have done, and come out, for it is better than staying at home.'[135] 'I very often think of the slaves in England and the empty bellies.'[136]

Then there were the instances of an open flouting of authority, obvious statements of disrespect. '[Y]ou Can Just kiss my Ass. I am now in America living in the land of the free', was the way that a Devonshire carpenter ended his letter to the parish authorities, from the safety of another conti-nent.[137] A Sussex man shouted out to the Reverend Egerton of Burwash 'that he always found beer much more profitable to him than preaching; he also began to . . . [urinate] & told me he was coming to church as soon as he had done'.[138] But there were also little individual acts of defiance, statements of principle rather than threats. William Brakespear, the son of an Oxfordshire lime-burner, began to question his parents' values after talking to a village radical who told him that he should never sell his labour cheaply because that was all he had. '[T]his man persuaded me to see life in a differ-ent way.' The boy began to refuse to sing deferential church songs and to doff his hat to his social superiors, except those he genuinely respected. 'I began to see things in a different light . . . before I left school I would not sing the rich man in his castle, the poor man at his gate, God made him high and mighty, and all of their estate.'[139] Some workers joked with serious purpose. When the chairman of a Sussex board of guardians told a labourer that his wife was not a good household manager, the man replied, 'Well Gentlemen I don't know nowt about my wife not being a good manager, but I be quite sure of one thing, she cd. manage a good deal more if she cd. get it.'[140] Others grumbled. Egerton heard daily complaints against farm machinery in Burwash, long after Swing. The grumbling could turn to open proclamation if the chance arose. At a prize-giving dinner for allot-ment tenants, attended by the minister, one of the cottagers took the oppor-tunity to speak out against threshing machines: 'if those thrashing machines were done away with all wd. be right'.[141] Open expression of discontent surfaced in a few of the meetings of agricultural labourers orga-nized by the Royal Commission of Labour in the 1890s. Aubrey J. Spencer, who visited Dorset, Wiltshire, Kent, Somerset, Essex, Worcestershire and Surrey, said that the labourers' spokesmen at public meetings 'often showed a bitter feeling towards their employers . . . in every district I heard a good deal of discontent from the lips of labourers'.[142]

* * *

Historians have argued that the ancestors of the nineteenth-century rioters wanted to regulate the price and flow of food and the impact of land improvement, and to ensure access to affordable grain and the produce of the commons. E. P. Thompson has famously described the ideology behind these forms of protest as the 'moral economy': 'these grievances operated within a popular consensus as to what were legitimate and what were ille-gitimate practices in marketing, milling, baking, etc. This in its turn was grounded upon a consistent traditional view of social norms and obliga-tions, of the proper economic functions of several parties within the community . . . An outrage to these moral assumptions, quite as much as actual deprivation, was the usual occasion for direct action.'[143] Riots were a form of 'community politics' in defence of what were perceived to be tradi-tional rights and customs.[144] This social philosophy of protest is normally associated with the food riots and anti-enclosure resistance of the period before 1800. However, Roger Wells has argued that it is possible to extend the moral economy of the poor into the 1830s and beyond. The compo-nents of this rural moral economy included the demand for fair prices (food, rent or fuel), adequate wages and the right to poor relief: 'a distinct rural variant of the moral economy, ensuring that all retained a legitimate place with a right to at least a basic standard of living'. With its attacks on competitive Irish labour and farm machinery as a way of protecting employment, its strikes, combinations and fires aimed at wage advancement, and its interventions against the local provisions of the poor law, Swing encapsulated the essentials of this rural moral economy.[145]

While the notion of a rural moral economy provides a tidy summary of the grievances outlined in the pages above, it is all a little too neat. It would be a mistake to present a picture of ideological consistency, a blueprint of an unswerving, socio-political world-view. Although dealing with a later period, Newby has made a case for a less systematic view of society, what, for want of a better term, he has called agricultural labourers' *ambivalence*. When he interviewed farm workers in Suffolk in 1972, assigning them 'deferential', 'proletarian', and 'ambivalent' social consciousness, he discovered that only minorities of his sample subscribed to the more unitary images of society – deferential (15 per cent) and proletarian (22 per cent) – and that the largest number (over 40 per cent) demonstrated ambivalence, that is, 'no single image of society'.[146] Identical proportions of those questioned (60 per cent) agreed with the propositions: (1) that farmers knew what was best for the farm and that workers should do just what they were told; and (2) that the ordinary man should play a greater role in running the country. It is possible to interpret Newby's findings slightly differently. In fact, these rural workers were divided fairly evenly between those with unitary (albeit opposing) social images (37 per cent) and those with a 'fragmented form of social consciousness' (43 per cent).[147] The combination of protest and deference that Newby found in the attitudes of rural workers was both a case of individual ambivalence – attitudinal splits within the same person – *and* the existence of coherent, contrasting group ideologies.

This fluidity of mentality is particularly noticeable in the languages of class that emerge when rural workers have been given a chance actually to describe their social environment. While there is a default towards a two-class model – what one labourer described as the 'snobs' or 'big men' versus 'the workers' or the 'little man' – what is interesting about these commentaries is the relative nature of people's perceptions of social ordering.[148] The Kent agricultural labourer, Len Austin, talked in terms of two classes, certainly, but he also used a whole number of other social lenses. Indeed, his descriptions of fellow working people frequently invoked occupation rather than class: fruit men, horsemen, shepherds, stockmen, waggoners, woodmen, those from the brickfields, those in service, those hired by the year, those who worked by the week. He also favoured a series of binary opposites of age, gender, religion, and so on, to classify the people he encountered. There were boys and girls, men and women, old and young, 'townies' and 'clodhoppers', those who had an education and those who did not, locals and outsiders, large families and small families, those on the land and those not, Liberals and Tories, the rebellious and those who accepted, the Methodist and the non-Methodist, and the rough and the respectable. In other words, while he saw the world in class terms, and was continually invoking the polarity of big and little to describe this world, Austin was by no means limited to this way of making sense of his experience and society.[149]

Newby also discovered 'great diversity' in class images. Although a majority of respondents leaned towards a two-class model (nearly 60 per cent), the number of classes distinguished ranged from none to five, and there were 24 different types of classification. Those interviewed would slide from one notion of class to another, according to situation or context. Newby concluded that class was 'not a fixed property' for the agricultural labourer; 'it is an amorphous, nebulous and fluid concept which he feels he recognizes when he is confronted by it, but a clear conception of which is not always necessary for him to engage in his everyday social encounters'.[150] Similarly, an anthropology of a northern dale village community has provided detailed interactive evidence for 'individuals ... adopting a number of different personae, and even close neighbours in a small village occupying a miscellany of highly diverse social worlds'.[151] When they did invoke the language of class to describe their environment, rural workers used a variety of categories. Their classifications were continually shifting, and the descriptions that they used varied from context to context.

* * *

There is an interesting undercurrent of religious influence in the rural protest of the nineteenth century. Biblical imagery pervaded the deferential bitterness of Keith Snell's rural workers: 'we will find the Bible referred to by the poor far more frequently than it ever is in the diaries of the reverends Woodforde, Kilvert, Holland or Skinner'.[152] The Hernhill rising of 1838 is the most obvious instance of this, a millenarian mobilization of agricultural labourers, led by a pretended messiah.[153] But there are other cases of religious influences in the languages of craft and class complaint, or when rural workers simply attempted to make sense of their situation. The Buckinghamshire farm worker, Mayett, used the Bible as something of a touchstone throughout his life. He met a follower of the millenarian prophet, Joanna Southcott, who lent him some books. Mayett was initially attracted but thought that their religion was inconsistent with the Bible and suspected a ruse 'to get money'. The Bible also helped him pick his way through the contrasting political messages of the early 1820s. On the one hand, he encountered the conservative tracts of Hannah More, attempting 'to perswade poor people to be satisfied in their situation . . . and in fact there was but little else to be heard from the pulpit or the press and those kind of books were often put into my hands in a dictatorial way in order to Convince me of my errors . . . which drove me almost into despair for I Could see their design'. On the other hand, there were the radical writings of William Cobbett, Thomas Wooler and Richard Carlile, which fellow-workers introduced him to, and to which he was momentarily attracted, persuaded of 'the sins of oppression in all those that had the supremacy over the lower order of people'. However, they also failed Mayett's test of consistency with his interpretation of the word of God: 'I would advise others to do the same and always prefer the bible before any other book however feasible the[y] may seem.'[154] The union leader, George Edwards, said something similar. 'With my study of theology, I soon began to realize that the social conditions of the people were not as God intended they should be.' When he became a union speaker, he would search the scriptures to make sure that he was doing the right thing. 'Then, as now, to me the Labour movement was a most sacred thing and, try how one may, one cannot divorce Labour from religion.'[155]

The various statements of nineteenth-century rural labouring protest are dotted with religious imagery. A Norfolk machine-breaker told the court in 1831 that he was 'doing God a service'.[156] Anti-Poor-Law protesters referred to the 'law of God . . . torn asunder by the Laws of Man', and quoted 'texts of scripture illustrative of the tyranny and injustice' of some of the provisions of the Act of 1834.[157] Snell has demonstrated that the 1830s Dorsetshire unionist, George Loveless, employed at least six biblical references in a mere two or three pages of his pamphlet, *The Victims of Whiggery* (1837).[158] The Staffordshire potter, Charles Shaw, recalled that the language of the nineteenth-century craft newspaper, *The Potter's Examiner*, 'was steeped in the forms and methods of biblical expression'.[159] We can also see religious imagery in some of the friendly-society or club banners: the Tysoe Club (Warwickshire) had 'God is our Help' as its motto;[160] the Ebrington Club banner (Gloucestershire) had a picture of the Good Samaritan.[161]

Biblical allusion, quotation and imagery were central to the discourse of the agricultural trade unionism of the 1870s. When the Kent Union was officially formed at a meeting in Maidstone in May 1872, one of the speakers said that the agricultural labourers 'were the creatures whom God had created, and God was no respecter of persons'. 'God said the labourer should plough the fields and hoe the land; if they done that they were entitled to a bit of the cheese.'[162] Ernest Selley observed that the National Union congress of 1872 'had all the characteristics of a religious revival . . . At times the conference bore a strong resemblance to a Methodist "love feast".' Many of the delegates were Methodist preachers, and their speeches reflected their affiliations. 'Sir, this be a blessed day: this ere Union be the Moses to lead us poor men up out o' Egypt.' 'King Daavid sed as ow the 'usbanman as labourers must be the fust partaker o' the fruit.' One delegate reflected that 'little things was often chus to du graat ones, and when e sa' the poor labrin' man comin' furrud in this ere movement, and a bringin' o' the faarmers to terms, he were remoinded o' many things in th' Scripters, more perticler o' th' ram's horns that blew down the walls o' Jericho, and frightened Pharaoh, King of Egypt'.[163] Methodism contributed a millenarian mood of anticipated change.[164] Joseph Arch, the leader of the National Agricultural Labourers' Union, wrote of 'These white slaves of England' who 'stood there with the darkness all about them, like the children of the land of Israel waiting for someone to lead them out of the land of Egypt.'[165] Similar language permeated the unions' advocacy of emigration. The *Labourers' Union Chronicle* saw New Zealand as 'a paradise', 'the Eden', 'the land of promise', 'A LAND WHEREIN THOU MAY'ST EAT BREAD WITH-OUT SCARCENESS'; 'Away, then, farm labourers, away! New Zealand is the promised land for you; and the Moses that will lead you is ready.'[166] So the religious repertoire was varied, and even included a catechism:

Question   Who created the land?
Answer   God.
Question   Who then has the sole right to order its disposal?
Answer   God.
Question   And what has He declared in His will respecting it?
Answer   That it should be divided among all people, to every man his portion. See Numbers 26, verses 51–56 to prove that God designed the land to be the common property of the people . . .'[167]

Appropriately, union songs were sung to the tunes of well-known hymns rather than to the beat of traditional folk-songs.[168]

These influences are not difficult to explain. There is strong evidence for the impact of Methodism on rural working-class culture: the maps derived from the Census of Religious Worship in 1851 show few registration districts unaffected either by Wesleyan or Primitive Methodism.[169] J. C. Buckmaster recollected that Methodists were active in and around the Buckinghamshire village of Slapton in the 1830s. The young farm worker attended their meetings, held in the homes of ordinary working folk. The 'ranting and groaning and the confessions of some of the converted were frightful. I had no idea that I had been living and working with men who ought to have been in prison.' 'They talked familiarly about Jesus Christ, as if He were a farm labourer keeping a family on nine shillings a week.'[170] The Primitives were particularly successful in the pit villages and among agricultural labourers.[171] They were known as a 'working-class sect' because of their social composition and perceived influences.[172] Labourers served as Primitive Methodist church officials and lay preachers, and most of those who baptized their children in Primitive chapels were either agricultural labourers or other rural workers.[173] Ninety per cent of the households in the Blean area of Kent in 1881 with children baptized in the Primitive Methodist chapel were those of labouring families.[174] Skilled, semi-skilled and unskilled workers made up 90 per cent of the fathers of those baptized by the Primitives in the Midlands, and most of these would have been rural workers employed either on the land or in rural industry or the mining villages.[175]

This is not to negate the impact of Wesleyanism, the most numerous alternative to the established church. The social profile of Wesleyan Methodism in the Blean villages in 1881 was almost identical to that of the Primitives.[176] Their social structure in the Midlands was weighted towards the skilled worker, and did not include many miners (they were less proletarian than the Primitives), but still contained a large contingent (nearly a third) of the semi-skilled and unskilled.[177] Wesleyan office-holders were definitely drawn from those above the labouring class. Although some were labourers (around 20 per cent in Lincolnshire), the majority of stewards, class-leaders and local preachers at mid-century were farmers, craftsmen and shopkeepers.[178] Together, the two Methodisms covered the occupational and social range of the rural worker.[179]

The Church of England and nonconformity were not rigidly separated in the minds of rural workers. Kitchen's Methodist parents sent their children to the Church of England Sunday school in the mornings and afternoons, and to the Methodist chapel in the evenings.[180] Joseph Ashby went to church in the morning and either the Primitive or the Wesleyan chapel at night.[181] Methodists in the Yorkshire fishing village of Staithes baptized their children in the Anglican Church (they called it 'having the baby done').[182] Local studies demonstrate what James Obelkevich has termed 'shopping around' by rural labourers: many households had children with either an Anglican or Methodist baptism.[183] Rural workers moved between church and chapel.[184]

The other influence on the languages of protest was the Church of England Sunday school. As we saw in the last chapter, the 1851 census showed a positive correlation between areas of rural child-labour and Sunday-school attendance, indicating that the Sunday school was the main source of education for many labouring children.[185] Ironically, 'those areas most exploiting child labour were the ones that leaned most heavily on primarily religious education for their youth'. The Church of England dominated Sunday-school provision, providing over 40 per cent of national enrolments, and as much as 70 per cent of attendance in the rural counties of Dorset and Sussex.[186] The farm worker Mayett was influenced by both Methodists and Baptists, but he also acknowledged that the Church of England Sunday school taught him to write and improved his reading abilities. It was the only available means of education once Mayett started labouring at an early age.[187] The potter Shaw was taught to read the Bible by an old woman in her cottage school: 'like that of thousands in my day'. But he too stressed the role of the Sunday school in his education; a parallel education going alongside and after that of the ABC school. School lasted from the age of four until he started work as a mould-runner at seven, but Sunday school continued until he was ten.[188] Later oral histories imply that Sunday school was still influential at the beginning of the twentieth century.[189]

The Sunday school supplemented, and in some cases replaced, an educational system that for much of the nineteenth century placed a heavy emphasis on basic religion. Reading and religious instruction went hand in hand.[190] Educational practices were reinforced by the literary supply to working-class homes. Statistical surveys of book-ownership in working-class households in the 1830s and 1840s discovered that the majority of rural workers had access to literature (normally between 70 and 90 per cent of households contained some sort of literature). However, they also found that the vast majority of this potential literary diet was religious in nature. The Bible and Prayer Book dominated the profile of book-ownership, whether it was in parishes with high or low access.[191] Of a group of 151 labouring households in several Kent villages and hamlets, where around 60 per cent of those interviewed possessed reading material, only 12 houses contained any non-religious literature.[192]

Charles Shaw was convinced that religion was a significant factor in the mentality of working-class people because of this cultural milieu.[193] The Bible was 'the sole lesson book of so many poor people in that day'. What Shaw perceptively described as 'a leaven of religious feeling' in the Potteries was true of many parts of rural England: 'The Sunday schools mainly fed this feeling. Though few could write, many could read, and in the Sunday schools the habit of reading the Bible was strongly fostered. Through reading, the sympathy and habit of the "man in the street", though he did not attend a place of worship, were in favour of religion.'[194] One certainly does not get the sense of a village England divorced from biblical influences – at any stage during our period of interest – and there are indications that this early religious exposure lasted throughout life. We find it in the early twentieth century as well. Fred Mills, born in 1899, the son of an Essex farm worker, said that his father, who could not write, 'could read the Bible and the Bible only, and he always read it out loud'.[195] Will Askham, who grew up in a Durham quarry community at much the same time, said that his father used to tell him that if he followed 'the Book' he would not go wrong. 'He believed in the Bible very very much so . . . me father used to sit at one end of the fireplace and me aunt at the other one, and they would sit and talk about the Bible. And every night before we went to bed she got the family Bible, she read a certain amount out of that Bible before we went to rest. Every night.'[196]

Of course, Methodism and the Church of England were merely two influences on the mentalities of the villages. In 1915, the folk-song collector, Janet Blunt, was told by an old Oxfordshire woman from Adderbury that in November it was possible to predict the weather for the winter. As midnight approached on Martinmas Eve, the Four Angels of the Earth circled the world, beating up the wind to determine the winter weather. If the wind came from the north, it would be cold. The woman's father and a friend, both farm workers, looked for this sign every year.[197] This was but a momentary glimpse of a whole mental framework, a hybrid Christianity that was widespread in rural England, lingering into the twentieth century.[198] The Church of England was notoriously compliant as far as folk-beliefs were concerned, and even Methodism did not so much replace local popular beliefs as accommodate them into a new framework.[199] Hence the religious world of rural workers comprised a mix of Christianity and folklore.[200] We can actually see this combination at work in the Kent rising of 1838. The millenarian enthusiasm, singing of hymns, and belief in the Christ-like qualities of the labourers' leader have the feel of a religious revival, possibly the influence of the Bible Christians (an offshoot of Methodism similar to the Primitives). Some of the beliefs of the protesting agricultural labourers smacked of folklore: their misconceived invulnerability to bullets, and the supposed extrasensory powers of their leader. Yet the core of those involved in the abortive rising were adherents of the Church of England, including the Hernhill church band and singers.[201]

* * *

We have encountered a long inventory of resistance. Rural workers were able to overcome some of the barriers to protest. Hence the importance of violence and coercion in rural protest, for the East Anglian rioters of 1816,

Swing and the anti-Poor-Law protesters all used coercion to recruit. The itinerant, press-ganging band accumulated the numbers needed for success, while moving action over an area beyond the individual village or farm. Although denied the associational possibilities of factory or town, rural inhabitants utilized the available sites: beer-shops and public houses, workforces on large farms, the gangs of men on directed labour for poor relief (found in both Swing and 1838), fairs, moments of festivity (Oak Apple Day and St Clements) and both church and chapel.[202]

Methodism helped to overcome some of the structural barriers to rural protest discussed at the start of this chapter, providing an organizational framework with leadership personnel, a structure of meetings, and actual venues. Primitive Methodist chapels were used extensively for meetings of the labourers' union in Norfolk in the 1870s.[203] The linkages of Methodism overcame some of the work-fragmentation of rural labour that made organized protest so difficult, and the union could build on this ready infrastructure. It also encouraged public speaking and the reading and writing skills that were helpful to union activities.[204] The evidence for the Methodist connection in unionism is strong. Four of the six Dorset unionists transported in 1834 were Methodists, as were just over half of the union leaders in Suffolk, Norfolk and Lincolnshire in the 1870s.[205] Methodism was pivotal to both Norfolk and Gloucestershire unionism.[206] The movement did not much influence the Kent and Sussex Labourers' Union, but a rival union in the same county, the National Agricultural Labourers' Union, did meet in the rooms of the Bible Christians.[207]

We should not emphasize the separation between the rural and urban, and agricultural and industrial protest. The machine-breaking of Swing included factory and industrial as well as farm machinery: woollen mills and paper-mills were among the targets.[208] Craftsmen from the small county towns may have had a radicalizing influence on the agricultural labourers in 1830 – though the initiative demonstrated by the latter in 1816 indicated that the flow did not have to be one-way.[209] One of the spokesmen in the early riots of 1830 was a radical shoemaker from Maidstone, and unionists in this Kent town were also active in the organization of the agricultural labourers in the 1860s and 1870s. The Kent and Sussex Labourers' Union was particularly successful in villages around market towns; indeed paper-mill hands and foundry workers were involved in the initial combinations. It was a *labourers'* union rather than an *agricultural* labourers' union. Felicity Carlton has argued that it was this alliance between the workers of village and town that accounts for the KSUL's strength relative to those unions (NALU) where the sole focus was on farm workers.[210] Interactions occurred on an informal basis as well. The Royal Commission of the 1890s noted that although unionism was non-existent among Cornish agricultural labourers, 'the proximity of mines and the constant going to and fro between Cornwall and America, make the men hang together more than elsewhere, and treat their interests as more decidedly distinct from, if not antagonistic to, those of their masters'.[211]

As we saw in an earlier chapter, there was in fact considerable movement between the spheres; it is inconceivable that rural workers always followed historians' rigid separation between urban and rural protest.[212] It is not as if there were no urban precursors to the sorts of activities we have been discussing. In Kent, for instance, rural trade unionism had the late eighteenth- and early nineteenth-century examples of combination in the dockyards, and among rope-makers, paper-makers, the building trades, and boot- and shoemakers.[213] There were certainly a number of national protest movements to draw upon: the Wiltshire shearmen of 1802, the Luddites in 1811–12, the Reform crisis of the 1830s, anti-Corn-Law agitation of the 1840s, Chartism, machine-breaking, industrial unionization, strikes, petitioning, riot and intimidatory violence.[214] The resistance of woollen-workers to mechanization in the early 1800s – in villages as well as towns, it should be noted – rehearsed the larger-scale Luddism of Swing and rural protest later in the century. The machinery was different, but the tactics of resistance are comparable: petitions, strikes, collective bargaining, combination, riot, intimidation and open violence.[215] Anthea Newman has shown that the Anti-Corn-Law League of the manufacturing northern towns was able to gain some support among Wiltshire agricultural labourers and workers in the decaying woollen industry in the 1840s, and has suggested that its tactics of non-confrontational mobilization, including handbills, meetings and touring speakers, sat comfortably with the methods of the unions of the 1870s. The rural workers of the Calne area were involved first with the League and then with the West of England Labourers' Association.[216] There were also many national examples of unionism at work, throughout the nineteenth century.[217] The revival of rural unionism in the 1890s was a direct result of the Dock Strike of the 1880s.[218]

The impact of rural Chartism is a vastly neglected topic, though there is evidence of printed Chartist and union handbills, including one by the union pioneer George Loveless appealing to the farm labourers and workers of Dorset to embrace unionization and Chartism, and another outlining the history of Loveless and the transported unionists. Distributed in Dorset beer-houses in 1838, they called on workers to 'obtain by peaceable means a fair return of wages for your labour, and a share in the making of the Laws by having a vote for Members of Parliament . . . and remain Firm to your Unions'.[219] We learn of farm workers in the 1840s walking to country towns on Saturdays, after work, to purchase their copies of the Chartist *Northern Star*. We know that village labourers joined the Chartist Land Company.[220] Doubtless the rural unionism of the 1870s, with its effective use of the press, mass meetings and organization beyond the county, drew on the urban Chartism of an earlier period as well as the structures of the Methodisms. In fact, the unions' wider discussion about the franchise could almost be interpreted as a Chartist revival.[221]

Finally, there is a quieter history yet to be written: the role of the friendly societies and self-help clubs discussed in an earlier chapter. The artisan, and one-time travelling player, Christopher Thomson, became the secretary of the branch of the Oddfellows in the Nottinghamshire village of Edwinstowe. For him, it was far more than a means of economic survival: 'The Lodge has, unquestionably, been of vast use to our village; it has been the means of drawing a large body of men to provident and self-caring considerations, checking drunkenness, promoting social concord, and sublimating, by intense fire-thought, gross lumps of ignorance into Christian men.' It was a matter of moral as well as financial betterment for Thomson, and he claimed to have helped to set up forty or fifty branches in a little over a decade during the 1830s and 1840s, travelling more than six thousand miles lecturing and advocating on behalf of these self-help societies. He thought that the Lodge 'raised the drooping spirit' of the labourers of Edwinstowe 'by small savings they have purchased a certain dependence, and now they feel themselves rising into manliness . . . It is not less a proof that men, once made to feel the dignity of their position in society, will use every effort to keep themselves.'[222] While we do not have to follow any retrospective pressing of the friendly societies into the service of anti-welfare-state, free-market philosophies, there is truth in the description of these self-help groups as examples of 'training grounds for democracy'.[223] They certainly demonstrate the strength of working-class self-help and its ability to organize.[224] The union movement of the nineteenth century must have built on thousands of similar hidden initiatives. The union of the Dorset farm labourers, transported in 1834 as a lesson to others with similar aims, was called the Tolpuddle *Friendly Society* of Agricultural Labourers.

John Stevenson once commented that rural workers, 'hindered by illiteracy and less frequent exposure to the world of pamphlets and news-papers, lagged almost a generation or more behind their urban counterparts in the forms of their protest'.[225] Yet what is most intriguing about the protest described in the pages above is the number of times that both rudimentary and more sophisticated literacies were called upon – in the anonymous letters, handbills, tickets stuck in hats, graffiti, poor-law and emigrant letters, autobiographies, club-banner mottoes and the organizational records of friendly society and union.[226] The union leader, George Edwards, used to get his wife to read the newspapers to him before he learned to read.[227] But even if participation was mediated, protest was by no means cut off from the influences of literacy and print. Union commentators were insistent about the role played by the newspaper in their momentary success.

We should therefore be wary of presenting rural protest as somehow isolated from modernity, or, worse still, as a late arrival to the advanced repertory of such activity. Superficially, the history of rural protest could be moulded into the framework of Charles Tilly's modernization theory of British contentious repertoires, with the parochial protest of 1816 at the beginning of our period, transformed into the more politically sophisticated social movement of unionism in the 1870s.[228] Hopefully, readers of this chapter will resist such teleological tendencies. My preference is for the history of varying strategies. Rather than charting great turning-points or patterns of the transformation of rural protest, it makes far better sense to see rural workers as practising the art of the possible, employing a varied repertoire of resistance, according to context and opportunity.

8 Picturing Rural Work

Patrick Wright has outlined what he has termed a conservative attachment to 'Deep England', based on a strong sense of evocation, of actually 'being there' and seeing, hearing and smelling. However, what is interesting is that while experience is essential to this sense of Englishness, labour is more peripheral. The landscape is certainly central, as indicated by H. A. L. Fisher in 1933:

> The unique and incommunicable beauty of the English landscape constitutes for most Englishmen the strongest of all the ties which bind them to their country. However far they travel, they carry the English landscape in their hearts. As the scroll of memory unwinds itself, scene after scene returns with its complex

8 John Brett, *The Stonebreaker* (1857–58)

association of sight and hearing, the emerald green of an English May, the carpet of primroses in the clearing, the pellucid trout-stream, the fat kine browsing in the park, the cricket matches on the village green, the church spire pointing upwards to the pale-blue sky, the fragrant smell of wood fires, the butterflies on chalk hills, the lark rising from the plough into the March wind, or the morning salutation of blackbird or thrush from garden laurels. These and many other notes blend in a harmony the elements of which we do not attempt to disentangle, for each part communicates its sweetness to the other.[1]

The animals that inhabit the countryside are important to this sense of Englishness, yet the workers of that landscape are almost invisible in these descriptions of primroses, trout-streams, larks rising, and cows. The tradition continues in Roger Scruton's recent elegy. His England under threat comprises 'English character', 'English religion', 'English culture' and – the book's shortest chapter – the 'English countryside'. Again, it is countryside without workers. There are certainly hedges and country-houses, especially the latter. The country-house represents 'an ideal of English civilisation – one in which hierarchy was softened by neighbourliness, and wealth by mutual aid'. 'They are the last signs of what England was like, when those who governed it also dwelled in it.'[2] Where are the workers in this heritage?

It is tempting to assume a continuing tradition of elision, linking the visual arts of the eighteenth century to these twentieth-century tropes. In George Stubbs's late eighteenth-century imagery of *Haymakers* (1783) and *Reapers* (1784), rural labour had appeared as the upper class in lower-class drag, although the clothing, it must be said, is rather clean and refined.[3] Whatever our take on the representability of 'historical reality', we are a long way from it with Thomas Gainsborough's incongruous figure, *Peasant Girl Gathering Faggots* (1782). We can be sure that this 'peasant girl' never so much as touched a faggot, and that the girl, whoever she was, was no peasant.[4] The temptation to treat the nineteenth century as a mere stage in a continuity of representation is reinforced by John Barrell's work on John Constable. Constable's rural workers inhabit the 'dark side of the landscape', in Barrell's famous phrase. 'The labourers do not step between us and the landscape – they keep their place, and it is a very small place, a long way away.'[5] The landscape dominates these paintings. Those who toiled the fields or worked in the woods are marginal, miniscule or invisible. But how characteristic was this marginalization in visual representations of the rural during the nineteenth century?

* * *

There is a great deal of visual evidence for the rural worker domesticated and tamed. We can see it in reproductions of George Morland's 'rustic scenes'.[6] It is there in paintings by Francis Wheatley.[7] Christiana Payne has stressed that the work of William Collins, Thomas Faed, Thomas Webster and David Wilkie presented early Victorian ideals of the poor but contented, rural working-class family. These images, engravings as well as actual paintings, were intended as comfort for their middle- and upper-class viewers and purchasers, but possibly also to impart a message to the working class about the virtues of rural life.[8] A similar argument has been made of the landscapes of the prolific John Linnell, whose harvest paintings appeared 25 times at the Royal Academy's annual exhibitions between 1852 and 1881. His richly coloured and thickly textured paintings presented 'an imaginary past … to ward off the anguish of the present'.[9] Timothy Barringer's analysis of the landscapes of Linnell and George Vicat Cole in the 1850s and 1860s demonstrates the tensions between representing workers in a landscape that middle- and upper-class viewers and consumers associated with leisure and pleasure.[10] The realities of dirty and hard harvest work are constantly anaesthetized by brilliant colours and glazes, and the subjects of these paintings, when not invisible, seem to be at play even when they are working.[11]

Nineteenth-century art is certainly littered with pictorial vignettes of pleased peasants, cheerful cottagers, and rural romps among the bluebells. It is particularly visible in the work of Myles Birket Foster and the colony of artists who lived in and around the village of Witley, in Surrey.[12] One of Birket Foster's neighbours, the watercolourist Helen Allingham, specialized in the genre of cottage art. An article in *The Art Journal* of 1888 described her oeuvre perfectly. 'Her little people belong to the rosy, light-hearted tribe . . . They are placed in the prettiest setting, and whether the fruit trees are in blossom, the commons are brilliant with heather and gorse, or leaves are brown at the waning of the year, these young rustics appear just where their presence is required.' Allingham produced more than a thousand paintings, all on much the same theme:

> She is a painter of Nature pure and simple – Nature in her brightest and most agreeable aspects, untouched by affectation, unspoiled by sorrow or any shadow of distress . . . The small children of the homesteads are in their prettiest frocks and whitest aprons; their elder sisters, busily sewing in the neat kitchen or parlour lit by soft sunshine, appear ideal mates for the rustic lovers of their dreams; and the young mothers, guarding the cradle or zealously preserving the brightness of the hearth and of their crockery and pans, are all that good house-wives should be. In Mrs. Allingham's Art there is no trace of sympathy with the stern realism to which we have grown accustomed in the works of so many modern painters. For her there would be little attraction of a pictorial kind in the marks of grime and toil on rugged hands and bronzed faces . . .[13]

Sunshine, cleanliness and the youth and feminine vulnerability of care-fully-chosen subjects erased the corporeal reality of poorly-paid rural labour. Unsurprisingly, the most-used colour on her palette was yellow.[14]

Commentaries on these metaphorical air-brushings completed the process. Allingham's *Crossing the Meadows* was a 'charming drawing of a lithe and slender country maiden walking in a meadow path and carrying a pail of milk', with 'movements almost rhythmical in their comeliness, and so much grace and beauty of line, and elegance of air'.[15] Davidson Knowles's drawing, *Honiton Lace Making*, was of a 'lovely child, whose beauty has been fostered in its softness of line and colour by the humid breezes of Devonshire downs and valleys . . . and the artist has given her docility a singular charm'.[16] Such imagery obviously had appeal for the social elite. William Collins's *Rustic Civility* (1832), with its peasant child touching his forelock, was bought by the Duke of Devonshire for 250 guineas.[17]

One is tempted to observe that the critics would not have known a rural worker if she had arrived at their doorstep. The writer for the *Magazine of Art* waxed lyrical on W. Q. Orchardson's *The Farmer's Daughter* (1884), 'a superb creature'. Yet it is hard to imagine anything less like a farming woman. She is more like one of the Greek Muses.[18] Christopher Wood has observed that we 'might be forgiven for thinking that all Victorian farm workers were married to artists' models'.[19] Frederick Walker, whose brief career as an illustrator and painter ended with his death in 1875, actually used one of his sisters as the main model in *The Vagrants* (1867), a painting of a gypsy camp: 'The vile gypsies had "struck camp" by the time I got there, so now I give them up, and go at my models here. The fools! to let money slip through their fingers.'[20] The Pre-Raphaelite, Ford Madox Brown, painted vibrant, compelling landscapes, but the figures (genteel, urban, leisured) in the fore-ground of *An English Autumn Afternoon* (1852–55) and *Walton-on-the-Naze* (1860) are clearly not those who worked that land.[21] When the *real thing* intruded, they were an unwelcome and uncomfortable distraction. Madox Brown (*Carrying Corn* [1854–55] and *The Hayfield* [1855–56]) was entranced by the colours of the hayfields in the twilight, but merely irritated by a 'degraded wretch' who tried to hit upon him for beer money.[22]

Even when the working subject is in the foreground, and that subject is engaged in hard, non-romantic labour, artistic composition can conspire. Two powerful portraits of male workers engaged in the exhausting occupa-tion of stone-breaking, both called *The Stonebreaker* and both exhibited in 1858, are arguably subverted by the paintings' colours. The flint in John Brett's work, like the shirt of the young worker, is an adjunct to the blues and violets of a vibrant Surrey landscape, while the rich autumnal colours of Henry Wallis's painting of the same name is resonant of leafy repose rather than death among broken stone. The stones in one picture look more like plants; the rocks in the other appear as fallen leaves.[23] Contemporary critics, however, tended to contrast the works, exhibited in different rooms at the Royal Academy. Wallis's portrait of a dead, elderly worker, though admired, was suspected of social didacticism. Brett's young stone-breaker, which may have contained a religious message, was viewed as a beautiful landscape that happened to have a human figure in its foreground.[24] The model for the figure in Brett's painting, by the way, was not a young labourer but the artist's brother.[25] (See Plate 8.)

William Holman Hunt's study of rural courtship, *The Hireling Shepherd* (1851), broke many of the unwritten rules of rural representation. His 'workers' are not working. They are not neutralized by being miniaturized into the landscape. The flirting shepherd and shepherdess are centre stage in the composition, and Hunt used a genuine farm girl as a model. Moreover, critics were scandalized by what they took to be the indecorous realism of the work, writing, in shocked tones, of the traces of class inscribed on the couple's bodies, in their wiry hair, large feet and sunburned complexions. 'These rustics are of the coarsest breed,' wrote the art critic of the *Athenaeum*, 'literal transcriptions of stout, sunburnt, out-of-door labourers.' Yet the Pre-Raphaelite clothing of these literal rustics, and the painting's beauty, lighting, colours and landscape create resonances far removed from anything approaching labouring realism. Hunt, it is worth recalling, intended the painting as an allegory of the minister dallying while his flock wandered.[26]

As Deborah Cherry has explained, landscape art was a luxury commodity in the nineteenth century, and its purchasers and dealers wanted the inhabitants and workers of the rural to be equally picturesque.[27] Thus the bodies of workers rendered as 'they really were' compromised the desired pleasing beauty. We see this clearly in the *Athenaeum*'s reactions to the servant in Joanna Wells's *Peep-bo* (1861): 'No doubt the servant-girl's face is excellent as a portrait, and so interesting to her acquaintances and friends; but without desiring invariable beauty in pictures, we do feel objection to sheer ugliness as not desirable in Art. Her hands are large beyond natural requirements or the habit of labour.'[28] This was a criticism later levelled at the work of the realists. Domestic service could be represented in paint, and in sculpture, but it had to be offered in the appropriate form. *The Housemaid* (1894), a life-size bronze statue by Thomas Woolner, was praised by *The Art Journal*, even though it was of a servant on her knees at a bucket. Indeed, it marked 'a new departure in sculpture, because it applies to a subject of common life the canons of the noblest style'.[29] The paintings of Alice Havers often dealt with potentially unsettling subjects: women's hard labour, death and rural sexuality. However, the poses of her working subjects were drawn from the repertoire and conventions of Greek and Roman sculpture. To quote Cherry, 'the starkness of the event is mitigated by the painting's visual and narrative strategies'.[30]

Arthur Munby, a minor poet and collector of images of women's labour, was scathing of the erasure of working women's bodies in Victorian art, raising the subject with John Ruskin in 1859, when viewing the latter's collection of paintings by J. M. W. Turner and William Henry Hunt. He told Ruskin that someone should 'paint peasant girls & servant maids as they are – coarse & hearty & homely – and so shame the false whitehanded wenches of modern art. *These* have been painted as they are, but *women*, never: spurious refinement & false delicacy prevent it – as if a housemaid was not as well worth painting as a lady – & as if, being painted, she ought to be idealised & varnished with the halfgentility of a lady's maid!'[31] Munby and others fetishized breaches of pleasing beauty.[32] But their fetishism could not have existed without the dominance of the aesthetically pleasing.

* * *

There are exceptions to the alternatives of romanticization and invisibility, to the bucolic bumpkins on, or behind, the hill. There is certainly no intended competition with the landscape in the later Victorian social realist paintings of Sir George Clausen, Henry Herbert La Thangue, Sir Hubert von Herkomer and Stanhope Alexander Forbes. (See Plate 9.) It is difficult to overlook the body and the stare of the labouring woman in Jules Bastien-Lepage's *Les Foins* [*Haymakers*] (1878), one of the best-known works of the French Naturalist artist so influential upon Clausen, La Thangue and Forbes.[33] When the painting was exhibited in London at the Grosvenor Gallery in 1880, the *Illustrated London News* alluded to the gorilla-like appearance of the young peasant woman, while the *Magazine of Art* described 'the passive dreaming of an animal'.[34] Nevertheless, even these paintings have their agendas.[35]

Although Herkomer used real workers as his models for his famous *Hard Times* (1885), the effect is of a Roman general in worker's guise.[36] (See Plate 10.) The neo-classicism of *Hard Times* is very similar to the work of Alice Havers, referred to earlier, particularly her painting, *The End of Her Journey* (1877).[37] Frederick Walker, who influenced the realists, was praised by Herkomer for 'combining the grace of the antique with the realism of our everyday life in England. His navvies are Greek gods, and yet not a bit the less true to nature. True poet that he was, he felt that all nature should be represented as a poem.'[38] Herkomer's lifestyle was

9 Henry La Thangue, *Harrowing* (*c*.1899)

Although the man and woman are central to the painting, engaged in hard work, and have dirty clothing (browns dominate the image), they are represented as noble figures. The painting also shows the influences of Impressionism

rather different from that of his rural working subjects. He was a renowned portraitist of society figures, royalty and industrialists; his painting of the Directors of Krups brought him £10 000 in 1912. He lived in the intriguingly named Lululaund, a Gothic/Art Nouveau mansion in his ideal village, Bushey, and was certainly capable of idealized notions of rural folk. He later described his painting, *Our Village* (1889), as capturing the essence of 'a sleepy, picturesque village ... women and children were standing about in picturesque groups awaiting the husbands and fathers coming from their daily labours. There was a somnolence and there was a peace unattainable in our day.' One critic described it as 'a sort of bucolic idyll'. Interestingly, Herkomer was responsible for the illustrations for Thomas Hardy's *Tess of the d'Urbervilles*, when it was serialized in *The Graphic* in 1891.[39]

10 Hubert von Herkomer, *Hard Times* (1885)

Christiana Payne has pointed out that Clausen's realism was distasteful to the buying public, forcing him to modify his art.[40] Reactions to his painting, *A Field-Hand* (1882), also known as *Head of a Peasant Woman* (used as the cover for this book), were certainly intense. It was condemned as 'excessively ugly, . . . painted for its ugliness' sake, and nothing else'.

> It is a bust-portrait of an elderly field-hand. She has little or no forehead; her cheeks, all weather-worn and coarse with exposure, are purpled in their staring redness; her mouth is a mere gash; her hands, clasped on the top of a hay-fork, are brutalised with work, with fingers worn to the bone, and stubby, grubby, grimy nails, each one carefully crescented with black. She wears an old black bonnet, a grey shawl, a white *fichu*, and a lilac dress, and she confronts you – dull, squalid, uninteresting – with all the solemn stupidity of what by a contradiction in terms is called 'realistic art'.[41]

Similarly, Clausen's *Labourers after Dinner* (1884) provoked considerable hostility. When it was displayed several years later, George Moore used the opportunity to pen a savage critique:

> Realism, that is to say the desire to compete with nature, to be nature, is the disease from which art has suffered most in the last twenty years. The disease is

now at wane, and when we happen upon a canvas of the period like 'Labourers after Dinner', we cry out, 'What madness! were we ever as mad as that?' . . . Until I saw Mr. Clausen's 'Labourers' I did not fully realise how terrible a thing art becomes when divorced from beauty, grace, mystery, and suggestion. It would be difficult to say where and how this picture differs from a photograph; it seems to me to be little more than the vices of photography magnified. . . .

The subject of this picture is a group of field labourers finishing their mid-day dinner in the shade of some trees. They are portrayed in a still even light, exactly as they were; the picture is one long explanation; it is as clear as a newspaper, and it reads like one. We can tell how many months that man in the foreground has worn those dreadful hobnailed boots; we can count the nails, and we notice that two or three are missing. Those disgusting corduroy trousers have hung about his legs for so many months; all the ugliness of these labourers' faces and the solid earthiness of their lives are there; nothing has been omitted, curtailed, or exaggerated. There is some psychology. We can see that the years have brought the old man cunning rather than wisdom. The middle-aged man and the middle-aged woman live in mute stupidity – they have known nothing but the daily hardship of living, and the vacuous face of their son tells how completely the life of his forefathers has descended upon him. . . . Mr. Clausen has seen nothing but the sordid and the mean, and his execution in this picture is as sordid and as mean as his vision.

Moore concluded, 'I can imagine no valid reason for the portrayal of so much ugliness.'[42]

It is intriguing that images relatively unchallenging to our sensibilities should provoke such reactions. Ironically, these paintings were sanitized versions of the photographs Clausen took as his life studies. The clothing of the female mangold cutter in *Winter Work* (1883–84), the same model used in *A Field-Hand*, is far less ragged than the original.[43] (See Plates 11 and 12.) The responses to Clausen tell us more about genteel male assumptions about the bodily aesthetics of class and gender than they do about rural labour. The *Magazine of Art* was kinder, even enthusiastic, about his later – and softer – paintings. *A Girl's Head*, reviewed in 1887, was 'the best picture in the exhibition'. *The Girl at the Gate*, reviewed in 1890, was 'reality . . . based on a true picturesque conception'. *The Shepherdess*, reviewed in 1891, was 'an admirable specimen of Mr. Clausen's best manner'. Unlike the despised *A Field-Hand*, the subjects of these paintings are all 'girls'.[44] Karen Sayer has suggested that Clausen's tendency towards monumentalism also removed him from his subjects. Furthermore, he was caught up in representing rural labour as a symbol of national strength and character: 'By this time celebration of the rural could not be separated from the celebration of Englishness, nation and empire.'[45]

11 George Clausen, *Winter Work* (1883–84)

Naturalism in the visual arts more or less corresponds to the later period covered in this book, from the late 1870s through to the early 1900s. Gabriel Weisberg has characterized its English variant, represented by Clausen, La Thangue, Stanhope Forbes, Herkomer and the photographer, Peter Henry Emerson, as attempting to present a 'slice of life', situating its subjects in their natural environment, often at work, bathing them in light and colour, and attending to detail (of dress, for example) through preparatory use of photography.[46] The whole purpose of realism or naturalism was to move out of the studio into the open air (or to make the studio as close to nature as possible: glass studios were sometimes used) and to record its workers in their natural environment. In the fishing settlement of Newlyn in Cornwall, the artists' studios were concentrated in a meadow overlooking the bay. Villagers became accustomed to posing. 'And what better material could artists have wished for', Stanhope Forbes observed in 1898, 'A fine-knit race of men and women, engaged in healthy and picturesque occupation, and one which by its nature gives the painter his opportunity, when storms and tempests arise, to secure the necessary sittings; swarms of children, many of them charmingly pretty; no wonder that enough material has been

12 George Clausen, Woman in a turnip field, *c.* 1883
A photographic study used in *Winter Work*

found to keep us engaged these many years.'[47] Although working human subjects were in the foreground of their paintings, the naturalists' interest in their subjects was as a part of a larger whole. Though visually central, their models were as ideologically invisible as the miniaturized figure in a Constable. Forbes reflected that 'The people seemed to fall naturally into their places, and to harmonise with their surroundings . . . [with fishermen] obliged to don their quaint souwesters and duck-frocks and all the rest of their picturesque attire which one is always struck with in strolling through a fishing village . . . not only the dress, but its wearers were alike weather-stained, and tanned into harmony by the sun and the salt wind, so that the whole scene was in keeping and of one piece.'[48] Note the words 'naturally', 'harmonise' and 'harmony', combined with 'quaint' and 'picturesque'.

* * *

The relationship between landscape and the human figure continued as an important consideration for the arbiters of Victorian artistic taste. Poses of rural workers were acceptable for the *Magazine of Art*'s reviewer if the figures were 'inseparably associated with the atmosphere and tone of their surroundings'. It was the field behind rather than the figure of the worker that determined the 'naturalism' of a picture.[49] Herkomer's *Hard Times* (see Plate 10) was unthreatening because it melded landscape and figures. 'The triangular group in the foreground . . . suggests, no doubt, a foreground conclusion; but it is perfectly natural, and has as much verisimilitude about it as the delicately drawn trees on the extreme right, and the road below it which takes such a magnificent sweep. All these are elements in the composition which the artist has blended most pleasantly'; all the intentions of the artist are thus neatly bypassed.[50] Conversely, one of the offending characteristics of Clausen's *A Field-Hand*, exhibited at the Royal Institute in 1885, was the lack of a background to detract from the 'fact of the model's actuality', a telling phrase indicating the force of her face and hands. 'Seen under certain appropriate conditions of light and air, placed in a right environment, the centre of interest in a fitting scheme of values, the personality of Mr. Clausen's model might have been made acceptable as artistic material, and its representation have been shown to be a legitimate achievement in art.'[51]

Moore's savage reaction to *Labourers*, discussed earlier, contrasted to his praise of Clausen's later painting, *The Mowers* (1891). The difference lay in the *Mowers'* lighting, the beauty of its setting, and the lack of detail in the workers' clothing and faces: 'Things ugly in themselves become beautiful by association; or perhaps I should say that they become picturesque.'[52] A book on Clausen, published in 1923, all but ignored his early work, but also isolated *The Mowers* as representing the artist's shift to a softer Impressionism. The difference between the early (unapproved) Clausen and his later (approved) work hinged on the relation between his rural workers and their landscape. Form is less distinct in the later art, and there is 'subordination of the human figures to the scene in which they are placed'.[53] La Thangue also moved 'towards Impressionism'. His dappled and unfocused figures in a light-conscious landscape created images vastly different from his earlier realism. The *Graphic* noted this shift in a review in 1899: 'Mr. La Thangue shows by the lack of expression in his figures' faces that he sympathises more with nature and effects of atmosphere and light than with the men and women whose hard lives he paints.'[54] The farm worker in his *The Water-plash* (1900) is a distant adjunct to the rather more prominent geese.[55]

The logic of containment applied to earlier, more unsettling works. George Morland's occasionally subversive late eighteenth-century images of the rural poor were perfectly acceptable a century later. *The Art Journal* wrote in 1898 of his *Gipsy Encampment* (then in the collection of the Earl of Normanton) that 'it is so pervaded by a sense of style that its realism gives no hint of vulgarity, and its truth tends not the least in the direction of coarseness. The scene represented is frankly taken from low life, and the people who play their part in the rustic drama are but a set of wandering outcasts; but the artist has had the good judgment to subordinate squalor to picturesqueness.'[56]

There was certainly no diminution of interest in rural imagery as the century ended. Paintings exhibited at the Royal Academy in 1899, for instance, included Frank Bramley's *The Gossips*; Clausen's *Going to Work*; H. W. B. Davis's *Approaching Night* and *Going Home*; Alfred East's *A Coombe in the Cotswolds*; Rudolph Onslow Ford's *A February Morning*; C. E. Johnson's *Silver Poplars*; Walter Langley's *Wandering Musicians*; B. W. Leader's *Evening's Last Gleam* and *Summer Eve by Haunted Stream*; G. D. Leslie's *The Peaceful Highway*; J. MacWhirter's *Crabbed Age and Youth*; David Murray's *The Church Pool*; the Impressionist Edward Stott's *The Harvester's Return*; and E. A. Waterlow's *Forest Oaks*. Some of these paintings – *Going to Work*, *The Gossips*, *The Harvester's Return* and *Wandering Musicians* – made rural workers central to their composition. However, most were of animals, trees, buildings and water, with people either absent or peripheral.[57] *The Art Journal* of the preceding year declared its preferences in a feature on the work of the watercolourist, David Cox, who had exhibited nearly a thousand works by the time he died in 1859. 'No man ever painted figures and other incidents in landscape with finer fitness or truer character, and in depicting the leading features, such as trees, buildings, and skies, he was a veritable master.'[58]

The rural inhabitants of landscapes were incidental; trees and skies were pre-eminent.

Appropriately, the work of John Constable (with which we began the discussion of this chapter) had increased in visibility and popularity. There were prints of his famous *The Hay-wain* (1820–21) all over London at the end of the nineteenth century, and cheap picture cards in many humble house-holds.[59] *The Hay-wain* has figures in its foreground, but they may as well not be there, for the viewer's eye is immediately drawn towards the light of the horizon. Indeed Barrell uses the work to demonstrate his 'dark side of the landscape' thesis.[60] An early twentieth-century critic referred even less kindly to the painting as 'merely an aggregate of circumstances suggesting fine weather'.[61]

There are various ways of dividing the history of British landscape art. Peter Howard has come up with a series of overlapping periods: the Picturesque, 1790–1830; the Romantic, 1830–70; and the Heroic, 1870–1910. Actual people feature in these representations of rural life only in the last phase, and here, as the name suggests, they are heavily idealized as the heroic worker. The prevailing subject matter – with chronological variation and varying emphasis upon county – is rivers, ruins, castles, cathedrals, woods, estuaries, lakes, mountains, waterfalls, moors, valleys, churches, trees, cottages and villages.[62]

* * *

Male photographers and collectors, even those acclaimed as pioneers of photographic realism, also objectified and distanced through lighting and pose.

Misconceptions of empathy vanish when the work of such men is exam-ined in conjunction with their diaries. In other words, far from being an unproblematic representation of rural lives, photography really got no closer to its subjects. Indeed, one leading photographer, Henry Peach Robinson, persuaded his friends and family to pose as 'peasants' for his compositions. A ' "fresh caught peasant" was rarely capable of serving as a capable model.'[63] He would buy the clothing of working women for his stand-ins, and considered a professional model 'nearer to nature' than the genuine article. The language behind his photography is notable in its condescending use of animal imagery and notions of capture, as in his reference to 'a picturesque model caught wild, but too stupid to be of any use. Naturally she had a delightful smile, and although I tried all I knew for a fortnight to overcome her timidity – mixed her with tame models, as they train wild elephants – she remained camera-shy, and I could do nothing with her. I did the next best thing. I bought her clothes.'[64] 'I seldom find the "real thing" to quite answer my purpose', Robinson wrote, in a manual still consulted by art students, 'The aboriginal is seldom sufficiently intelligent to be of use, especially if you have "intention" in your work.'[65] For this photographer, then, a portrait of a rural worker, to 'natural effect', could consist of a child of the gentry on a moving platform made up of 'turf, ferns, heath, &c.', in front of a painted screen in an artist's studio![66] (See Plate 13.) Robinson's famous *Bringing Home the May* (1862) was composed over several days, and consisted of a composite of nine different negatives.[67] Robinson was a great fan of Birket Foster, and he followed the artist's fondness for posed and idealized rural work – 'implausibly arcadian', as one critic has termed it.[68] (See Plate 14.)

It is tempting to contrast Robinson with another Victorian rural photographer, P. H. Emerson, with the latter as the realist ethnographer of actual labour. Compare *A Holiday in the Wood* (1860) with *During the Reed Harvest* (1886) or *Polling the Marsh Hay* (1886). (See Plates 14, 15, and 16.) However, it would be a mistake to overlook the artifice of Emerson's images.[69] You 'must choose your models most carefully', he advised, 'and they must without fail be picturesque and typical. The student should feel that there never was such a fisherman, or such a ploughman, or such a poacher, or such an old man, or such a beautiful girl, as he is picturing.'[70] He was constantly on the lookout for 'picturesque models'.[71] Although Emerson's powerful photographs may be viewed differently by twenty-first century readers of this book, there is no denying the evidence of his lack of empathy for his subjects. Consider this explanation of his photograph of a ploughman, *A Stiff Pull* (1888): 'Our plate shows us a stiff pull, such as is life for many. Like the horses and the ploughman in the plate, they must look neither to the right nor to the left, but straight before them, putting all their strength into their work. Slowly they climb the steep ascent of years, and finally, when they have reached the top, they sink down exhausted under the disappointments of life's imperfections. But this honest peasant, a true son of Suffolk, dogged, grasping, not overly intelligent, and rather boorish, little recks he of such thoughts.'[72] 'Who can probe the workings of his simple mind?' he said of the subject for his *Haymaker with Rake* (1888).[73]

As portrayed in either Emerson's photographs, or in his long captions, rural workers are part of the landscape, specimens rather than individuals.[74] The text accompanying *Coming Home from the Marshes* (1886) (see Plate 2) begins, 'Along the marsh wall comes a group of labourers returning from their short day's work. Typical specimens these of the Norfolk peasant, – wiry in body, pleasant in manner, intelligent in mind. Their lot, though hard, is not unpleasant.' Or here is the description of *Haymaker with Rake* (1888):

13 One of H. P. Robinson's models, 1860s

An illustration from his book, *Pictorial Effect in Photography* (1869)

14 H. P. Robinson, *A Holiday in the Wood* (1860)
An early example of photomontage, and a highly artificial depiction of rural life

From a superficial examination of the Norfolk peasant we find two predomi-
nating types; the commoner being men of average height, with rather small
massive heads, high cheek-bones, dark bright eyes, and black hair. These men
are very active, intelligent, and wiry. The other type is of larger muscular
development, with light or reddish hair and grey or blue eyes. These also are
good workers, and, though not so active as the smaller men, are mentally
superior to them. Both here and in Suffolk the smallness of the hands and feet
is very noticeable. In the plate of the haymaker resting we have a specimen of
the smaller dark type of peasant. The marsh-hay has been cut, and he has
been sent with others on a threatening afternoon to rake it into cocks, lest the
coming rainstorm should wet it during the night. He has nearly done his
work, and is resting on his rake. Behind him the marsh is dotted with
haycocks; before him, in the distance, stretches the broad, across which he
can just see his cottage-home silhouetted against the sky. His face and the
haycocks are softly lighted up by the setting sun, which is nearly clouded over
by the coming storm.[75]

As Jennifer Green has observed, Emerson's workers were of 'no more
consequence than a marsh heron, an eel, a cottage, yet as necessary to the

15 P. H. Emerson, *During the Reed Harvest* (1886)

'The cutting and harvesting of the reed afford profitable employment to the Broadman, marshman, or farm-hand during the winter months, when other work is scarce': P. H. Emerson and T. F. Goodall, *Life and Landscape on the Norfolk Broads* (London, 1886). Goodall, an artist, considered reed cutting 'picturesque labour'

elements of the picturesque as all these'.[76] His *Pictures of East Anglian Life* (1888) was a 'Natural History of the English Peasantry and Fisherfolk', and it was indeed written like a natural history.[77]

The records of the London Camera Club for the late 1880s and 1890s reflect the tastes of a wider photographic fraternity. They were not discordant with the tendencies of the artists explored in the pages above. Their photographic excursions to picturesque Surrey villages – picturesque was a key word for this fraternity – were almost always in search of scenery, buildings, and flora and fauna. Their subjects were cottages, water mills, fine trees, old sheds, village pumps, streams, bridges, and sandpits and sand martins.[78] A trip to Gomshall focused on 'fine views', flowering gorse, and sheep under a tree. The models during the outing to Godstone were ducks, roosters and swans.[79] The excursion to Nutfield resulted in plates of groups of cattle and farm buildings, as

16 P. H. Emerson, *Polling the Marsh Hay* (1886)

From P. H. Emerson and T. F. Goodall, *Life and Landscape on the Norfolk Broads* (London, 1886)

well as the area's 'exquisite scenery'. A more distant expedition to the Norfolk Broads 'bagged' images of 'a family of little porkers, ducks, horses, all, of course, properly located among local scenery, Norfolk dykes, reed-lined marshes, &c.'[80] Although hop-pickers appear to have been photographed at Heathfield in Sussex, there was a tendency to avoid worker subjects. One member of the Club explained that the real thing was too awkward when confronted by the camera, or had a tendency to move, but that upper-class models dressed in 'imitation-rustic garb' looked unreal. 'Owing to the many difficulties in obtaining suitable figures, it is well, I think, in a great number of instances to ask such persons as are present to "move on", and to take the view without them . . . Still, if the grouping and posing are satisfactory, and the figures harmonise with the view, there is no doubt that they add greatly to the artistic effect.'[81] Another member thought that there was little point in capturing the image of a woman knitting or an old man at his pipe: 'Now, in the sky what a field of work for the photographer there is.'[82] For these weekend photographers, the rural workers had a provisional place in their own landscape.

As with landscape painters, some of these photographers were deliberately seeking 'untouched villages'. They wanted to capture a rural England threatened by modernity: 'Scientific farming has done much to injure the beauty of the country, and the picturesqueness of agricultural life.' Their photography intended to capture 'the picturesque side of country life' that was 'rapidly becoming a thing of the past'. Hence the fascination with thatched cottages in the face of corrugated iron.[83] (See Plate 17.) J. Gale, a master of the genre, favoured the 'wild commons' and 'charming cottages' of Surrey, the wattle and daub of rural Berkshire, and the whitewash and thatch of Essex. He also focused on windmills and watermills, other icons of that disappearing countryside. Costume and tools were included in his list: the labourer's smock, Kentish and Sussex ploughs, and the sickle and flail. But the wearers of the clothing and the wielders of the tools were almost there by sufferance. Shepherds positioned the sheep; carters controlled the teams of horses that were the primary concern of the

17 George Dawson, *A Berkshire Village Street* (1895)
Note the artificiality of the scene

photographer. A shepherd was only of interest if he wore 'an out-of-date military cloak'.[84]

* * *

Several of the great collectors of rural art were based in industrial and commercial urban centres. The City Art Gallery of Manchester purchased Herkomer's *Hard Times*. (See Plate 10.) Councillor John Maddocks, a self-made and very wealthy cloth-exporter, owned work by La Thangue, Bramley, Stanhope Forbes and Stott, and the more than two hundred pictures he loaned to the Bradford Gallery in 1891 included 11 Clausens.[85] The Bradford alderman and mohair-manufacturer, Abraham Mitchell, who had his own private gallery, was a patron of La Thangue.[86] Another Bradford local politician, the mill-owner, Isaac Smith, Mayor of Bradford in the 1880s, had Clausens and La Thangues. His collection included the latter's *Leaving Home* (1890), a painting of a young woman leaving home for work as a domestic servant.[87] Sharpley Bainbridge, a Lincoln merchant and manufacturer of ready-made clothing, was yet another great patron of images of rural labour; fitting, given that much of his money was from the clothing that they wore. He was a patron of Clausen, and owned 50 paintings by Birket Foster, and others by Herkomer, La Thangue and Stanhope Forbes. His collection contained social criticism as well as social conservatism, ranging from Stanhope Forbes's subversive *By Order of the Court* (1890) to Birket Foster's large watercolour of happy workers, *The Haymakers*. He also owned Clausen's *The Mowers* and La Thangue's *The Old Peasant*.[88] These men, agents of the very process that was transforming so many rural worlds and lives, displayed images of that disappearing world on the walls of their drawing rooms and galleries. (See Plate 18.) These images varied in their selective amnesia: there were paintings to trouble as well as to salve consciences.

The existence of these collections suggests that the narrative of nineteenth-century rural representations belongs in the realm of *urban* history. The demand for landscape imagery in the early nineteenth century, in purchase, exhibition, prints, and in journal and newspaper publicity and reproduction, was city-based.[89] Similarly, the French bourgeoisie sought relief from the pressures of modernity by seeking immersion in nature and 'natural life'; 'the fantasy was of a complete but temporary immersion which would restore the mental and spiritual equilibrium ruptured by the city's frenzy'.[90] This could be achieved by a walk in a city garden or park, by an excursion to the country, or merely by a glance at a picture. A landscape painting, or even a critic's description of

18 Mr Sharpley Bainbridge's drawing-room

A photograph from an article in the *Art Journal*, 1898, discussing his collection. Birket Foster's *Haymakers* is the large painting above the cabinet

their response to that representation, could transport the viewer or reader into the realm of a conjured, lived experience.[91] One can assume similar fantasies in bourgeois England. Thus the late Victorian art of Leslie Thomson 'is sympathetic with the quiet mood of the fisherman, with the dreaminess that comes over the solitary walker on moors in grey weather, or at the fall of evening when his eye, overlooking the sticks and stones and trivialities at his feet, broods on a vast sky and distance'.[92] Alice Meynell likewise bathed readers of *The Art Journal* of 1889 in the misty calm of rural, coastal Cornwall, captured in the paintings of the Newlyn School:

> There is a singular charm in the repose of this scene involved in soft summer mist, with no one left behind upon the seaward hill but children and women, and the dogs who so energetically encourage the enterprises in which they can take no more active part, and the old man whose fishing days are over . . . The pretty backs of boys' heads direct our attention to the interest of this little coast – the sails soon to be absorbed by the warm and tender mist. The backs of young children's heads have always a certain beauty of mere youth and innocence, which they have in common with the same part of the construction of kittens and cygnets. And lying round the peaceful coast Mr. Detmold has painted a yet more peaceful sea, a sea as it is on the English south-west littoral, with the beautiful lucid surface capable of reflections which are themselves an intricate yet distinctively impressionary study.[93]

The rural signified the tranquillity of a lost age in the face of change. One of the clues to the appeal of Victorian and Edwardian rural imagery lies with that constantly recurring word, 'picturesque'. By aestheticizing the landscape and its occupants, the picturesque provided a literal or virtual site for leisure and pleasure in momentary escape from modernity. The 'charm of country life' in a painting imparted 'the restfulness and repose of those rural retreats which still remain happily untouched by the restless influences of modern civilization'.[94]

Barringer has suggested that the process of rural objectification intensified in England with the development of the railway that linked London to a network of villages within easy access. Escape and refreshment were a short trip away. Several prominent landscape artists, we have seen, moved to villages in the immediate south-east. Vicat Cole and Linnell lived near commuter railway stations in Hampshire and Surrey.[95] Richard Redgrave had a summer residence in Abinger, Surrey, believed to be the setting for his painting, *The Emigrant's Last Sight of Home* (1858).[96] (See Plate 19.) Stott and La Thangue lived in Sussex villages.[97] Indeed, one reviewer suggested rural Sussex as England's equivalent to Barbizon, the French peasant village colonized by nineteenth-century artists in search of the picturesque.[98]

19 Richard Redgrave, *The Emigrant's Last Sight of Home* (1858)

The rural ideal lay in the realms of the imaginary. We capture the process at work in *The Art Journal*'s description of the etching, *Godalming*. The old Surrey town was close to Charterhouse, so presumably the leisure activities of several hundred public school boys regularly disturbed its tranquillity. And its aesthetics were marred by the redbrick villas of its northern slopes, and the converted farmhouses of the numerous writers and artists who (ironically) had moved there in search of rural escape. The etching's commentary was aware of these blemishes, but constructed an idyllic core, an 'untouched, old world' spot amidst 'such innovations':

> Down in the flat green meadows the little old town lies sleepy and peaceful, its streets of half-timbered or old red-brick houses as quaint and narrow as ever, crawling up to the woods of the south-western hills; every garden rich with flowers in their warm shelter; while its noble church stands guard between the meadows and the town.
>
> In his admirable Etching, Mr. Percy Robertson has given us, besides a well-conceived composition, the real charm and character of the place. The sluggish Wey, creeping along between the marly banks, so slow, so lazy, that the current does not stir the lily pads. The haymakers carrying their last loads of the lush grass of the water-meadows. The passing cloud in the hot summer sky, that throws the church and middle distance into strong but luminous shadow against the sunlit town and hills.

Although the pollution from a very non-picturesque tanning yard pricks the conceit of the rural aesthetic, it is easily accommodated in the written landscape. 'While the smoke from the tall chimney of the tan-yard gives a pleasant accent to the picture, which has evidently been thought out with loving appreciation of nature.'[99] Industrial pollution is transformed into a 'pleasant accent'. Evidently, the natural is infinitely malleable.

The role of labour in the rural ideal varies, but it is usually as subordinate as its role in the real world. Labourers are haymaking in the foreground of the etching, *Godalming*, yet *The Art Journal* views them in terms of their relationship to the lush grass of the water meadows. Their cart is as prominent as the church, but it is invisible in the commentary. The haymakers are dwarfed by the landscape in Vicat Cole's *Hayfield, near Day's Lock, Oxford* (1891). (See Plate 20.) The water, trees, sky and newly-mown hay dominate the painting. Workers are often tolerated as part of a greater whole. Stott's hazy shapes express the 'link which binds the peasant to his environment, the subtle correspondence between human life and nature'.[100] La Thangue's ploughboy is almost a means of delivering sunlight. It is the sunlight rather than the subject that is responsible for the painting's 'quickening, life-enhancing qualities', and that so fills the viewer with 'pleasure'.[101] R. W. Macbeth's peasant woman 'is a personification . . . not a mere individual cottager who was persuaded to pose for her portrait'. She typifies 'life that is . . . unspoiled by the sordid struggle after things not worth possessing'. She represents 'the motherhood of nature and the vital principle that governs all creation'. Those with the things not worth possessing could thus possess this life-enhancing image, and momentarily escape the corrupting influences of their own existence. It was quite a role for a rural working woman.[102]

Sometimes the workers of rural England were banished entirely from their own 'picturesque' environment: Benjamin Williams Leader was carrying out Constable-like deflections into the twentieth century.[103] Yet even when workers were in the foreground of the landscape, art commentators – and presumably many viewers – passed them over in favour of the stubble or the sky.[104] Redgrave's *Emigrant's Last Sight of Home* (see Plate 19) places its large figures in the right foreground of the landscape; a departing carpenter with his family at his side, and at his feet, bids farewell to his village across the Surrey valley. There is no doubting the centrality of the group in the composition. Yet the famous critic Ruskin merely referred to the 'beautiful distance' in this oil.[105] Ruskin performed a similar trick in his comments on Brett's *Stonebreaker* (see Plate 8), overlooking the young stone-breaker in his enthusiasm for the painting's thistledown, chalk hills, and 'lovely . . . distance'.[106]

Absences are as significant as presences. There are almost no representations of the hybrid communities and varied occupations discussed in the

20 George Vicat Cole, *Hayfield near Day's Lock, Oxford* (1891)

previous chapters of this book. The rural worker is invariably a farm worker or village blacksmith or carpenter, and, if female, the archetypal gleaner or milkmaid. (See Plate 21.) The horse signifies the rural but, as Richard Jefferies noted in the 1890s, machinery was invisible: 'So many pictures and so many illustrations seem to proceed upon the assumption that steam-plough and reaping-machine do not exist, that the landscape contains nothing but what it did a hundred years ago.'[107]

Many of the images are of a society in decline. Art and photography were preserving the last glimpses of a doomed world. Fittingly, they did so by stressing age through old buildings and elderly people. The photographic archive that accompanied Cecil Sharp's folk-song recording is a visual catalogue of rural authenticity as gerontocracy: most of the images are of old men and women.[108] The magazine, *Country Life*, captured this moment in 1901–02, when it catalogued its readers' photographs of 'English Village Types', including a 75-year-old Norfolk woodcutter and an 87-year-old dairymaid: 'It is in old age that the labourer becomes most picturesque.'[109] La Thangue's *The Last Furrow* (1895), with the (exhausted, dying?) old man on his knees on the ground, while one of his horses turns to investigate, could be emblematic of the perceived demise of a culture.[110] The same could be said of his portrait of a smock-clad agricultural worker, *The Old Peasant*, reproduced in the 1898 edition of *The Art Journal*.[111] Alternatively, Hamo Thornycroft's incongruous, homoerotic bronze statue, *The Mower* (1884), displayed at the Royal Academy in 1894, appears as a fantastical homage to the youthful, rural masculinity of a bygone era. (See Plate 22.) It is ironic that agricultural labourers had been least visible in art when they were a commonplace sight in rural England, and then became most visible in late Victorian England, when perceived to be an old and disappearing species. When La Thangue met a fellow-artist at the Chelsea Arts Club on the eve of the First World War, he asked the latter if he 'knew of a quiet old-world village where he could live and find real country models'. 'Again and again when we met in the club there was the same unsettled, unhappy look in his eye – the same question – and a tinge of sadness in his voice ... I believe he never found his spot.'[112] Realism had given way to nostalgia.

Clearly, representations of the rural and its workers performed a great deal of ideological labour. Early nineteenth-century artists exulted the open fields of England and their gleaners at the very moment of enclosure.[113] John Crome, John Sell Cotman and other members of the Norwich school presented picturesque nostalgia as landscape in one of the most aggressively modernizing agricultural areas of England. Mousehold Heath, enclosed in 1799, was magically transformed back into an open,

21 Milkmaid postcard, 1900s

One of a collection of similar rural images available in postcard form in the early
twentieth century

22 Hamo Thornycroft, *The Mower* (1884)
From a photograph in the *Art Journal*, 1894

uncultivated common in the paintings and etchings of 1810–20.[114] Painters produced sunny images of harvests and harvesters during the years of depression and mechanization in the latter half of the nineteenth century, when both harvests and harvesters seemed doomed.[115] The most seemingly innocuous image could be the most political. Birket Foster's comforting conservatism comforted conservatives of successive generations. 'His toilers stand erect; they are not bowed down and hopelessly struggling against fate; they carry out their appointed tasks with a due measure of pleasure and interest', an admirer wrote in 1906.[116]

* * *

However, it would be misleading to finish with closure. Representations are complex, and I am not claiming that the *only* alternatives in images of rural workers are invisibility or misrepresentation. We have seen that contemporaries saw some paintings as threatening. The *Athenaeum* interpreted Wallis's *Stonebreaker* as a protest against the New Poor Law. 'This may be a protest against the Poor law – against a social system that makes the workhouse or stonebreaking the end of the model peasant; but it may also be a mere attempt to excite and to startle by the poetically horrible.'[117] There are disruptive images among the sixty or so Victorian works of art dealing with emigration, itself one of the strategies used by rural workers as a form of protest and a source of potential economic improvement. Emigration could be both a sign of hope and an explicit critique of the conditions that had made such departure necessary. Herkomer's *Pressing to the West* (1884), a painting of the processing of migrants in New York, was greeted by critics as a depressing scene of dreariness, misery and dejection.[118]

It is true that there is a tendency to present woman as patient sufferer in ways that confirm rather than challenge Victorian stereotypes. (See Plate 23.) The female worker subject is tied firmly to family and the domestic sphere, and invariably either weeping or in a state of gender appropriate, prostrate passivity. The title of Walter Langley's *But Men Must Work and Women Must Weep* (1882) proclaims the trope perfectly. However, these paintings also deal with subjects that were troublesome in the nineteenth-century context: death, displacement, eviction, homelessness and the trauma of unmarried motherhood. A. H. Marsh's *Homeless* (1882), Blandford Fletcher's *Evicted* (1887), Walter Langley's *On the Road* (1887), Fred Hall's *Adversity* (1889) and La Thangue's *The Runaway* (1887), *Leaving Home* (1889) and *Some Poor People* (1894) are merely a few examples.[119] Frank Holl's dark images of labouring poverty, death and despair – *I am the Resurrection*

23 Frank Bramley, *A Hopeless Dawn* (1888)

and the Life [*Village Funeral*] (1872), *Her First Born* (1877), *Gone* (1877), *Hush!* (1877), *Hushed* (1877) and *Besieged* (1880) – are poles apart from the picturesque.[120] 'Who would choose to live in constant contemplation of such a domestic tragedy?', one critic wrote of a Holl.[121] Such works were like Roland Barthes' photographic punctum, disturbing and destabilizing the power of the collective complacency of nineteenth-century rural art.[122] The Newlyn artists' representations of Cornish fisherwomen – Stanhope Forbes's *A Fish Sale on a Cornish Beach* (1885) and Langley's *The Breadwinners* (1886) – with their women working rather than weeping, present powerful statements about the female role in the social economy of the rural poor.[123] (See Plate 24.)

We could also revisit the accompanying texts to Emerson's photographs, for they sometimes slip into shockingly realist observations on the plight of the rural poor. Here is the description of Emerson's photograph, *A Slippery Path – Winter Scene* (1888):

The cottages in our plate are tenanted by peasants more prosperous than some we know; yet even here what a life! The scanty cubic space filled with air poisoned with the organic exhalations of the eight human beings we saw sitting in the one room, where the hard-worked mother, dragged down by penury and child-bearing, was preparing a coarse meal for the delicate children, each of

24 Stanhope A. Forbes, *A Fish Sale on a Cornish Beach* (1885)

whom was suffering from eczema. Pure air and good food they needed, and neither could they get. Unconscious of their grinding fate, they raised to us their large blue serious eyes full of innocent wonder. The day was bitingly cold, but we were glad to get out once more into the air, and escape from that ill-smelling dwelling.[124]

It is a strange combination of sympathetic representation, fear of contamination, and purported innocence. Emerson wrote of people who, 'like savages . . . eat when they get an opportunity', 'pathological specimens of humanity, brought to their present habits only too often by hereditary taints'.[125] But the same book also contains the following passage:

we in our house-boat have often mused on the nightly visions of the country phantasmagoria. In large houses the brightly lighted rooms greeted the richly-dressed dames, and the well-fed lackeys served the dainty meats and sparkling wines, whilst a hundred yards down the road in a leaky cottage an old couple with chilled frames huddled over a slender smoky fire of damp green crackling faggots . . . The burly well-to-do farmer throws pieces of meat to his dogs or plies his groom with drams of drink, while a poor young mother with phthisical husband and dying child, its features all pale and pinched . . . takes forth her last shilling with which to buy everything . . .[126]

Emerson's work was full of such contradictions. The oeuvre of Emerson's artist friend, Clausen, also included realism as well as romanticism. As we saw, Clausen's *Winter Work* and his study of the head of a peasant woman were strongly criticized by contemporary critics for their delight in the 'ugly': 'Nothing indeed is represented but the fact of the model's actuality.'[127] It is an ironic vote of confidence in the representation of at least one rural worker.

Conclusion

This book began and ended with the invisibility of rural workers in the oeuvre of their class superiors. However, it would be wrong to suggest that our quarry is hidden from history. Workers were quite capable of their own laconic interventions: 'I shall not fatigue the reader by tracing the branches of our genealogical tree, for the best of all reasons – we never had one.'[1] 'Who or what my father was it is not at all necessary to state; but in case there should be any doubt upon the subject, I positively assert that I had one, and that he had a wife, who was my mother.'[2] Autobiographies, oral histories, parliamentary reports, social surveys, newspapers, school records, folk-songs, letters, memoirs, journals, court files, poor-law records, and medical and sanitary reports are just some of the sources that have been reworked to produce the history in the pages above.

While this book is a series of arguments on specific topics, several themes have emerged: the importance of the north and west (I have rejected English rural history's tendency to focus on the villages of the south and east); the hybridity of the rural and the urban (communities on the margins of the rural and the urban); the role of rural industry (rural work is not synonymous with agricultural labour); the sheer range of work engaged in by rural workers; the centrality of the work of women and children in rural history; the incredible range of strategies involved in household survival; the localization of the experiences of life and death; the richness of rural leisure patterns; the varied repertoire of rural protest; and the discovery of substantial visual imagery of rural workers (photographs, paintings, prints, postcards), though with interesting silences, absences and romanticization.

It is a heterogenous quarry. P. H. Emerson's natural history of the 'The Suffolk Peasantry' observed that:

> The peasant of the Dunwich district differs in nearly every respect from the Westleton peasant, although but a little more than a league separates the two villages. The Dunwich peasant is a quiet, plodding, harmless man, the type that delights the heart of a tyrannical landlord, for he can be driven like a dumb beast; whereas the men of Westleton are of more mercurial dispositions. They are good workmen, but fiery in temper, and will not brook oppression . . . Even

their modes of exclamation are quite distinct; for the man of Dunwich receives a communication with a 'Dar! sar!' – I dare say; whilst the Westleton man greets it with a more cautious and questionable 'Wal! wal!'[3]

Of course, we would reject Emerson's condescending classifications, but the point is that he was grappling with local complexities. Even the terms for work varied from region to region. Day-labourers were datal men in Northumberland, darrickers in Cumberland, and slingers in Cornwall.[4] Those who worked with cattle or cows were called yardmen or garthmen in Lincolnshire and Yorkshire, byremen in Northumberland, and foggers in the south and west of England.[5] As one commissioner put it in 1893–94, 'The character and condition of the labourers in the several districts vary almost as much as the soil and climate.'[6] Hence, local variation is a recurring theme. Whatever the topic – settlement type, the extent of rural industrialization, patterns of work, wages, unemployment, economic opportunities for women and children, mortality and fertility, sports, folk customs, literacies, protest ('Bread or Blood in Brandon') – regional and local variation are much more than some minor variant to be incorporated into a larger picture. The extent of localization is so compelling that it forces a rethinking of any conception

25 Thomas Sydney Cooper, *Fording a Brook, Suburbs of Canterbury* (1834)

of a 'rural England'. As suggested in the title of this book, we need to replace it with rural *Englands*.

I would like to finish with the imagery in a painting, because it touches visually on some of the concerns of this book. (See Plate 25.) Thomas Sidney Cooper's *Fording a Brook, Suburbs of Canterbury* (1834) is of a group of cows in a landscape, with the obligatory trees and clouds. However, the Kent urban centre of Canterbury interposes where there might normally be hills or more trees. Moreover, some labouring figures intrude in the left corner of the canvas; not just the cow-keeper, who is actually working, but also some itinerants, camped on the edge of the wood. It is a fitting marginality. People tangential to histories of rural England are peripheral in this painting. And yet, their mere presence – a punctum! – unsettles and disturbs, just as Canterbury disrupts the order of a traditional rural scene. Like the painting, this book has found a place for the town in the history of the rural. Like the painting, it has troubled imaginary rural worlds. In the process, it has relocated rural workers away from the margins towards the centre. The cows have had to move over.

Notes

Preface

1. Recent surveys include, G. E. Mingay (ed.), *The Victorian Countryside*, 2 vols (London, 1981); H. Newby, *Country Life: A Social History of Rural England* (London, 1987); G. E. Mingay (ed.), *The Rural Idyll* (London, 1989); G. E. Mingay (ed.), *The Unquiet Countryside* (London, 1989); G.E. Mingay (ed.), *The Vanishing Countryman* (London, 1989); G. E. Mingay, *A Social History of the English Countryside* (London, 1990). The exceptions include A. Howkins, *Reshaping Rural England: A Social History 1850-1925* (London, 1991) and B. Short (ed.), *The English Rural Community* (Cambridge, 1992).

2. The book is Alan Armstrong's *Farmworkers: A Social and Economic History 1770–1980* (London, 1988); the review is by K. D. M. Snell, 'Agrarian Histories and our Rural Past', *Journal of Historical Geography*, 17 (1991), p. 198. Snell is the author of one of the best books written on the rural poor: *Annals of the Labouring Poor: Social Change and Agrarian England, 1660–1900* (Cambridge, 1985).

3. See E. Higgs, 'Occupational Censuses and the Agricultural Workforce in Victorian England and Wales', *Economic History Review*, 48 (1995), pp. 700–16.

4. Adjusted census figures, provided by E. Higgs, 'Occupational Censuses and the Agricultural Workforce in Victorian England and Wales', *Economic History Review*, 48 (1995), pp. 709–11; A. Howkins, 'Peasants, Servants and Labourers: The Marginal Workforce in British Agriculture, *c*.1870-1914', *Agricultural History Review*, 92 (1994), p. 57.

5. A. M. Everitt, *Transformation and Tradition: Aspects of the Victorian Countryside* (Norwich, 1982), pp. 2–3.

6. For examples of different surveys of the period, based on chronology: see Armstrong, *Farmworkers*; Howkins, *Reshaping Rural England*; R. Perren, *Agriculture in Depression, 1870–1940* (Cambridge, 1995).

7. See P. Cloke and N. Thrift, 'Refiguring the "Rural"', in P. Cloke and others, *Writing the Rural: Five Cultural Geographies* (London, 1994), p. 1. Especially ch. 1: D. Matless, 'Doing the English Village, 1945–90: An Essay in Imaginative Geography'.

Introduction

1. Note that it was the 'English'; and note the regional focus.
2. Cecil J. Sharp, *English Folk-Song, Some Conclusions* (London, 1907), pp. 32, 106.
3. Quoted in D. Harker, 'May Cecil Sharp be Praised?', *History Workshop*, 14 (1982), p. 54. For the folk-song revival movement, see also, R. S. Thomson, 'The Development of the Broadside Ballad Trade and its Influence upon the Transmission of English Folksongs' (University of Cambridge Ph.D. thesis, 1974); V. Gammon, 'Folk Song Collecting in Sussex and Surrey 1843–1914', *History Workshop*, 10 (1980), pp. 61–89; J. Marsh, *Back to the Land: The Pastoral Impulse in England, from 1880–1914* (London, 1982), ch. 5; M. Pickering, *Village Song and Culture* (London, 1982); D. Harker, *Fakesong* (Milton Keynes, 1985); G. Boyes, *The Imagined Village: Culture, Ideology and the English Folk Revival* (Manchester, 1993); R. Sykes, 'The Evolution of Englishness in the English Folksong Revival, 1890–1914', *Folk Music Journal*, 6 (1993), pp. 446–90; and the rather pedantic piece by C. J. Bearman, 'Who were the Folk? The Demography of Cecil Sharp's Somerset Folk Singers', *Historical Journal*, 43 (2000), pp. 751–75.
4. J. Reeves, *The Idiom of the People* (London, 1958), p. 9. See also, S. Baring-Gould, *Further Reminiscences 1864–1894* (London, 1925), pp. 189–90.
5. *Journal of the Folk-Song Society*, 1 (1899–1904), p. 140.
6. E. MacColl and P. Seeger, *Travellers' Songs from England and Scotland* (Knoxville, TN, 1977), p. 165.
7. Sharp, *English Folk-Song*, p. 119.
8. Ibid, p. 137.
9. R. Wortley and M. Dawney (eds), 'George Butterworth's Diary of Morris Dance Hunting', *Folk Music Journal*, 3 (1977), pp. 193–207.
10. Quoted in V. Gammon, 'Song, Sex, and Society in England, 1600–1850', *Folk Music Journal*, 4 (1982), p. 219.
11. Grainger Museum, University of Melbourne, Restricted Access Photos, W106–14.
12. J. Bird, *Percy Grainger* (Oxford, 1999), pp. 127–31.
13. Grainger Museum, SL1 MG13/1–12, 'History and Anecdotes of Folksingers': Joseph Taylor.
14. K. Dreyfus (ed.), *The Farthest North of Humanness: Letters of Percy Grainger 1901–14* (London, 1985), p. 206. It is difficult to credit Grainger's next observation that the labourer was 'quite calm and self-possessed' (ibid.).
15. Ibid., pp. 72–3.
16. Ibid., p. 305.
17. S. Denith, *Society and Cultural Forms in Nineteenth-Century England* (London, 1998), pp. 81–3.
18. J. Austen, *Mansfield Park* (London, 1814), vol. 1, pp. 119, 170, 280 (repr. 1994).
19. For example, *Sylvia's Lovers* (1863) and *Cousin Phillis* (1865): see K. Flint, *Elizabeth Gaskell* (Plymouth, 1995), pp. 45, 53.
20. E. Gaskell, *Four Short Stories*, intro. by Anna Walters (London, 1983).

21. E. Gaskell, *Cranford, The Cage at Cranford, The Morland Cottage* (Oxford, repr. 1924).

22. A. Howkins, 'From Hodge to Lob: reconstructing the English Farm Labourer', in M. Chase and I. Dyck (eds), *Living and Learning: Essays in Honour of J. F. C. Harrison* (London, 1996), ch. 15; M. Freeman, 'The Agricultural Labourer and the "Hodge" Stereotype, *c.* 1850–1914', *Agricultural History Review*, 49 (2001), pp. 172–86.

23. See his introduction to G. Eliot, *Adam Bede* (Oxford, 1996), pp. vii–xl.

24. Ibid., p. 19.

25. Ibid., p. 49.

26. Ibid., pp. 83–5.

27. G. Eliot, *Silas Marner* (London, 1996), pp. 4–5.

28. G. Eliot, *Scenes of Clerical Life* (Oxford, 1988), pp. 21–3, 195.

29. H. James, *The House of Fiction*, ed. L. Edel (London, 1957), p. 269.

30. For the essay, see T. Hardy, 'The Dorsetshire Labourer' (1883), in J. Moynahan (ed.), *The Portable Hardy* (Harmondsworth, 1977), pp. 714–36.

31. T. Hardy, *Far from the Madding Crowd* (Harmondsworth, 1979), chs 10, 42; T. Hardy, *The Mayor of Casterbridge* (London, 1975), ch. 36; T. Hardy, *Tess of the d'Urbervilles* (Ware, 2000), chs 1–3; and K. D. M. Snell, *Annals of the Labouring Poor: Social Change and Agrarian England, 1660–1900* (Cambridge, 1985), ch. 8. For a recent restatement of Hardy's 'innovative realism' that seems oblivious of Snell's criticisms, see S. L. Rogers, ' "The Historian of Wessex": Thomas Hardy's Contribution to History', *Rethinking History*, 5 (2001), pp. 217–32.

32. James, *House of Fiction*, pp. 268–73. The review of *Far from the Madding Crowd* was published in 1874.

33. This story appeared in the summer number of *The Graphic*, 1883.

34. R. Jefferies, *Wild Life in a Southern County* (London, n.d.), p. vii.

35. R. Jefferies, *The Life of the Fields* (London, 1893), p. 144.

36. R. Jefferies, *Hodge and his Masters*, 2 vols (London, 1966). First published in 1880.

37. To cite the Contents pages of Jefferies, *Wild Life in a Southern County*.

38. A. Somerville, *The Whistler at the Plough*, ed. K. D. M. Snell (London, 1989), pp. 41–2. First published in 1852.

39. For a detailed and sophisticated account of rural social investigators, see M. Freeman, *Social Investigation and Rural England, 1870–1914* (Woodbridge, 2003).

40. M. Freeman, 'Rider Haggard and *Rural England*: Methods of Social Enquiry in the English Countryside', *Social History*, 26 (2001), pp. 209–16.

41. Freeman found that Haggard used part of the letter but cut out some of the criticism, including the quote above: ibid, p. 216.

42. L. L. Price, 'Reviews: *Rural England*', *Economic Journal*, 13 (1903), p. 209.

43. The cover note on G. Sturt, *The Bettesworth Book* (Firle, 1978).

44. G. Bourne [Sturt], *Change in the Village* (Harmondsworth, 1984), pp. 69–71. First published in 1912.

45. Ibid., pp. 72–3.

46. E. D. Mackerness (ed.), *The Journals of George Sturt 1890–1927* (Cambridge, 1967), vol. 1, p. 121 (his emphasis).

47. Ibid., p. 270.

48. Mackerness (ed.), *Journals of George Sturt*, vol. 2, p. 541.

49. E. Grey, *Cottage Life in a Hertfordshire Village* (Harpenden, 1977), introduction by F. M. L. Thompson, pp. iii–v. (First published in 1934.)

50. Ibid., pp. 17, 30, 129, 159.

51. W. Rose, *Good Neighbours* (Bideford, 1988), pp. 17, 37.

52. See back cover of the 1988 edition, published by Green Books.

53. C. Holdenby, *Folk of the Furrow* (London, 1913), p. 9. Holdenby's real name was Ronald George Hatton. He was educated at Balliol College, Oxford.

1 Rural Worlds

1. K. Worpole, 'Village School or Blackboard Jungle?', in R. Samuel, *Patriotism: The Making and Unmaking of British National Identity, Volume 3: National Fictions* (London, 1989), p. 125.

2. S. Dentith, *Society and Cultural Forms in Nineteenth-Century England* (London, 1998), p. 101.

3. There is a vast literature for the above. For a range of approaches, see J. Barrell, *The Dark Side of the Landscape: The Rural Poor in English Painting* (Cambridge, 1980); M. Wiener, *English Culture and the Decline of the Industrial Spirit, 1850–1980* (Cambridge, 1981); J. Marsh, *Back to the Land: The Pastoral Impulse in England, from 1880–1914* (London, 1982); A. Howkins, 'The Discovery of Rural England', in R. Colls and P. Dodd (eds), *Englishness, Politics and Culture, 1880–1920* (London, 1986), pp. 62–88; L. Nead, *Myths of Sexuality: Representations of Women in Victorian Britain* (Oxford, 1988), pp. 39–44; C. Shaw and M. Chase (eds), *The Imagined Past: History and Nostalgia* (Manchester, 1989); B. Short, 'Images and Realities in the English Rural Community: An Introduction', in B. Short (ed.), *The English Rural Community* (Cambridge, 1992), ch. 1; S. Laing, 'Images of the Rural in Popular Culture 1750-1990', in Short (ed.), *English Rural Community*, ch. 7; G. Bennett, 'Folklore Studies and the English Rural Myth', *Rural History*, 4 (1993), pp. 77–91; G. Boyes, *The Imagined Village: Culture, Ideology and the English Folk Revival* (Manchester, 1993); C. Payne, *Toil and Plenty: Images of the Agricultural Landscape in England, 1780-1890* (New Haven, CT, 1993); F. Trentmann, 'Civilization and its Discontents: English Neo-Romanticism and the Transformation of Anti-Modernism in Twentieth-Century Western Culture', *Journal of Contemporary History*, 29 (1994), pp. 583–625; K. Sayer, *Women of the Fields: Representations of Rural Women in the Nineteenth Century* (Manchester, 1995); L. Driscoll, ' "The Rose Revived": Derek Jarman and the British tradition', in C. Lippard (ed.), *By Angels Driven: The Films of Derek Jarman* (Westport, CT, 1996), pp. 65–83; E. K. Helsinger, *Rural Scenes and National Representation: Britain, 1815-1850* (Princeton, NJ, 1997), esp. introduction; P. Mandler, 'Against "Englishness": English Rural Culture and the Limits to Rural Nostalgia,

1850–1940', *Transactions of the Royal Historical Society*, 6th series, 7 (1997), pp. 155–75; D. Matless, *Landscape and Englishness* (London, 1998); J. Vernon, 'Border Crossings: Cornwall and the English (Imagi)nation', in G. Cubitt (ed.), *Imagining Nations* (Manchester, 1998), ch. 9; J. V. Beckett, 'Our Green and Pleasant Land', *Journal of British Studies*, 38 (1999), pp. 252–61; K. Sayer, *Country Cottages; A Cultural History* (Manchester, 2000); A. Howkins, 'Rurality and English identity', in D. Morley and K. Robins (eds), *British Cultural Studies* (Oxford, 2001), ch. 9; J. Burchardt, *Paradise Lost: Rural Idyll and Social Change in England since 1800* (London, 2002).

4. P. J. Taylor, 'The English and their Englishness', *Scottish Geographical Magazine*, 107 (1991), pp. 146–61.

5. A. D. Hall, *A Pilgrimage of British Farming 1910–1912* (London, 1913), pp. vii, 6, 15, 24.

6. Ibid., pp. 38–9, 47.

7. Ibid., pp. 86–93, 101–7.

8. Ibid., p. 124.

9. Ibid., pp. 173, 222, 252, 408.

10. Ibid., p. 121.

11. Ibid., p. 54.

12. Ibid., pp. 348–9.

13. Ibid., pp. 33–4.

14. Quoted in N. Scotland, *Methodism and the Revolt of the Field: A Study of the Methodist Contribution to Agricultural Trade Unionism in East Anglia, 1872–96* (Gloucester, 1981), p. 135.

15. J. C. Buckmaster, *A Village Politician: The Life-Story of John Buckley* (Horsham, 1982), p. 164. First published in 1897.

16. R. Hillyer, *Country Boy* (London, 1966), p. 33.

17. J. Obelkevich, *Religion and Rural Society: South Lindsey 1825–1875* (Oxford, 1976), p. 36.

18. H. Rider Haggard, *Rural England: Volume 1* (1902), pp. 160–1.

19. Centre for Kentish Studies (hereafter CKS), IR 4/37/1, Valuation Book 1910, Boughton, Dunkirk, Hernhill.

20. Templeman Library (hereafter TL), University of Kent, Oral History Project: Life in Kent Before 1914, A. Packman, b. 1892.

21. A. M. Everitt, *Transformation and Tradition: Aspects of the Victorian Countryside* (Norwich, 1982), pp. 14, 32–3.

22. Calculated from *Parliamentary Papers* (hereafter PP), 1896, lxvii, 'Return of the Number and Size of Agricultural Holdings Exceeding an Acre in Extent in Great Britain in 1895', p. 525.

23. Ibid., pp. 538–9, 542–3.

24. Ibid., pp. 538–9.

25. J. V. Beckett, 'Agricultural Landownership and Estate Management', in E. J. T. Collins (ed.), *The Agrarian History of England and Wales, VII, 1850–1914, Part 1* (Cambridge, 2000), p. 703.

26. J. D. Marshall and J. K. Walton, *The Lake Counties from 1830 to the Mid-Twentieth Century* (Manchester, 1981), p. 103.

27. C. Rawding, 'The Iconography of Churches: A Case Study of Landownership and Power in Nineteenth-Century Lincolnshire', *Journal of Historical Geography*, 16 (1990), p. 160; C. Rawding, 'Society and Place in Nineteenth-century North Lincolnshire', *Rural History*, 3 (1992), pp. 59–85; C. K. Rawding, *The Lincolnshire Wolds in the Nineteenth Century* (Lincoln, 2001), pp. 56–68.

28. Everitt, *Transformation*, p. 15.

29. Rawding, 'Iconography of Churches', p. 157.

30. G. Darley, *Villages of Vision* (London, 1975), ch. 4.

31. W. Howitt, *The Rural Life of England* (Shannon, 1971), p. 88. First published in 1838.

32. Everitt, *Transformation*, pp. 6–12.

33. These figures are derived from M. Winstanley, 'Industrialization and the Small Farm: Family and Household Economy in Nineteenth-Century Lancashire', *Past and Present*, 152 (1996), pp. 166–7: Table 1.

34. See M. Chamberlain, *Fenwomen: A Portrait of Women in an English Village* (London, 1983).

35. Rawding, 'Society and Place', p. 75. For the wealthier farmer, see also Rawding, *Lincolnshire Wolds*, ch. 3.

36. The best summary of this subject is A. Howkins, 'Types of Rural Communities', in Collins (ed.), *Agrarian History of England and Wales, VII, 1850–1914, Part 2*, ch. 22. See also B. K. Roberts, *The Making of the English Village* (Harlow, 1987).

37. The most recent accounts of open and close parishes are to be found in Howkins, 'Types of Rural Communities'; and B. Short, 'The Evolution of Contrasting Communities in Rural England', in Short (ed.), *English Rural Community*, ch. 2.

38. I am referring to the latest volume of *Agrarian History of England and Wales*: B. A. Holderness and others, 'Farming Regions', in Collins (ed.), *Agrarian History of England and Wales, VII, Part 1*, ch. 5. For quote, see p. 420.

39. Obelkevich, *Religion and Rural Society*, p. 6.

40. For particularly informative accounts of the role of agriculture in the industrial development of textiles in Lancashire and Yorkshire, see J. K. Walton, 'Proto-Industrialisation and the First Industrial Revolution: The Case of Lancashire', and P. Hudson, 'Capital and Credit in the West Riding Wool Textile Industry *c.* 1750–1850' both in P. Hudson (ed.), *Regions and Industries: A Perspective on the Industrial Revolution in Britain* (Cambridge, 1989), chs 2 and 3.

41. M. W. Dupree, *Family Structure in the Staffordshire Potteries 1840–1880* (Oxford, 1995), esp. pp. 36–40, 76.

42. A. D. M. Phillips, 'The Growth of the Conurbation', in A. D. M. Phillips (ed.), *The Potteries: Continuity and Change in a Staffordshire Conurbation* (Stroud, 1993), ch. 8, esp. pp. 124–8.

43. T. W. Rammell, *Report to the General Board of Health . . . of the Parish of Wotton-Under-Edge* (London, 1854), pp. 4–7.

44. A. M. Urdank, *Religion and Society in a Cotswold Vale: Nailsworth, Gloucestershire, 1780–1865* (Berkeley and Los Angeles, CA, 1990), pp. 21–7.

45. M. F. Davies, *Life in an English Village* (London, 1909), pp. 41–5, 84–5.

46. G. C. Allen, *The Industrial Development of Birmingham and the Black Country 1860–1927* (London, 1929), pp. 3–83.

47. W. Lee, *Report to the General Board of Health . . . of the Township of Heanor* (London, 1853), pp. 18–19; W. Lee, *Report to the General Board of Health . . . of the Parish of Eastwood* (London, 1853), p. 13.

48. *Second Report of the Commissioners on the Employment of Children, Young Persons, and Women in Agriculture*, PP, 1868–9, xiii, p. 154.

49. W. Lee, *Report to the General Board of Health . . . of the Parish of Alfreton* (London, 1850), pp. 6–7.

50. *Royal Commission on Labour: The Agricultural Labourer: Reports . . . Upon . . . Selected Districts*, PP, 1893–4, xxxv, pp. 617, 620.

51. Marshall and Walton, *Lake Counties*, pp. 3, 11–12, 27.

52. C. Hallas, *Rural Responses to Industrialization: The North Yorkshire Pennines 1790–1914* (Bern, 1999), esp. chs 3, 7–8, 11. Quote from p. 295.

53. R. Lawton, 'The Economic Geography of Craven in the Early Nineteenth Century', in D. Mills (ed.), *English Rural Communities: The Impact of a Specialised Economy* (London, 1973), ch. 7.

54. Winstanley, 'Industrialization and the Small Farm', pp. 157–95.

55. Public Record Office (hereafter PRO), RG 12/1299, Littleport Census 1891.

56. P. Sharpe, *Adapting to Capitalism: Working Women in the English Economy, 1700–1850* (London, 1996), p. 8.

57. C. Phythian-Adams, 'Introduction: An Agenda for English Local History', in Phythian-Adams (ed.), *Societies, Cultures and Kinship, 1580–1850* (Leicester, 1993), ch. 1.

58. M. Carter, 'Town or Urban Society? St Ives in Huntingdonshire, 1630–1740', in Phythian-Adams (ed.), *Societies, Cultures and Kinship*, ch. 3.

59. J. Cooper, *The Well-ordered Town: A Story of Saffron Walden, Essex 1792–1862* (Saffron Walden, 2000).

60. Quoted in C. W. Chalklin, 'Country Towns', in G. E. Mingay (ed.), *The Victorian Countryside*, 2 vols (London, 1981), vol. 1, p. 277.

61. N. Goose, *Population, Economy and Family Structure in Hertfordshire in 1851: St Albans and its Region* (Hatfield, 2000), pp. 33, 70–7; *Morning Chronicle*, 5 April 1850: 'Labour and the Poor: The Rural Districts'.

62. G. F. R. Spenceley, 'The English Pillow Lace Industry 1840–80: A Rural Industry in Competition with Machinery', *Business History*, 19 (1977), pp. 69–70; P. Horn, *Victorian Countrywomen* (Oxford, 1991), p. 168.

63. PP, 1868–9, xiii, Second Report, p. 154.

64. Ibid., pp. 205–7.

65. J. Ginswick (ed.), *Labour and the Poor in England and Wales 1849–1851, Vol. 2:*

Northumberland and Durham, Staffordshire, the Midlands (London, 1983), pp. 158, 162.

66. R. Samuel, 'Comers and Goers', in H. J. Dyos and M. Wolff (eds), *The Victorian City: Images and Realities*, vol. 1 (London, 1976), ch. 5. Quote from p. 139.

67. H. Llewellyn Smith, 'Influx of Population', in C. Booth (ed.), *Life and Labour of the People in London* (London, 1892), vol. 3, p. 96.

68. Ibid., p. 91.

69. W. A. Armstrong, 'The Flight from the Land', in G. E. Mingay (ed.), *The Vanishing Countryman* (London, 1989), pp. 66–7.

70. H. Shpayer-Makov, 'Country Workers in the Metropolitan Police', *Historical Research*, 64 (1991), p. 197.

71. T. Richardson, 'Labour', in A. Armstrong (ed.), *The Economy of Kent 1640–1914* (Woodbridge, 1995), pp. 241, 243, 257.

72. *PP*, 1893–4, xxxv, pp. 513, 581–2.

73. The diaries and letters of Arthur J. Munby (1828–1910) and Hannah Cullwick (1833–1909), Trinity College Library, Cambridge, Volume 80, pp. 92–3.

74. R. Samuel, 'Village Labour', in R. Samuel (ed.), *Village Life and Labour* (London, 1982), p. 4; G. E. Evans, *Where Beards Wag All: The Relevance of the Oral Tradition* (London, 1977), pp. 241–70, 283–5.

75. N. Rapport, *Diverse World-Views in an English Village* (Edinburgh, 1993), pp. 18, 22. 'Wanet' is a pseudonym.

76. See J. E. Archer, ' "A Reckless Spirit of Enterprise": Game-Preserving and Poaching in Nineteenth-Century Lancashire', in D. W. Howell and K. O. Morgan (eds), *Crime, Protest and Police in Modern British Society* (Cardiff, 1999), pp. 149–75.

77. My calculations based on Census of 1871: *PP*, 1873, lxxi, Part 1.

78. *PP*, 1868–9, xiii, Second Report, p. 276.

79. S. Hussey, 'Low Pay, Underemployment and Multiple Occupations: Men's Work in the Inter-War Countryside', *Rural History*, 8 (1997), p. 219.

80. A. Williams, *Life in a Railway Factory* (London, 1915). Quote from p. 127.

81. Marshall and Walton, *Lake Counties*, pp. 2–3.

82. Llewellyn Smith, 'Influx of Population', pp. 61–2, and map facing p. 68.

83. A. August, *Poor Women's Lives: Gender, Work, and Poverty in Late-Victorian London* (London, 1999), pp. 37, 178.

84. Llewellyn Smith, 'Influx of Population', p. 134.

85. T. Sokoll, 'Negotiating a Living: Essex Pauper Letters from London, 1800–1834', *International Review of Social History*, 45 (2000), pp. 19–46.

86. E. Higgs, 'Domestic Service and Household Production', in A. V. John (ed.), *Unequal Opportunities: Women's Employment in England 1800–1918* (Oxford, 1986), pp. 139, 140; Horn, *Victorian Countrywomen*, pp. 141–2; Sharpe, *Adapting to Capitalism*, ch. 5.

87. A. Armstrong, *The Population of Victorian and Edwardian Norfolk* (Norwich, [2001]), pp. 22, 28.

88. Phillips, 'Growth of Conurbation', pp. 107–9.

89. M. W. Greenslade, 'The Potteries: A Question of Regional Identity', in Phillips (ed.), *Potteries*, ch. 11.

90. G. T. Clark, *Report to the General Board of Health . . . of the Parishes of Nuneaton and Chilvers Coton* (London, 1849), p. 5.

91. R. Rawlinson, *Report to the General Board of Health . . .Township of Willenhall* (London, 1854), pp. 7–9; *PP* 1873, xxi, pt 2, p. 128.

92. W. Lee, *Report to the General Board of Health . . . of Bacup* (London, 1849), p. 1; *PP* 1873, xxi, pt 2, p. 129.

93. R. Rawlinson, *Report to the General Board of Health . . . Parish of Wallasey* (London, 1851), pp. 8–10; *PP* 1873, xxi, pt 2, p. 129.

94. R. I. Woods, 'The Population of Britain in the Nineteenth Century', in M. Anderson (ed.), *British Population History from the Black Death to the Present Day* (Cambridge, 1996), p. 298.

95. R. Lawton, 'Population Changes in England and Wales in the Late Nineteenth Century: An Analysis of Trends by Registration Districts', *Transactions of the Institute of British Geographers*, 44 (1968), pp. 55–74, table on p. 70.

96. Woods , 'Population of Britain', p. 303.

97. J. Ginswick (ed.), *Labour and the Poor in England and Wales 1849–1851, Vol. 1: Lancashire, Cheshire, Yorkshire* (London, 1983), pp. 3, 33, 142.

98. Ginswick (ed.), *Labour and the Poor*, vol. 2, p. 17.

99. P. J. Taylor, 'Which Britain? Which England? Which North?', in Morley and Robins (eds), *British Cultural Studies*, p. 135.

2 Working Men

1. Alexander Somerville, *The Whistler at the Plough*, ed. K. D. M. Snell (London, 1989), p. 18. First published in 1852.

2. Ibid., pp. 142–6.

3. A. Howkins, 'The English Farm Labourer in the Nineteenth Century: Farm, Family and Community', in B. Short (ed.), *The English Rural Community: Image and Analysis* (Cambridge, 1992), p. 102.

4. Figures partly adapted from A. J. Gritt, 'The "Survival" of Service in the English Agricultural Labour Force: Lessons from Lancashire, *c.* 1650–1851', *Agricultural History Review*, 50 (2002), pp. 32–3.

5. For an important study of smallholders, see A. Hall, *Fenland Worker-Peasants: The Economy of Smallholders at Rippingdale, Lincolnshire, 1791–1871* (Agricultural History Review, Supplement Series, 1, 1992). See also, M. Reed, 'The Peasantry of Nineteenth-Century England: A Neglected Class?', *History Workshop*, 18 (1984), pp. 53–76; A. Howkins, 'Peasants, Servants and Labourers: The Marginal Workforce in British Agriculture, *c.* 1870–1914', *Agricultural History Review*, 92 (1994), pp. 49–62.

6. See table in M. Overton, *Agricultural Revolution in England: The Transformation of the Agrarian Economy 1500–1850* (Cambridge, 1996), p. 179.

7. These figures are derived from *Parliamentary Papers* (hereafter PP), 1896, lxvii,

'Return of the Number and Size of Agricultural Holdings Exceeding an Acre in Extent in Great Britain in 1895', pp. 525, 542–3. See also, M. Winstanley, 'Industrialization and the Small Farm: Family and Household Economy in Nineteenth-Century Lancashire', *Past and Present*, 152 (1996), pp. 166–7.

8. Winstanley, 'Industrialization and the Small Farm', pp. 165–71.

9. That is, those described respectively as (1) 'neither employer nor employed' or (2) 'employed'. Public Record Office (hereafter PRO), RG 12/4325, Ravenstonedale Census 1891.

10. See the excellent discussion of small farmers in A. Howkins, *Reshaping Rural England: A Social History 1850–1925* (London, 1991), ch. 2.

11. R. C. Allen, *Enclosure and the Yeoman: The Agricultural Development of the South Midlands 1450–1850* (Oxford, 1992), p. 57.

12. A. Mutch, 'The "Farming Ladder" in North Lancashire, 1840–1914: Myth or Reality?', *Northern History*, 27 (1991), p. 169.

13. J. Obelkevich, *Religion and Rural Society: South Lindsey 1825–1875* (Oxford, 1976), p. 47.

14. *Royal Commission on Labour: The Agricultural Labourer: Reports . . . Upon . . . Selected Districts*, PP, 1893–4, xxxv, pp. 24, 55.

15. B. Reay, *Microhistories: Demography, Society and Culture in Rural England, 1800–1930* (Cambridge, 1996), pp. 19–20.

16. H. Rider Haggard, *Rural England: Volume 1* (1902), pp. 324–9. There were a further 233 holdings of less than an acre.

17. 'Tom Mullins, Farm Labourer', in J. Burnett (ed.), *Useful Toil: Autobiographies of Working People from the 1820s to the 1920s* (Harmondsworth, 1977), p. 67.

18. Obelkevich, *Religion and Rural Society*, p. 48.

19. *PP*, 1893–4, xxxv, p. 49.

20. Ibid., p. 97.

21. Templeman Library (hereafter TL), University of Kent, Oral History Project: Life in Kent Before 1914, A. Austin, b. 1889.

22. The definitive account of allotments is J. Burchardt, *The Allotment Movement in England, 1793–1873* (Woodbridge, 2002).

23. J. Ashby and B. King, 'Statistics of Some Midland Villages', *Economic Journal*, 3 (1893), pp. 8–20 (quote from p. 12).

24. E. A. Wrigley, 'Men on the Land and Men in the Countryside: Employment in Agriculture in Early-Nineteenth-Century England', in L. Bonfield, R. M. Smith, and K. Wrightson (eds), *The World We Have Gained* (Oxford, 1986), ch. 11.

25. A. M. Everitt, *Transformation and Tradition: Aspects of the Victorian Countryside* (Norwich, 1982), pp. 26–7.

26. For the above, see E. J. T. Collins, 'The Coppice and Underwood Trades', in G. E. Mingay (ed.), *The Agrarian History of England and Wales*, VI, 1750–1850 (Cambridge, 1989), pp. 484–501.

27. *Second Report of the Commissioners on the Employment of Children, Young Persons, and Women in Agriculture*, PP, 1868–9, xiii, p. 78.

28. Ibid., p. 632.

29. *PP*, 1893–4, xxxv, pp. 88–91.

30. E. J. T. Collins, 'Farming and Forestry in Central Southern England in the Nineteenth and Early Twentieth Centuries', in H. Brandl (ed.), *Geschichte der Kleinprivatwaldwirtschaft, Geschichte des Bauernwaldes, Tagungsvorträge* (Freiburg, 1993), pp. 290–306.

31. G. Timmins, *The Last Shift: The Decline of Handloom Weaving in Nineteenth-Century Lancashire* (Manchester, 1993), pp. 60–3.

32. Ibid., pp. 72, 77, 78, 134. (Quote from p. 72.) See also, J. D. Marshall, 'The Lancashire Rural Labourer in the Early Nineteenth Century', *Transactions of the Lancashire and Cheshire Antiquarian Society*, 71 (1963), p. 92; D. Bythell, *The Sweated Trades: Outwork in Nineteenth-Century Britain* (New York, 1978), ch. 1.

33. D. Hey, 'Industrialized Villages', in G. E. Mingay (ed.), *The Victorian Countryside*, 2 vols (London, 1981), vol. 1, pp. 358–61; J. Chartres, 'Rural Industry and Manufacturing', in E. J. T. Collins (ed.), *The Agrarian History of England and Wales, VII, 1850–1914, Part 2* (Cambridge, 2000), pp. 1138–47. For the miners, see also R. Church, A. Hall, and J. Kanefsky, *The History of the British Coal Industry, Vol. 3, 1830–1913: Victorian Pre-Eminence* (Oxford, 1986), pp. 611–37.

34. *PP*, 1893–4, xxxv, pp. 180, 279.

35. R. Fieldhouse and B. Jennings, *A History of Richmond and Swaledale* (London, 1978), p. 229.

36. M. Jones, 'Combining Estate Records with Census Enumerators' Books to Study Nineteenth-Century Communities: The Case of the Tankersley Ironstone Miners, *c*. 1850', In D. Mills and K. Schürer (eds), *Local Communities in the Victorian Census Enumerators' Books* (Oxford, 1996), ch. 17.

37. R. Samuel, 'Mineral Workers', in R. Samuel (ed.), *Miners, Quarrymen and Saltworkers* (London, 1977), pp. 65–6.

38. *PP*, 1868–9, xiii, Second Report, p. 209.

39. M. Bragg, *Speak for England* (London, 1976), ch. 2.

40. J. L. Green, *Village Industries: A National Obligation* (London, 1915), pp. 22–5.

41. H. Fitzrandolph and M. D. Hay, *The Rural Industries of England and Wales: II: Osier Growing and Basketry and . . . Rural Factories* (Oxford, 1926, repr. 1977).

42. J. Chartres, 'Rural Industry and Manufacturing', and 'The Retail Trades and Agricultural Services', in Collins (ed.), *Agrarian History of England and Wales, VII, 1850–1914, Part 2*, chs 18 and 19. (Quote from p. 1211.)

43. Chartres, 'Rural Industry' (p. 1129 for quote).

44. Fitzrandolph and Hay, *Rural Industries, II*, pp. 117–56 (p. 117 for quote).

45. Bythell, *Sweated Trades*, chs 1–3.

46. Ibid., pp. 123–31.

47. Chartres, 'Rural Industry', pp. 1138–47; Samuel, 'Mineral Workers', pp. 12, 25–6.

48. Hey, 'Industrialized Villages'; J. D. Marshall, 'Industrial Colonies and the Local Historian', *Local Historian*, 23 (1993), pp. 146–54.

49. J. H. Porter, 'The Development of Rural Society', in Mingay (ed.), *Agrarian History of England and Wales, VI*, p. 855.

50. M. F. Davies, *Life in an English Village* (London, 1909), pp. 122–4.

51. C. Shaw, *When I was a Child* (Firle, 1977), pp. 23–4. First published in 1903.

52. Reay, *Microhistories*, p. 22.

53. A. McInnes, 'A Forgotten People: The Craftsmen of Pre-industrial England', in C. Richmond and I. Harvey (eds), *Recognitions* (Aberystwyth, 1996), p. 442.

54. Davies, *Life in an English Village*, p. 105.

55. J. Robin, *Elmdon: Continuity and Change in a North-West Essex Village 1861–1964* (Cambridge, 1980), p. 11.

56. N. Goose, *Population, Economy and Family Structure in Hertfordshire in 1851: St Albans and its Region* (Hatfield, 2000), pp. 78–9.

57. Ashby and King, 'Statistics', pp. 2–3.

58. TL, B. H. Fagg, b. 1894.

59. Reay, *Microhistories*, p. 22.

60. D. R. Mills, 'The Nineteenth-Century Peasantry of Melbourn, Cambridgeshire', in R. M. Smith (ed.), *Land, Kinship and Life-Cycle* (Cambridge, 1984), pp. 496–9.

61. Census, 1871 – Report: *PP* 1873, xxi, Part 2, pp. 44–5.

62. Reay, *Microhistories*, p. 146.

63. *PP*, 1868–9, xiii, Second Report, p. 266.

64. S. Caunce, *Amongst Farm Horses: The Horselads of East Yorkshire* (Stroud, 1991), pp. 46, 74–6.

65. W. A. Armstrong, 'Labour 1', in Mingay (ed.), *Agrarian History of England and Wales*, VI, p. 671.

66. A. Kussmaul, *Servants in Husbandry in Early Modern England* (Cambridge, 1981), ch. 7: 'Extinction'.

67. Ibid., p. 4.

68. Census of 1871: *PP*, 1873, lxxi, Part 1, p. 39. My calculations.

69. M. Reed, 'Indoor Farm Service in 19th-Century Sussex: Some Criticisms of a Critique', *Sussex Archaeological Collections*, 123 (1985), p. 225; Howkins, 'Peasants, Servants, and Labourers', pp. 57–60.

70. See G. Moses, '"Rustic and Rude": Hiring Fairs and their Critics in East Yorkshire *c.* 1850–75', *Rural History*, 7 (1996), pp. 151–75; G. Moses, 'Proletarian Labourers? East Riding Farm Servants *c.* 1850–75', *Agricultural History Review*, 47 (1999), pp. 78–94; Gritt, 'Service in the English Agricultural Labour Force'.

71. Mutch, 'Farming Ladder', p. 182.

72. Caunce, *Amongst Farm Horses*.

73. Kussmaul, *Servants in Husbandry*, pp. 130–1. For a recent critique of Kussmaul's data for 1831, see A. J. Gritt, 'The Census and the Servant: A Reassessment of the Decline and Distribution of Farm Service in Early Nineteenth-Century England', *Economic History Review*, 53 (2000), pp. 84–106.

74. My calculations based on Census of 1871: *PP*, 1873, lxxi, Part 1.

75. Goose, *St Albans and its Region*, pp. 110–14.

76. Reay, *Microhistories*, pp. 26–7.

77. B. Short, 'The Decline of Living-in servants in the Transition to Capitalist Farming: A Critique of the Sussex Evidence', *Sussex Archaeological Collections*, 122 (1984), pp. 147–64; Reed, 'Indoor Farm Service', pp. 228–9.

78. My calculations based on Census of 1871: *PP*, 1873, lxxi, Part 1.

79. TL, L. Austin, b. 1902.

80. Reay, *Microhistories*, p. 24; Robin, *Elmdon*, p. 11.

81. My calculations from PRO, RG 12/896, Godshill Census 1891.

82. D. Jones, 'Thomas Campbell Foster and the Rural Labourer; Incendiarism in East Anglia in the 1840s', *Social History*, 1 (1976), p. 7.

83. K. Apps, 'Portrait of a Village in Crisis! A Study of Changes in Household Structures in a Small Dartmoor Village from 1851 to 1891', in L. Faulkner and R. Finnegan (eds), *Project Reports in Family and Community History* (Open University CD-ROM, 2001).

84. G. Nair, *Highley: The Development of a Community 1550–1880* (Oxford, 1988), pp. 169, 181, 183. This does not include farm servants.

85. Ashby and King, 'Statistics', pp. 1–3.

86. Armstrong, 'Labour 1', p. 675.

87. W. E. Bear, 'The Farm Labourers of England and Wales', *Journal of the Royal Agricultural Society of England*, 4 (1893), pp. 660–1.

88. Collection of Sandys Dawes, Mt Ephraim, Hernhill, Farming Account Book of Crockham Farm 1836–46.

89. F. Liardet, 'State of the Peasantry in the County of Kent', in *Central Society of Education, Third Publication* (London, 1968), p. 107. First published in 1839.

90. J. Burnette, 'Labourers at the Oakes: Changes in the Demand for Female Day-Labourers at a Farm Near Sheffield During the Agricultural Revolution', *Journal of Economic History*, 59 (1999), p. 49. I have reworked the data in Table 3.

91. Marshall, 'Lancashire Rural Labourer', pp. 109–13 (quote on p. 112).

92. Bear, 'Farm Labourers', pp. 660–1.

93. See also Reed, 'Indoor Farm Service', p. 228.

94. Allen, *Enclosure and the Yeoman*, pp. 248–9.

95. A. Miles and D. Vincent, 'A Land of "Boundless Opportunity"?: Mobility and Stability in Nineteenth-Century England', in S. Dex (ed.), *Life and Work History Analyses: Qualitative and Quantitative Developments* (London, 1991), p. 54; D. Mitch, ' "Inequalities which Every One May Remove": Occupational Recruitment, Endogamy, and the Homogeneity of Social Origins in Victorian England', in A. Miles and D. Vincent (eds), *Building European Society: Occupational Change and Social Mobility in Europe 1840–1940* (Manchester, 1993), ch. 7.

96. Reay, *Microhistories*, pp. 142–3; Jones, 'Thomas Campbell Foster and the Rural Labourer', p. 7.

97. Reay, *Microhistories*, pp. 143–4.

98. Robin, *Elmdon*, pp. 76–7.

99. Reay, *Microhistories*, pp. 142–4.

100. B. S. Rowntree and M. Kendall, *How the Labourer Lives* (London, 1913), pp. 18–19.

101. S. Horrell and J. Humphries, 'Old Questions, New Data, and Alternative Perspectives: Families' Living Standards in the Industrial Revolution', *Journal of Economic History*, 52 (1992), p. 858, n. 31.

102. G. R. Boyer and T. J. Hatton, 'Did Joseph Arch Raise Agricultural Wages? Rural Trade Unions and the Labour Market in Late Nineteenth-Century England', *Economic History Review*, 47 (1994), pp. 310–34.

103. C. H. Feinstein, 'Pessimism Perpetuated: Real Wages and the Standard of Living in Britain During and After the Industrial Revolution', *Journal of Economic History*, 58 (1998), p. 642. Feinstein's findings modify the more optimistic arguments of Peter Lindert and Jeffrey Williamson: P. H. Lindert and J. G. Williamson, 'English Workers' Living Standards During the Industrial Revolution: A New Look', *Economic History Review*, 36 (1983), pp. 1–25. However, Gregory Clark's most recent calculations argue that Feinstein was 'too pessimistic about living standards for workers in the years from 1815 onwards': G. Clark, 'Farm Wages and Living Standards in the Industrial Revolution: England, 1670–1869', *Economic History Review*, 54 (2001), pp. 477–505 (quote at p. 496). So the debate continues.

104. S. King and G. Timmins, *Making Sense of the Industrial Revolution* (Manchester, 2001), pp. 308–11.

105. Bear, 'Farm Labourers', p. 663.

106. A. L. Bowley, *Wages in the United Kingdom in the Nineteenth Century* (Cambridge, 1900), table at end of book.

107. *PP*, 1868–9, xiii, Second Report, p. 266.

108. Davies, *Life in an English Village*, pp. 116–18.

109. P. H. Mann, 'Life in an Agricultural Village in England', *Sociological Review*, 1 (1904), p. 192.

110. Ashby and King, 'Statistics', p. 5.

111. Clark, 'Farm Wages', p. 497.

112. *Report . . . into the Administration . . . of the Poor Laws . . . Answers to Rural Queries*, *PP*, 1834, xxx, p. 439.

113. Ibid., p. 515.

114. *PP*, 1893–4, xxxv, p. 33.

115. *PP*, 1834, xxx, pp. 445, 488, 515.

116. F. Carlton, ' "A Substantial and Sterling Friend to the Labouring Man": The Kent and Sussex Labourers' Union 1872–1895' (University of Sussex M. Phil. thesis, 1977), p. 31.

117. *PP*, 1893–4, xxxv, pp. 21, 42, 49, 81, 98, 149, 186, 700; *Royal Commission on Labour: The Agricultural Labourer: General Report*, *PP*, 1893–4, xxxvii, Part 2, pp. 67–8.

118. Ashby and King, 'Statistics', p. 19.

119. Clark, 'Farm Wages', p. 488.

120. Allen, *Enclosure and the Yeoman*, pp. 248–9. (A study of Berkshire, Oxfordshire, Buckinghamshire, Bedfordshire, Cambridgeshire, Huntingdonshire, Northamptonshire, Rutland, Leicestershire and Warwickshire.)

121. L. Bellamy and T. Williamson (ed), *Life in the Victorian Village: The Daily News*

Survey of 1891: Vols 1 and 2 (London, 1999); *PP*, 1893–4, xxxv; *PP*, 1893–4, xxxvii, Part 2.

122. Clark, 'Farm Wages', pp. 489–90.

123. See Reay, *Microhistories*, p. 103.

124. G. R. Boyer, 'An Economic Model of the English Poor Law circa 1780–1834', *Explorations in Economic History*, 22 (1985), p. 153.

125. *PP*, 1893–4, xxxv, p. 472.

126. Over the period 1863–1922: J. C. Riley, *Sick, Not Dead: The Health of British Workingmen During the Mortality Decline* (Baltimore, MD, 1997), p. 173 (and pp. 154–6 for methods of calculation).

127. *PP*, 1834, xxx, pp. 380, 409, 412, 448, 451, 528.

128. Ibid., pp. 13, 500.

129. G. R. Boyer, *An Economic History of the English Poor Law, 1750–1850* (Cambridge, 1990), p. 89.

130. M. Chamberlain, *Fenwomen: A Portrait of Women in an English Village* (London, 1983), pp. 78–9.

131. TL, F. Pack, b. 1897.

132. Mann, 'Life in an Agricultural Village', pp. 176–8.

133. *PP*, 1868–9, xiii, Second Report, p. 268.

134. *PP*, 1868–9, xiii, Second Report, p. 276.

135. R. Samuel, '"Quarry Roughs": Life and Labour in Headington Quarry, 1860–1920. An Essay in Oral History', in R. Samuel (ed.), *Village Life and Labour* (London, 1982), pp. 139–263. (Quote on p. 184.)

136. *PP*, 1834, xxx, p. 13.

137. Ibid., p. 40.

138. Ibid., p. 381.

139. Ibid., p. 422.

140. T. Richardson, 'Labour', in A. Armstrong (ed.), *The Economy of Kent 1640–1914* (Woodbridge, 1995), pp. 254–5.

141. N. Rapport, *Diverse World-Views in an English Village* (Edinburgh, 1993), p. 13.

142. Rider Haggard, *Rural England: Volume 1*, p. 341.

143. PRO, RG 12/1163, Headington Quarry Census 1891. My calculations.

144. PRO, RG 12/4338, Berry Hill (Coleford) Census 1891. My calculations.

145. Potter was fascinated by the juxtaposition between the green and pleasant idyll of the woods that surrounded the miners, and the gloom and 'opposing tightness' of their lives in the small pits and tiny mining villages that dotted the Forest: D. Potter, *The Changing Forest* (London, 1996), pp. 13, 36. First published in 1962.

146. Almost half of the Calverton households in 1881 were headed by a framework knitter: P. Sharpe, 'The Shiners: Framework-Knitting Households in Nottinghamshire and Derbyshire, 1840–1890', *Family and Community History*, 3 (2000), pp. 105–20.

147. T. Wailey, 'Community: Life in the Inshore Village of Marshside', in P. Thompson, T. Wailey and T. Lummis, *Living the Fishing* (London, 1983), ch. 5.

148. For the remarkable range of the countryside's natural resources (food, fuel, raw materials, agricultural by-products) in the early modern period, see D. Woodward, 'Straw, Bracken, and the Wicklow Whale: The Exploitation of Natural Resources in England Since 1500', *Past and Present*, 159 (1998), pp. 43–76. For the innovation and diversity of farmers (both successful and less successful), from the Middle Ages to the present, see J. Thirsk, *Alternative Agriculture: A History from the Black Death to the Present Day* (Oxford, 1997).

149. B. Short, 'Conservation, Class and Custom: Lifespace and Conflict in a Nineteenth-Century Forest Environment', *Rural History*, 10 (1999), pp. 127–54.

150. B. J. Davey, *Ashwell 1830–1914: The Decline of a Village Community* (Leicester, 1980), pp. 17–18, 37–8. The Cambridgeshire coprolite works also provided 'much employment for the young of both sexes of the agricultural labouring class . . . The digging work is done by men and grown lads; boys are employed in wheeling barrows, and children of both sexes in sorting the fossils in the mills.' See *PP*, 1867–8, xvii, First Report, p. 168.

151. Samuel, 'Quarry Roughs', pp. 139–263.

3 Working Women and Children

1. The best accounts of rural women's work in the nineteenth century are J. Kitteringham, 'Country Work Girls in Nineteenth-Century England', in R. Samuel (ed.), *Village Life and Labour* (London, 1982), pp. 75–138; and N. Verdon, *Rural Women in Nineteenth-Century England: Gender, Work, and Wages* (Woodbridge, 2002).

2. See P. Horn, *Victorian Countrywomen* (Oxford, 1991), ch. 5.

3. B. Reay, *Microhistories: Demography, Society and Culture in Rural England, 1800–1930* (Cambridge, 1996), pp. 17–18.

4. Census, 1871 – Summary Tables: *Parliamentary Papers* (hereafter *PP*), 1873, lxxi, Part 1, pp. 44–5.

5. Horn, *Victorian Countrywomen*, pp. 186, 187.

6. Reay, *Microhistories*, p. 22.

7. M. F. Davies, *Life in an English Village* (London, 1909), pp. 124–30.

8. *PP*, 1873, lxxi, Part 1, p. 44. These figures are for the whole of England and Wales (not just the rural areas).

9. Templeman Library (hereafter TL), University of Kent, Oral History Project: Life in Kent Before 1914, E. Clark, b. 1885.

10. TL, F. Dadson, b. 1895.

11. E. Higgs, 'Women, Occupations and Work in the Nineteenth-Century Censuses', *History Workshop*, 23 (1987), p. 75. Figures adjusted by Higgs.

12. My calculations based on Census of 1871: *PP*, 1873, lxxi, Part 1, p. 45.

13. However, see Verdon, *Rural Women*, ch. 3.

14. M. Bragg, *Speak for England* (London, 1976), pp. 48–50.

15. D. Gittins, 'Marital Status, Work and Kinship, 1850–1930', in J. Lewis (ed.), *Labour and Love* (Oxford, 1986), p. 251; Higgs, 'Women, Occupations and Work', p. 60.

16. E. Higgs, 'Occupational Censuses and the Agricultural Workforce in Victorian England and Wales', *Economic History Review*, 48 (1995), p. 706.

17. C. Miller, 'The Hidden Workforce: Female Field Workers in Gloucestershire, 1870–1901', *Southern History*, 6 (1984), pp. 139–55.

18. H. V. Speechley, 'Female and Child Agricultural Day Labourers in Somerset, *c.* 1685–1870' (University of Exeter Ph.D. thesis, 1999), pp. 29–30.

19. Miller, 'Hidden Workforce', p. 145.

20. E. Roberts, *Women's Work 1840–1940* (London, 1990), p. 31.

21. Higgs, 'Women, Occupations and Work', p. 75.

22. M. Drake, 'Domestic Servants', in J. Golby (ed.), *Communities and Families* (Cambridge, 1994), pp. 38–9.

23. P. Taylor, 'Daughters and Mothers – Maids and Mistresses: Domestic Service Between the Wars', in J. Clarke, C. Critcher, and R. Johnson (eds), *Working Class Culture* (London, 1979), ch. 5. For change over time, see E. M. Garrett, 'The Dawning of a New Era? Women's Work in England and Wales at the Turn of the Twentieth Century', *Histoire Sociale/Social History*, 28 (1995), pp. 428–9, 441, 450–1, 457–8.

24. Census, 1891: *PP*, 1893–4, cvi, pp. 121–2.

25. Drake, 'Domestic Servants', p. 48.

26. Drake, 'Domestic Servants', pp. 39–44. Data from the 13 study areas of the Cambridge Group for the History of Population and Social Structure points to an ageing of domestic servants over the twentieth century: the percentage under the age of 25 drops every ten years from 68% in 1891 to 37% in 1921: Garrett, 'Dawning', p. 458 (Table 9).

27. Reay, *Microhistories*, p. 32; E. Higgs, 'Domestic Servants and Households in Victorian England', *Social History*, 8 (1983), p. 208.

28. TL, V. Turner, b. 1896.

29. University of Essex, Essex Oral History Collection (hereafter EOHC), Family Life and Work Experience Before 1918, Int. 310, M. Childs, b. 1901.

30. Bragg, *Speak for England*, p. 47.

31. Reay, *Microhistories*, pp. 30–1.

32. TL, G. Post, b. 1896; V. Turner, b. 1896; E. Burgess, b. 1890; L. Austin, b. 1902.

33. K. D. M. Snell, *Annals of the Labouring Poor: Social Change and Agrarian England, 1660–1900* (Cambridge, 1985), ch. 1; R. C. Allen, *Enclosure and the Yeoman: The Agricultural Development of the South Midlands 1450–1850* (Oxford, 1992), chs. 11–12, esp. pp. 215, 235–6; P. Sharpe, 'The Female Labour Market in English Agriculture During the Industrial Revolution: Expansion or Contraction?', *Agricultural History Review*, 47 (1999), pp. 161–82.

34. *Second Report of the Commissioners on the Employment of Children, Young Persons, and Women in Agriculture, PP*, 1868–9, xiii, p. 16.

35. *Royal Commission on Labour: The Agricultural Labourer: Reports . . . Upon . . . Selected Districts, PP*, 1893–4, xxxv, p. 337.

36. Extracts from *PP*, 1868–9, xiii, Second Report, p. 88.

37. K. Sayer, *Women of the Fields: Representations of Rural Women in the Nineteenth Century* (Manchester 1995). Quote from p. 125.

38. J. Bourke, Housewifery in Working-Class England 1860–1914', *Past and Present*, 143 (1994), pp. 167–97. Quote from p. 174.

39. *PP*, 1868–9, xiii, Second Report, pp. 127–8.

40. See the evidence of rural workers, ibid., pp. 520–30.

41. *First Report of the Commissioners on the Employment of Children, Young Persons, and Women in Agriculture, PP*, 1867–8, xvii, p. 438.

42. *Reports of Special Assistant Poor Law Commissioners on the Employment of Women and Children in Agriculture, PP*, 1843, xii, p. 19.

43. *PP*, 1868–9, xiii, Second Report, p. 88.

44. My calculations based on Census of 1871: *PP*, 1873, lxxi, Part 1.

45. *PP*, 1868–9, xiii, Second Report, p. 109.

46. *PP*, 1893–4, xxxv, pp. 429–32. For women workers in Northumberland, see J. Long, *Conversations in Cold Rooms: Women, Work and Poverty in Nineteenth-Century Northumberland* (Woodbridge, 1999), ch. 4.

47. E. Hostettler, 'Women Farm Workers in 18th and 19th Century Northumberland', *North East Labour History*, 16 (1982), p. 40.

48. Northumberland Record Office (hereafter NRO), 1193/T97, Oral History, M. Bruce, b. 1897.

49. *PP*, 1868–9, xiii, Second Report, p. 750.

50. Ibid., pp. 210–11, 750–9.

51. Ibid., p. 758.

52. Ibid., p. 78.

53. Ibid., p. 89.

54. Ibid., pp. 127–8.

55. Ibid., p. 81.

56. C. Black (ed.), *Married Women's Work* (London, 1983), p. 233. First published in 1915.

57. Most of the oral history informants mention hop-picking. See also, M. Lewis (ed.), *Old Days in the Kent Hop Gardens* (Maidstone, 1981). G. O'Neill, *Pull No More Bines: An Oral History of East London Women Hop Pickers* (London, 1990), deals with memories of picking as late as the 1970s.

58. *PP*, 1868–9, xiii, Second Report, pp. 273, 277, 279.

59. *Morning Chronicle*, 13 February 1850: 'Labour and the Poor: The Rural Districts'.

60. *Report . . . into the Administration . . . of the Poor Laws . . . Answers to Rural Queries, PP*, 1834, xxx.

61. N. Verdon, 'The Rural Labour Market in the Early Nineteenth Century: Women's and Children's Employment, Family Income, and the 1834 Poor Law Report', *Economic History Review*, 55 (2002), pp. 299–323, esp. pp. 304–8.

62. *PP*, 1893–4, xxxv, p. 118.

63. *PP*, 1867–8, xvii, First Report, p. 155.

64. J. Golby, 'Married Women and Work', in Golby (ed.), *Communities and Families*, pp. 50–3.

65. See R. Samuel, ' "Quarry Roughs": Life and Labour in Headington Quarry, 1860–1920. An Essay in Oral History', in Samuel (ed.), *Village Life and Labour*, pp. 179–83. And for 1891, not covered in Samuel's account, see Public Record Office (hereafter PRO), RG 12/1163, Headington Quarry Census 1891. My calculations.

66. Black (ed.), *Married Women's Work*, pp. 235–7.

67. *PP*, 1868–9, xiii, Second Report, p. 205.

68. J. W. G. Powlesland, 'The Work Experience of Women in Montacute, Somerset, During the Period 1851–1891', in L. Faulkner and R. Finnegan (eds), *Project Reports in Family and Community History* (Open University CD-ROM 1996).

69. *PP*, 1868–9, xiii, Second Report, p. 246.

70. *PP*, 1843, xii, pp. 102–3.

71. R. Wall, 'Work, Welfare and the Family: An Ilustration of the Adaptive Family Economy', in L. Bonfield, R.M. Smith, and K. Wrightson (eds), *The World We Have Gained* (Oxford, 1986), pp. 280–1.

72. P. Coker, 'Married Women's Paid Work in Kensworth Village and the Parish of Bolnhurst in 1851', and H. Hull, 'The Extent of Married Women's Work in Two Bedfordshire Lace-Making Villages in 1851', in Faulkner and Finnegan (eds), *Project Reports* (2001).

73. My calculations from PRO, RG 12/1262, Ridgmont Census 1891.

74. PRO, RG 12/1299, Littleport Census 1891.

75. *PP*, 1893–4, xxxv, p. 363.

76. R. A. Whitta, 'An Analysis of the Population of Brandon, Suffolk, in the Second Half of the Nineteenth Century', in Faulkner and Finnegan (eds), *Project Reports* (1996).

77. P. Sharpe, *Adapting to Capitalism: Working Women in the English Economy, 1700–1850* (London, 1996), chs. 2–3.

78. *PP*, 1867–8, xvii, First Report, pp. 168, 311, 439.

79. Black (ed.), *Married Women's Work*, pp. 239–41.

80. N. Goose, *Population, Economy and Family Structure in Hertfordshire in 1851: The Berkhamsted Region* (Hatfield, 1996), p. 38; N. Goose, *Population, Economy and Family Structure in Hertfordshire in 1851: St Albans and its Region* (Hatfield, 2000), pp. 89–91. For a wider study of straw-plaiting, see P. Sharpe, 'The Women's Harvest: Straw-Plaiting and the Representation of Labouring Women's Employment, *c.* 1793–1885', *Rural History*, 5 (1994), pp. 129–42; Verdon, *Rural Women*, ch. 5. By 1891, only 13 per cent of married women in Harpenden were classified as having an occupation: straw-hat-making was the occupation of nearly 30 per cent of women with an occupation, but the number of working women had clearly declined: PRO, RG 12/1114, Harpenden Census 1891.

81. *PP*, 1868–9, xiii, Second Report, p. 89.

82. Ibid., p. 9.

83. See Kitteringham, 'Country Work Girls', pp. 75–138; Reay, *Microhistories*, pp. 231–2.

84. Kitteringham, 'Country Work Girls', p. 81.

85. Reay, *Microhistories*, p. 231.

86. See P. Horn (ed.), *Village Education in Nineteenth-Century Oxfordshire: The Whitchurch School Log Book* (Oxfordshire Record Society, 51, 1979).

87. H. Cunningham, 'The Employment and Unemployment of Children in England *c.* 1680–1851', *Past and Present*, 126 (1990), pp. 115–50.

88. *PP*, 1868–9, xiii, Second Report, p. 282.

89. For a good overview of child-labour trends, see A. Davin, 'Child Labour, the Working-Class Family, and Domestic Ideology in 19th Century Britain', *Development and Change*, 13 (1982), pp. 633–52.

90. TL, Mr. and Mrs. Arnold, b. 1907 and 1910.

91. Sharpe, *Adapting to Capitalism*, p. 13.

92. TL, H. Adley, b. 1886.

93. A. Davin, 'When is a Child not a Child?', in H. Corr and L. Jamieson (eds.), *Politics of Everyday Life* (London, 1990), p. 39. See also, A. Davin, 'Working or Helping? London Working-Class Children in the Domestic Economy', in J. Smith, I. Wallerstein, and H. D. Evers (eds.), *Households and the World Economy* (Beverley Hills, 1984), ch. 14; and her rich case-study of children in London, *Growing up Poor: Home School and Street in London 1870–1914* (London, 1996).

94. Reay, *Microhistories*, p. 116.

95. Davin, *Growing up Poor*, pp. 85, 86, 175.

96. P. King, 'Customary Rights and Women's Earnings: The Importance of Gleaning to the Rural Labouring Poor, 1750–1850', *Economic History Review*, 44 (1991), pp. 461–76; J. P. Kay, 'Earnings of Agricultural Labourers in Norfolk and Suffolk', *Journal of the Royal Statistical Society*, 1 (1838), p. 183.

97. *PP*, 1868–9, xiii, Second Report, pp. 229, 789–92. For an excellent account of the opportunities for rural working children in nineteenth-century Lancashire, including cockling and potato work, see S. Coombs and D. Radburn, 'Children and Young People on the Land', in M. Winstanley, *Working Children in Nineteenth-Century Lancashire* (Preston, 1995), ch. 4.

98. *PP*, 1868–9, xiii, Second Report, p. 658.

99. Cunningham, 'Employment and Unemployment of Children', pp. 115–50.

100. However, he allowed for labouring households within such counties that did not enjoy the security and income of the 'constant man': *PP*, 1868–9, xiii, Second Report, p. 9.

101. Ibid. He cites Bedfordshire, Berkshire, Buckinghamshire, Essex, Gloucestershire, Norfolk, Oxfordshire and Suffolk wrongly as high-wage areas. He is correct with his inclusion of Northumberland and Yorkshire.

102. Ibid., p. 11.

103. Ibid., p. 254.

104. Ibid., pp. 211–12.

105. N. Verdon, 'The Employment of Women and Children in Agriculture: A Reassessment of Agricultural Gangs in Nineteenth-century Norfolk', *Agricultural History Review*, 49 (2001), p. 51.

106. *PP*, 1868–9, xiii, Second Report, pp. 195–7, 683.

107. Ibid., p. 12.

108. Ibid., pp. 77–8.

109. Ibid, p. 56.

110. Ibid.

111. Ibid.

112. Ibid, p. 89.

113. M. Lavalette, 'The Changing Form of Child Labour *circa* 1880–1918', in M. Lavalette (ed.), *A Thing of the Past? Child Labour in Britain in the Nineteenth and Twentieth Centuries* (Liverpool, 1999), ch. 5.

114. D. Vincent, *The Rise of Mass Literacy: Reading and Writing in Modern Europe* (Cambridge, 2000), p. 65.

115. Reay, *Microhistories*, pp. 223–33.

116. A. Williams, *A Wiltshire Village* (London, 1920), p. 207.

117. Reay, *Microhistories*, pp. 223–33.

118. W. B. Stephens, *Education, Literacy and Society, 1830–70: The Geography of Diversity in Provincial England* (Manchester, 1987), p. 41.

119. Reay, *Microhistories*, pp. 221, 226.

120. For these (sometimes rather slippery) links, see Stephens, *Education, Literacy and Society*, esp. pp. 19, 21, 79–80, 191–2, 248–50, 265.

121. H. Bradley, *Men's Work, Women's Work* (Cambridge, 1989), p. 38.

122. Verdon, *Rural Women*, pp. 98–106.

123. Ibid., pp. 115–16.

124. J. Burnette, 'Labourers at the Oakes: Changes in the Demand for Female Day-Labourers at a Farm Near Sheffield During the Agricultural Revolution', *Journal of Economic History*, 59 (1999), pp. 41–67.

125. Goose, *St Albans and its Region*, pp. 106–9.

126. Goose, *The Berkhamsted Region*, p. 39; Goose, *St Albans and its Region*, p. 114.

127. *PP*, 1893–4, xxxv, pp. 32, 36.

128. E. Jordan, 'Female Unemployment in England and Wales 1851–1911: An Examination of the Census Figures for 15–19 Year Olds', *Social History*, 13 (1988), pp. 175–90.

129. For children aged ten to 14: Cunningham, 'Employment and Unemployment of Children', pp. 144–5. Boys' rates varied from over 50 per cent in the West Riding and Bedfordshire to less than 20 per cent in Middlesex.

130. From 1 per cent to 42 per cent (women), and from 5 per cent to 33 per cent (children): Speechley, 'Female and Child Agricultural Day Labourers in Somerset', pp. 57, 150.

131. *PP*, 1843, xii, pp. 19–20.

132. Miller, 'Hidden Workforce', pp. 139–55.

133. A. M. James, 'The Working Women of Alton, Hampshire in 1891; A Study of Female Employment in a Traditional English Market Town', in Faulkner and Finnegan (eds), *Project Reports* (2001).

134. *PP*, 1893–4, xxxv, pp. 50–1.

135. This is in keeping with the findings of the most recent history of rural women workers: Verdon, *Rural women*.

4 Household Strategies

1. Templeman Library (hereafter TL), University of Kent, Oral History Project: Life in Kent Before 1914, L. Austin, b. 1902; P. H. Mann, 'Life in an Agricultural Village in England', *Sociological Review*, 1 (1904), p. 169.
2. S. Horrell and J. Humphries, 'Old Questions, New Data, and Alternative Perspectives: Families' Living Standards in the Industrial Revolution', *Journal of Economic History*, 52 (1992), pp. 855, 858–9.
3. *Second Report of the Commissioners on the Employment of Children, Young Persons, and Women in Agriculture Parliamentary Papers* (hereafter *PP*), 1868–9, xiii, p. 154.
4. Ibid., p. 625.
5. J. P. Kay, 'Earnings of Agricultural Labourers in Norfolk and Suffolk', *Journal of the Royal Statistical Society*, 1 (1838), calculated from the summary table on p. 183.
6. *Reports of Special Assistant Poor Law Commissioners on the Employment of Women and Children in Agriculture*, *PP*, 1843, xii, p. 32.
7. Mann, 'Life in an Agricultural Village', p. 189.
8. Of 99 couples, the wife worked in 32 cases (32%), and either a wife or child (or both) were given occupations in 63 cases (64%). My calculations from Public Record Office (hereafter PRO), RG 12/1262, Ridgmont Census 1891.
9. A. Randell, *Fenland Memories* (London, 1969), pp. 77, 80.
10. See L. H. Lees, 'Getting and Spending: The Family Budgets of English Industrial Workers', in J. M. Merriman (ed.), *Consciousness and Class Experience in Nineteenth-Century Europe* (New York, 1979), ch. 8; E. Roberts, 'Women and the Domestic Economy, 1890–1970: The Oral Evidence', in M. Drake (ed.), *Time, Family and Community: Perspectives on Family and Community History* (Oxford, 1994), ch. 6; N. Verdon, *Rural Women in Nineteenth-Century England: Gender, Work, and Wages* (Woodbridge, 2002), ch. 6. See also Ellen Ross, *Love and Toil: Motherhood in Outcast London 1870–1918* (New York, 1993), ch. 2.
11. *PP*, 1868–9, xiii, Second Report, p. 618.
12. D. Vincent, *Poor Citizens: The State and the Poor in Twentieth-Century Britain* (London, 1991), p. 6.
13. A. Tweedy, 'Recollections of a Farm Worker', *Bulletin of the Cleveland and Teeside Local History Society*, 21 (1973), p. 1.
14. See the discussions in E. H. Hunt, *British Labour History 1815–1914* (London, 1988), pp. 81–8; D. J. Oddy, 'Food, Drink and Nutrition', in F. M. L. Thompson (ed.), *The Cambridge Social History of Britain 1750–1950, Vol. 2, People and their Environment* (Cambridge, 1990), ch. 5; C. Shammas, *The Pre-Industrial Consumer in England and America* (Oxford, 1990), ch. 5. See also, although for London, A. Davin, 'Loaves and Fishes: Food in Poor Households in Late Nineteenth-Century London', *History Workshop Journal*, 41 (1996), pp. 167–92.
15. *PP*, 1868–9, xiii, Second Report, p. 102.

16. Ibid., p. 300.
17. Compare the budgets in E. C. Tufnell, 'The Dwellings and General Economy of the Labouring Classes in Kent and Sussex' [1841], in J. Simon, *Report on the Sanitary Condition of the City of London* (London, 1853), with the later budgets in M. F. Davies, *Life in an English Village* (London, 1909).
18. B. S. Rowntree and M. Kendall, *How the Labourer Lives* (London, 1913), p. 40.
19. C. Holdenby, *Folk of the Furrow* (London, 1913), pp. 43, 44.
20. University of Essex, Essex Oral History Collection (hereafter EOHC), Family Life and Work Experience Before 1918, Int. 22, C. Hills, b. 1904.
21. B. Reay, *Microhistories: Demography, Society and Culture in Rural England, 1800–1930* (Cambridge, 1996), pp. 121–2.
22. R. Floud, K. Watcher, and A. Gregory, *Height, Health and History: Nutritional Status in the United Kingdom, 1750–1980* (Cambridge, 1990), p. 198.
23. J. Nye, *A Small Account of My Travels Through the Wilderness* (Brighton, n.d.), p. 11. This autobiography of an agricultural labourer was written between the 1860s and 1888, and edited by Vic Gammon for QueenSpark Books.
24. EOHC, Int. 22, C. Hills, b. 1904.
25. Reay, *Microhistories*, p. 122.
26. Cyril Rice, in S. Humphries and B. Hopwood, *Green and Pleasant Land* (London, 1999), pp. 14–15. See also R. Malcolmson and S. Mastoris, *The English Pig: A History* (London, 1998), ch. 5.
27. Malcolmson and Mastoris, *English Pig*, p. 64.
28. See J. G. Rule, 'Social Crime in the Rural South in the Eighteenth and Early Nineteenth Centuries', *Southern History*, 1 (1979), pp. 135–53; A. Howkins, 'Economic Crime and Class Law: Poaching and the Game Laws, 1840–1880', in S. Burman and B. E. Harrell-Bond (eds), *The Imposition of Law* (New York, 1979), ch. 15; D. Jones, 'The Poacher: A Study in Victorian Crime and Protest', in his *Crime, Protest, Community and Police in Nineteenth-Century Britain* (London, 1982), ch. 3.
29. R. Samuel, '"Quarry Roughs": Life and Labour in Headington Quarry, 1860–1920. An Essay in Oral History', in R. Samuel (ed.), *Village Life and Labour* (London, 1982), pp. 218–23.
30. Northumberland Record Office (hereafter NRO), 1706/T139, Oral History, A. Patten.
31. EOHC, Int. 265, F. Harker, b. 1895.
32. TL, L. Austin, b. 1902.
33. EOHC, Int. 22, C. Hills, b. 1904.
34. Ibid.
35. TL, J. W. Manuel, b. 1903.
36. R. Palmer (ed.), 'The Minstrel of Quarry Bank', *Oral History*, 11, no. 1 (1983), p. 64.
37. R. Arnold, *The Farthest Promised Land: English Villagers, New Zealand Immigrants of the 1870s* (Wellington, 1981), pp. 127, 193, 194, 198, 244.
38. [Benjamin Smith], *Twenty-Four Letters from Labourers in America* (London, 1829), pp. 12, 16, 28.

39. British Library of Political and Economic Science, University of London, Emigrants' Letters, 1/45.
40. Rowntree and Kendall, *How the Labourer Lives*, p. 307.
41. TL, L. Austin, b. 1902.
42. J. Ashby and B. King, 'Statistics of Some Midland Villages', *Economic Journal*, 3 (1893), pp. 13–20.
43. J. Burchardt, *The Allotment Movement in England, 1793–1873* (Woodbridge, 2002), pp. 130, 150, 154, 156, 162, 232.
44. Ibid, pp. 182–3, 228.
45. Hernhill Oral History, E. Wade, b. 1908. The Hernhill Oral History Tapes are interviews that I carried out in 1991–92. For 'making do', see E. Hostettler, '"Making Do": Domestic Life Among East Anglian Labourers, 1890–1910', in L. Davidoff and B. Westover (eds), *Our Work, Our lives, Our Words* (London, 1986), ch. 2.
46. TL, F. Pack, b. 1897.
47. Hostettler, 'Making Do'; Reay, *Microhistories*, pp. 124–5; Verdon, *Rural Women*, p. 175.
48. J. E. Archer, *By a Flash and a Scare: Incendiarism, Animal Maiming, and Poaching in East Anglia 1815–1870* (Oxford, 1990), p. 14.
49. Quoted in ibid., p. 15.
50. T. Shakesheff, 'Wood and Crop Theft in Rural Herefordshire, 1800–60', *Rural History*, 13 (2002), pp. 1–18.
51. TL, L. Austin, b. 1902.
52. P. Johnson, *Saving and Spending: The Working-Class Economy in Britain 1870–1939* (Oxford, 1985), ch. 3; D. Neave, *Mutual Aid in the Victorian Countryside: Friendly Societies in the Rural East Riding 1830–1914* (Hull, 1991); Reay, *Microhistories*, pp. 126–8; E. Lord, 'The Friendly Society Movement and the Respectability of the Rural Working Class', *Rural History*, 8 (1997), pp. 165–73.
53. J. C. Riley, *Sick, Not Dead: The Health of British Workingmen During the Mortality Decline* (Baltimore, MD, 1997), pp. 29–30.
54. Ashby and King, 'Statistics', p. 203. The figure was 5,200 estimated total membership: 1.25 per family.
55. Neave, *Mutual Aid*, ch. 5.
56. M. Gorsky, 'The Growth and Distribution of English Friendly Societies in the Early Nineteenth Century', *Economic History Review*, 51 (1998), pp. 489–511.
57. My calculations from figures provided in *PP*, 1868–9, xiii, Second Report, pp. 215–16.
58. *Royal Commission on Labour: The Agricultural Labourer: Reports . . . Upon . . . Selected Districts*, PP, 1893–4, xxxv, p. 98 (for Friendly Society numbers); *PP*, 1893–4, cvi, pp. 120–7 (for occupation totals).
59. W. E. Bear, 'The Farm Labourers of England and Wales', *Journal of the Royal Agricultural Society of England*, 4 (1893), p. 676; PP, 1893–4, xxxv, pp. 36, 63, 98, 126–7, 205, 585, 602, 619, 642–3, 689, 772.

60. For a useful survey, see M. Gorsky, 'Self Help and Mutual Aid: Friendly Societies in 19th Century Britain', *ReFresh*, 28 (1999), pp. 1–4.

61. Ashby and King, 'Statistics', p. 19.

62. See P. Mandler (ed.), *The Uses of Charity: The Poor on Relief in the Nineteenth-Century Metropolis* (Philadelphia, PA, 1990), particularly the chapters by Mandler, Lynn Hollen Lees and Ellen Ross. The phrase 'neighbourhood resource' comes from Ross's chapter, 'Hungry Children: Housewives and London Charity, 1870–1918', in ibid., ch. 6.

63. C. Booth, *The Aged Poor in England and Wales* (London, 1894), p. 330.

64. Mann, 'Life in an Agricultural Village', p. 192.

65. B. S. Rowntree, *Poverty: A Study of Town Life* (London, 1902), p. 137.

66. For an excellent recent discussion of the potentials of welfare at the local level during the long durée of the Old Poor Law, see J. Broad, 'Parish Economies of Welfare, 1650–1834', *Historical Journal*, 42 (1999), pp. 985–1006.

67. K. D. M. Snell, *Annals of the Labouring Poor: Social Change and Agrarian England, 1660–1900* (Cambridge, 1985), ch. 3; L. H. Lees, *The Solidarities of Strangers: The English Poor Laws and the People, 1700–1948* (Cambridge, 1998), pp. 64–73.

68. T. Sokoll (ed.), *Essex Pauper Letters 1731–1837* (Oxford, 2001).

69. P. Thane, *Old Age in History: Past Experiences, Present Issues* (Oxford, 2000), p. 155.

70. S. King, *Poverty and Welfare in England, 1700–1850: A Regional Perspective* (Manchester, 2000), chs 6–7. Indeed his argument is for two systems of welfare: see p. 221.

71. S. King and G. Timmins, *Making Sense of the Industrial Revolution* (Manchester, 2001), p. 319.

72. B. Reay, *The Last Rising of the Agricultural Labourers* (Oxford, 1990), index: 'poor', 'poor-relief'; Reay, *Microhistories*, p. 129.

73. G. R. Boyer, *An Economic History of the English Poor Law, 1750–1850* (Cambridge, 1990), esp. chs 1 and 3.

74. The best account of the operation of the New Poor Law is Lees, *Solidarities of Strangers*, chs 4–6.

75. Reay, *Microhistories*, p. 129.

76. TL, S. Twist, b. 1899.

77. Lees, *Solidarities of Strangers*, p. 182.

78. M. Woollard, 'The Employment and Retirement of Older Men, 1851–1881: Further Evidence From the Census', *Continuity and Change*, 17 (2002), pp. 445–6.

79. Census of 1871: *PP*, 1873, lxxi, Part 1, p. 39. My calculations.

80. Booth, *Aged Poor*, pp. 329–30.

81. J. M. Faragher, 'Open-Country Community: Sugar Creek, Illinois, 1820–1850', in S. Hahn and J. Prude (eds), *The Countryside in the Age of Capitalist Transformation* (Chapel Hill, NC, 1985), p. 251.

82. TL, L. Austin, b. 1902.

83. For the older view, see R. M. Smith, 'Fertility, Economy, and Household Formation in England Over Three Centuries', *Population and Development Review*, 7 (1981), pp. 595–622; D. Thomson, 'Welfare and the Historians', in L.

Bonfield, R. M. Smith, and K. Wrightson (eds), *The World We Have Gained* (Oxford, 1986), ch. 13; P. Laslett, 'Family, Kinship and Collectivity as Systems of Support in Pre-Industrial Europe: A Consideration of the "Nuclear-Hardship" Hypothesis', *Continuity and Change*, 3 (1988), pp. 153–75.

84. For these recent challenges to the orthodoxy about the shallowness of English kinship, see Reay, *Microhistories*, ch. 6; King and Timmins, *Making Sense of the Industrial Revolution*, ch. 8; and D. Kertzer, 'Living with Kin', in D. I. Kertzer and M. Barbagli (eds), *Family Life in the Long Nineteenth Century, 1789–1913* (New Haven, CT, 2002), ch. 2.

85. J. Robin, 'Family Care of the Elderly in a Nineteenth-Century Devonshire Parish', *Ageing and Society*, 4 (1984), p. 515; S. O. Rose, 'The Varying Household Arrangements of the Elderly in Three English Villages: Nottinghamshire, 1851–1881', *Continuity and Change*, 3 (1988), pp. 108–9; Reay, *Microhistories*, pp. 170–1. Elderly women were more likely to live on their own or with non-relatives than elderly men were, but most lived with a spouse or child: for a recent wide-ranging survey of the household arrangements of the elderly in English history, see R. Wall, 'The Residence Patterns of Elderly English Women in Comparative Perspective', in L. Botelho and P. Thane (eds), *Women and Ageing in British Society Since 1500* (London, 2001), ch. 7.

86. Rose, 'Household Arrangements of the Elderly', p. 118. See also, S. O. Rose, 'Widowhood and Poverty in Nineteenth-Century Nottinghamshire', in J. Henderson and R. Wall (eds), *Poor Women and Children in the European Past* (London, 1994), ch. 13.

87. Booth, *Aged Poor*, pp. 377–80.

88. The argument of Reay, *Microhistories*, ch. 6; Thane, *Old Age*, chs 8–9; King and Timmins, *Making Sense of the Industrial Revolution*, ch. 8.

89. Booth, *Aged Poor*, pp. 339–41. The survey was of all village elderly, not just the poor, and included nearly 25 per cent who lived off their own means.

90. E. Ross, 'Survival Networks: Women's Neighbourhood Sharing in London Before World War One', *History Workshop*, 15 (1983), pp. 4–27; For the villages, see Verdon, *Rural Women*, pp. 189–93.

91. Vincent, *Poor Citizens*, p. 14.

92. Booth, *Aged Poor*, p. 425.

93. Ibid., p. 380.

94. TL, H. Matthews, b. 1890.

95. J. Glyde, *Suffolk in the Nineteenth Century* (London, [1856]), p. 359.

96. Rowntree and Kendall, *How the Labourer Lives*, pp. 19–20.

97. Davies, *Life in an English Village*, p. 80.

98. D. Baines, 'The Economics of Migration in Nineteenth Century Britain', *ReFresh*, 27 (1998), pp. 5–8.

99. V. Worship, 'Cotton Factory or Workhouse: Poor Law Assisted Migration from Buckinghamshire to Northern England, 1835–1837', *Family and Community History*, 3 (2000), pp. 33–48.

100. J. Ginswick (ed.), *Labour and the Poor in England and Wales 1849–1851, Vol. 1: Lancashire, Cheshire, Yorkshire* (London, 1983), pp. 174, 180.

101. D. Baines, *Migration in a Mature Economy: Emigration and Internal Migration in England and Wales 1861–1900* (Cambridge, 1985), p. 228.

102. The counties are Sussex, Berkshire, Hertfordshire, Buckinghamshire, Huntingdonshire, Oxfordshire, Bedfordshire, Cambridgeshire, Suffolk, and Norfolk. Baines defines Surrey, Kent, and Essex as partly suburban and therefore does not include them: Ibid., p. 162.

103. Baines, 'Economics of Migration'.

104. Baines, *Migration in a Mature Economy*, p. 63.

105. Ibid., p. 128.

106. J. Robin, *Elmdon: Continuity and Change in a North-West Essex Village 1861–1964* (Cambridge, 1980), p. 190; J. V. Beckett and T. Foulds, 'Beyond the Micro: Laxton, the Computer and Social Change Over Time', *Local Historian*, 16 (1985), pp. 451–6; B. Wojciechowska, 'Brenchley: A Study of Migratory Movements in a Mid-Nineteenth Century Rural Parish', *Local Population Studies*, 41 (1988), pp. 28–40; K. Schürer, 'The Role of the Family in the Process of Migration', in C. G. Pooley and I. D. Whyte (eds), *Migrants, Emigrants and Immigrants: A Social History of Migration* (London, 1991), ch. 6, esp. table on p. 113; Reay, *Microhistories*, pp. 158, 258.

107. M. Anderson, 'The Social Implications of Demographic Change', in F.M.L. Thompson (ed.), *The Cambridge Social History of Britain 1750-1950, Vol. 2, People and Their Environment* (Cambridge, 1990), pp. 11–12.

108. P. S. Herridge, 'The Exodus of Burlescombe: A Study of the Out-Migration of the Natives of Burlescombe, Devon, in 1881', in L. Faulkner and R. Finnegan (eds), *Project Reports in Family and Community History* (Open University CD-ROM, 2001).

109. D. Mills and K. Schürer, 'Migration and Population Turnover', in Mills and Schürer (eds), *Local Communities in the Victorian Census Enumerators' Books* (Oxford, 1996), p. 225, Table 18.3.

110. C. Pooley and J. Turnbull, *Migration and Mobility in Britain Since the Eighteenth Century* (London, 1998), p. 65, Table 3.4.

111. D. Fitzpatrick, *Irish Emigration 1801–1921* (Dublin, 1984), pp. 29–30.

112. W. Cameron, S. Haines, and M. M. Maude (eds), *English Immigrant Voices: Labourers' Letters from Upper Canada in the 1830s* (Montreal, 2000), p. 50.

113. Ibid., p. 87.

114. Ibid., p. 44.

115. Ibid., p. 371.

116. R. Haines, '"Shovelling Out Paupers"? Parish-Assisted Emigration From England to Australia 1834–1847', in E. Richards (ed.), *Poor Australian Immigrants in the Nineteenth Century* (Canberra, 1991), p. 57.

117. G. Howells, '"For I Was Tired of England Sir": English Pauper Emigrant Strategies, 1834–60', *Social History*, 23 (1998), pp. 181–94. Quote from p. 185. See also, G. Howells, 'Emigration and the New Poor Law: The Norfolk Emigration Fever of 1836', *Rural History*, 11 (2000), pp. 145–64.

118. British Library of Political and Economic Science, Emigrants' Letters, 1/46.

119. See Arnold, *Farthest Promised Land*, chs 2–4.

120. Baines, *Migration in a Mature Economy*, pp. 76–7, 78.

121. For the US, see C. J. Erickson, 'Emigration From the British Isles to the U.S.A. in 1841: Part II. Who Were the English Migrants', *Population Studies*, 44 (1990), pp. 21–40, esp. p. 27. R. L. Cohn, 'The Occupations of English Immigrants to the United States, 1836–1853', *Journal of Economic History*, 52 (1992), pp. 377–87, has disputed these findings, arguing for a greater contingent of agricultural labour in US emigration. For Australia, see R. F. Haines, *Emigration and the Labouring Poor: Australian Recruitment in Britain and Ireland, 1831–60* (London, 1997), esp. pp. 58–9. For a comparative approach, see also, C. Erickson, *Leaving England: Essays on British Emigration in the Nineteenth Century* (London, 1994).

122. E. Richards, 'British Poverty and Australian Immigration in the Nineteenth Century', in Richards (ed.), *Poor Australian Immigrants*, p. 26.

123. C. Macdonald, *A Woman of Good Character: Single Women as Immigrant Settlers in Nineteenth-Century New Zealand* (Wellington, 1990), ch. 2.

124. Arnold, *Farthest Promised Land*, p. 103.

125. Ibid., p. 346.

126. Ibid., chs 6–10.

127. Ibid., p. 182.

128. Ibid., chs 12–13.

129. Of course it was far too orderly for a real English village. For Camden, see A. Atkinson, *Camden: Farm and Village Life in Early New South Wales* (Melbourne, 1988), esp. pp. 38–40, 126, 213–21.

130. R. Dalziel, 'Emigration and Kinship: Migrants to New Plymouth 1840–1843', *New Zealand Journal of History*, 25 (1991), pp. 112–28.

131. P. Hudson and D. Mills, 'English Emigration, Kinship and the Recruitment Process: Migration From Melbourn in Cambridgeshire to Melbourne in Victoria in the Mid-Nineteenth Century', *Rural History*, 10 (1999), pp. 55–74.

132. D. Hitch, 'Cambridgeshire Emigrants to Australia, 1842–74: A Family and Community Perspective', *Family and Community History*, 5 (2002), pp. 85–97.

133. *PP*, 1867–8, xvii, First Report, pp. 134, 365, 532, 624; *PP*, 1868–9, xiii, Second Report, p. 308, 310, 452–3, 457, 648, 755, 792–3; *PP*, 1893–4, xxxv, pp. 146, 431, 581, 847; *PP*, 1893–4, xxxvii, Part 2, p. 62.

134. *PP*, 1867–8, xvii, First Report, p. 134.

135. D. H. Morgan, *Harvesters and Harvesting 1840–1900* (London, 1982), ch. 5.

136. A. Mutch, *Rural Life in South-West Lancashire 1840–1914* (Lancaster, 1988), p. 39.

137. L. Fontaine and J. Schlumbohm, 'Household Strategies for Survival; An Introduction', *International Review of Social History*, 45 (2000), pp. 1–17, esp. pp. 5–6. Laura Oren anticipated their argument some thirty years earlier, appropriately in the first volume of the journal, *Feminist Studies*: L. Oren, 'The Welfare of Women in Labouring Families: England, 1860–1950', *Feminist Studies*, 1 (1973), pp. 107–25.

138. M. Bragg, *Speak for England* (London, 1976), pp. 46–7.

139. Li-Ming Hu, 'Reworking Oral Histories: Masculinity and Rural Workers' Representations of Self, 1890–1930' (University of Auckland MA thesis, 2001).
140. Oren, 'Welfare of Women', pp. 107–25.
141. *PP*, 1868–9, xiii, Second Report, p. 625.
142. Ibid., pp. 41–2.
143. Oren, 'Welfare of Women' (quote from p. 121).
144. EOHC, Int. 22, C. Hills, b. 1904.
145. R. Wall, 'Some Implications of the Earnings, Income and Expenditure Patterns of Married Women in Populations in the Past', in J. Henderson and R. Wall (eds), *Poor Women and Children in the European Past* (London, 1994), p. 329.
146. H. Cunningham, 'The Decline of Child Labour: Labour Markets and Family Economies in Europe and North America Since 1830', *Economic History Review*, 53 (2000), pp. 409–28, esp. pp. 409–10, 420.
147. S. Horrell and J. Humphries, 'The Origins and Expansion of the Male Breadwinner Family: The Case of Nineteenth-Century Britain', in A. Janssens (ed.), *The Rise and Decline of the Male Breadwinner Family?* (Cambridge, 1997), p. 37.
148. For the adaptive family economy, see R. Wall, 'Work, Welfare and the Family: An Illustration of the Adaptive Family Economy', in Bonfield, Smith, and Wrightson (eds), *World We Have Gained*, ch. 10.

5 Life and Death

1. F. Thompson, *Lark Rise to Candleford* (Harmondsworth, 1977), pp. 19, 136, 169. First published in 1939.
2. B. English, '*Lark Rise* and Juniper Hill: A Victorian Community in Literature and History', *Victorian Studies*, 29 (1985–6), pp. 7–34, esp. pp. 28–9, 31.
3. Ibid., p. 34.
4. M. Anderson, 'Highly Restricted Fertility: Very Small Families in the British Fertility Decline', *Population Studies*, 52 (1998), p. 178; R. Woods, *The Demography of Victorian England and Wales* (Cambridge, 2000), p. 118.
5. M. Anderson, 'The Social Implications of Demographic Change', in F. M. L. Thompson (ed.), *The Cambridge Social History of Britain 1750-1950, Vol. 2, People and Their Environment* (Cambridge, 1990), p. 27, Table 1.2. By the 1970s, only about 1 to 2 per cent of children were dead by the age of five.
6. R. I. Woods, 'The Population of Britain in the Nineteenth Century', in M. Anderson (ed.), *British Population History from the Black Death to the Present Day* (Cambridge, 1996), p. 305.
7. E. van de Walle and J. Knodel, 'Europe's Fertility Transition: New Evidence and Lessons for Today's Developing World', *Population Bulletin*, 34 (1979), pp. 1–43. R. I. Woods, 'Approaches to the Fertility Transition in Victorian England', *Population Studies*, 41 (1987), p. 309, also stresses the rapid change in England in the 1870s, 1880s and 1890s.
8. C. Wilson, 'Natural Fertility in Pre-Industrial England, 1600-1799', *Population*

Studies, 38 (1984), pp. 225–40; Woods, 'Approaches', p. 283; C. Wilson and R. Woods, 'Fertility in England: A Long-Term Perspective', *Population Studies*, 45 (1991), pp. 399–400.

9. Wilson and Woods, 'Fertility', p. 399.

10. W. Seccombe, 'Starting to Stop: Working-class Fertility Decline in Britain', *Past and Present*, 126 (1990), p. 153; Woods, 'Approaches', p. 291. In spacing, or non-parity-specific limitation, couples prolong the intervals between births – that is, space out the births. Stopping behaviour, or parity-specific limitation, occurs when couples avoid having children after they have a certain number – that is, stop.

11. R. Woods, 'Working-Class Fertility Decline in Britain', *Past and Present*, 134 (1992), pp. 201–2. The most recent treatment of the issue is the impressive book by S. Szreter, *Fertility, Class and Gender in Britain, 1860–1940* (Cambridge, 1996), pp. 45–66.

12. Woods, *Demography*, pp. 21–3. Based on the original formulation of J. Hajnal, 'Two Kinds of Pre-Industrial Household Formation System', in R. Wall, J. Robin, and P. Laslett (eds), *Family Forms in Historic Europe* (Cambridge, 1983), ch. 2.

13. M. Anderson, 'Population Change in North-Western Europe, 1750-1850', in Anderson (ed.), *British Population History*, pp. 238–40; R. Schofield, 'British Population Change, 1700–1871', in R. Floud and D. McCloskey (eds), *The Economic History of Britain Since 1700* (Cambridge, 1994 edn), ch. 4.

14. E. A. Wrigley and R. S. Schofield, 'English Population History from Family Reconstitution: Summary Results 1600–1799', *Population Studies*, 37 (1983), p. 162; E. A. Wrigley and R. S. Schofield, *The Population History of England 1541-1871* (Cambridge, 1989 edn), p. 255; E. A. Wrigley, R. S. Davies, J. E. Oeppen and R. S. Schofield, *English Population History from Family Reconstitution 1580–1837* (Cambridge, 1997), pp. 134–7. Male marriage ages declined from 27 to 25.

15. Woods, *Demography*, pp. 23–4; M. Anderson, 'Households, Families and Individuals: Some Preliminary Results From the National Sample From the 1851 Census of Great Britain', *Continuity and Change*, 3 (1988), p. 427.

16. Nuptiality = the index of the proportion of women married. Woods, *Demography*, pp. 24, 81, 84–6. See also, the earlier work of Michael Anderson, 'Marriage Patterns in Victorian Britain: An Analysis Based on Registration District Data for England and Wales', *Journal of Family History*, 1 (1976), pp. 55–78.

17. R. I. Woods and P. R. A. Hinde, 'Nuptiality and Age at Marriage in Nineteenth-Century England', *Journal of Family History*, 10 (1985), pp. 119–44; P. R. Andrew Hinde, 'The Marriage Market in the Nineteenth Century English Countryside', *Journal of European Economic History*, 18 (1989), pp. 383–92.

18. B. Reay, *Microhistories: Demography, Society and Culture in Rural England, 1800-1930* (Cambridge, 1996), p. 42; See the summary Table 7 in D. R. Mills, *Aspects of Marriage: An Example of Applied Historical Studies* (Milton Keynes, 1980), p. 21.

19. Reay, *Microhistories*, pp. 44, 64.

20. D. Levine, 'Sampling History: The English Population', *Journal of Interdisciplinary History*, 28 (1998), pp. 605–32 (quote from p. 626).
21. G. Santow, 'Coitus Interruptus and the Control of Natural Fertility', *Population Studies*, 49 (1995), pp. 19–43; and Woods, *Demography*, p. 134, although he continues to employ the concept. See also R. T. Vann, 'Unnatural Fertility, or Whatever Happened in Colyton?', *Continuity and Change*, 14 (1999), pp. 91–104. One of the problems for demographers trying to chart the pattern of the onset of family limitation is arriving at an agreed measurement. The influential standard of unrestrained Hutterite fertility (which lay behind most demographic work) has been challenged as setting unrealistic levels of so-called natural fertility, and showing insufficient sensitivity to the range of English fertility before the transition to fertility control. A new measurement has been proposed using British figures for the period 1650–1799 to determine natural levels (before the transition), and employing figures for England and Wales for 1938 as a standard for fertility control (fertility after the transition). The problem that arises from this reworking of the demographic models is that much of the work on family limitation (including Richard Vann's and this writer's own) is undermined. Communities that were believed to be practising family limitation now fall under the revised concept of 'natural' fertility. See Woods, *Demography*, pp. 124–40. While it is not appropriate to go into specifics here, one of the problems with Woods' challenge to these studies is that he ignores a great deal of other supporting evidence for family limitation.
22. I am responding to Levine's suggestion (in his critique of the Cambridge Group's latest population history) that someone remove a cohort of family controllers from the aggregate and subject them to more searching analysis. Levine, 'Sampling History', p. 629.
23. Szreter, *Fertility*, pp. 335–46. For the link between early fertility decline and late marriage, see also M. Anderson, 'Fertility Decline in Scotland, England and Wales, and Ireland: Comparisons From the 1911 Census of Fertility', *Population Studies*, 52 (1998), pp. 1–20.
24. Szreter, *Fertility*, p. 346.
25. See ibid., ch. 8.
26. Ibid., p. 381.
27. E. M. Garrett, 'The Trials of Labour', *Continuity and Change*, 5 (1990), pp. 121–54; Szreter, *Fertility*, p. 375. Vann and Eversley have raised the possibility of spacing behaviour among newly-married Quakers in pre-industrial southern England: R. T. Vann and D. Eversley, *Friends in Life and Death* (Cambridge, 1992), p. 162.
28. Szreter, *Fertility*, p. 433.
29. A further interesting contrast to the 'natural fertility' cohort is that it had a large number of families (37 per cent) neither spacing nor stopping and a negligible number (5 per cent) never starting at all, whereas in the family-controlling cohort only 3 per cent did not practise any form of control, and 27 per cent never started.

30. Szreter, *Fertility*, pp. 389–98.
31. Reay, *Microhistories*, pp. 44, 62, 65.
32. The title of ch. 7 of Szreter, *Fertility*. See also, his comments on pp. 534–46.
33. For the above, see ibid., ch. 7, esp. Figure 7.1, and Appendix C (pp. 608–13).
34. Ibid., ch. 7.
35. Anderson, 'Marriage Patterns'. The higher the percentage employed as domestic servants, the higher the marriage ages and proportion of women not married.
36. Szreter, *Fertility*, ch. 8 (quote from p. 502).
37. B. Hill, 'The Marriage Age of Women and the Demographers', *History Workshop*, 28 (1999), pp. 129–47 (quote from p. 140).
38. Woods, *Demography*, p. 137.
39. Farmers probably contributed substantially to this decline; hence the difference between the rates for agricultural labourers and agricultural areas. But the fertility of the wives of agricultural labourers did drop too. See E. Garrett, A. Reid, K. Schürer, and S. Szreter, *Changing Family Size in England and Wales: Place, Class and Demography, 1891–1911* (Cambridge, 2001), ch. 5, esp. pp. 226–9, 241–8, 258–60, 290–1.
40. Ibid., pp. 246–7.
41. Woods, *Demography*, ch. 4.
42. D. Friedlander and B. S. Okun, 'Pretransition Marital Fertility Variation over Time: Was There Deliberate Control in England?', *Journal of Family History*, 29 (1995), pp. 139–58.
43. Reay, *Microhistories*, p. 64; Szreter, *Fertility*, p. 418.
44. Reay, *Microhistories*, ch. 2; Anderson, 'Highly Restricted Fertility', pp. 177–99.
45. Reay, *Microhistories*, p. 63. Nationally, the percentage of couples with no more than one child rose from 13.6 per cent for those married in the 1870s to 26.1 per cent for the cohort of 1900–09 and 41.3 for marriages in 1925: Anderson, 'Highly Restricted Fertility', p. 178.
46. Hernhill Oral History, D. Tong, b. 1912. The Hernhill Oral History Tapes are interviews that I carried out in 1991–92.
47. M. Chamberlain, *Fenwomen: A Portrait of Women in an English Village* (London, 1983), p. 77.
48. A. Parker, 'Oxfordshire Village Folklore (1840–1900)', *Folk-Lore*, 24 (1913), p. 76.
49. Santow, 'Coitus Interruptus'; pp. 29, 41–3; Reay, *Microhistories*, p. 67; Szreter, *Fertility*, p. 447. See also, important recent work by Kate Fisher, dealing with birth control practices in working-class Wales and Oxford in the 1920s through to the 1940s: K. Fisher, 'Uncertain Aims and Tacit Negotiations: Birth Control Practices in Britain, 1925–50', *Population and Development Review*, 26 (2000), pp. 295–317, esp. comments on pp. 300–6.
50. Woods, 'Approaches', p. 291; Seccombe, 'Starting to Stop'; A. McLaren, *A History of Contraception* (Oxford, 1990), ch. 6; Santow, 'Coitus Interruptus'; Szreter, *Fertility*, pp. 50–5, 389–439; Woods, *Demography*, pp. 122–4; Fisher, 'Uncertain Aims'; and K. Fisher, '"She Was Quite Satisfied With the

Arrangements I Made": Gender and Birth Control in Britain 1920–1950', *Past and Present*, 169 (2000), pp. 161–93.

51. Fisher, 'Uncertain Aims', p. 305. Most had no more than three children, though some of the Welsh families had more than five.

52. For a wider literature that questions the uniformity of the European fertility decline as presented by the demographers of the Princeton European Fertility Project, see J. and P. Schneider, 'Demographic Transitions in a Sicilian Rural Town', *Journal of Family History*, 9 (1984), pp. 245–72; D. Levine, 'Recombinant Family Formation Strategies', *Journal of Historical Sociology*, 2 (1989), pp. 89–115; K. Ittmann, 'Family Limitation and Family Economy in Bradford, West Yorkshire 1851–1881', *Journal of Social History*, 25 (1991–2), pp. 547–73; J. R. Gillis, L. A. Tilly and D. Levine (eds), *The European Experience of Declining Fertility: A Quiet Revolution, 1850–1970* (Oxford, 1992). As Levine has put it, we should think of 'multiple paths', 'not one but many fertility declines': D. Levine, 'Moments in Time: A Historian's Context of Declining Fertility', in Gillis *et al.* (eds), *European Experience of Declining Fertility*, p. 329.

53. For the period 1800–80, the average number of children in those families unbroken by the death of one of the partners (and where the woman reached the age of 45) was 6.8. It was 4.1 in those families where one of the partners died before the family was completed. Based on my family reconstitutions for Hernhill, Dunkirk and Boughton: see Reay, *Microhistories*, pp. xix–xxi for the procedure.

54. Ibid. For the period 1800–80, a mean number of 1.1 children per family did not live to the age of five. This is a conservative figure because it does not allow for the under-registration of infant mortality.

55. Wrigley et al., *English Population History*, ch. 9; E.A. Wrigley, 'Explaining the Rise in Marital Fertility in England in the "Long" Eighteenth Century', *Economic History Review*, 51 (1998), pp. 435–64; P. Razzell, 'The Conundrum of Eighteenth-Century English Population Growth', *Social History of Medicine*, 11 (1998), p. 499.

56. See the discussion in Woods, *Demography*, pp. 295–300. It is also clear that prolonged breast-feeding has an inhibiting effect on both infant fertility and mortality; a change in practice can render infants more vulnerable as well as leading to higher fertility.

57. This applies to the basic texts, F. B. Smith, *The People's Health 1830–1910* (London, 1979), and A. S. Wohl, *Endangered Lives: Public Health in Victorian Britain* (London, 1983), as well as the best recent monograph on nineteenth-century diseases, A. Hardy, *The Epidemic Streets: Infectious Disease and the Rise of Preventive Medicine 1856–1900* (Oxford, 1993).

58. R. I. Woods, P. A. Watterson, and J. H. Woodward, 'The Causes of Rapid Infant Mortality Decline in England and Wales, 1861-1921 Part I', *Population Studies*, 42 (1988), pp. 343–66; R. I. Woods, P. A. Watterson, and J. H. Woodward, 'The Causes of Rapid Infant Mortality Decline in England and Wales, 1861-1921 Part II', *Population Studies*, 43 (1989), pp. 113–32; R. Woods, 'Infant Mortality in

Britain: A Survey of Current Knowledge on Historical Trends and Variations', in A. Bideau, B. Besjardins, H. P. Brignoli (eds), *Infant and Child Mortality in the Past* (Oxford, 1997), ch. 5; Woods, *Demography*, ch. 7. Clearly our knowledge of the patterns of infant mortality in the nineteenth and early twentieth centuries depends very heavily on the work of Robert Woods.

59. Woods, 'Infant Mortality in Britain', pp. 80–2; Woods, *Demography*, ch. 9.

60. Woods, *Demography*, tables and figures on pp. 365, 369, 372.

61. C. H. Lee, 'Regional Inequalities in Infant Mortality in Britain, 1861–1971: Patterns and Hypotheses', *Population Studies*, 45 (1991), p. 57: 15 experienced their highest infant-mortality rates in 1861, 19 in 1871, none in 1881, three in 1891, and four in 1901.

62. For the maps, see Woods, *Demography*, Figures 7.5 and 7.6 (between pp. 96–7); and R. Woods and N. Shelton, *An Atlas of Victorian Mortality* (Liverpool, 1997). For variation, see also R. Woods, 'Mortality Patterns in the Past', in R. Woods and J. Woodward (eds), *Urban Disease and Mortality in Nineteenth-Century England* (New York, 1984), ch. 2.

63. Woods *et al.*, 'Causes of Rapid Infant Mortality Decline . . . Part I', p. 359.

64. Woods, *Demography*, p. 262; and especially ch. 9.

65. See Figure 5.3 in Woods, 'Infant Mortality in Britain', p. 79.

66. Woods, *Demography*, pp. 368, 372.

67. Ibid., p. 369.

68. S. Szreter and G. Mooney, 'Urbanization, Mortality, and the Standard of Living Debate: New Estimates of the Expectation of Life at Birth in Nineteenth-Century British Cities', *Economic History Review*, 51 (1998), pp. 93–4.

69. Woods, *Demography*, p. 267.

70. A point made by Garrett *et al.*, *Changing Family Size*, p. 141.

71. Woods, *Demography*, pp. 252–4.

72. P. Huck, 'Infant Mortality in Nine Industrial Parishes in Northern England, 1813–1836', *Population Studies*, 48 (1994), pp. 513–26; Reay, *Microhistories*, pp. 72–5; S. King, 'Dying With Style: Infant Death and its Context in a Rural Industrial Township 1650–1830', *Social History of Medicine*, 10 (1997), p. 12.

73. Reay, *Microhistories*, pp. 72–5.

74. Or twentieth-century Nepal or Bangladesh: Reay, *Microhistories*, pp. 74–5.

75. Calculated from the table in M. W. Dupree, *Family Structure in the Staffordshire Potteries 1840–1880* (Oxford, 1995), p. 86.

76. Huck, 'Infant Mortality', p. 519.

77. D. Levine, *Family Formation in an Age of Nascent Capitalism* (New York, 1977), p. 68.

78. B. H. Babbage, *Report to the General Board of Health . . . of the Hamlet of Haworth* (London, 1850), pp. 7, 26.

79. King, 'Dying with Style', pp. 19–23.

80. Woods, *Demography*, p. 263.

81. The same problem occurs in Alan Armstrong's recent study of Norfolk when he provides figures for the main towns and 'rural Norfolk': A. Armstrong, *The Population of Victorian and Edwardian Norfolk* (Norwich, [2001]), ch. 3.

82. Razzell, 'Conundrum', pp. 490–1; Levine, 'Sampling History', pp. 617–18. The nineteenth-century rural parishes in Razzell's sample show lower levels, it is true, but my point is that these figures demonstrate the potential range of rural childhood mortality.

83. Levine, 'Sampling History', pp. 617–18.

84. W. Lee, *Report to the General Board of Health . . . of the Parish of Arnold* (London, 1850).

85. J. Skinner, *Journal of a Somerset Rector 1803–1834* (Oxford, 1984).

86. Reay, *Microhistories*, pp. 78–85.

87. R. Rawlinson, *Report to the General Board of Health . . . of the Townships of Alnwick and Canongate* (London, 1850), p. 38.

88. B. H. Babbage, *Report to the General Board of Health . . . of the Town of Bromyard* (London, 1850), pp. 10–11.

89. W. Lee, *Report to the General Board of Health . . . of the Parish of Longbridge Deverill* (London, 1850).

90. W. Lee, *Report to the General Board of Health . . . of the Parish of Holbeach* (London, 1849).

91. T. W. Rammell, *Report to the General Board of Health . . . of the Parish of Burnham* (London, 1849), pp. 6–11.

92. V. Fildes, 'Infant Feeding Practices and Infant Mortality in England, 1900–1919', *Continuity and Change*, 13 (1998), pp. 251–80. See also, Woods, *Demography*, pp. 280–95.

93. Fildes, 'Infant Feeding', pp. 263–7; Public Record Office (hereafter PRO), MH 12/5067, Report of Rural Sanitary Authority for 1881; PRO, MH 12/5069, Reports of Medical Officer of Health of Rural District for 1885 and 1886.

94. *Parliamentary Papers* (hereafter PP), 1864, xxviii, p. 35, and Appendix 14, pp. 454–62: 'Report by Dr. Henry Julian Hunter on the Excessive Mortality of Infants in Some Rural Districts of England'.

95. Fildes, 'Infant Feeding', p. 259.

96. Reay, *Microhistories*, pp. 81–2.

97. Fildes, 'Infant Feeding'.

98. M. J. Dobson, *Contours of Death and Disease in Early Modern England* (Cambridge, 1997), pp. 2–3.

99. Ibid., pp. 168–74.

100. Ibid., pp. 176–8.

101. Ibid., ch. 6. See also, M. Dobson, ' "Marsh Fever"– The Geography of Malaria in England', *Journal of Historical Geography*, 6 (1980), pp. 357–89.

102. PP, 1864, xxviii, Appendix 13, pp. 430–54: 'Report by Dr. George Whitley as to the Quantity of Ague and Other Malarious Diseases Now Prevailing in the Principal Marsh Districts of England'; and Appendix 14, pp. 454–62 (quote on p. 456).

103. C. Creighton, *A History of Epidemics in Britain*, Vol. 2 (London, 1965 edn), pp. 664, 672, 729, 742–3; Smith, *People's Health*, pp. 104–11, 136–52; Hardy, *Epidemic Streets*, pp. 28, 59; A. Hardy, 'Rickets and the Rest: Child-Care, Diet and the

Infectious Children's Diseases, 1850–1914', *Social History of Medicine*, 5 (1992), pp. 392–5.

104. Smith, *People's Health*, p. 143; L. Bradley, 'An Enquiry into Seasonality in Baptisms, Marriages and Burials. Part 3: Burial Seasonality', in M. Drake (ed.), *Population Studies From Parish Registers* (Matlock, 1982), p. 89; Hardy, *Epidemic Streets*, p. 45.

105. Smith, *People's Health*, p. 136.

106. See Smith, *People's Health*, pp. 147–8; Hardy, *Epidemic Streets*, pp. 44, 88.

107. Woods, *Demography*, ch. 8.

108. Vann and Eversley, *Friends in Life and Death*, p. 186.

109. Reay, *Microhistories*, pp. 85–8.

110. PRO, MH 12/5069, Report of Medical Officer of Health of Rural District for 1887.

111. J. C. Riley, *Sickness, Recovery and Death: A History and Forecast of Ill Health* (London, 1989), p. 192.

112. Wrigley and Schofield, *Population History of England*, p. 296.

113. Woods, *Demography*, ch. 8.

114. Ibid., pp. 332–40. See also, G. Cronjé, 'Tuberculosis and Mortality Decline in England and Wales, 1851–1910', in Woods and Woodward (eds), *Urban Disease and Mortality*, ch. 4.

115. W. Lee, *Report to the General Board of Health . . . of the Township of Baildon* (London, 1852), pp. 7–10.

116. T. W. Rammell, *Report to the General Board of Health . . . of the Town and Parish of Ottery St. Mary* (London, 1850), pp. 17–19. The agricultural workers lived in town and worked in the surrounding farms.

117. W. Lee, *Report to the General Board of Health . . . of the Parish of Mileham* (London, 1849), pp. 6–7, 16–17.

118. T. W. Rammell, *Report to the General Board of Health . . . of the Borough and Parish of Banbury* (London, 1850), pp. 16–17.

119. Rawlinson, *Report . . . Alnwick and Canongate*, p. 30.

120. Lee, *Report . . . Mileham*; W. Lee, *Report to the General Board of Health . . . of the Township of March* (London, 1851); T.W. Rammell, *Report to the General Board of Health . . . of the Parish of Wotton-under-Edge* (London, 1854); Rawlinson, *Report . . . Alnwick and Canongate*.

121. R. Woods and J. Woodward, 'Mortality, Poverty and the Environment', in Woods and Woodward (eds), *Urban Disease and Mortality*, p. 27. See also, Wohl, *Endangered Lives*, pp. 280–2; A. Armstrong, *Farmworkers: A Social and Economic History 1770–1980* (London, 1988), p. 140; M. R. Haines, 'Conditions of Work and the Decline of Mortality', in R. Schofield, D. Reher and A. Bideau (eds), *The Decline of Mortality in Europe* (Oxford, 1991), ch. 10.

122. Woods, *Demography*, pp. 207–8, and, more generally, ch. 6 (though agricultural labourers are not one of the occupations discussed in any detail). For the whole issue of occupation and environment, see E. Garrett and A. Reid, 'Satanic Mills, Pleasant Lands: Spatial Variation in Women's Work, Fertility

and Infant Mortality as Viewed from the 1911 Census', *Historical Research*, 67 (1994), pp. 156–77; A. Reid, 'Locality or Class? Spatial and Social Differentials in Infant and Child Mortality in England and Wales', in C. A. Corsini and P. P. Viazzo (eds), *The Decline of Infant and Child Mortality: The European Experience: 1750–1990* (The Hague, 1997), ch. 7; Garrett *et al.*, *Changing Family Size*, ch. 4. And for a fascinating case-study of the interaction between environment and class, see N. Williams, 'Death in its Season: Class, Environment and the Mortality of Infants in Nineteenth-Century Sheffield', *Social History of Medicine*, 5 (1992), pp. 71–94.

123. J. C. Riley, *Sick, Not Dead: The Health of British Workingmen During the Mortality Decline* (Baltimore, MD, 1997), p. 11.

124. A. Lochee, *A Descriptive and Tabular Report of the Medical and Surgical Cases Treated in the Kent and Canterbury Hospital . . . 1838 to 1840* (Canterbury, 1841), p. 19.

125. Ibid., pp. 8, 10, 17, 55.

126. *PP*, 1864, xxviii, Appendix 13, pp. 438–9, 453.

127. Lochee, *A Descriptive and Tabular Report*, pp. 9, 11, 20, 36; V. Berridge, 'Opium in the Fens in Nineteenth-Century England', *Journal of the History of Medicine*, 34 (1979), p. 297.

128. Hernhill Oral History, D. Tong, b. 1912.

129. Centre for Kentish Studies (hereafter CKS), G/F RA 12-14, Faversham Union Relieving Officer's Application and Report Books, 1859-61.

130. Riley, *Sick, Not Dead*, Table 7.2, p. 192.

131. *Reports of Special Assistant Poor Law Commissioners on the Employment of Women and Children in Agriculture*, *PP*, 1843, xii, p. 21.

132. This even applies to Garrett *et al.*, *Changing Family Size*, ch. 7, esp. comments on pp. 410, 412.

133. Compare: Reay, *Microhistories*, pp. 88–9 with Wrigley *et al.*, *English Population History*, p. 313.

134. Lee, *Report . . . March*, pp. 19, 46. For March in earlier periods, see Dobson, *Contours of Death and Disease*, pp. 173, 176: March had an IMR of over 250/1,000 in the period 1550–1740.

135. *Royal Commission on Labour: The Agricultural Labourer: Reports . . . Upon . . . Selected Districts*, *PP*, 1893–4, xxxv, p. 250.

136. Wrigley *et al.*, *English Population History*, pp. 232–3; Dobson, *Contours of Death and Disease*, p. 176.

6 Leisure

1. J. E. and P. A. Crowther (eds), *The Diary of Robert Sharp of South Cave: Life in a Yorkshire Village 1812–1837* (Oxford, 1997), p. 345.

2. Surely there is an element of not-so-hidden harrassment here.

3. *Diary of Robert Sharp*, p. 93.

4. Ibid., pp. 97, 240, 293, 372, 442.

5. Ibid., pp. 126, 254, 452, 556.

6. *Diary of Robert Sharp*, pp. 206, 262.

7. Ibid., pp. 208, 210, 312, 374–5, 496, 497, 524, 525.

8. Ibid., p. 419.

9. Ibid., p. 149.

10. Ibid., pp. 82, 170, 231, 476, 542. Quote on p. 231.

11. Ibid., pp. 232, 234, 287, 339, 477.

12. M. F. Davies, *Life in an English Village* (London, 1909), pp. 276–84.

13. The long hours of those in work in the early twentieth century come through clearly in the case studies provided in B. S. Rowntree and M. Kendall, *How the Labourer Lives* (London, 1913).

14. Northumberland Record Office (hereafter NRO), 1706/T139, Oral History, A. Patten.

15. For the development of leisure during the nineteenth century, see H. Cunningham, *Leisure in the Industrial Revolution* (London, 1980).

16. See C. Thomson, *The Autobiography of an Artisan* (London, 1847); D. P. Miller, *The Life of a Showman* (London, 1849).

17. Miller, *Life of a Showman*, pp. 14–15, 53, 69.

18. Miller, *Life of a Showman*, pp. 24, 111.

19. Thomson, *Autobiography of an Artisan*, p. 269.

20. University of Essex, Essex Oral History Collection (hereafter EOHC), Family Life and Work Experience Before 1918, Int. 182, R. Robinson, b. 1891.

21. F. Kitchen, *Brother to the Ox: The Autobiography of a Farm Labourer* (London, 1984), pp. 164–7. Kitchen was born in 1891.

22. EOHC, Int. 265, F. Harker, b. 1895.

23. For much of the above, see H. Cunningham, 'Leisure', in J. Benson (ed.), *The Working Class in England 1875–1914* (London, 1985), ch. 5.

24. For example, Rowntree and Kendall's description of the recreational offerings in a Leicestershire village: 'no anything!': *How the Labourer Lives*, p. 228.

25. For a recent survey and critique of the way in which the perceived impact of the industrial revolution has dominated studies of eighteenth- and nineteenth-century leisure, see E. Griffin, 'Popular Culture in Industrializing England', *Historical Journal*, 45 (2002), pp. 619–35.

26. H. Cunningham, 'Leisure and Culture', in F. M. L. Thompson (ed.), *The Cambridge Social History of Britain 1750–1950, Vol. 2, People and Their Environment* (Cambridge, 1990), ch. 6, esp. pp. 302–5. Significantly, his discussion of rural leisure ends with a description of Corsley. This characterization is surprising, given Cunningham's sophisticated approach to *national* change during the period 1780–1880, where, indeed, he argued against notions of a leisure vacuum in the early nineteenth century. See his earlier book, *Leisure in the Industrial Revolution*.

27. R. Wells (ed.), *Victorian Village: The Diaries of the Reverend John Coker Egerton of Burwash 1857–1888* (Stroud, 1992), p. 237.

28. R. Hutton, *The Stations of the Sun: A History of the Ritual Year in Britain* (Oxford, 1996), p. 59. Hutton found that it was confined to counties south of (but

including) Cheshire and the West and East Ridings of Yorkshire. Hutton's book is the best general history of British calendar customs.

29. Wells (ed.), *Victorian Village*, pp. 106, 131.
30. Hutton, *Stations of the Sun*, p. 127.
31. F. W. L. Jewitt, 'On Ancient Customs and Sports of the County of Derby', *Journal of the British Archaeological Association*, 7 (1851), p. 202.
32. Hutton, *Stations of the Sun*, p. 96.
33. P. Maylam, *The Hooden Horse, an East Kent Christmas Custom* (Canterbury, 1909); E. C. Cawte, *Ritual Animal Disguise* (Cambridge, 1978), pp. 85–93; Hutton, *Stations of the Sun*, p. 83.
34. Maylam, *Hooden Horse*, p. 4.
35. S. Bamford, *Early Days* (London, 1849), p. 138.
36. Ibid., pp. 143–4.
37. Hutton, *Stations of the Sun*, pp. 200–1.
38. C. Phythian-Adams, 'Milk and Soot: The Changing Vocabulary of a Popular Ritual in Stuart and Hanoverian London', in D. Fraser and A. Sutcliffe (eds), *The Pursuit of Urban History* (London, 1983), ch. 4.
39. Hutton, *Stations of the Sun*, pp. 237–41.
40. P. Horn (ed.), *Oxfordshire Village Life: The Diaries of George James Dew (1846–1928), Relieving Officer* (Abingdon, 1983), p. 39. See also, pp. 13, 31, 50, 58, 65, 69, 79, 89.
41. Ibid., p. 65.
42. J. Ayres (ed.), *Paupers and Pig Killers: The Diary of William Holland a Somerset Parson, 1799–1818* (Harmondsworth, 1986), p. 35.
43. Horn (ed.), *Oxfordshire Village Life*, p. 51.
44. Cunningham, 'Leisure and Culture', pp. 303–4.
45. Cunningham, *Leisure in the Industrial Revolution*, p. 122.
46. A. Howkins, 'The Taming of Whitsun: The Changing Face of a Nineteenth-Century Rural Holiday', in E. and S. Yeo (eds), *Popular Culture and Class Conflict 1590–1914: Explorations in the History of Labour and Leisure* (Brighton, 1981), ch. 7.
47. Howkins, 'Taming of Whitsun'.
48. Horn (ed.), *Oxfordshire Village Life*, pp. 51, 66. See also, pp. 41, 70, 90.
49. Wells (ed.), *Victorian Village*, pp. 68, 80, 89, 99, 115, 137, 138, 245, 268, 269, 287–8, 294.
50. Ibid, pp. 89, 137.
51. Quoted in K. Chandler, *'Ribbons, Bells and Squeaking Fiddles': The Social History of Morris Dancing in the English South Midlands, 1660–1900* (London, 1993), p. 87. For the legendary drinking of morris dancers, see Chandler, *Ribbons, Bells*, pp. 200–2.
52. E. Brill, *Life and Tradition on the Cotswolds* (London, 1973), pp. 166–7, and plates 238 and 243. The original banner also contains an image of the Good Samaritan, with the words 'Go and do Likewise' and 'Let Brotherly Love Continue', a message of working strength and Christian compassion.
53. Wells (ed.), *Victorian Village*, pp. 141, 145. Egerton did not disapprove of the proceedings.

54. E. Grey, *Cottage Life in a Hertfordshire Village* (Harpenden, 1977), pp. 214–17.

55. J. K. Walton and R. Poole, 'The Lancashire Wakes in the Nineteenth Century', in R. D. Storch (ed.), *Popular Culture and Custom in Nineteenth-Century England* (London, 1982), ch. 5.

56. A. Kussmaul, *A General View of the Rural Economy of England, 1538-1840* (Cambridge, 1990); J. Thirsk, 'A Time to Weed, a Time to Wed', *Times Higher Educational Supplement*, 16 November 1990.

57. J. Obelkevich, *Religion and Rural Society: South Lindsey 1825–1875* (Oxford, 1976), pp. 82–3, 136.

58. R. D. Storch, ' "Please to Remember the Fifth of November": Conflict, Solidarity and Public Order in Southern England, 1815-1900', in Storch (ed.), *Popular Culture and Custom*, ch. 4.

59. B. Bushaway, *By Rite: Custom, Ceremony and Community in England 1700-1880* (London, 1982), pp. 74–80, 209–10; Hutton, *Stations of the Sun*, ch. 27.

60. See A. R. Wright, *British Calendar Customs*, 3 vols (London, 1936–40); C. Hole, *A Dictionary of British Folk Customs* (London, 1984).

61. L. Murfin, *Popular Leisure in the Lake Counties* (Manchester, 1990), ch. 3.

62. Murfin, *Popular Leisure*, p. 64; B. Reay, *The Last Rising of the Agricultural Labourers* (Oxford, 1990), pp. 54–8; B. Reay, *Microhistories: Demography, Society and Culture in Rural England, 1800–1930* (Cambridge, 1996), pp. 106, 107, 118, 126–7.

63. See Templeman Library (hereafter TL), University of Kent, Oral History Project: Life in Kent Before 1914, S. Twist, b. 1899.

64. Obelkevich, *Religion and Rural Society*, p. 86.

65. R. Jefferies, *The Toilers of the Field* (London, 1893), pp. 100–1.

66. Murfin, *Popular Leisure*, p. 72; Reay, *Microhistories*, p. 116; Reay, *Last Rising*, p. 58.

67. D. K. Cameron, *The English Fair* (Stroud, 1998), p. 1. See also, D. A. Reid, 'Interpreting the Festive Calendar: Wakes and Fairs as Carnivals', in Storch (ed.), *Popular Culture and Custom*, ch. 6.

68. Kitchen, *Brother to the Ox*, ch. 6 (p. 93 for the quote).

69. Murfin, *Popular Leisure*, p. 47.

70. NRO, 1193/T97, Oral History, M. Bruce, b. 1897.

71. Obelkevich, *Religion and Rural Society*, pp. 82–3.

72. Grey, *Cottage Life in a Hertfordshire Village*, pp. 209–13.

73. S. Alexander, *St. Giles Fair, 1830–1914* (Oxford, 1970).

74. A. Williams, *Folk-Songs of the Upper Thames* (London, 1923), pp. 20–1.

75. R. A. Houston, *Scottish Literacy and the Scottish Identity: Illiteracy and Society in Scotland and Northern England, 1600-1800* (Cambridge, 1985), p. 206. See also, D. M. Dugaw, 'Anglo-American Folksong Reconsidered: The Interface of Oral and Written Forms', *Western Folklore*, 43 (1984), pp. 102–3; D. Dugaw, *Warrior Women and Popular Balladry, 1650–1850* (Cambridge, 1989).

76. M. Spufford, 'The Pedlar, the Historian and the Folklorist: Seventeenth Century Communications', *Folklore*, 105 (1994), p. 20.

77. E. Robinson and D. Powell (eds), *John Clare by Himself* (Ashington, 1996), p. 68.

78. E. Robinson and D. Powell (eds), *The Early Poems of John Clare 1804-1822* (Oxford, 1989), vol. 1, p. 175. Clare was born in 1793.

79. Robinson and Powell (eds), *John Clare by Himself*, pp. 101, 109–10.

80. Ibid., p. 2.

81. Henry Burstow, *Reminiscences of Horsham* (Horsham, 1911), pp. 108–9.

82. H. Mayhew, *London Labour and the London Poor*, 4 vols (New York, 1968 edn), vol 1, p. 227.

83. Ibid., pp. 234–5.

84. Ibid., pp. 222–3.

85. Ibid., p. 223.

86. Ibid., pp. 280–1.

87. Grey, *Cottage Life in a Hertfordshire Village*, p. 44.

88. E. D. Mackerness (ed.), *The Journals of George Sturt 1890–1927* (Cambridge, 1967), vol. 1, pp. 282–3.

89. F. Thompson, *Lark Rise to Candleford* (Harmondsworth, 1977), p. 69. First published in 1939.

90. TL, A. Packman, b. 1892.

91. V. Gammon, 'Song, Sex, and Society in England, 1600–1850', *Folk Music Journal*, 4 (1982), pp. 208–45; A. Howkins and C. I. Dyck, ' "The Time's Alteration": Popular Ballads, Rural Radicalism and William Cobbett', *History Workshop*, 23 (1987), pp. 20–38.

92. Original version of *Gently Johnny My Jingalo*, collected by Cecil Sharp in 1907 and rewritten: see J. Reeves, *The Idiom of the People* (London, 1958), pp. 113–14. He thought the words 'too coarse for publication', so rewrote the offending lines and published the song in *Folk Songs from Somerset*, and *English Folk Songs*.

93. Thompson, *Lark Rise*, pp. 57, 66.

94. For the latest overview of this milieu, see V. and S. Gammon, 'The Musical Revolution of the Mid-Nineteenth Century', in T. Herbert (ed.), *The British Brass Band: A Musical and Social History* (Oxford, 2000), ch. 3.

95. Wells (ed.), *Victorian Village*, p. 166.

96. See Obelkevich, *Religion and Rural Society*, pp. 146–50; V. Gammon, ' "Babylonian Performances"; The Rise and Suppression of Popular Church Music, 1660–1870', in Yeo (eds), *Popular Culture and Class Conflict*, ch. 3.

97. J. Skinner, *Journal of a Somerset Rector 1803–1834* (Oxford, 1984), pp. 162, 200, 203, 207.

98. Ibid., p. 206.

99. Horn (ed.), *Oxfordshire Village Life*, p. 83.

100. T. Nicholson, 'Masculine Status and Working-Class Culture in the Cleveland Ironstone Mining Communities, 1850–1881', in K. Laybourn (ed.), *Social Conditions, Status and Community 1860–c.1920* (Stroud, 1997), ch. 8, esp. p. 143.

101. A. Metcalfe, 'Organized Sport in the Mining Communities of South Northumberland, 1800–1889', *Victorian Studies*, 25 (1982), pp. 469–95; A. Metcalfe, 'Sport and Community: A Case Study of the Mining Villages of East

Northumberland, 1800–1914', in J. Hill and J. Williams (eds), *Sport and Identity in the North of England* (Keele, 1996), ch. 2.

102. R. Palmer (ed.), 'The Minstrel of Quarry Bank . . . Part Two', *Oral History*, 11, no. 2 (1983), pp. 61–8. Quote from p. 64.

103. Murfin, *Popular Leisure*, ch. 4.

104. J. Ginswick (ed.), *Labour and the Poor in England and Wales 1849–1851, Vol. 1: Lancashire, Cheshire, Yorkshire* (London, 1983), pp. 111, 150.

105. Brill, *Life and Tradition on the Cotswolds*, p. 170.

106. C. Shaw, *When I Was a Child* (Firle, 1977), pp. 31–2. First published in 1903.

107. V. Newall, 'Throwing the Hood at Haxey: A Lincolnshire Twelfth-Night Custom', *Folk Life*, 18 (1980), pp. 7–23.

108. M. Alexander, 'Shrove Tuesday Football in Surrey', *Surrey Archaeological Collections*, 77 (1986), pp. 197–205.

109. See TL, H. Matthews, b. 1890; S. Twist, b. 1899; L. Austin, b. 1902.

110. Grey, *Cottage Life in a Hertfordshire Village*, pp. 202–3; A. Randell, *Fenland Memories* (London, 1969), p. 76. They recur in oral histories.

111. Tony Mason's history, covering this period, is essentially a history of the urban working class: T. Mason, *Association Football and English Society 1863–1915* (Brighton, 1980). Although his purpose is to explore the older tradition of football, Richard Holt's article again focuses on the city: R. Holt, 'Working Class Football and the City: The Problem of Continuity', *British Journal of Sports History*, 3 (1986), pp. 5–17.

112. TL, L. Austin, b. 1902; H. Ash, b. 1898.

113. Wells (ed.), *Victorian Village*, pp. 269, 294.

114. Grey, *Cottage Life in a Hertfordshire Village*, p. 202.

115. TL, L. Austin, b. 1902.

116. TL, H. Matthews, b. 1890. See also, TL, H. Ash, b. 1898.

117. EOHC, Int. 42, W. Breakspear, b. 1893.

118. Murfin charts the change in Cumbria over the period: *Popular Leisure*, ch. 4.

119. Palmer (ed.), 'The Minstrel of Quarry Bank . . . Part Two', p. 61.

120. Li-Ming Hu, 'Reworking Oral Histories: Masculinity and Rural Workers' Representations of Self, 1890–1930' (University of Auckland MA thesis, 2001), pp. 41–2.

121. Murfin, *Popular Leisure*, p. 11.

122. *Royal Commission on Labour: The Agricultural Labourer: Reports . . . Upon . . . Selected Districts, Parliamentary Papers* (hereafter *PP*), 1893–4, xxxv, pp. 513, 581–2.

123. Quoted in M. Winstanley, *Life in Kent at the Turn of the Century* (Folkestone, 1978), p. 79.

124. Reay, *Microhistories*, ch. 8.

125. EOHC, Int. 154, E. V. Franklin, b. 1893.

126. Mackerness (ed.), *Journals of George Sturt*, vol. 1, p. 245.

127. See Hu, 'Reworking Oral Histories', ch. 2.

128. M. Pickering, *Village Song and Culture* (London, 1982), p. 134. See also, Williams, *Folk-Songs of the Upper Thames*, pp. 20–1.

129. G. Porter, '"Work the Old Lady Out of the Ditch": Singing at Work by English Lacemakers', *Journal of Folklore Research*, 31 (1994), pp. 35–55.

130. Palmer (ed.), 'The Minstrel of Quarry Bank . . . Part Two', p. 67.

131. A. Howkins and L. Merricks, 'The Ploughboy and the Plough Play', *Folk Music Journal*, 6 (1991), pp. 187–208.

132. NRO, 1706/T139, A. Patten.

133. C. K. Nelson, *To be a Farmer's Boy* (Stroud, 1991), pp. 8–9.

134. Hutton, *Stations of the Sun*, p. 422. See also, Bushaway, *By Rite*, esp. pp. 180-90, for the prevalence of dole-seeking in the eighteenth and nineteenth centuries; although he was unaware of discontinuities with the sixteenth and seventeenth centuries.

135. Chandler, *Ribbons, Bells*, pp. 93–5.

136. EOHC, Int. 265, F. Harker, b. 1895.

137. This section on the life-cycle draws on Cunningham, 'Leisure'. For the implications of poverty, see my chapter 4 above.

138. A. Davies, 'Leisure in the "Classic Slum"' 1900–1939', in A. Davies and S. Fielding (eds), *Workers' Worlds: Culture and Communities in Manchester and Salford, 1880–1939* (Manchester, 1992), ch. 5. Quote from p. 111.

139. Rowntree and Kendall, *How the Labourer Lives*, p. 313.

140. Davies, 'Leisure in the "Classic Slum"', p. 121.

141. See EOHC, Int. 22, C. Hills, b. 1904; EOHC, Int. 5, J. Troy, b. 1888; EOHC, Int. 182, R. Robinson, b. 1891.

142. TL, S. Twist, b. 1899.

143. A point made by Cunningham, 'Leisure'; and Davies, 'Leisure in the "Classic Slum"'.

144. Though he also complained that they flouted his rules: Skinner, *Journal of a Somerset Rector*, pp. 174, 335.

145. EOHC, Int. 265, F. Harker, b. 1895.

146. Reay, *Microhistories*, pp. 198–9. See also, S. D'Cruze, *Crimes of Outrage: Sex, Violence and Victorian Working Women* (DeKalb, IL, 1998), ch. 6.

147. Murfin, *Popular Leisure*, ch. 2.

148. Apart from the work of Hutton, cited throughout this chapter, see T. Buckland and J. Wood (eds), *Aspects of British Calendar Customs* (Sheffield, 1993).

149. Obelkevich, *Religion and Rural Society*, pp. 57–8.

150. Maylam, *Hooden Horse*.

151. Hutton, *Stations of the Sun*, pp. 58–60.

152. Hutton, *Stations of the Sun*, ch. 7.

153. G. M. Ridden, 'The Goathland Plough Monday Customs', *Folk Music Journal*, 2 (1973), pp. 352–88.

154. R. Wortley and M. Dawney (eds), 'George Butterworth's Diary of Morris Dance Hunting', *Folk Music Journal*, 3 (1977), pp. 193–207, esp. p. 198.

155. Chandler, *Ribbons, Bells*, provides the best study of the nineteenth-century morris.

156. J. Forrest and M. Heaney, 'Charting Early Morris', *Folk Music Journal*, 6 (1991), pp. 169–86; Hutton, *Stations of the Sun*, p. 276.

157. Although the focus was on the urban regions: R. D. Storch, 'The Policeman as Domestic Missionary: Urban Discipline and Popular Culture in Northern England, 1850–1880', *Journal of Social History*, 9 (1976), pp. 481–509; R. Malcolmson, 'Leisure', in G. E. Mingay (ed.), *The Victorian Countryside*, 2 vols (London, 1981), vol. 2, ch. 44.

158. Mackerness (ed.), *Journals of George Sturt*, vol. 1, p. 273.

159. G. Smith, 'Winster Morris Dance', in T. Buckland (ed.), *Traditional Dance* (Crewe, 1982), vol. 1, pp. 93–107; R. Judge, 'D'Arcy Ferris and the Bidford Morris', *Folk Music Journal*, 4 (1984), pp. 443–80; R. Judge, 'May Day and Merrie England', *Folklore*, 102 (1991), pp. 131–48; and Hutton, *Stations of the Sun*, chs 25, 28, which provides the best overview.

160. B. Bushaway, ' "Things Said or Sung a Thousand Times": Customary Society and Oral Culture in Rural England, 1700–1900', in A. Fox and D. Woolf (eds), *The Spoken Word: Oral Culture in Britain 1500–1850* (Manchester, 2002), ch. 9.

161. Reay, *Microhistories*, ch. 8.

162. D. Vincent, *Literacy and Popular Culture: England 1750-1914* (Cambridge, 1989), p. 23.

163. Wells (ed.), *Victorian Village*, p. 98.

164. Ginswick (ed.), *Labour and the Poor, Vol. 1*, pp. 61–4.

165. For variability, see W. B. Stephens, *Education, Literacy and Society, 1830–70: The Geography of Diversity in Provincial England* (Manchester, 1987).

166. Vincent, *Literacy and Popular Culture*, p. 97.

167. Ibid., pp. 24–6.

168. See Vincent, *Literacy and Popular Culture*, pp. 1, 47, 97, 212, 274; D. F. Mitch, *The Rise of Popular Literacy in Victorian England: The Influence of Private Choice and Public Policy* (Philadelphia, PA, 1992), ch. 3; D. Vincent, *The Rise of Mass Literacy: Reading and Writing in Modern Europe* (Cambridge, 2000), p. 19.

169. Kitchen, *Brother to the Ox*, pp. 72–3. For the weekly comic, *Ally Sloper's Half-Holiday*, see the essay, 'Ally Sloper's Half-Holiday: Comic Art in the 1880s', in Peter Bailey's marvellous book, *Popular Culture and Performance in the Victorian City* (Cambridge, 1998), ch. 3. The farm servants' familiarity with the comic suggests that its mass appeal included the rural areas.

170. For the impact of print at the rural level, see J. Rose, *The Intellectual Life of the British Working Classes* (London, 2001), pp. 9–10, 28–31, 33, 34–5, 84–5, 97–8, 102, 113, 114, 127, 131, 372. Though it has to be said that Rose provides relatively little on the impact of the book on nineteenth-century rural workers.

171. Kitchen, *Brother to the Ox*, pp. 146–8.

172. G. Bourne [Sturt], *Change in the Village* (Harmondsworth, 1984), pp. 154, 170–1. First published in 1912.

173. Rose, *Intellectual Life of the British Working Classes.*, p. 84.

174. TL, F. Kemsley, b. 1887.

175. A. R. Randell, *Sixty Years a Fenman* (London, 1966), p. 13.

176. Reay, *Microhistories*, p. 242.
177. See, for example, Murfin, *Popular Leisure*, ch. 5.
178. K. D .M. Snell and P. S. Ell, *Rival Jerusalems: The Geography of Victorian Religion* (Cambridge, 2000), ch. 9.
179. The types of work referred to here are those encountered earlier in this volume: agricultural labouring, family labour on small farms, and rural crafts such as lace-making, straw-plaiting, weaving, and framework-knitting. The correlation between the Sunday schools and child labour includes factory work in the towns.
180. Shaw, *When I Was a Child*, pp. 7–8.
181. See both the Kent (TL) and Essex (national) (EOHC) collections. See, also, Hugh McLeod's reworking of the Essex collection: H. McLeod, 'New Perspectives on Victorian Class Religion: The Oral Evidence', *Oral History Review*, 14 (1986), pp. 31–49.
182. Mackerness (ed.), *Journals of George Sturt*, vol. 1, p. 274.
183. EOHC, Int. 16, R. Jaggard, b. 1882.
184. EOHC, Int. 272, L. Watson, b. 1888.
185. EOHC, Int. 265, F. Harker, b. 1895.
186. TL, B. H. Fagg, b. 1894.
187. TL, A. Packman, b. 1892.
188. Even though he lived at Great Bentley, only about five miles from the coast: EOHC, Int. 22, C. Hills, b. 1904.
189. J. Rule, 'Methodism, Popular Beliefs and Village Culture in Cornwall, 1800–50', in Storch (ed.), *Popular Culture and Custom*, pp. 48–60.
190. EOHC, Int. 16, R. Jaggard, b. 1882.
191. TL, E. Burgess, b. 1890.
192. EOHC, Int. 453, M. Abbot, b. 1902.
193. Randell, *Fenland Memories*, p. 94.
194. Obelkevich, *Religion and Rural Society*, p. 212.
195. TL, A. Austen, b. 1889.
196. EOHC, Int. 42, W. Breakspear, b. 1893.
197. EOHC, Int. 265, F. Harker, b. 1895.
198. NRO, 3339/T200, J. Cranston, b. 1907.
199. EOHC, Int. 22, C. Hills, b. 1904.
200. TL, A. Packman, b. 1892. Quoted in Winstanley, *Life in Kent*, pp. 224, 229. Michael Winstanley collected all the remarkable oral histories in the Kent archive.

7 Protest

1. F. L. Olmsted, *Walks and Talks of an American Farmer in England*, intro. by C. C. McLaughlin (Amherst, 2002), pp. 98–9, 107, 369. First published in 1852.
2. Ibid., pp. 353–4.
3. Ibid., pp. 152–3, 352, 353–4, 357, 369.

4. Alexander Somerville, *The Whistler at the Plough*, ed. K. D. M. Snell (London, 1989), pp. 41–3. First published in 1852.

5. J. C. Scott, *Weapons of the Weak: Everyday Forms of Peasant Resistance* (New Haven, CT, 1985), p. 246.

6. E. Gaskell, *North and South* (Harmondsworth, 1981), p. 382. First published in 1854–55.

7. G. Bourne [Sturt], *Change in the Village* (Harmondsworth, 1984), p. 63. First published in 1912.

8. H. Newby, *The Deferential Worker: A Study of Farmworkers in East Anglia* (London, 1977), p. 369.

9. Templeman Library (hereafter TL), University of Kent, Oral History Project: Life in Kent Before 1914, J. W. Manuel, b. 1903.

10. TL, L. Austin, b. 1902.

11. A. J. Peacock, *Bread or Blood: A Study of the Agrarian Riots in East Anglia in 1816* (London, 1965), pp. 92–3, 126–7.

12. *The Cambridge Chronicle*, 5 July 1816, quoted in ibid, p. 128.

13. E. J. Hobsbawm and G. Rudé, *Captain Swing* (Harmondsworth, 1973), p. 224.

14. J. Marlow, *The Tolpuddle Martyrs* (St Albans, 1974).

15. See R. Wells, 'Southern Chartism', in J. Rule and R. Wells, *Crime, Protest and Popular Politics in Southern England 1740–1850* (London, 1997), ch. 7, esp. p. 150.

16. Ibid., p. 134.

17. *Kent Messenger and Maidstone Telegraph*, 8 June 1872.

18. W. Hasbach, *A History of the English Agricultural Labourer* (London, 1920), p. 285.

19. E. T. Hurren, 'Agricultural Trade Unionism and the Crusade Against Outdoor Relief: Poor Law Politics in the Brixworth Union, Northamptonshire, 1870–75', *Agricultural History Review*, 48 (2000), pp. 200–22.

20. A. Tweedy, 'Recollections of a Farm Worker', *Bulletin of the Cleveland and Teeside Local History Society*, 21 (1973), p. 6.

21. For these ties, see K. D. M. Snell, 'The Culture of Local Xenophobia', *Social History*, 28 (2003), pp. 1–30.

22. Hasbach, *History of the English Agricultural Labourer*, pp. 286–7.

23. See *Kent Messenger and Maidstone Telegraph*, 8 June 1872.

24. J. P. D. Dunbabin, 'The Incidence and Organization of Agricultural Trades Unionism in the 1870s', *Agricultural History Review*, 16 (1968), pp. 124–5; C. Bell and H. Newby, 'The Sources of Variation in Agricultural Workers' Images of Society', *Sociological Review*, 21 (1973), pp. 238–9.

25. Lodgers, those on poor relief, those not resident for 12 months, and servants; this, combined with various problems with registration, must have severely impacted on rural workers. Neal Blewett estimated that as late as 1911, 40 per cent of adult males were not on the electoral register: N. Blewett, 'The Franchise in the United Kingdom 1885–1918', *Past and Present*, 32 (1965), pp. 27–56.

26. See, for example, *Kent Messenger and Maidstone Telegraph*, 8 June 1872.

27. L. M. Springall, *Labouring Life in Norfolk Villages 1834–1914* (London, 1936), p. 92.

28. H. Shpayer-Makov, 'Country Workers in the Metropolitan Police', *Historical Research*, 64 (1991), pp. 191, 193.

29. A. Armstrong, *Farmworkers: A Social and Economic History 1770–1980* (London, 1988), p. 249.

30. Springall, *Labouring Life*, p. 92.

31. Scott, *Weapons of the Weak*, p. 325.

32. Newby, *Deferential Worker*, p. 28.

33. K. D. M. Snell, 'Deferential Bitterness: The Social Outlook of the Rural Proletariat in Eighteenth- and Nineteenth-Century England and Wales', in M. L. Bush (ed.), *Social Classes in Europe Since 1500* (London, 1992), ch. 9.

34. For Chartist complaint, see J. Rule, 'The Chartist Mission to Cornwall', in Rule and Wells, *Crime, Protest and Popular Politics*, p. 69.

35. For Downham, see Peacock, *Bread or Blood*, pp. 87–94.

36. Ibid., pp. 87–8.

37. Ibid., pp. 89, 95, 102.

38. A. Charlesworth, 'The East Anglian Protests of 1816', in Charlesworth (ed.), *An Atlas of Rural Protest in Britain 1548–1900* (London, 1983), pp. 146–8.

39. A village of 1200 people: Peacock, *Bread or Blood*, pp. 78–9.

40. A. Charlesworth, 'The Agricultural Labourers' Protests of 1822', in Charlesworth (ed.), *Atlas of Rural Protest*, pp. 148–51.

41. J. E. Archer, *By a Flash and a Scare: Incendiarism, Animal Maiming, and Poaching in East Anglia 1815–1870* (Oxford, 1990), p. 81.

42. Ibid., p. 83. See also, P. Muskett, 'The East Anglian Riots of 1822', *Agricultural History Review*, 32 (1984), pp. 1–13.

43. A. Charlesworth, 'The Captain Swing Protests of 1830–1', in Charlesworth (ed.), *Atlas of Rural Protest*, pp. 151–4. Hobsbawm and Rudé, *Captain Swing*, remains the best general account of Swing. See, also, the fascinating study by D. Kent and N. Townsend, *The Convicts of the Eleanor: Protest in Rural England, New Lives in Australia* (London, 2002), which traces a cohort of Berkshire, Hampshire, Wiltshire and Dorset rioters to their transportation and experiences in Australia.

44. C. Griffin, ' "There was no Law to Punish that Offence". Re-Assessing "Captain Swing": Rural Luddism and Rebellion in East Kent, 1830–31', *Southern History*, 22 (2000), pp. 131–63, esp. pp. 140, 143–6; P. Hastings, 'Radical Movements and Workers' Protests to *c*. 1850', in F. Lansberry (ed.), *Government and Politics in Kent, 1640–1914* (Woodbridge, 2001), pp. 116–17.

45. Hobsbawm and Rudé, *Captain Swing*, p. 163.

46. B. Reay, *The Last Rising of the Agricultural Labourers* (Oxford, 1990), pp. 75–6.

47. D. Kent and N. Townsend (eds), *Joseph Mason Assigned Convict, 1831–1837* (Melbourne, 1996), pp. 9–11.

48. A. Charlesworth, 'The Captain Swing Protests of 1830–1', in Charlesworth (ed.), *Atlas of Rural Protest*, pp. 151–4. Also stressed in A. Charlesworth, 'A Comparative Study of the Spread of the Agricultural Disturbances of 1816, 1822 and 1830 in England', *Peasant Studies*, 11 (1984), pp. 91–110.

49. Kent and Townsend, *Convicts*, p. 31.

50. Hobsbawm and Rudé, *Captain Swing*, pp. 78–9.
51. Reay, *Last Rising*, p. 74.
52. Hastings, 'Radical Movements', p. 115.
53. Hobsbawm and Rudé, *Captain Swing*, p. 166.
54. Kent and Townsend, *Convicts*, p. 30.
55. Somerville, *Whistler at the Plough*, pp. 261–5.
56. For the role of folk ritual in protest, see B. Bushaway, *By Rite: Custom, Ceremony and Community in England 1700-1880* (London, 1982), pp. 190–202; Kent and Townsend, *Convicts*, ch. 4.
57. The fascinating observation of Kent and Townsend, *Convicts*, pp. 104–5. Though it is only one peak in some counties.
58. Hobsbawm and Rudé, *Captain Swing*, pp. 174–6.
59. *Kentish Gazette*, 9 June 1835.
60. Report from Headington Union, 22 August 1835: Public Record Office (hereafter PRO), MH 12/9658 Local Government Board: Correspondence with Poor Law Union, co. Oxfordshire, Headington 1834–8.
61. Reay, *Last Rising*, p. 53.
62. R. Wells, 'Resistance to the New Poor Law in the Rural South', in Rule and Wells, *Crime, Protest and Popular Politics*, ch. 6.
63. Including arson: J. Lowerson, 'Anti Poor Law Movements and Rural Trade Unionism in the South-East 1835', in Charlesworth (ed.), *Atlas of Rural Protest*, p. 156.
64. A. Digby, 'Protest in East Anglia Against the Imposition of the New Poor Law', in Charlesworth (ed.), *Atlas of Rural Protest*, pp. 158–62.
65. Wells, 'Resistance to the New Poor Law'.
66. See J. Knott, *Popular Opposition to the 1834 Poor Law* (London, 1986).
67. The best accounts are: D. Jones, 'Thomas Campbell Foster and the Rural Labourer: Incendiarism in East Anglia in the 1840s', *Social History*, 1 (1976), pp. 5–43, reprinted in his *Crime, Protest, Community and Police in Nineteenth-Century Britain* (London, 1982), ch. 2; and Archer, *By a Flash and a Scare*.
68. P. Hastings, 'Crime and Public Order', in Lansberry (ed.), *Government and Politics in Kent*, pp. 232–4.
69. Archer, *By a Flash and a Scare* , p. 69.
70. Hastings, 'Crime and Public Order', p. 231.
71. E. Newman, 'The Anti-Corn Law League and the Wiltshire Labourer: Aspects of the Development of Nineteenth-Century Protest', in B.A. Holderness and M. Turner (eds), *Land, Labour and Agriculture, 1700–1920* (London, 1991), p. 91.
72. Calculated from figures in Archer, *By a Flash and a Scare*, p. 178; Hastings, 'Crime and Public Order', pp. 231–2.
73. Archer, *By a Flash and a Scare*, pp. 136, 140, 142, 147.
74. Ibid., pp. 133–4.
75. Jones, 'Thomas Campbell Foster', p. 30
76. Ibid., p. 31.
77. From 1844: Archer, *By a Flash and a Scare*, p. 113.

78. In East Anglia the incendiary was working for, or had worked for, the target of the fire in nearly 50 per cent of cases: Archer, *By a Flash and a Scare*, p. 191.

79. Jones, 'Thomas Campbell Foster', pp. 20–1.

80. Quoted by A. J. Peacock, 'Village Radicalism in East Anglia 1800–50', in J. P. D. Dunbabin, *Rural Discontent in Nineteenth-Century Britain* (London, 1974), p. 57.

81. Quoted in E. P. Thomson, 'The Crime of Anonymity', in D. Hay, P. Linebaugh, J. G. Rule, E. P. Thompson, and C. Winslow, *Albion's Fatal Tree: Crime and Society in Eighteenth-Century England* (Harmondsworth, 1977), p. 273.

82. For example, Thompson, 'Crime of Anonymity', p. 290.

83. A Sussex letter, 1830: Thompson, 'Crime of Anonymity', pp. 315–16.

84. A letter 'To the Gentlemen of Ashill', May 1816, in Peacock, *Bread or Blood*, pp. 65–6.

85. A letter sent to a Briningham (Norfolk) overseer in the 1830s by a pauper blacksmith: Archer, *By a Flash and a Scare*, pp. 49, 99.

86. Lowerson, 'Anti Poor Law Movements and Rural Trade Unionism', pp. 157–8; R. Wells, 'Tolpuddle in the Context of English Agrarian Labour History, 1780–1850', in J. Rule (ed.), *British Trade Unionism 1750–1850* (London, 1988), ch. 5.

87. F. Carlton, ' "A Substantial and Sterling Friend to the Labouring Man": the Kent and Sussex Labourers' Union 1872–1895' (University of Sussex M. Phil. thesis, 1977), pp. 45–9.

88. See a series of articles by J. P. D. Dunbabin: Dunbabin, 'The "Revolt of the Field": The Agricultural Labourers' Movement in the 1870s', *Past and Present*, 26 (1963), p. 68; Dunbabin, 'The Incidence and Organization of Agricultural Trades Unionism', pp. 117–18; Dunbabin, 'Agricultural Trade Unionism in England 1872–94', in Charlesworth (ed.), *Atlas of Rural Protest*, pp. 171–3.

89. Dunbabin, 'Incidence and Organization of Agricultural Trades Unionism', pp. 117–18.

90. Conveyed dramatically in the map in Dunbabin, 'Agricultural Trade Unionism in England 1872–94', p. 172. See also, G. R. Boyer and T. J. Hatton, 'Did Joseph Arch Raise Agricultural Wages? Rural Trade Unions and the Labour Market in Late Nineteenth-Century England', *Economic History Review*, 47 (1994), p. 318: table of union density by county.

91. N. Scotland, *Agricultural Trade Unionism in Gloucestershire 1872–1950* (Cheltenham, 1991), p. 17.

92. F. E. Green, *A History of the English Agricultural Labourer 1870–1920* (London, 1920), pp. 46–7.

93. R. Wells (ed.), *Victorian Village: The Diaries of the Reverend John Coker Egerton of Burwash 1857–1888* (Stroud, 1992), pp. 135–6.

94. N. Scotland, 'The National Agricultural Labourers' Union and the Demand for a Stake in the Soil, 1872–1896', in E. F. Biagini (ed.), *Citizenship and Community: Liberals, Radicals and Collective Identities in the British Isles, 1865–1931* (Cambridge, 1996), ch. 6.

95. *Kent Messenger and Maidstone Telegraph*, 18 July 1874.

96. *Kent and Sussex Times*, 16 November 1878.

97. *Kent Messenger and Maidstone Telegraph*, 18 July 1874.

98. Carlton, 'Substantial and Sterling Friend', p. 75. For club days, see chapter 6 above.

99. Wells (ed.), *Victorian Village*, pp. 161, 168–9, 174, 183–4.

100. K. Sayer, *Women of the Fields: Representations of Rural Women in the Nineteenth Century* (Manchester, 1995), ch. 7. Quote from p. 125.

101. The union leader, Alfred Simmons, 1873, quoted in Carlton, 'Substantial and Sterling Friend', p. 58.

102. Hastings, 'Radical Movements', pp. 108–9, 112–13.

103. J. Glyde, *Suffolk in the Nineteenth Century* (London, [1856]), p. 171.

104. For Wiltshire, see A. Randall and E. Newman, 'Protest, Proletarians and Paternalists: Social Conflict in Rural Wiltshire, 1830–1850', *Rural History*, 6 (1995), p. 221.

105. *Royal Commission on Labour: The Agricultural Labourer: Reports . . . Upon . . . Selected Districts, Parliamentary Papers* (hereafter *PP*), 1893–4, xxxv, p. 280.

106. Ibid., pp. 585, 643.

107. Ibid., p. 209.

108. A poor-law official's description of the Otmoor rising against enclosure in Oxfordshire: Report from Headington Union, 22 August 1835: PRO MH 12/9658. For enclosure in Otmoor, see D. Eastwood, 'Communities, Protest and Police in Early Nineteenth-Century Oxfordshire: The Enclosure of Otmoor Reconsidered', *Agricultural History Review*, 44 (1996), pp. 35–46.

109. K. P. Bawn, 'Social Protest, Popular Disturbances and Public Order in Dorset, 1790–1838' (University of Reading Ph.D. thesis, 1984), pp. 26–7.

110. J. M. Neeson, 'The Opponents of Enclosure in Eighteenth-Century Northamptonshire', *Past and Present*, 105 (1984), pp. 114-39; M. Turner, 'Economic Protest in Rural Society: Opposition to Parliamentary Enclosure in Buckinghamshire', *Southern History*, 10 (1988), pp. 94–128.

111. Turner, 'Economic Protest', p. 99.

112. The best discussion of tactics of resistance is to be found in J. M. Neeson, *Commoners: Common Right, Enclosure and Social Change in England, 1700–1820* (Cambridge, 1993), ch. 9: 'Resisting Enclosure'.

113. F. Kitchen, *Brother to the Ox: The Autobiography of a Farm Labourer* (London, 1984), p. 100. Kitchen was born in 1891.

114. See I. Carter, 'Agricultural Workers in the Class Structure: A Critical Note', *Sociological Review*, 22 (1974), pp. 271–9; I. Carter, 'Class and Culture among Farm Servants in the North-East, 1840–1914', in A. A. McLaren (ed.), *Social Class in Scotland* (Edinburgh, 1976), ch. 6.

115. *PP*, 1893–4, xxxv, p. 436.

116. A. Kussmaul (ed.), *The Autobiography of Joseph Mayett of Quainton (1783–1839)* (Buckinghamshire Record Society, no. 23, 1986), pp. xxi, 8, 10, 11–12, 83.

117. Carter, 'Agricultural Workers', pp. 276–7.

118. J. C. Scott, *Domination and the Arts of Resistance: Hidden Transcripts* (New Haven, CT, 1990).

119. J. Walter, 'Public Transcripts, Popular Agency and the Politics of Subsistence in Early Modern England', in M. J. Braddick and J. Walter (eds), *Negotiating Power in Early Modern Society: Order, Hierarchy and Subordination in Britain and Ireland* (Cambridge, 2001), ch. 5, and p. 124 for the quote.

120. Archer, *By a Flash and a Scare*, pp. 199, 208, 215, 216. We should exclude horses accidentally poisoned by over-zealous horsemen administering potions to improve their coats.

121. 'Here's First to those Farmers', collected from Alfred Smith, Watchfield, Berks, in A. Williams, *Folk-Songs of the Upper Thames* (London, 1923, repr. 1971), p. 104.

122. Williams, *Folk-Songs of the Upper Thames*, p. 105.

123. For song and protest in rural England, see A. Howkins and C. I. Dyck, ' "The Time's Alteration": Popular Ballads, Rural Radicalism and William Cobbett', *History Workshop*, 23 (1987), pp. 20–38; I. Dyck, 'Towards the "Cottage Charter": The Expressive Culture of Farm Workers in Nineteenth-Century England', *Rural History*, 1 (1990), pp. 95–111.

124. M. Yates, ' "Stand Up Ye Men of Labour": the Socio-Political Songs of Walter Pardon', *Musical Traditions*, 1 (1983), p. 26. (I owe this reference to Dyck, 'Towards the "Cottage Charter" ', p. 104.)

125. E. Richards, '"Captain Swing" in the West Midlands', *International Review of Social History*, 19 (1974), pp. 98–9. My emphasis.

126. Kitchen, *Brother to the Ox*, p. 132.

127. Tweedy, 'Recollections of a Farm Worker', p. 3.

128. Ibid. Snell cites the examples of Kitchen and Tweedy in his piece, 'Deferential Bitterness', which also deals with this topic, but they are too good to leave out.

129. T. Sokoll (ed.), *Essex Pauper Letters 1731–1837* (Oxford, 2001), p. 107.

130. Ibid., pp. 69–70. Instances are too numerous to list. See Sokoll's index: 'removal, danger of, as strategic argument ("if not relieved")'; 'sending family to home parish, intention of, as strategic argument'.

131. Ibid., p. 124.

132. Ibid., p. 138. The man obtained his relief.

133. Ibid., p. 11.

134. Letter from parish of Besthorpe, PRO MH 12/8616 Local Government Board: Correspondence with Poor Law Union, co. Norfolk, Wayland 1834–7.

135. *Kent Messenger and Maidstone Telegraph*, 23 August 1873.

136. *The Labourers' Herald*, 27 November 1874.

137. See p. 88, above.

138. Wells (ed.), *Victorian Village*, p. 29

139. University of Essex, Essex Oral History Collection (hereafter EOHC), Family Life and Work Experience Before 1918, Int. 42, W. Breakspear, b. 1893.

140. Wells (ed.), *Victorian Village*, p. 179. The story clearly appealed to Egerton.

141. Ibid., pp. 29, 43.

142. *PP*, 1893–4, xxxv, p. 643.

143. E. P. Thompson, *Customs in Common* (London, 1991), p. 188.

144. The phrase 'community politics' comes from J. Bohstedt, *Riots and Community Politics in England and Wales 1790-1810* (Cambridge, MA, 1983).

145. R. Wells, 'The Moral Economy of the English Countryside', in A. Randall and A. Charlesworth (eds), *Moral Economy and Popular Protest: Crowds, Conflict and Authority* (London, 2000), ch. 9, esp. pp. 210, 235–6. This is an argument antic-ipated by both Knott, *Popular Opposition to the 1834 Poor Law*; and G. Seal, 'Tradition and Rural Protest in Nineteenth-Century England', *Folklore*, 99 (1988), pp. 146–69.

146. Newby, *Deferential Worker*, ch. 7.

147. Ibid., p. 406.

148. B. Reay, *Microhistories: Demography, Society and Culture in Rural England, 1800–1930* (Cambridge, 1996), pp. 151–5.

149. TL, L. Austin, b. 1902.

150. Newby, *Deferential Worker*, pp. 387–8, 395.

151. N. Rapport, *Diverse World-Views in an English Village* (Edinburgh, 1993), p. 157. Thus the craftsman, Syd, had seven different personae: 1. Sid as a craftsman; 2. Sid as a local; 3. Sid as a husband; 4. Sid as a pal; 5. Sid as a father; 6. Sid as a man ; 7. Sid as English. See ibid., pp. 106–7.

152. Snell, 'Deferential Bitterness', p. 171.

153. Reay, *Last Rising*, pp. 106–7, 144–8.

154. Kussmaul (ed.), *Autobiography of Joseph Mayett*, pp. 52, 70–2.

155. G. Edwards, *From Crow-Scaring to Westminster* (London, 1957), pp. 36, 42–3. Edwards was born in 1850.

156. Quoted in G. Rudé, *Ideology and Popular Protest* (London, 1980), p. 156.

157. Wells, 'Resistance to the New Poor Law', pp. 102, 108.

158. Snell, 'Deferential Bitterness', pp. 172–3.

159. C. Shaw, *When I Was a Child* (Firle, 1977), p. 193. First published in 1903.

160. M. K. Ashby, *Joseph Ashby of Tysoe, 1859–1919* (Cambridge, 1961), p. 69.

161. E. Brill, *Life and Tradition on the Cotswolds* (London, 1973), pp. 166–7.

162. *Kent Messenger and Maidstone Telegraph*, 11 May 1872.

163. Ernest Selley, *Village Trade Unions in Two Centuries* (New York, 1919), p. 47.

164. N. Scotland, *Methodism and the Revolt of the Field: A Study of the Methodist Contribution to Agricultural Trade Unionism in East Anglia, 1872–96* (Gloucester, 1981), pp. 87–100, 129–45, 147–60.

165. J. G. O'Leary (ed.), *The Autobiography of Joseph Arch* (London, 1966), p. 43. First published in 1898.

166. Quoted in Dunbabin, 'Revolt of the Field', p. 79.

167. The *English Labourers' Chronicle* of 1881, quoted in Scotland, 'National Agri-cultural Labourers' Union', p. 157.

168. Yates, 'Stand Up Ye Men of Labour', p. 25.

169. See K. D. M. Snell and P. S. Ell, *Rival Jerusalems: The Geography of Victorian Religion* (Cambridge, 2000), pp. 125, 128, 138, 140.

170. J. C. Buckmaster, *A Village Politician: The Life-Story of John Buckley* (Horsham, 1982), pp. 38–40. First published in 1897.

171. R. Colls, *The Pitmen of the Northern Coalfield: Work, Culture, and Protest, 1790–1850* (Manchester, 1987), ch. 9; Snell and Ell, *Rival Jerusalems* pp. 142–3.

172. J. Obelkevich, *Religion and Rural Society: South Lindsey 1825–1875* (Oxford, 1976), p. 221. For the Primitives, see his ch. 5.

173. Obelkevich, *Religion and Rural Society*, pp. 239–40; A. Howkins, *Poor Labouring Men: Rural Radicalism in Norfolk 1870–1923* (London, 1985), p. 45.

174. Based on unpublished research carried out as part of the project resulting in Reay, *Microhistories*.

175. K. D. M. Snell, *Church and Chapel in the North Midlands: Religious Observance in the Nineteenth Century* (Leicester, 1991), pp. 42–5.

176. Based on unpublished research carried out as part of the project resulting in Reay, *Microhistories*.

177. Snell, *Church and Chapel*, pp. 42–5.

178. Calculated from Obelkevich, *Religion and Rural Society*, p. 195.

179. Snell, *Church and Chapel*, p. 45.

180. Kitchen, *Brother to the Ox*, p. 27.

181. Ashby, *Joseph Ashby of Tysoe*, p. 77.

182. D. Clark, *Between Pulpit and Pew: Folk Religion in a North Yorkshire Fishing Village* (Cambridge, 1982), p. 118.

183. Obelkevich, *Religion and Rural Society*, pp. 240–1. Just over 20 per cent of households in the Blean villages and hamlets in 1881 contained children baptized either by the Wesleyans or Primitives, and these Kent communities were by no means strongholds of Methodism: based on unpublished research carried out as part of the project resulting in Reay, *Microhistories*.

184. See also, F. Knight, *The Nineteenth-Century Church and English Society* (Cambridge, 1995), pp. 24–32.

185. Snell and Ell, *Rival Jerusalems*, ch. 9.

186. Ibid., pp. 298, 317, 319.

187. Kussmaul (ed.), *Autobiography of Joseph Mayett*, pp. xi, 2.

188. Shaw, *When I Was a Child*, pp. 1–3, 6–7.

189. See both the Kent (TL) and Essex (national) (EOHC) collections.

190. See, for example, P. Horn (ed.), *Village Education in Nineteenth-Century Oxfordshire: The Whitchurch School Log Book* (Oxfordshire Record Society, 51, 1979).

191. D. Vincent, 'Reading in the Working-Class Home', in J. K. Walton and J. Walvin (eds), *Leisure in Britain 1780–1939* (Manchester, 1983), ch. 11.

192. Reay, *Microhistories*, p. 238.

193. A point also made by H. McLeod, 'New Perspectives on Victorian Class Religion: The Oral Evidence', *Oral History Review*, 14 (1986), pp. 31–49; H. McLeod, *Religion and Irreligion in Victorian England* (Bangor, 1993), pp. 35–9.

194. Shaw, *When I Was a Child*, pp. 143, 192–3.

195. P. Thompson, *The Edwardians* (London, 1984), p. 147.

196. Ibid., p. 156.
197. M. Pickering, 'The Four Angels of the Earth: Popular Cosmology in a Victorian Village', *Southern Folklore Quarterly*, 45 (1981), pp. 10–11.
198. The term 'hybrid Christianity' is Pickering's: ibid., p. 12.
199. J. Rule, 'Methodism, Popular Beliefs and Village Culture in Cornwall, 1800–50', in R. D. Storch (ed.), *Popular Culture and Custom in Nineteenth-Century England* (London, 1982), pp. 61–7; Clark, *Between Pulpit and Pew*, pp. 57, 65.
200. Obelkevich, *Religion and Rural Society*, ch. 6. For other accounts of this world, see: C. Phythian-Adams, 'Rural Culture', in G. E. Mingay (ed.), *The Victorian Countryside*, 2 vols (London, 1981), vol. 2, ch. 45; Clark, *Between Pulpit and Pew*; B. Bushaway, ' "Tacit, Unsuspected, but still Implicit Faith": Alternative Belief in Nineteenth-Century Rural England', in T. Harris (ed.), *Popular Culture in England, c. 1500-1850* (London, 1995), ch. 9. The situation among the working-class population of the towns may not have been vastly different: S. Williams, 'Urban Popular Religion and the Rites of Passage', in H. McLeod (ed.), *European Religion in the Age of Great Cities 1830–1930* (London, 1995), ch. 8. For witchcraft, see O. Davies, *Witchcraft, Magic and Culture 1736–1951* (Manchester, 1999); R. Hutton, *The Triumph of the Moon: A History of Modern Pagan Witchcraft* (Oxford, 1999), ch. 6.
201. Reay, *Last Rising*, pp. 64–8, 106–7, 144–8.
202. I first attempted to think about these issues in 1988 for a paper given at the 'Peasants' seminar at the Institute of Commonwealth Studies, University of London. Further musings are scattered through my book, *Last Rising*.
203. Howkins, *Poor Labouring Men*, p. 47.
204. Scotland, *Methodism and the Revolt of the Field*, pp. 9, 22; Howkins, *Poor Labouring Men*, pp. 52–3.
205. Marlow, *Tolpuddle Martyrs*, pp. 12–18; Scotland, *Methodism and the Revolt of the Field*, p. 58.
206. Howkins, *Poor Labouring Men*, p. 63–5; Scotland, *Agricultural Trade Unionism in Gloucestershire*, pp. 33–7.
207. Carlton, 'Substantial and Sterling Friend', p. 41.
208. Hobsbawm and Rudé, *Captain Swing*, pp. 97, 114–15.
209. Ibid., pp. 76–7, 184–6.
210. Carlton, 'Substantial and Sterling Friend', pp. 26–7, 46, 51–2, 178.
211. *PP*, 1893–4, xxxv, p. 280.
212. Roger Wells is one of the few historians constantly aware of the possibilities of this interaction. See, for example, R. Wells, ' Rural Rebels in Southeastern England in the 1830s', in C. Emsley and J. Walvin (eds), *Artisans, Peasants & Proletarians 1760–1860* (London, 1985), ch. 6.
213. Hastings, 'Radical Movements', pp. 98–9.
214. The best short surveys are J. Stevenson, *Popular Disturbances in England, 1700–1832* (London, 1992); and M. W. Steinberg, *Fighting Words: Working-Class Formation, Collective Action, and Discourse in Early Nineteenth-Century England* (Ithaca, NY, 1999), ch. 1.
215. See A. Randall, 'The Shearmen and the Wiltshire Outrages of 1802: Trade

Unionism and Industrial Violence', *Social History*, 7 (1982), pp. 283–304; A. Randall, *Before the Luddites: Custom, Community and Machinery in the English Woollen Industry, 1776–1809* (Cambridge, 1991).

216. Newman, 'Anti-Corn Law League and the Wiltshire Labourer'.
217. See E. Hopkins, *Working-Class Self-Help in Nineteenth-Century England* (London, 1995), Part Two: 'The Trade Unions', which, ironically, barely mentions the agricultural labourers!
218. Hasbach, *History of the English Agricultural Labourer*, p. 297.
219. PRO, Home Office Papers, 73/54: Information regarding the formation of labourers' unions, 21 Nov. 1838.
220. D. Thompson, *The Chartists* (London, 1984), pp. 173–5.
221. A point made long ago by Springall, *Labouring Life*, p. 91.
222. See C. Thomson, *The Autobiography of an Artisan* (London, 1847), pp. 322, 329, 332, 333–4.
223. Though perhaps not the sort of democracy that free marketeers have in mind: D. G. Green, *Reinventing Civil Society* (London, 1993), p. 39.
224. See Hopkins, *Working-Class Self-Help*, which deals with friendly societies, unions, and the co-operative movement, in that order.
225. Stevenson, *Popular Disturbances in England*, p. 270.
226. For a fascinating study of the interaction of orality and print in nineteenth-century political culture, and for the ultimately limiting role of print on electoral politics, see J. Vernon, *Politics and the People: A Study in English Political Culture, c. 1815–1867* (Cambridge, 1993), esp. ch. 3.
227. Edwards, *From Crow-Scaring to Westminster*, p. 42.
228. For example, C. Tilly, 'Contentious Repertoires in Great Britain, 1758–1834', in M. Traugott (ed.), *Repertoires and Cycles of Collective Action* (Durham, 1995), pp. 15–42. This article is a summary of Tilly's book, *Popular Contention in Great Britain 1758–1834* (Cambridge, MA, 1995).

8 Picturing Rural Work

1. P. Wright, *On Living in an Old Country* (London, 1991), pp. 82–3.
2. R. Scruton, *England: An Elegy* (London, 2000), ch. 10.
3. See J. Barrell, *The Dark Side of the Landscape: The Rural Poor in English Painting* (Cambridge, 1980), pp. 25–6. I remain mystified by Michael Rosenthal's claim that Stubbs's figures look like 'actual labourers': M. Rosenthal, *British Landscape Painting* (Oxford, 1982), p. 92.
4. See the image in Barrell, *Dark Side of the Landscape*, p. 83.
5. Barrell, *Dark Side of the Landscape*, esp. ch. 3: 'John Constable' (quote from p. 134). Although, see the critique by A. Bermingham, *Landscape and Ideology: The English Rustic Tradition, 1740–1860* (London, 1987), ch. 3.
6. Barrell, *Dark Side of the Landscape*, ch. 2: 'George Morland'.
7. J. Barrell, 'Sportive Labour: The Farmworker in Eighteenth-Century Poetry and Painting', in B. Short (ed.), *The English Rural Community* (Cambridge, 1992), ch. 6.

8. C. Payne, 'Rural Virtues for Urban Consumption', *Journal of Victorian Culture*, 3 (1998), pp. 45–68.

9. P. Street, 'Painting Deepest England: The Late Landscapes of John Linnell and the Uses of Nostalgia', in C. Shaw and M. Chase (eds), *The Imagined Past: History and Nostalgia* (Manchester, 1989), ch. 5. Quote from p. 79.

10. T. M. Barringer, 'Representations of Labour in British Visual Culture, 1850–1875' (University of Sussex Ph.D. thesis, 1994), ch. 2.

11. Ibid. Barringer distinguishes Cole's exclusion of labour from Linnell's naturalization of labour, but the response of critics to both artists was usually to concentrate on the landscape and to ignore its workers.

12. D. Cherry, *Painting Women: Victorian Women Artists* (London, 1993), p. 178. C. Wood, *Paradise Lost: Paintings of English Country Life and Landscape 1850–1914* (London, 1988), discusses Foster and many others and provides examples of their work: 'It is difficult to resist the charge . . . that the majority of Victorian landscapes are machines for evasion' (p. 12).

13. *The Art Journal*, 1888, p. 199.

14. D. Cherry, 'Paradise Lost: Histories Regained', *Art History*, 12 (1989), p. 377.

15. *The Art Journal*, 1888, p. 123.

16. *The Art Journal*, 1884, illustration facing p. 200.

17. C. Payne, *Toil and Plenty: Images of the Agricultural Landscape in England, 1780-1890* (New Haven, CT, 1993), pp. 30, 71.

18. *Magazine of Art*, 1884, p. 442.

19. Wood, *Paradise Lost*, p. 14.

20. J. Treuherz, *Hard Times: Social Realism in Victorian Art* (London, 1987), pp. 49–52.

21. The paintings are reproduced, with discussion, in Bermingham, *Landscape and Ideology*, Plate 7 (between pp. 142–3), and pp. 174–80. See also, A. Staley, *The Pre-Raphaelite Landscape* (New Haven, CT, 2001) [first published in 1973], ch. 3. For the Pre-Raphaelites and landscape, see also T. Barringer, *The Pre-Raphaelites* (London, 1998), ch. 2.

22. Payne, *Toil and Plenty*, pp. 109–12.

23. For the paintings, see Wood, *Paradise Lost*, pp. 14–15. The interpretation is mine, however. See also, Treuherz, *Hard Times*, pp. 36–8; Bermingham, *Landscape and Ideology*, pp. 185–91; Staley, *Pre-Raphaelite Landscape*, pp. 115–16, 172–3.

24. For a study of the purpose of Brett's work, and the reactions of critics to both paintings, see M. Hickox and C. Payne, 'Sermons in Stones: John Brett's *The Stonebreaker* Reconsidered', in E. Harding (ed.), *Re-Framing the Pre-Raphaelites* (Aldershot, 1995), ch. 6.

25. Staley, *Pre-Raphaelite Landscape*, p. 172.

26. Wood, *Paradise Lost*, pp. 195–6 (painting on p. 196); K. D. Kriz, 'An English Arcadia Revisited and Reassessed: Holman Hunt's *The Hireling Shepherd* and the Rural Tradition', *Art History*, 10 (1987), pp. 475–91 (quote on p. 477).

27. Cherry, *Painting Women*, p. 166.

28. Quoted in Cherry, *Painting Women*, p. 149. The painting is Plate 25 in her book.

29. *The Art Journal*, 1894, pp. 85–6.

30. Cherry, *Painting Women*, pp. 173–4.

31. D. Hudson, *Munby Man of Two Worlds: The Life and Diaries of Arthur J. Munby 1828–1910* (London, 1974), p. 31.

32. See G. Pollock, ' "With My Own Eyes": Fetishism, the Labouring Body and the Colour of its Sex', *Art History*, 17 (1994), pp. 342–82; B. Reay, *Watching Hannah: Sexuality, Horror and Bodily De-Formation in Victorian England* (London, 2002), esp. ch. 4.

33. A. Jenkins, *Painters and Peasants: Henry La Thangue and British Rural Naturalism 1880–1905* (Bolton, 2000).

34. K. McConkey, 'Rustic Naturalism at the Grosvenor Gallery', in S. P. Casteras and C. Denney (eds), *The Grosvenor Gallery: A Palace of Art in Victorian England* (London, 1996), pp. 134–5.

35. See Wood, *Paradise Lost*, ch. 3: 'Work'.

36. The models for *Hard Times* were the Quarry family of the village of Bushey, Hertfordshire. For Herkomer, see L. M. Edwards, 'Hubert von Herkomer', in Treuherz, *Hard Times*, ch. 11; and her *Herkomer a Victorian Artist* (Aldershot, 1999), esp. ch. 6. See also, L. Nead, 'Paintings, Films and Fast Cars: A Case Study of Hubert von Herkomer', *Art History*, 25 (2002), pp. 240–55.

37. For this painting, see Cherry, *Painting Women*, Plate 33.

38. Treuherz, *Hard Times*, pp. 49–52.

39. Edwards, *Herkomer*, chs 7, 9; H. von Herkomer, *My School and My Gospel* (London, 1908), pp. 1–2.

40. Payne, *Toil and Plenty*, p. 126. For Clausen, see K. McConkey, *Sir George Clausen, R.A. 1852–1944* (Gateshead, 1980).

41. *Magazine of Art*, 1885, p. 134.

42. G. Moore, *Modern Painting* (London, n.d.), pp. 116–18.

43. Payne, *Toil and Plenty*, pp. 200–2.

44. *Magazine of Art*, 1887, pp. 111–13; 1890, p. 326; 1891, p. 338.

45. K. Sayer, *Women of the Fields: Representations of Rural Women in the Nineteenth Century* (Manchester, 1995), pp. 164, 168–9.

46. G. P. Weisberg, *Beyond Impressionism: The Naturalist Impulse in European Art 1860–1905* (New York, 1992), Preface, and ch. 4.

47. S. A. Forbes, 'A Newlyn Retrospect', *The Cornish Magazine*, July 1898, pp. 81–93.

48. Stanhope Forbes, quoted in J. Vernon, 'Border Crossings: Cornwall and the English (Imagi)nation', in G. Cubitt (ed.), *Imagining Nations* (Manchester, 1998), p. 160. On the naturalists in Cornwall, see also B. Deacon, 'Imagining the Fishing: Artists and Fishermen in Late Nineteenth-Century Cornwall', *Rural History*, 12 (2001), pp. 159–78.

49. *Magazine of Art*, 1884, pp. 443, 446.

50. *Magazine of Art*, 1888, p. 215.

51. *Magazine of Art*, 1885, p. 134.

52. Moore, *Modern Painting*, pp. 119, 122.

53. A. Rutherston (ed.), *Contemporary British Artists: George Clausen* (London, 1923), pp. 18, 20.

54. Quoted in Jenkins, *Painters and Peasants*, p. 145.

55. See the illustration in ibid., p. 153.

56. *The Art Journal*, 1898, p. 326. For Morland in the eighteenth century, see Barrell, *Dark Side of the Landscape*, ch. 2.

57. *The Art Journal*, 1899, pp. 161–84.

58. *The Art Journal*, 1890, p. 67. For Cox, see K. Baetjer (ed.), *Glorious Nature: British Landscape Painting 1750–1850* (New York, 1993), pp. 220–3.

59. S. Daniels, 'John Constable and the Making of Constable Country', in his *Fields of Vision* (Oxford, 1993), pp. 207–11. Constable died in 1837. *The Hay-wain* was gifted to the National Gallery in 1886.

60. Barrell, *Dark Side of the Landscape*, pp. 146–9.

61. Charles Holmes, 1902, quoted by Daniels, *Fields of Vision*, p. 212.

62. P. Howard, *Landscapes: The Artists' Vision* (London, 1991).

63. M. F. Harker, *Henry Peach Robinson: Master of Photographic Art, 1830–1901* (Oxford, 1988), ch. 6; B. Lukacher, 'Powers of Sight: Robinson, Emerson, and the Polemics of Pictorial Photography', in E. Handy (ed.), *Pictorial Effect Naturalistic Vision: The Photographs and Theories of Henry Peach Robinson and Peter Henry Emerson* (Norfolk, VA, 1994), p. 41.

64. Quoted in J. M. Green, '"The Right Thing in the Right Place": P. H. Emerson and the Picturesque Photograph', in C. T. Christ and J. O. Jordan (eds), *Victorian Literature and the Victorian Visual Imagination* (Berkeley, CA, 1995), p. 93.

65. H. P. Robinson, *Picture-Making by Photography* (London, 1895), p. 52.

66. H. P. Robinson, *Pictorial Effect in Photography* (London, 1869), p. 109.

67. Harker, *Henry Peach Robinson*, pp. 34–7.

68. E. Handy, 'Pictorial Beauties, Natural Truths, Photographic Practices', in Handy (ed.), *Pictorial Effect*, p. 11.

69. See the interesting critique of P. H. Emerson in J. Taylor, *A Dream of England: Landscape, Photography and the Tourist's Imagination* (Manchester, 1994), ch. 3.

70. Handy, 'Pictorial Beauties', p. 10.

71. P. H. Emerson, *Pictures of East Anglian Life* (London, 1888), p. 97.

72. Ibid., p. 72, quoted in Lukacher, 'Powers of Sight', p. 46.

73. Emerson, *Pictures of East Anglian Life*, p. 141.

74. Green, 'Right Thing', pp. 94–5.

75. Both examples are from P. Turner and R. Wood, *P. H. Emerson: Photographer of Norfolk* (Boston, MA, 1974), pp. 97, 104.

76. Green, 'Right Thing', p. 95.

77. Emerson, *Pictures of East Anglian Life*, Preface.

78. *The Journal of the Camera Club*, 2 (1888), p. 81.

79. *The Journal of the Camera Club*, 3 (1889), pp. 137, 146.

80. *The Journal of the Camera Club*, 4 (1890), pp. 139, 168–9.

81. *The Journal of the Camera Club*, 3 (1889), p. 171.

82. *The Journal of the Camera Club*, 7 (1893), p. 68.

83. Ibid., p. 67.
84. *The Journal of the Camera Club*, 4 (1890), pp. 203–7.
85. *Magazine of Art*, 1888, p. 216; *Magazine of Art*, 1891, pp. 298–303, 337–44; K. Holden, 'George Clausen and Henry Herbert La Thangue: Rural Painting, Urban Patronage', *Apollo*, 149 (1999), pp. 17–18. For middle-class collecting generally, see D. S. Macleod, *Art and the Victorian Middle Class: Money and the Making of Cultural Identity* (Cambridge, 1996).
86. K. McConkey, *A Painter's Harvest: Works by Henry Herbert La Thangue, R.A. 1859–1929* (Oldham, 1978), pp. 22–3; K. McConkey, *Impressionism in Britain* (London, 1995), pp. 36–8.
87. Holden, 'George Clausen and Henry Herbert La Thangue', p. 17.
88. Ibid., pp. 13–15; *The Art Journal*, 1898, pp. 225–9, 272–5.
89. A. Hemingway, *Landscape Imagery and Urban Culture in Early Nineteenth-Century Britain* (Cambridge, 1992).
90. N. Green, *The Spectacle of Nature: Landscape and Bourgeois Culture in Nineteenth-Century France* (Manchester, 1990), quote from p. 70.
91. Ibid., p. 109.
92. *The Art Journal*, 1898, p. 57.
93. *The Art Journal*, 1889, p. 140.
94. *The Art Journal*, 1897, p. 326.
95. Barringer, 'Representations of Labour', pp. 111–13, 119.
96. S. P. Casteras and R. Parkinson (eds), *Richard Redgrave 1804–1888* (London, 1988), p. 138.
97. Jenkins, *Painters and Peasants*, pp. 126, 146. La Thangue, who had previously lived in rural Norfolk, moved to Sussex in 1890.
98. *The Art Journal*, 1898, p. 164. For Barbizon, see Green, *Spectacle of Nature*, pp. 116–26.
99. *The Art Journal*, 1898, pp. 338 and facing.
100. *The Art Journal*, 1900, p. 182.
101. Ibid., p. 176.
102. Ibid., p. 292.
103. See image file for Leader in Witt Library, Courtauld Institute of Art, London.
104. Hemingway, *Landscape Imagery and Urban Culture*, p. 151; Barringer, 'Representations of Labour', ch. 2.
105. S. P. Casteras, ' "Green Lanes and Chequered Shade": The Landscapes of Richard Redgrave', in Casteras and Parkinson (eds), *Richard Redgrave*, p. 80.
106. Quoted in Staley, *Pre-Raphaelite Landscape*, p. 173.
107. R. Jefferies, *The Life of the Fields* (London, 1893), p. 144.
108. See the Cecil Sharp Photograph Collection, Vaughan Williams Memorial Library, Cecil Sharp House, London.
109. See *Country Life*, 12 October 1901, p. 479; 26 October 1901, p. 543; 22 November 1902, p. 671; 29 November, 1902, p. 703; 6 December 1902, p. 760; 20 December 1902, p. 824; 12 April 1902, p. 480; 14 June 1902, pp. 768–71 (quote from p. 770).

110. Wood finishes his book with an image of this painting: Wood, *Paradise Lost*, p. 216. For La Thangue, see McConkey, *Painter's Harvest*; and Jenkins, *Painters and Peasants*.

111. *The Art Journal*, 1898, p. 228.

112. Quoted in Jenkins, *Painters and Peasants*, p. 162.

113. C. Payne, 'Boundless Harvests: Representations of Open Fields and Gleaning in Early Nineteenth Century England', *Turner Studies*, 2 (1991), pp. 7–15.

114. D. B. Brown, A. Hemingway, and A. Lyles, *Romantic Landscape: The Norwich School of Painters* (London, 2000), esp. pp. 16, 51–2, 62–3, 92–3.

115. Street, 'Painting Deepest England'; Barringer, 'Representations of Labour', ch. 2.

116. W. S. Sparrow (ed.), *In Rustic England* (London, 1906), pp. 116–17, 121.

117. Quoted in Treuherz, *Hard Times*, p. 38.

118. S. P. Casteras, ' "Oh! Emigration! Thou'rt the Curse . . . Victorian Images of Emigration Themes', *Journal of Pre-Raphaelite Studies*, 6 (1985), pp. 1–23 (p. 13 for the quote about Herkomer).

119. For these, see Cherry, *Painting Women*, Plate 33 and pp. 173–4 (Havers); *The Art Journal*, 1884, facing p. 84 and p. 87 (Marsh); A. Trumble, *Love & Death: Art in the Age of Victoria* (Adelaide, 2002), p. 45 (Fletcher); T. Cross, *The Shining Sands: Artists in Newlyn and St Ives 1880–1930* (Tiverton, 1994), p. 30, and file in Witt Library (Langley); *The Art Journal*, 1890, facing p. 353 (Hall); McConkey, 'Rustic Naturalism', pp. 140–1; Jenkins, *Painters and Peasants*, pp. 126–7, 136 (La Thangue).

120. See Treuherz, *Hard Times*, ch. 9, and file in Witt Library.

121. Quoted in Treuherz, *Hard Times*, p. 80.

122. For the punctum, see R. Barthes, *Camera Lucida* (London, 1993), esp. pp. 26–7.

123. For these paintings, see Cross, *Shining Sands*, pp. 51, 54; Jenkins, *Painters and Peasants*, pp. 92–3; Weisberg, *Beyond Impressionism*, p. 131.

124. Emerson, *Pictures of East Anglian Life*, p. 120, quoted in Turner and Wood, *P H Emerson Photographer of Norfolk*, p. 104.

125. Emerson, *Pictures of East Anglian Life*, pp. 38, 142.

126. Ibid., pp. 119–20.

127. Weisberg, *Beyond Impressionism*, p. 111.

Conclusion

1. C. Thomson, *The Autobiography of an Artisan* (London, 1847), p. 26.

2. D. P. Miller, *The Life of a Showman* (London, 1849), p. 1.

3. P. H. Emerson, *Pictures of East Anglian Life* (London, 1888), p. 1.

4. *Royal Commission on Labour: The Agricultural Labourer: Reports . . . Upon . . . Selected Districts*, Parliamentary Papers (hereafter PP), 1893–4, xxxv, pp. 274, 430, 471.

5. *Royal Commission on Labour: The Agricultural Labourer: General Report*, PP, 1893–4, xxxvii, Part 2, p. 55.

6. PP, 1893–4, xxxv, p. 175.